Second Edition

Introduction to Rhetorical Theory

Second Edition

Introduction to Rhetorical Theory

Gerard A. Hauser
University of Colorado

WAVELAND
PRESS, INC.
Long Grove, Illinois

For information about this book, contact:
    Waveland Press, Inc.
    4180 IL Route 83, Suite 101
    Long Grove, IL 60047-9580
    (847) 634-0081
    info@waveland.com
    www.waveland.com

10-digit ISBN 1-57766-221-0
13-digit ISBN 978-1-57766-221-1

Printed in the United States of America

17   16   15   14   13

To my father,
with appreciation for sharing
his admiration of a good argument

Contents

Preface

The first edition of *Introduction to Rhetorical Theory* appeared in 1986. At that time the study of rhetoric was enjoying a renaissance in a number of academic disciplines apart from Speech Communication and English Studies. Rhetorical uses of language were becoming widely recognized as central to the social construction of reality, although rhetorical theory was not well known outside its traditional academic domains and, apart from specialists, its concepts were not commonly deployed for the analysis and criticism of human symbolic joining. At that time students interested in learning about rhetoric did not have available a systematic, easy-to-understand exposition of the subject. I wrote *Introduction to Rhetorical Theory* to meet that need. During the intervening years, interest in rhetoric has continued to increase. Scholarship has advanced the sophistication of our understanding of traditional concepts, and scholars in a surprisingly broad range of humanities and social sciences have entered the interdisciplinary conversation on rhetoric. Yet most of the work that presents rhetorical theory includes it as part of a discussion of the composing process, rhetorical criticism, or the history of ideas.

This revised edition discusses rhetorical theory as a subject in its own right. It strives to make a rhetorical approach to human communication accessible to readers. It sets forth a humanistic account of what transpires when people communicate for some purpose. It discusses ancient and contemporary thinking about influential uses of language and the value of symbolic inducements for social cooperation. This, then, is a book about fundamental rhetorical precepts and their implications for shaping human realities.

The revised edition includes two new chapters concerned with areas of theory that have emerged since 1986: publics theory (chapter 5) and narrative theory (chapter 10). The significant body of thought devoted to rhetoric as a constituting agency of social reality guides the general discussion throughout the book. The remaining chapters have been revised to include developments in the ongoing discussion of rhetoric that affect its basic theoretical constructs. The explanations are written for the reader being introduced to rhetoric, avoiding scholarly debates that require a more extensive background. The illustrations of precepts draw on events, persons, and experiences familiar to the traditional undergraduate reader.

I have retained the organizational structure of the first edition, providing readers with an overview of the subject and working progressively through the more subtle and demanding aspects of rhetoric. For this reason, the book begins with five chapters on the nature of rhetoric that are intended to introduce broad themes and issues essential for a rhetorical approach to communication. The next four chapters (6–9) provide a discussion of the content of rhetoric—namely, methods of invention and the three ancient modes of argument: logos, ethos, and pathos. Chapter 10, dealing with narrative theory, serves as a transition from concerns with argument and rhetorical validity to more language-based concerns that developed in twentieth century rhetorical thought under the influence of Kenneth Burke. The concluding four chapters (11–14) emphasize symbolic processes as the means by which humans not only induce social cooperation but also constitute social reality.

I have retained the book's general topical structure, which affords the flexibility of incorporating insights from past and present and allows instructors to adapt its use to the structure of courses in which rhetorical concepts are of central importance. Since the topics addressed apply to a number of media, I have sought to illustrate the relevance of rhetoric to a broad range of communication modes and settings. Combining the inventive stage in developing proofs and the analysis of language as the basis for inducing social action underscores the power of language to present a particular reality.

I am grateful to many students who have joined me in dialogue on rhetoric in the introductory level rhetorical theory course at Penn State University and the University of Colorado. Since 1971 our dialogue has continually refreshed my curiosity about and altered my understanding of rhetorical transactions. My graduate assistants have been invaluable companions in exploring rhetoric. They have used our weekly staff meetings as an opportunity to examine rhetorical theory as it concretely applies to undergraduates and to interrogate the integrity of rhetorical theory at large.

My work on this revision was aided considerably by a sabbatical leave from the University of Colorado. Thanks to Amy Grim who composed the Instructor's Manual for this edition. I am grateful to Carol Rowe, who has been a source of constant encouragement to write a second edition and who was patient beyond reason when administrative duties prevented me from meeting deadlines that were long overdue. Her editorial suggestions when it finally arrived on her desk were intelligent and masterful, and I am in her debt. I wish to thank my wife, Jean Hauser, for her continued support, understanding, and charming Irish sense of gentle persuasion. Finally, I wish to thank my father, Al Hauser, to whom this edition is dedicated.

Gerard Hauser
Boulder, CO

1

The Eventfulness of Rhetoric

Communication is universally recognized as vital to our everyday lives. It is recognized as essential in business, in the professions, in science and technology, in interpersonal relations, in community affairs, in political processes, in institutions of all sorts. References to communication as either a problem or a salvation have been common since the first quarter of the twentieth century. Most ideas about communication subscribe to the *Cool Hand Luke* school of thought. The foul-ups, mishaps, misunderstandings, discontent, frustrations, and even carnage that mark bungled attempts at social coordination are characterized as, "What we have here is failure to communicate." Having said that, the analysis usually quits. One reads between the lines, "When you say 'communication problem,' you've said it all."

The obvious inference from this way of thinking is that if we communicated better, our "problem" would be solved. If we really got carried away, we might imagine some perfectly conditioned communicator sailing through life with nary a problem. We sometimes do think of diplomats in this way, though their memoirs reveal that even diplomats get the blues.

We never notice when people don't have communication problems. When we do have communication problems, we want to know what went wrong and how to fix it. We aren't helped very much if our analysis stops with advice to communicate better. That's obvious and too general. We need to know what elements to examine as sources of our difficulty and the alternatives available as possible remedies. In short, we need to know more about what we mean by communication and about its specific function in social coordination. While it almost goes without saying that communica-

1

tion is vital to our everyday lives, it won't do to stop there. Until we study in greater detail what happens when person A communicates for some purpose with person B, we risk ignorance of how and why this statement is true.

୨୭

Communication and Rhetoric

Let's begin at the beginning and ask what kind of beast we have in hand when we study communication, especially the type of communication called rhetoric. People commonly use the term *rhetoric* to refer to propaganda or empty speech, but that is not what we have in mind when we investigate rhetoric as an important type of communication. As a first step, we need to determine the boundaries of our subject and its concerns. This will improve our chances of avoiding some pitfalls that come with terms used in a variety of ways.

A great many disciplines now study communication. Biology, botany, zoology, and anthropology include studies of the diverse exchanges that occur in nature among plants, animals, and their environments. Mechanical and electrical engineering and computer science examine technologically based exchanges among machines, computers, and their users. Business administration, sociology, and political science examine how institutions communicate among one another and within their subdivisions. Our concern is with human communication. *We are interested in what happens when at least one person engages at least one other person in an act of shared meaning and interpretation through the use of symbols.*

In its most basic form, human communication includes face-to-face talk, such as occurs between friends and family. It may extend, however, to include such complicated business as political campaigns, collective bargaining, and television broadcasting. As a general area of study, it does not eliminate the unintentional or nonverbal uses of symbolic forms from its study. It includes among its concerns all forms where there is meaningful engagement through shared symbols. Research into human communication and human communication theory are therefore concerned with (1) all the ways in which people experience communication, (2) the processes that define how people engage one another through symbols, and (3) the relationships necessary to sustain shared meanings and interpretations.[1]

There are many types of human communication. These include forms of communication where people use language to accomplish some goal, as in sales or politics. Some forms deliberately focus on expressing ideas for insights and enjoyment. Literature is communication of this sort. Other forms focus on conveying information accurately for precise record keeping, such as research reports. Still others focus on managing language to influence conduct—for example, public speeches.

Rhetoric, as an area of study, is concerned with how humans use symbols, especially language, to reach agreement that permits coordinated effort of some sort. In its most basic form, rhetorical communication occurs whenever one person engages another in an exchange of symbols to accomplish some goal. It is not communication for communication's sake; rhetorical communication, at least implicitly and often explicitly, attempts to coordinate social action. For this reason, rhetorical communication always contains a pragmatic intent. Its goal is to influence human choices on specific matters that require attention, often immediately. Such communication is designed to achieve desired consequences in the relative short run. Finally, rhetoric is most intensely concerned with managing verbal symbols, whether spoken or written.

Clearly, other communication forms can have practical consequences, and communication designed for an immediate issue sometimes continues to exert influence beyond its specific context and across time. There are times, as well, when we influence practical choices even though we did not intend to do so or are unaware of having done so. Further, symbolic modes other than the verbal, such as music and dance, also can exert influence. The initial description of rhetorical communication is not intended to deny any of these possibilities. Rather, we begin by drawing the concerns of rhetoric narrowly so that at the outset we can have a clear idea of its essential characteristics. *Rhetoric*, then, *is concerned with the use of symbols to induce social action.*

Communication Processes and Rhetorical Events

We commonly think of natural and artificial systems in terms of process. We conceptualize life as passing through continuous stages of development from conception to death. We pattern our thinking about machines in terms of how they process information. We talk about biological processes of organisms, the energy processes of matter, the geological processes of the planet, the astral processes of the universe, and, of course, the social, economic, developmental, psychological, and political processes of humans. Not surprisingly, in the last 20 years we have come to speak of communication in the same way.[2]

Communication has been conceptualized and investigated in terms of the interaction among elements when persons engage one another with symbols. Process thinking does not focus on communication as a product or output—speech or address or essay. It does focus on such features as these: the internal sequence of cognitions or thinking experienced by symbol users; the impact of environment, broadly conceived, on these changes; the chain of developments whenever we send and receive messages; the continuous oscillation of feedback that places sender-receiver-meaning in a special and ever-changing relationship; and the ongoing environmental modifications that receive direct or indirect impetus through symbol use.

Since the use of process thinking is pervasive among communication scholars, it is important that we clarify its significance to rhetorical theory. What do we mean by process? Should rhetoric be thought of as a process? What alternatives are there?

Things, Events, and Processes

Things and events can be set apart from processes. Things exist; events occur; processes continue.[3] **Things** have sensible qualities. We can describe them in terms of attributes such as shape, size, weight, and color. These are the palpable characteristics that distinguish one thing from another.

Events occur. Each takes place at a specific place and time. Each has a beginning and an end that can be noted in time. An event may consist of a single episode (say, the publication of a novel) or a set of episodes (say, the individual games in the World Series). Regardless, events are bounded or bracketed in ways that processes are not. Our interest in events, even those with multiple episodes, is in terms of their uniqueness as occurrences. Events have causes and outcomes, but we attend to these features for their specific relevance to an occurrence we can locate in time. We are not interested in them as a continuous sequence, even though they may be part of such a sequence. Take a rainstorm of some duration. It may occur on the East Coast; begin on Monday, May 28, and last until Thursday, May 31; and pour with such intensity that rivers and lakes swell, flooding a number of eastern communities and forcing residents to evacuate. There are episodes of rain, rising water, flooding, and evacuation. When our friends call to ask how we fared in the storm, we know which one they mean—the one that occurred between May 28 and May 31.

Processes are continuous. They consist of sequential developments that involve changes. In general, we characterize these changes as *causes* and *effects*. But our accounts of causes and effects focus on the continuity of their sequential development and the changes that follow. For instance, social Darwinism is a theory that says humans evolve as social creatures better adapted to survive their social environment through the process of social natural selection. The continuous selection process is a series of causes and effects that weed out the weaker, socially speaking.

Although processes may have sensible qualities, these are not the distinguishing characteristics; continuity of sequential development is the important aspect. Sensible qualities become relevant only if there is an unexpected appearance or absence of a quality. That may signal a discontinuity—the end of one sequence and the beginning of another. For example, the appearance of leaves on a birch tree is not remarkable in itself. They appear annually as part of the continuous active and dormant periods that are natural to the tree's life cycle. Should the leaves suddenly turn yellow in June and begin to fall, that is remarkable. It is a discontinuity that possibly marks the end of one process—life—and the beginning of another—death.

Finally, there are times when we talk of processes in terms of events and when we talk of events in terms of processes. In the rainstorm example, we may talk of this event in terms of the sequences of causes and effects within the frame: The rain caused the rivers and lakes to rise; these waters overflowed their banks, causing towns to be flooded; the floodwaters caused the citizens to evacuate. We can speak of ancillary or secondary sequences within the frame: Property damage caused by the flooding was in the billions of dollars; the governors in the affected states responded by declaring states of emergency; because of the flood damage, tens of thousands of insurance claims were filed. Ancillary sequences outside the frame may also be observed: The higher prices for produce later that summer were due to the substantial crop losses incurred during the flood; the flood damaged much lakefront rental property, causing losses of resort income in many areas. In these instances we are inquiring about processes that are related to or within the event of the rainstorm.

Similarly, we may treat the process described by social Darwinism as an event if, for example, we inquire into G. B. Shaw's views about Darwin's theory. We may investigate the events that led Shaw to formulate his views. When did he first publish his views? What do his diaries and correspondence indicate as a likely date when he formulated his views? What happened at that time? Did he read Darwin? Did he have noteworthy discussions? Did he write to friends on the matter? Did someone writing to him instigate his thought process? Here we are searching for a specific occurrence at a specific time.

If we can speak of processes as events and events as processes, how do we know which one we're considering at any given moment? It all depends on the questions we ask. If we want to know about the causes of some X that can be identified by its date, we are asking about an event. If we want to know about a sequence of developments and changes with regard to its continuity, we are asking about a process.[4]

Continuity and Discontinuity

Bearing these distinctions in mind, it should be evident that *communication is not a thing*. It is not a physical object and to think of it as such would lead to many erroneous opinions. However, communication can be thought of as a process or as an event. As we noted earlier, the prevailing view for some time has been to view communication as a process. Process thinking has been essential for research that reveals what occurs in generating and sharing symbols and in the scope of communication as a major source of influence on our psychological and social behaviors.

In short, when we think of and study communication, we raise questions of process—about continuous sequences of causes and effects. This is especially true in areas where personal and social evolution are grounded in communication. Communication is seen as a process that unfolds in a never-ending set of interlocking relationships that create our personal awareness, our sense of other, our public institutions, and our cultural patterns. As noted previously, communication is vital to all aspects of our everyday lives.

However, there is a danger of pushing too far the idea that everything is related to everything else. As Michel Foucault observed, if we conceptualize our experiences as unified, we are forced to search for the connections that demonstrate continuity.[5] We start analyzing our communication experiences in ways best described as self-fulfilling prophesies: We find continuity because we assume experience is unified.

In fact, however, experience is frequently marked by discontinuities or breaks in the sequence. There are discontinuities in legal processes when the Supreme Court restricts search-and-seizure rules for gathering admissible evidence; in economic processes when the stock market plummets at news of lower than expected earnings; in the nature of warfare when "Star Wars" technologies are perfected; in scientific knowledge when theoretical paradigms—our conceptual frameworks—are changed; in national self-image when an unpopular and unsuccessful war is fought; in our personal lives when birth and death, love gained or lost, careers made or ruined, and countless other formative experiences disrupt ongoing sequences of causes and effects and introduce new ones in their place. These gaps or breaks in the normal processes of experience are eventful. They have initial causes, they occur, and they have outcomes that are consequential for the future.

The discontinuities of experience are as important as the unities when we study communication, especially rhetorical communication. We not only experience communication as an ongoing process but also experience discontinuities in communication. This is especially true when we have a communication breakdown. For example, when the Supreme Court restricts search-and-seizure rules, it changes the way the police may operate. Law enforcement can break down until the police adjust to the new rules. The person who picks your pocket may be freed because the police made an error.

Similarly, when a person with whom you are having a casual conversation begins to get intimate, communication may break down until you decide how to respond to this unexpected development. At such moments we become painfully aware of the function our symbols play in inducing social action. At these moments we consciously strive to manage our symbols for specific goals. In short, the moments of discontinuity in our communication processes bring rhetoric into play.

Discontinuity is important in another way to our understanding of rhetoric. In all the areas of experience not narrowly thought of as primarily communication processes—legal processes, economic processes, military processes, scientific processes, political processes, and so forth—the need for discourse arises most pointedly at times when disruptions or gaps occur in the normal course of affairs. Again we find ourselves consciously selecting and using symbols to coordinate social action; we are practicing rhetoric.

Discontinuity is the culture in which rhetoric germinates, the soil in which it grows. A world without gaps, breaks, and discontinuities would be utterly predictable and utterly manageable and without need for consciously controlling the use of symbols to coordinate social actors. Everyone would know their part and play the role as scripted by the regular nature of the world. However, the human world is not a regular one. It is potholed and bumpy, riddled with unpredictable acts and sudden needs. In the human world, people have choices; they alter the course of affairs by the decisions they make. Rhetoric comes into play precisely because choices are advised and decisions coordinated through language.

The discontinuities that invite rhetorical acts also are events. They occur at specific times and places. They have initial causes, develop episodically, and eventually are brought to a conclusion. For instance, the new fire marshal in Hometown, USA, decided during last Christmas season to enforce the city code prohibiting decorated plants over three feet tall in public buildings. Since all the Christmas trees in downtown stores, restaurants, and taverns were taller than the law permitted, the fire marshal threatened to fine and close all establishments that displayed decorated Christmas trees. This act is a discontinuity because it interrupts the traditions of the community; it exists as an event. It occurs at a specific time and place and invites rhetorical acts from those affected—the proprietors of these establishments and their patrons. The initial cause of the fire marshal's act serves to elicit speeches, interviews with the local press, petitions, and even a city council debate, each of which is an episode in the development of the event to its conclusion—the marshal was fired, the ordinance was changed, or the local customs were altered.

The rhetoric addressed to the concerns, needs, issues, and alternatives that are present in these episodes is itself an event. Rhetorical communication takes place at a specifiable time and place. It occurs. Sometimes it occurs as an episode of a single message; at other times it has multiple episodes of debates, campaigns, or other serial messages. Regardless, rhetorical communication can be bracketed in ways that permit us to specify its initial causes, its episodic development, and its eventual outcomes.

For these reasons, a rhetorical approach to the ways in which people engage one another through their uses of symbols takes on a different cast than is typically found in the more general study of communication. While rhetoric can be investigated in terms of process questions, it is essentially manifested as an event. Accordingly, rhetorical theory conceptualizes communication as eventful. This conceptual orientation has important ramifications for the way rhetoric is studied and understood.

Characteristics of Rhetorical Eventfulness

Obviously, each event is a unique occurrence. It would be very difficult to develop a systematic body of thought about matters of this sort unless some meaningful characteristics could be found that were typical of all events. These typical features are found by shifting focus from the uniqueness of each event to the shared qualities of an **event type**. An *event type consists of the general characteristic or set of characteristics that distinguishes one group of events from another* (say, rhetorical events from astronomical ones).

As an event type, rhetoric falls within the general category of **action**. This category implies an agent who does something as a result of choices. It is distinguished from the general category of **motion**, which refers to the natural processes of the physical world. Within the category of action, there is a subset of six modes of action that typify rhetoric and provide a conceptual framework for rhetorical theory:

- Situated action
- Symbolic action
- Transaction
- Social action
- Strategic action
- Constitutive Action

Situated Action. Considered rhetorically, communication is a specific manifestation of language use at a specific time. We are usually disappointed by speeches or essays that are too general, failing to take into account our specific interests and concerns; they could have been addressed to anybody at any time under a wide variety of circumstances. Effective rhetoric is addressed to somebody specific and is contingent on the dynamics of the given case.

The nonrhetorical elements that are a part of the complex of forces in which communication occurs (such as prior attitudes, legal restrictions, the deadline for a decision, or existing policy commitments) serve as opportunities or limitations for the management of symbols. They provide an environment within which communicative engagement of another will take place. If we had only the words but not these situating features, rhetoric would lose much of its intelligibility as communication. It would be just words. Consequently, the salient factors of the situation in which rhetoric occurs modify and contextualize rhetorical action.[6]

For example, when 14-year-old Nathaniel Brazill was found guilty of second-degree murder for shooting his teacher, the boy's age became a mitigating concern in imposing a sentence. Brazill had shot Barry Grunow, his favorite teacher, in the face when Grunow would not permit Brazill to enter his class on the last day of school to say goodbye to two girls. Florida law specifies that a person who harms or kills another with a gun while committing a crime face a minimum sentence of 25 years without parole or credit for time served. All things being equal, we might expect that this crime would not generate interest outside West Palm Beach, where the trial took place. We also might expect that community sentiment for shooting a 35-year-old person—a law-abiding citizen who was a husband and father—for being denied access to a space under his supervision would be for the maximum sentence of life. However, Brazill's age—13 when he killed Grunow—situated his crime and his sentencing in a national discussion of juvenile crime involving a capital offense.

The offender' age, the gravity of the offense, the context of its commission, the character of the victim, and the statutory sentencing requirements modified and contextualized arguments at sentencing, as witnesses for the prosecution and the defense pleaded for the maximum sentence of life or the minimum sentence of 25 years. Beyond the court, Brazill's age situated his crime and his sentence in a national discussion conducted in television and press interviews, in news-service chat rooms and letters to the editor, and in other media outlets by the prosecuting and defense attorneys, members of the legal community, various spokespersons representing concerned interest groups, and citizens who weighed into the controversy. Their statements for or against leniency made sense because they were situated acts—rhetorical acts explicitly aimed at inducing social action in a given situation ("Treat juveniles as juveniles," "Send a message to youths that there are consequences for their actions," "Devote national resources to determine why youths are committing such crimes so we can put an end to them," and so forth). Finally, they were acts that might not make sense in any other context (say, the community's views on the sentencing of an older offender). What is pertinent to action in one situation may not apply in another.

Symbolic Action.   Humans are distinctive in their ability to use symbols. In communication, this ability is manifested most commonly in language. Languages are arbitrary systems. They are human inventions; the laws of nature do not dictate them. Languages are the means we use to ascribe meaning to reality. The action in a rhetorical event is that of uniting with or dividing from each other based on the way we talk about things. Every utterance conveys an attitude. Since the symbols of language are arbitrary and make only selective and partial reference to reality, they reflect our perception of what is important and relevant to convey meaning.[7]

In the Brazill case, was the judge's sentence of 28 years without parole a legitimate recognition of the offender's youth or was it an insensitive disregard of the Grunow family's loss? Here, as in all language use, each utterance about the propriety of the sentence suggests one point of view of the world—one attitude among many. Every attitude is also an *incipient act*, an act waiting to be done. Attitudes project what the future might be like by the presentations they make in the present. Thus the attitude that regards the sentence as just projects a world where the capital offenses of youths deserve leniency because their age does not allow them to comprehend fully the gravity of their acts. Those who regard the sentence as excessively lenient project a world where the taking of life is a criminal act that must be punished with the same absoluteness as the murderer inflicted on his victim. As we contemplate these appeals, we join or divide insofar as our symbolic presentations coincide. Rhetoric involves the actions of humans seeking agreement on their interpretations of specific experiences.

Transaction. A rhetorical event is one in which dynamic symbolic exchanges occur among the communicating parties. Rhetorical theory does not conceptualize one party as active and the other as passive or merely reactive. Although there are communicators who treat their audiences in these ways, their communication is generally deficient or nonrhetorical in character. Propaganda is an example. An audience, whether it be one person who is a conversational partner or a nation viewing a televised presidential address, is interactive. Audiences form opinions and beliefs, come to conclusions, and express themselves in a variety of ways, both verbal and nonverbal. Rhetorical action is a product of the interactions that occur within a rhetorical event. It is jointly constructed action involving all the participants acting together.[8]

Social Action. Rhetoric is a form of social action because it involves at least one person attempting to engage at least one other person. The specific mode of engagement is through symbols. Symbols are managed to influence the perceptions others have of their situations and to coordinate their subsequent responses in acts of cooperation. In other words, humans cooperate by means of the social act of constructing mutually compatible interpretations of their situations.[9] The jurors in the Brazill case had to agree that his age was not a factor in determining guilt. While events actually occur (the murder did take place), their significance in the ways they are perceived and understood and in the ways they are resolved are social constructs.

Strategic Action. Action for a particular goal is strategic. It is intentional and takes into account what can and cannot be done to achieve the goal under prevailing circumstances.[10] Judge Wennett, who ruled on the Brazill case, did not try to persuade the Grunow family or the community of the justness of his sentence; instead he informed them of his reasoning. Rhetoric is an action event in that those communicating within the event set goals and frame their messages to meet these goals. They deliberately choose means suited to their objectives, such as the types of appeals used, presentation of self, and engagement of audience responses. Further, strategy is evident in the forms of argument, language, medium of presentation, and other salient features that may shape audience perceptions. In this sense, rhetoric is an instrumental form of communication, or a means to an end.

Constitutive Action. Action that constructs a reality is constitutive. It constructs situational truths that give meaning to social behavior. Rhetoric functions as a constitutive action in that it can frame a world of moral actions and consequences for its audience. Unlike strategic action, in which we focus on the instrumental purposes of rhetoric, or its explicit attempts to influence, constitutive rhetoric is a mode of creativity. The power of symbols as a mode of constitutive action is not to persuade so much as to evoke a consciousness in the audience that discloses a world—a symbolic universe with its own values, ethical standards, and norms of conduct—and positions its members in it as responsive subjects.[11] In the debate over what punishment to impose on Nathaniel Brazill, the specific tragedy of his act became part of a larger discussion over the causes of youth violence and the norms for administering justice when that violence leads to murder. These rhetorical acts were attempts to negotiate a communal reality for a nation heartsick over carnage committed by children.

ॐ

The Rhetorical Domain

We have considered the ways in which rhetorical communication occurs as an event and how its eventfulness influences the way rhetoricians, or people who study rhetoric, conceptualize communication. While processes are involved in rhetorical communication, they are subordinated to understanding those factors that define how rhetorical events transpire. Moreover, we found that rhetorical events were of a certain type, called action events. The specific subtypes of rhetorical action highlight that rhetoric is a particular kind of action event: one in which social action is coordinated through the selective use of symbols.

Like politics, economics, and law, rhetoric is a **practical art**. It is concerned with matters where humans must make choices about conducting their affairs. Typically, these are matters where opinions are divided and there is no certain course of action to follow. Sometimes these problems are of major consequence to our community, our nation, or the world, but they also include the mundane concerns of everyday life where folks do not always see things eye-to-eye. Even in such nonearthshaking matters as getting a C in a course in which we expected an A, the need for rhetoric arises. We want to persuade the instructor to modify the grade. We plan something to say and we say it. Yet no matter how hard we try to say the right thing, we can be disappointed.

Rhetoric is an art; its practice, no matter how intelligently executed, does not guarantee a favorable outcome. Still, adhering to its precepts usually improves our chances of success. For this reason, problematic matters impel us to consider the alternatives available to us and to use prudent judgment in making a decision. Usually these decisions are about actions we should take, such as passing a zoning ordinance, finding a defendant innocent or guilty, investing our money or spending it, or even where we should go for a family vacation. At other times our choices may be more subtle in character and less obvious than overt deliberation: a child's bolstered confidence from the manner in which his mother speaks to him, a couple's sense of their relationship by the language they choose to narrate shared experiences, or a politician's manner of speech and dress to assure constituents that she is one of them. In the New York senatorial race of 2000, Hillary Clinton responded to a question about whether she could cook—an open invitation to cast her in a stereotypical female role and, therefore, not qualified for Congress. She replied that she made a mean tossed salad and a wicked omelet. These are not dishes that require much culinary skill and are often the claim to cooking fame of single males! She avoided the trap in a way that allowed both women and men to relate to her. Regardless of its form, rhetorical theory is concerned with the relationship between our selection and use of symbols—especially language in spoken or written discourse—and the choices that people make in managing their affairs.

The special focus of rhetorical theory is on the use of symbolic forms, especially persuasive appeals, to engender social action. Its subject matter includes the techniques of managing symbols as well as what transpires through their management in a rhetorical transaction. These two interrelated dimensions indicate that rhetoric is both a method and a practice.

As a method, proper usage means adhering to a set of principles. A master rhetorician follows these principles when constructing appeals. We study these appeals in courses on message preparation and the critical analysis of messages. They provide guidance in determining how a message was adapted to a situation, an audience, and a goal and how it managed available resources to shape a specific outcome.

As a practice, rhetoric achieves its finished artful form in the actual performance of a communicative transaction. A master of the art is adept at commanding personal resources of thought, strategy, and language to give ideas effective expression. The study of actual performances is frequently the subject matter of courses explicitly devoted to analyzing communication. Such studies are useful for understanding the way communication shaped specific practical choices. They are also useful as a source of data for advancing our knowledge of what happens when person A communicates for some purpose with person B. So the study of rhetoric includes two concerns: *(1) the methods followed in constructing intentional discourse—an intellectual discipline, and (2) the way symbolic performances influence practical choices—a social practice.*

Practical choices necessarily involve questions of value. Since values are involved, the personal and social stakes in these matters run high. We are confronted with choices because values differ among people, and their relevance is affected as circumstances change. Humans decide how their social world will develop; outcomes are not predetermined. However, we always run the risk that our decisions may be mistaken or faulty or that we may be misled. We risk choosing a world with social realities that are actually harmful.

A study of rhetoric thus takes us to the very core of our humanly made realities. An enlightened rhetoric can lead us to a world of hope, decency, and mutual respect. An uninformed or devious rhetoric can lead us to a world of despair and intolerance. Understanding the nature of rhetorical communication can enhance the role each of us necessarily plays as social actors who contribute to the shape our world takes. Wherever we have choices we also have freedom. There are no better alternatives in social exchanges among people who prize freedom and respect the legitimacy of different points of view.

৵

Summary

We have been discussing rhetoric, a way of thinking about human communication as a conscious art. Rhetoric is conscious because it is a way of planning talk or writing and executing the plan in order to accomplish human goals. It is an art because it is uncertain. In the following chapter we will talk about how we think when we engage in rhetoric.

❧ 2 ❧

Rhetorical Thinking

In the western United States, the region where I live, the ballot initiative is a prominent part of the political process. The driving hope of nineteenth-century Populists and Progressives was to give citizens a direct say on the laws that govern them. But sometimes the appearance of democratic process can be deceiving. David Broder, the senior political writer for the *Washington Post*, spent some time studying the initiative process and concluded that the process recently has fallen into the hands of the wealthy, who have given it a decidedly undemocratic turn. The powerful few hire professional firms to gather signatures and mount high profile publicity campaigns aimed at swaying electors to vote for spending public monies for private interests, such as spending public funds on sports facilities for teams owned by wealthy investors. Further, because successful ballot initiatives are not laws passed by representatives who are responsible to the voters for their actions, they may produce consequences harmful to the public good without making anyone accountable for these harms. An example of harmful consequences occurred a few years ago when Californians passed proposition 181, which denied public services to the children of illegal aliens. In Broder's words, "Simply put, the initiative's growing popularity has given us something that once was unthinkable—not a government of laws, but laws without government."[1]

Broder touches on a serious problem of contemporary mass societies. Writing shortly after World War I, noted American philosopher and educator John Dewey[2] argued that with a population as large, diverse, and dispersed as that of the United States, citizens could no longer rely on the politics of kin groups and small towns, in which everybody had an opportunity to voice their opinions on decisions affecting their lives. Dewey argued that in the arena of public decision making, the actions of powerful

15

individuals and groups carried *indirect* consequences for the lives of millions of citizens who were not part of the decision-making process. For example, the declaration by the Roman Catholic Church that 2000 was a Holy Year indirectly affected Italian businesses. Millions of pilgrims traveled to Rome to visit the Vatican that year. Usually Rome hosts about 18 million tourists; the government estimated that as many as 60 million would visit during the Holy Year. In fact, only about 26 million actually visited. About 60 percent of those tourists were pilgrims who spent their money on votive candles, not Versace blouses. They stayed in bed-and-breakfasts or convents, not pricey hotels. Further, due to fear of a millennium-year gridlock, Rome's city officials banned most tour buses. Consequently, pilgrims who went from site to site on foot were usually too exhausted to engage in serious shopping. For the merchants of Rome, the Church's declaration of 2000 as a Holy Year, the Department of Tourism's overestimate of the numbers who would visit Rome, and the city's decision to ban tour buses combined to visit *indirect* consequences on those who made their living from tourist trade. In the words of one city tour guide, "Mama mia. This Holy Year has brought us only religious pilgrims, not the quality money-spending tourists we're used to. Pilgrims don't spend; they eat box lunches on the steps of St. Peter's."[3]

Dewey reasoned that those who suffer the indirect consequences of another group's actions constitute "the public"—a large, diverse, and mobile aggregate of citizens who rely on representatives to protect their interests. The public, or publics, is an important concept in a liberal democracy, such as the United States, and increasingly important in rhetorical theory, as we will see in chapter 5. In this chapter, we underscore Dewey's emphasis on communication as the key practice necessary to guarantee that representatives learn of the public's interests and act in the interests of the general good. For Dewey, resolving the problems of the society rested on improved methods of debate, discussion, and persuasion.[4]

Broder, writing 75 years later, also projects communication as important to the decision-making process. He warns citizens to be aware of efforts to subvert what could be viewed as citizen participation in important decisions but actually represents the exclusion of interested citizens from the decision-making process. Says Broder:

> These players—often not even residents of the states whose laws and constitutions they seek to rewrite—have learned that the initiative is a more efficient way of achieving their ends *than the cumbersome and often time-consuming process of supporting candidates for public office and then lobbying them to pass legislation.*[5] [emphasis added]

You will notice that there is a difference between communication as Dewey and Broder imagine it: the difference between speaking and writing with an open or closed mind. In one case, communication is a means to explore and resolve public problems; it is *a discursive method for think-*

ing. In the other, communication is a means to achieve predetermined ends; it is a practice unable to escape its own partisanship. This difference is not new to the modern age. From the time Sophists wrote about rhetoric and young students paid hefty sums of drachmas to learn the art of influential speech, there has been controversy over the consequences that followed from the way people communicated on public issues.

These differences reveal some basic insights into both the boundless possibilities and the limitations of human beings. Speaking and writing are basic ways to influence the shape of the human world. Rhetorical communication can be used to foster or to inhibit participatory processes. Agency—the ability to act and to accept responsibility for action—is essential for developing political and social relations. While we depend on our use of symbols to coordinate human actions—that is, we depend on rhetoric—we also share concern about the credibility and fidelity of verbal presentations that influence practical decisions.

In chapter 1 we saw that rhetoric is eventful because it occurs at a specific time and place for a specific reason. One of the significant features of rhetoric is that it makes appeals. Because it provides reasons to believe, feel, and act in a particular way, rhetorical discourse is a mode of thinking. In this chapter we want to clarify the type of reasoning that is involved in rhetoric. In the first part of the chapter, we will consider rhetoric as a social practice: What are the characteristics of rhetorical thought *as it is actually presented*? In the second part we will consider rhetoric as a method: What are the characteristics of rhetorical thought when our focus is on *the eventfulness of a question or issue to be decided*? In both cases we will develop our discussion historically to help us maintain a clear focus and to provide a concrete context for understanding what is unique about a rhetorical perspective toward communication.

സo

Rhetoric as a Social Practice

The earliest speculations about rhetoric in the Western tradition occurred in ancient Greece through analysis of how Greeks experienced oratory in their political and military assemblies. There was a method to the modes of argument and to the uses of language; most effective speeches shared certain traits. Rhetoric also was powerful in bringing about agreements that could change human relations. For example, in 432 B.C.E. the Peloponnesian War erupted between the city-states of ancient Greece. At first, Athens pursued the war against Sparta and its allies with the youthful conviction of a rising power self-confident in its superiority. But its invasion of Attica exacted a cruel price. It fell to the Athenian leader Pericles to console and fortify his fellow Athenians—to make sense of the sacrifice of sons and husbands, fathers and friends to a city stricken with grief. He delivered his "Funeral Oration"[6] seemingly to celebrate the valor of Athenians killed in battle, but its true focus was on celebrating the virtues of public life. Pericles concluded that involvement and service, open deliberation, and putting the state's welfare above personal gain made Athens "an education for Greece." His remarks were powerful in creating an image through which grieving citizens might see beyond their personal loss to a model of citizenship practices and future aspirations of what it meant to be an Athenian. In a sense, his speech created an understanding of Athens. Today we look to our leaders to perform a similar rhetorical task of deriving sense from shared tragedy, whether the April 1999 slaughter of students and faculty members at Columbine High School or the destruction of lives and property on September 11, 2001.

In *On Rhetoric*, Aristotle (384–322 B.C.E.) was the first to codify the two dominant aspects of public discourse—method and social consequences. He taught that rhetoric was a practical art; it was a *praxis* (mode of action) that had consequences in the world. Its specific *praxis* was the social practice of speaking in a way that might influence the community's actions. By engaging culturally understood norms to influence the community's judgment, this *praxis* exercised a *dynamis* (power) to constitute political, legal, and social arrangements. Aristotle also taught that rhetoric was a **productive art**; it was a mode of thinking that produced something concrete—a speech in Aristotle's day, although today we would include any mode of discourse that might influence the judgment of its audience. Rhetoric's modes of analyzing a topic and of constructing actual discourse formed a *techné* (art) that could be described and taught.[7] Rhetorical thinking involves both aspects. We will consider its power (*dynamis*) as a social practice first and then its method as an art (*techné*).

The concept of a social practice is not easily defined, since different traditions involve meaning suited to particular ends. For our purposes, *social practice will refer to modes of conduct that are constitutive of an act*. When we refer to a practice as "constitutive," we mean that a way of doing something, such as speaking according to certain conventions, is necessary to bring some other condition or state into being. These may be everyday micropractices, such as the daily words of encouragement parents offer their children as a way of building self-confidence, or the more macropractices of public speakers who commonly use the pronoun "we" to develop a shared sense of identity with their audiences. Or they may be more momentous practices, such as the Declaration of Independence, through which a group of British colonials established a new political identity independent of the crown and defined the core of their new identity by guaranteeing in writing certain inalienable rights—life, liberty, and the pursuit of happiness. These conditions of life—a sense of self-confidence, group identification, and political identity—are inextricably bound to the vocabularies we use to express them.

In addition to the "state of being" brought about by communicating in a certain way, the idea of "constitutive act" also includes the actual "mode of

communication" itself. For example, activities such as deliberating or negotiating are social practices that constitute social relations, they bring them
into being. When we deliberate about gun control, for example, we understand our activity to be pointed toward resolving such issues as the conditions of purchase, registration, and ownership of firearms. These are
matters on which we might disagree and experience uncertainty about what
we should do. We understand that we cannot deliberate without a partner
who can voice opinions other than our own, even if the partner is our own
internal voice helping to test our thinking. When we deliberate we try to
discover the issues involved, consider all relevant points of view, allow partners to express opinions, and so forth. Each of these activities is part of the
practice of deliberation, and none would be possible without discourse.

A social practice also assumes a relationship between those who engage in the practice and the rest of society. In this respect, social practices
are culture specific. I once visited the bazaar in the "old town" section of
Mostar in Bosnia with a group of American academicians. As we visited the
merchants' booths at our own speed and to suit our own tastes, we eventually became separated. One member of our group, a colleague from the
Philippines, rejoined me after a while. When I asked how her day had been,
she informed me that she was negotiating. How could that be, I wondered,
since she was talking to me? She told me that she had found a carpet she
fancied and had offered the brothers who ran the shop about half their asking price in U.S. dollars, highly prized for its stability against their inflation-
ridden national currency. One brother thought it was a good offer, but the
other wanted to hold out for more. "They're thinking it over," she assured
me. Apparently they were because as we passed their storefront she patted
her handbag and continued walking down the street. I looked over my
shoulder and saw the brothers fall into heated discussion. Later she told me
she had closed the deal at her offered bid. To my Western eyes, this mode
of negotiation—the offer, the leave-taking, the stroll past the storefront,
patting the handbag—was outside my cultural experience. But for my colleague from the Philippines, it was a social practice in which she obviously
was well versed, as were the Bosnian merchants with whom she was negotiating. There were "rhetorical rules" in play, so to speak, that constituted
the very act of negotiation and all parties had to know them to carry out
the transaction. The cultural specificity of social practices reveals that their
meanings are shared and not the property of any single individual.

In antiquity, the social practice of rhetoric as an art of practical discourse (the speech making that occurred in assemblies, law courts, and
public commemorations) emerged in relation to other discursive social
practices pertaining to public life: narrative and dialectic. Narrative, dialectic, and rhetoric remain important for public decision making, and we
still engage in these discursive social practices as modes of communal
thinking about life and experience. Examining the social practices in ancient Greece offers us some basic contrasts that help to clarify rhetoric as a

distinctive mode of thinking. In later chapters, we will consider additional ways in which rhetoric and dialectic interact. In chapter 10, we will return to narrative to examine in greater detail how rhetoricians today consider its relationship to rhetoric.

Narrative

Imagine for a moment that we are back in the time of Homeric Greece, around the ninth century B.C.E. Most of us would live in small villages or in the countryside. Those of us who are males likely would have a trade; we would be farmers, shepherds, sailors, potters, artisans, merchants, traders, and the like. Those who are females likely would be managers of the household, and if of sufficient means responsible for the slaves who worked on estates. Females also could occupy positions of leadership in religious practices and festivals.[8] Because we live in communities, our survival requires social cooperation; we depend on others and they on us to provide necessary goods and services. Unlike humans in the wild who might act as beasts by ripping food from the weak, having indiscriminate sexual relations, or killing prey, our congregation into social units requires that these behaviors not occur, lest the unit destroy itself. Social survival requires cooperation to provide food for the community, regulation to protect against unwanted sexual relations, and organization to defend our settlement against hostile attack.

Cooperation requires agreement among individuals concerning common interests and, usually, norms that express them. For example, our contemporary communities express their standards of conduct and belief in formal documents: norms of conduct may be expressed in student handbooks; in the charters of organizations; or in a religion's articles of faith. These formal documents are only part of the picture. For example, your college or university is unique; its personality is expressed through dress, special events, local hangouts, student attitudes, preferred curricula, and especially traditions. The traditions of your college or university have an "official" expression, which usually is perpetuated by the administration and faculty on appropriate occasions. But schools also have "unofficial" traditions perpetuated by the student grapevine and passed from each class to its successor. Mostly this aspect of tradition takes the form of stories about groups, events, courses, professors, and students whose unusual conduct becomes legendary. It also includes accounts of magnanimous acts, of contributions to campus and community life, and of other acts that bring honor to your group or school. To be a member in good standing in the student community requires that you acquire knowledge of the lore: memorable pranks played by your fraternity, sorority, or campus group; your chemistry professor's reputation; what to expect from this course; why your sorority, fraternity, or club sponsors a particular event; and so on. Much of our initiation into the norms of our community—our acculturation as members—occurs through such narrative tales.

So it was with the Homeric Greeks. Because they lived in communities, had interests to protect, depended on one another for vital goods or services, and occasionally found themselves at cross-purposes, they were in need of political and social guidance. Homeric tales were a principal source of this guidance. Narratives tell stories. They give us an account of human events in the form of a plot, with characters who act and react, and with a conclusion that resolves the story's issues. Homeric tales were heroic stories. They were tales of great men and women, including the gods, who were locked in momentous struggles. They depicted conflict between good and evil, represented challenges to virtue, portrayed exemplary conduct, and also illustrated the problems of a people living in perilous times. Through the resolution of these issues, Homer's narratives established paradigms for acting. If you understood his story, then in addition to being entertained, you also were instructed on how to live in your community by partaking of its traditions.

The Homeric tradition was an oral tradition. Since listeners lacked alphabetic skills of reading and writing, they learned the tales by hearing them intoned repeatedly. And since the tales were used as guides for resolving disputes, solving problems, and doing the right thing, the bards who sang them achieved great cultural status. They became the custodians of community traditions, which meant they were the moral teachers of Hellas.

As a social practice, narratives transmit norms. Though norms come to us most dynamically through narratives, they do not exist in narratives. Norms exist in the culture of a community. Narratives act as bridges between cultural standards of conduct and belief and the material realities confronting members of that culture. They are bridges of a special type and require a bit more explanation if we are to appreciate the differences between a normative pattern in thinking and other modes.

A narrative is scripted. It tells a particular tale in which the world is represented in one way rather than another. For a tale to be accepted, its boundaries for action must make sense within the intellectual, emotional, and moral framework of the community to which it is addressed. Tales can be false and still be acceptable if they represent the world in a manner that agrees with the vision of the community. But a tale that violates the framework of meaning in a culture, no matter how true its lesson, will likely be rejected. Consequently, narratives work within a tradition and tend to perpetuate the tradition.[9] Narrative thinking transmits norms; it does not challenge them. Modern narrative theory modifies some of these claims, as we will see in chapter 10. However, within the oral culture in which Homer created his tales, or from roughly the ninth through the fifth centuries B.C.E., narratives initiated the ancient Greeks into normative patterns of thinking without provoking their audience to be critical of the norms they transmitted. Narratives tended not to be reflexive—to ponder their assertions—vis-à-vis the culture they transmitted. This lack of critical attitude was the basis for Plato's famous attack against narrative tales set forth in his indictment of the poets.

Dialectic

In *The Republic*, Plato (428–328 B.C.E.) attacked the poets for teaching the youth in ways that did not permit critical examination of premises. The poets sang tales that accepted cultural belief as conventional wisdom and taught them to the youth. Because the poets transmitted culture uncritically, Plato banned them from his school, the Academy, and replaced them with philosophers who were practitioners of a different mode of communication.

The philosophers did not reject the importance of norms for communal living. But they maintained that the quality of communal life would be diminished if the norms were not based on truth. For example, suppose that through stories in which the brave and strong always prevail, a tradition perpetuates the norm that "might makes right." A philosopher would want to inspect that norm, not grant it as an assumption. What if the mighty person is a bully, or places personal gain above communal well-being, or through stupidity fights the wrong foe? Such possibilities should be considered to determine whether this norm is valid.

Plato believed that by questioning the opinions of the day, he could expose those that were false. If people recognized the fallacies in their thinking, he believed they would be forced to cultivate different habits of thought better suited to uncover the truth. The new habit he hoped to cultivate was the method of question and answer, called *dialectic*, which he had learned from his teacher Socrates. Dialectical thinking posed objections to all doubtful propositions until the objections were refuted or the original proposition was replaced by one better able to withstand critical examination.

Plato believed that there are Truths and that we can have insight into them. However, he also believed that we could never capture these Truths in words, rather we could only approximate them. Moreover, he doubted that we would recognize the force of insights afforded by dialectic unless we discovered the insights ourselves. In other words, it wasn't enough for someone else to reveal insights about the Truth; you had to discover it for yourself through active discussion. For these reasons, Plato did not write a philosophical treatise on dialectic and the Truth but portrayed the human quest for the Truth in dramatic works called dialogues. In them, each of the characters—usually a person who claims to be an expert and Socrates who claims to be ignorant but wants to learn the Truth from the supposed expert—engage in conversation. In this conversation Socrates acts as a gadfly by "bugging" the supposed expert with questions that both reveal the expert's ignorance and produce new insights into the subject matter. These new insights are not the result of teaching a doctrine external to the conversational partners. Instead the inner truth surfaces in the dialogue. Hence, Plato's Socrates calls his practice of dialectic his "midwife art." This powerful female image of helping a partner give birth to his or her ideas depicts discourse—speaking and writing—as an act that requires us to love and to seek to help our conversational mates. Consequently, by the end of each dialogue, Socrates' prodding questions pay off if they succeed in giving birth to truths on which both parties agree. But these conclusions are only "provisional truths," since further dialectical examination might give birth to new insight. Plato's dialogues illustrate the need to explore issues through question and answer.

Today we call Plato's dialectic critical thinking. We engage in critical thinking whenever we want to test the strength of an idea. We do this by raising counterexamples to show where the idea does not apply or by searching for inconsistencies or raising arguments in refutation. Like Socrates, we engage in critical thinking with a partner, called an *interlocutor*, and we seek our partner's agreement on which criticisms hold and which do not. However, sometimes we fail to achieve agreement. The same is true in Plato's dialogues. Not every dialogue ends in agreement, and sometimes Socrates comes out second best in the exchange.

The dialogues that do not quite work out the way Socrates intends reveal a special characteristic of analytic thought. The truths that dialectic attempts to establish depend on a set of shared assumptions. For example, Plato assumes that no person consciously chooses to do evil. Thus, whenever Socrates engages in a conversation in which moral conduct is the issue, he always argues that if the person whose behavior is in question knew the Truth about virtue, that person would cease to act in evil ways. At the conclusion of such discussions, Socrates and his interlocutor are interested in certifying or refuting the proposition in doubt. But they can reach agreement only if the interlocutor shares Socrates' assumption that humans do not consciously choose to be evil. Two additional conclusions follow.

Dialectic works out the truth of an assertion on the basis of certain assumptions. But there is no guarantee that the world is reflected accurately in those assumptions. We can just as easily imagine a world in which humans consciously choose to do evil as we can imagine Plato's world in which they do not. For example, it is difficult to imagine that individuals who knowingly cheat—whether card sharks playing poker, merchants selling inferior goods to their customers, citizens filing false tax returns—do not know that their actions lack virtue. Regardless of the assumption, the point remains that dialectically established propositions are true only if we grant that the world agrees with the interlocutors' assumptions. Dialectic gives us an analysis of a *possible* world (i.e., what the world would be like *if* we grant certain assumptions) without a guarantee that the real world in which we live is the same (i.e., whether these assumptions *actually* apply).

In addition to this, there is no guarantee that dialectic will lead to appropriate action in accord with its truths. Dialectic does not always coordinate truth with action because it addresses our reason without regard for our motivations. In other words, we may be unable to refute or even may be convinced by a person's argument, but we still may be unmoved to act. For example, we may be convinced by the arguments of Karl Marx about the vices of capitalism but still not become socialists and, in fact, support and reap the benefits from the capitalist system. Dialectical analysis does not necessarily lead to action because it concerns itself with the rational certainty of a claim, while human action requires more than reason alone. Action stems from the intersection of reason with experience in ways that also engage feelings and values.[10] This realization prompts a third mode of thinking, the rhetorical mode, that attempts to intersect the secured premise with the ways people experience that premise in everyday existence.

Rhetoric

In their narrative tales, the Greeks found normative patterns of thinking. These norms provided the necessary stability for communities to share a common orientation to social life. In the critical thought of dialectical oppositions, the Greeks found analytic patterns of thinking. Analytic thinking sought the stability of truths that transcended the uncertainties of day-to-day living. By contrast, rhetoric was much less attuned to permanence and much more attuned to change. As the Greek city-state developed and as the participation of citizens increased—especially in Athens—the need to achieve communal consensus on issues of the day gained in importance. These were issues for which there were no certain answers. The answers to issues depended on whose testimony was credible, the factors that weighed most heavily as evidence, or what point of view was adopted—matters of **contingency**.

The experience of the Greeks is not far removed from our own. We know, for example, that some matters are beyond our control; they are subject to the laws of nature. We cannot make lead float in water by casting a vote, or decide by fiat that radioactive isotopes will no longer be harmful to humans, or change by whimsy the ebb and flow of the tides. These are matters of nature. They have fixed properties that we must understand and be able to explain if we wish to use lead, isotopes, or the tides to our advantage. On the other hand, a great deal in our world is not determined by the laws of nature but by the actions of humans. Our laws, our literature, and our economic systems are arbitrary in the sense that they were not foreordained by nature but are products of human design. Consequently, when we confront social problems, we usually lack an obviously correct course of action. What we decide to do is *contingent* on what we want to accomplish, what we value, and what we find intellectually, emotionally, and ethically appealing. In a word, such contingent situations are open ended. They provided the original need for rhetorical communication and have sustained this need through today. Faced with the uncertainty of contingencies and the need to act, we seek arguments that will help us decide what to do.

As I was writing this chapter, for instance, I happened to read an article in *Discover* magazine. *Discover* publishes articles on scientific discoveries. It contains articles on such topics as outer space, the World Wide Web, the physics of guitars, disease, global warming, and interactive museums—open-ended topics that call for rhetorical thinking. The article began with the announcement:

> Scientists studying Earth's ancient history have received an exciting
> message in a bottle. Hollow carbon molecules, called buckyballs, are
> raining down from outer space—and trapped inside are samples of
> what the solar system was like billions of years ago, before the forma-
> tion of our planet.[11]

The article continued to set forth the way buckyballs were first discovered,
the tests scientist Luann Becker administered to confirm her hunches, and
the results of her tests. Becker's questions and the procedures she followed
to answer them illustrated how dialectic operates within science. Becker
and her associates assumed that there was a discoverable answer to the
composition of buckyballs, that their molecular structure would or would
not be like known molecular structures on Earth, and that the results of
the tests would support inferences that informed scientists would take seriously about Earth's origins. However, this type of argument, which can
be highly contested, does not raise an issue for most communities.

Another article in the same issue of *Discover* was on the Asian swamp
eel, which had been discovered in drainage ditches near the Everglades.[12]
The eels, which were not native to Florida and were probably imported as
pets or for exotic food, were probably dumped in drainage ditches near the
Everglades, where they multiplied. Their diet consists of small fish and
crayfish that hide from wading birds as marshes dry out. If the eels con-
sume them first, not only will the population of these fish drop precipi-
tously but the birds will starve. This article also relied on scientific
observation and procedures to reach its conclusion, but unlike our first example this threat to the balance of nature raises the question of what to
do. Should the forces of nature be left to sort this out on their own? Or
should there be human intervention, such as electroshocking the invaders,
as proposed by ecologist John Curnutt of the U.S. Geological Survey?

Both articles hold out the promise that there is a truth that can be discovered about causes and consequences. The second raises an additional
question about conduct that is open to disagreement and about which
there is no clear truth to be discovered. The best we can do is to offer probable answers—likelihoods of what will result if we leave nature to its own
devices, say, or actively try to kill the intruding eels. The second article reflects the type of decision we commonly must make in our social lives and
in dealing with civic issues in a democracy. Discussions about how to address such questions had their origins in Athenian democracy, which
placed a premium on civic participation.

Civic participation, which had been growing in Athens since the rule
of Solon during the sixth century B.C.E., gained significant steam in the
fifth century with the rise of a new breed of politician.[13] Originally Greek
politics had been largely controlled by aristocratic and wealthy elites. They
commonly conferred in private prior to an assembly meeting to determine
how they wished issues to be decided. Then, speaking as a cohesive voice
in the assembly, they created the impression that a large majority had

formed an opinion. This strategy worked until an aspiring politician, Kleon, rose one day to proclaim he was a lover of the *demos* (the people). His direct appeals to common citizens effectively circumvented the powerful elites. Kleon's appeal had an electric effect on the previously unorganized masses. Now there was a **rhetor** (the ancient Greek term for orator), soon followed by others of the same mold, who professed to speak directly to common citizens as advocates for their interests. Kleon's practice earned him the title "demagogue," leader of the people, derived from the Greek *demos* for the people and *agogos* for leader. As you can imagine, the power elite of fifth-century Athens didn't think much of these new politicians and reframed demagogue to connote the pejorative "leader of the mob," which is the connotation this term still carries today.

The tension between established political power and populist rhetoric is important for understanding the power of rhetoric and the intense fear and opposition it has aroused historically. Democracy has always been marked by tension between society's elites and common citizens, summarized by the observation that in a democracy the people reign while the elites rule. Historically, each has deeply distrusted the other. Prior to the rise of the demagogues, Athenian democracy was more nominal than real, with many measures enacted to keep the masses quiet and in line. The practice of direct appeal changed the political landscape. It both heightened Athenian awareness of the power of oratory to organize the masses and mold civic decisions that had consequences for their lives.

Sophistic rhetoric[14] was based on the idea of arguing from **probability**. Since human affairs offered no transcendent truths, the quality of civic life depended on the quality of agreements citizens reached in their assemblies and law courts. Protagoras (480–411 B.C.E.) expressed this doctrine succinctly in his aphorism: "Man is the measure of all things." He used the word "man" in the generic sense of "citizens of the polis" (the public realm of the Greek city-state). He taught that citizen consensus on public matters was a judgment about which arguments they found trustworthy. Consensus stood between absolute criteria (which Protagoras and the other Sophists rejected) and thoroughly relative standards (that Sophists are usually accused of advancing).[15] The Sophists endorsed a social truth that evolved from the polis and was not captured exclusively by any single partisan view. The assembly or the jury found this truth and approved it through its vote. In a world without absolute Truth, opinion prevails.

Protagoras's view that humans are the measure of social truths expressed the basic sophistic tenet that rhetoric constituted human **possibilities**. Every citizen had the expectation of participating in civic affairs, but in order to do that responsibly, each one had to have a sense of justice and civic virtue. Protagoras believed that the quality of the city is reciprocally related to the quality of its citizens. As the quality of civic life increases, citizenly virtue increases—people gain a higher sense of justice and civic virtue. As citizens behave with a greater sense of justice and civic virtue, the quality of life in the city increases. A later teacher of rhetoric, Isocrates, held a similar view. He believed that rhetoric was the master art for politics and emphasized that rhetorical education should be concerned with helping the student acquire command of language in order to advance civic ends.

How do you arrive at a sound opinion? Does whatever works count? Opponents of the Sophists thought that was what they trained their students to believe. But the actual pedagogy of Protagoras and Gorgias of Leontini (c. 490 B.C.E.–c. 380 B.C.E.), another important Sophist, suggests they were teaching their students to engage in a thought process that sought more than skill at making tricky arguments. They taught their students to argue both sides of an issue in order to discover which had the stronger arguments. They called this method **dissoi logoi**, or two-sided argument.

Let's return to the problem of the invading Asian swamp eels in the Everglades to illustrate this method. They produce environmental harm by disrupting the fragile ecology of the wetlands, which are the heart of an intricate ecosystem supporting water quality, vegetation, species reproduction, habitable water, and so forth. Disrupting wetlands, scientists have proven, has undesirable consequence of major proportions. This seems to justify human intervention to exterminate the unwanted invaders. Ecologist Curnutt proposed electroshocking them as **likely** to rid the Everglades of these invaders. On the other hand, fully effective extermination might require an auto-electroshock system. But such a system is **not likely** to be selective, and could produce undesired results by killing species indiscriminately, further upsetting the Everglades' delicate ecosystem. In that case, it is better to do nothing until a more selective method of extermination is available. The proposition that we should preserve the Everglades involves contradictory beliefs on what to do. Considering both sides, we would weigh the arguments for and against using electroshock to find the stronger among opposing opinions, the one that seemed to have the greater degree of likelihood. Are the Everglades more likely to be harmed if we use electroshock or if we do nothing? The Sophists held that in the absence of truth, *dissoi logoi* provided a method for determining the better course of public action. In order to decide a public issue, the *dissoi logoi* taught students that they had to confront arguments on both sides, pro and con, to determine which side was stronger.

In addition to promoting public deliberation as a method of two-sided argument, the Sophists also taught their students that the force of an argument depended on whether it was appropriate for the occasion, the audience, and the speaker. Sound rhetorical practice was characterized as having **prepon** (propriety), as being appropriate for a specific time and place. Speeches given in assemblies, courts, or at festivals demanded different modes of speaking, different attitudes toward the audience and the speaking occasion, and different uses of language. These differences are culturally negotiated and learned by members of the culture. By observation, and by guidance from our elders, we learn that we can sing and dance at festive occasions such as weddings, but we are expected to be reserved at somber occasions such as funerals. Equally, a leader will be expected to speak in the assembly and must know what may or may not be said about an issue, how far to go in attacking opponents, examples that will be acceptable or offensive to the audience, and so forth. *Prepon* implied its opposite *aprepes* (impropriety), which is also culturally learned. To excel as a rhetor required knowledge about propriety and impropriety to enhance esteem of the speaker by the audience and to avoid offending listeners.

Returning to the swamp eel example, we live at a time of increasing environmental consciousness, which makes it **inappropriate** to maintain we should be indifferent to the invasion but most **appropriate** to urge caution in selecting a solution. Within the community of wetlands ecologists, proposals to kill invading species are commonly regarded as the best course, which makes Curnutt's argument *prepon*—appropriate for that audience. But if the audience believed all life is sacred and humankind has no right to exterminate even unwanted creatures, Curnutt's proposal would be *aprepes*, or inappropriate, because it violated the audience's value structure.

The Sophists understood that, in addition to reinforcing tradition by adhering to norms of propriety, rhetoric was also a social practice that destabilized tradition by inventing fresh ways of thinking and acting. As a corollary to *prepon*, they taught their students to be alert for the opportune moment to make an argument. This sense for the moment was referred to as **kairos**. Literally, *kairos* carries two meanings: "right time" and "right measure." *Kairos* was the sense of time that related to knowing when to speak and when to be silent, when the time was right to make a particular argument and when it was best to wait. We commonly refer to it as having a sense of timing. In addition to "timing," the Greeks also used it to convey a sense of the occasion on which a particular argument could be made with maximum effect. In August 1963 Martin Luther King, Jr. had an occasion to address the entire nation on the meaning and purpose of the Civil Rights movement while speaking to the 200,000 people who had gathered around the Reflecting Pool between the Washington Monument and the Lincoln Memorial. This was a **kairotic** moment of "radical occasionality." For his speech to achieve its possibilities in reshaping American consciousness of civil rights, it had to convey the "right measure" of problem and hope. His "I Have a Dream" speech succeeded in moving the civil rights agenda from a regional problem to a national issue involving all citizens.

Kairos is a correlate of *prepon*, since remarks to seize the golden moment must be appropriate to that moment and its audience. The Sophists recognized that *kairos* provides the time frame for strategic action, for knowing when the moment is ripe to make an argument and when it is best to be silent. In addition to strategic opportunity, the radical occasionality of a kairotic moment provides an opening to invent a fresh argument, something not in the tradition yet responsive to it. Fresh arguments can challenge customary patterns of thought and action or offer insights that make us rethink our commitments and ways of acting. In this way, *kairos* destabilizes our "taken for granted" assumptions. But for this to occur, the moment must be right so that the audience will be receptive to a fresh point of view on the question before it and ready to respond.

For example, in 1995 former football star O. J. Simpson was on trial for allegedly stabbing to death his former spouse, Nicole Brown Simpson. Press coverage revealed that the marriage had a history of physical violence resulting in legal action against Mr. Simpson but that the courts had not imposed a stiff penalty on him for physically assaulting his spouse. Graphic pictures of her battered face and a 911 tape of Nicole calling for help during one of O. J.'s outbursts appeared regularly on television. This graphic evidence of physical and psychological assault sparked a national discussion on partner violence. The evidence provided the kairotic moment for advocates of greater police responsiveness and stiffer penalties to make their case to a national audience. The graphic evidence provided an opening for these advocates to invent a different public awareness of the severity of spousal abuse. This invention came in the form of shared examples (the pictures and the tape), a vocabulary to describe the act (*violence* became a more commonly used term than *abuse*; *spousal* replaced *domestic* to describe the violence), and arguments that took the act out of the private sphere of marital relations and into the public sphere of power (society's need to protect the weaker from the stronger) and law (assault and battery). When the issue was on everyone's mind, and the evidence was difficult to deny, the time was ripe to change people's attitudes and, possibly, their behavior.

Finally, because the Sophists thought political possibilities were open ended, they regarded language as a creative force for shaping possibilities. They adopted a **playful attitude** by experimenting with language. The most celebrated Sophist in this regard was Gorgias, who experimented with stylistic figures and who was fascinated with the psychological power of *logos* in the sense of speech. His famous argument "On Non-Being" makes this claim:

> Reality does not exist.
> If reality exists, it cannot be grasped.
> If reality could be grasped, it could not be communicated.[16]

Why would Gorgias spend his time worrying about rhetoric and *logos* with such a pessimistic view? He provides at least a partial answer in his famous speech, "Encomium of Helen." Gorgias attempts to build a case excusing Helen of Troy for starting the Trojan War by eloping with Paris. One of the excuses for her behavior lies in the power *logos* exerted over her. His argument offers a sense of the inherent power Gorgias found in language and speech. The *logos* is able to "stop fear and banish grief and create joy and nurture pity."[17] It works like a drug with irresistible power to bring us under its control. The power of language to arouse and calm emotions made it potent for guiding another person's soul. For the philosophers, this claim represented the chief danger of rhetoric, since anything this potent, if it were abused, posed a threat to the community. But for Gorgias and the Sophists, the philosophers were mistaken in assuming there could be any form of speech immune from this power. Actually, the philosophers' doctrine on transcendent Truth posed a greater threat because it deceived believers into falsely thinking they could escape opinion and act on the Truth. In fact, all we could ever have is an opinion about the truth and the options to act based on opinion.

Our brief comparison of narrative, dialectic, and rhetoric shows that each influences practical conduct (figure 2.1). Each also invites us to reason differently. Narratives provide stories that are representative of life. They invite us to imagine and to project reality in terms of a story line. The images they provide depend on and draw from shared traditions. Because narratives provide vivid verbal pictures of life, they can have enormous power to shape our perceptions of existential circumstances and judgments we based on those perceptions.

	Narrative	Dialectic	Rhetoric
Mode of Thinking	storytelling: normative, traditional, non-critical in nature	posing of objections to all doubtful propositions until objections are refuted or the original proposition is replaced by one better able to withstand critical examination	two-sided argument to arrive at likelihoods based on audience standards; intersection of reason with experience in ways that engage feelings and values
Used by	bards; everyone	experts	everyone
Outcome	transmits norms	criticism; explores and tests norms, assumptions, premises	probable conclusions
Structure	stories	question and answer; critical thinking	continuous discourse of speeches and essays
Focus	*infer* norms for appropriate/valorous action	rational certainty, not action	opinion or belief that leads to action
Subject Matter	traditions; reality reflected through storyline	generalizations, abstract principles	specific cases

Figure 2.1 Comparison of Narrative, Dialectic, and Rhetoric

In contrast, dialectic tries to abstract generalizations rather than to depict particular circumstances. Dialectic provides the clash of conflicting ideas about the basic principles of life. It invites us to conceptualize these principles as realities on which material existence depends. The principles it presents are drawn from seriously held opinions. Through question and answer, dialectic attempts an abstract inquiry into the principles that are the foundations of opinions. Because dialectic provides a compelling analysis of the rationality of our opinions, it can have enormous power in convincing us that a proposition is true or false within a given set of assumptions.

Unlike narrative, rhetoric does not present ideas in the form of stories; unlike dialectic, it does not address abstract generalizations. Rhetoric provides appeals that advise us about belief and conduct in a particular case. It invites us to interpret reality in terms of hypotheses about prudent conduct. Rhetoric's appeals depend on and are drawn from audience opinions. It attempts to evoke moral, emotional, and rational commitments to belief and actions through appeals designed to reach an intersection between ideas and experiences. Because rhetoric addresses specific cases, it has enormous power to focus thoughts and feelings and to shape practical judgments.

Though rhetoric differs from narrative and dialectic as a mode of thinking, it is not divorced from their basic concerns. Rhetorical events are themselves occurrences situated within larger contexts of a heritage. Consequently, rhetoric is never free from a tradition of assumed values. Further, rhetorical presentations in an open society may be subjected to the scrutiny of critical audiences or to the counterarguments of those who hold different opinions. Ultimately they require premises and reasoning that can ward off refutation during deliberation. However, rhetoric engages values and reason in its own unique fashion by addressing concrete cases in terms that are pertinent to how people experience the hopes and fears of life.

The need for rhetorical modes of thinking remains as important today as it was in antiquity. We still face problematic situations that require common effort to be resolved. We rely on our management of language to reason jointly to commonly acceptable solutions. We seek adherence and commitment to these solutions by projecting their impacts on our lives as feeling, valuing, and reasoning creatures.

Finally, the type of thinking typical to rhetorical events provides final insight into the role that rhetorical uses of language play in inducing and coordinating social action. The overall patterns of our experiences can take remarkably different paths. Some people lead lives devoted to service, some to greed, some to pleasure, some to survival. The fundamental questions remain: "What does our experience mean?" and "How can we enhance our lives?" Humans simply wouldn't be human if they did not ascribe meanings to their experiences, if they did not share these meanings with others, and if these shared meanings did not bring about an interpretation of what life has been and what it might become. The hallmark of human intelligence is our ability to use symbols to create and share meanings. Not only do we share our meanings with one another, but we also seek consensus on what our experiences mean, and we elicit and promote mutual cooperation on those of our experiences that involve common interests. This is the impulse for rhetoric.

໑
Rhetoric as a Method

In the fourth century B.C.E., Aristotle (384–322 B.C.E.) taught rhetoric at Plato's school, the Academy. His *Rhetoric* is a compilation of his lectures on the subject. Aristotle wanted his pupils to be clear on what was part of the subject and what was not. He noted that everyone in the polis speaks in ways that seek to influence the minds and hearts of others. Some do it well, some poorly, but in the public realm all humans speak with this purpose in mind. For him, the fact that some consistently spoke well meant that by observing their behavior, we could abstract the principles they followed when persuading. The principles constitute a framework for thinking communicatively about the eventfulness of rhetoric. We will outline this framework as our final consideration in this chapter.

Today rhetoric is most generally understood as using symbols to induce and coordinate social action. Most times, the rhetorical function of symbols is by design (although not always, as we will see in chapters 11 through 14). As an art or method, rhetoric is concerned with the purposive selection and arrangement of symbols; it is intentional discourse. Symbols refer to any meaningful system of signs that is referential. Music, dance, painting, mathematical notation, and cinema (to cite just five examples) comprise such systems. They can influence our perceptions, attitudes, beliefs, and even behaviors. Thus, in the contemporary sense of the term, they may be regarded as rhetorical at some level and, indeed, are examined as such by contemporary rhetoricians.

Among human symbol systems, language is the most basic. It is also the most pervasive and most complex of these systems and the one most clearly and explicitly used to influence others. To coordinate social action implies influence of some sort. At the very least it would include the inducement of an attitude, but it can extend to moving others to cooperative physical actions. The coordination of social actions covers a wide spectrum of concerns: from feelings such as elation or depression reflected in words, tones, or gestures; to beliefs reflected in opinions, arguments, and isms; to physical activities directed toward the management of social relations (such as soliciting a friend's help or campaigning for a political candidate) and the physical environment (such as riding a bike to conserve energy or changing diets to promote health). Mostly, we understand the inducement and coordination of social action to be concerned with the choices people make, especially choices about practical action. In sum, rhetoric's basic concern is with how party A (a rhetor) speaks or writes to party B (an audience) to affect that person's choices.

Clearly this concern is related to a number of disciplines. Rhetoric and psychology overlap insofar as psychology studies how the mind processes symbols and how this processing influences behavior. Rhetoric and political science overlap insofar as political science studies how interests are formed and represented to the state. Rhetoric and ethics overlap insofar as ethics studies the consequences of human choices. But rhetoric is not the same as, nor can it be reduced to, these studies. It is concerned exclusively with the interaction among thought-language-presentation-participants that occurs within the boundaries of a message, the options available to performers (rhetors) for managing this interaction in desired ways, and the consequences of the rhetors' choices. It is, as we have been saying, a mode of thinking.

As a mode of thinking, rhetoric differs from other disciplines in that it tends to be methodical rather than substantive. This does not mean that rhetoric lacks content but that its content is more concerned with the *hows* of what we're communicating about than the *whats* of what we're communicating about. This distinction was expressed most clearly when Aristotle observed in the opening sentence of the *Rhetoric* that "rhetoric is the counterpart of dialectic." Earlier we distinguished dialectic from rhetoric in a way that emphasized the difference between communication aimed at securing a transcendent Truth and one aimed at securing agreement of opinion. By claiming that rhetoric and dialectic are counterparts, Aristotle reminds us that these two modes of communication also are complements to, although different from, one another. They share many of the same traits, although in important ways they are distinct. These complementary features help us to understand the methodological side of rhetoric. Here we will begin to sketch these methodological features. Later, in chapters 6 through 9, we will develop them in greater detail.

First, both dialectic and rhetoric are modes of arguing. Dialectic is a mode of arguing that occurs when experts discuss their subjects in technical fashion. For example, when two physicists, two lawyers, or two photographers engage in conversation about a doubtful proposition unique to their field, they use a vocabulary, invoke a theory, and resort to abstractions that are specialized. Laypeople unfamiliar with the language and assumptions of the field generally do not understand the conversation. Rhetoric is a mode of arguing suited to laypeople. It presents contentions within the boundaries of lay opinion and experience.

Second, both dialectic and rhetoric are universal methods. They apply to all subjects but have no subject matter that is properly their own. Whenever experts make arguments among themselves, be they chemists, bankers, literary critics, or whatever, they use dialectic—arguments that critically test premises—to frame their technical proofs. Similarly, whenever laypeople have interests in a matter (the side effects of prescription drugs, lending policies of their credit union, censorship of novels), they use rhetoric—nontechnical appeals suited to the subject and audience (*prepon*), to help them render a sound judgment. As arguments become more technical, they become dialectical arguments proper to a specific discipline or domain of knowledge; as they become less technical and more focused on the needs for action, they enter the realm of rhetoric.

Third, dialectic and rhetoric are both modes of argument based on **opinion**. When experts speak among themselves, the objective of their inquiry is **criticism**. When an orator presents an appeal, the objective is **persuasion**. Dialectic systematically examines opinions and the necessary conclusions that must follow. The issue is always whether the opinion is sound. Rhetoric, on the other hand, examines problematic situations in terms of prevailing opinions. It tries to engage some opinions and refute others in order to urge a particular, partisan judgment.

Fourth, both are in the realm of the **contingent**. This is the realm of circumstance where certainty is unavailable. Rhetoric and dialectic begin with opinions. The dialectician asks the opinion of an interlocutor and then tests it through critical deliberation of question and answer. The rhetorician begins with audience-held opinions and uses these as a basis for constructing arguments. Because both begin with opinion, they are in the realm of open-ended thinking, where conflict is possible because we lack absolute certainty about the matters at hand. There is a stronger and weaker, a better and worse, but not necessarily a true or false solution to the problem. Consequently, the results of dialectic and of rhetoric are **probable** solutions. In dialectic, these probabilities may reach the point of virtual certainty. This would occur if we fail to find counterarguments to refute an opinion. In rhetoric, the likelihoods are less certain, always subject to the quality of the audience judging the remarks and the uncertainties of situations that are subject to last-minute changes—as happens all the time in politics or business.

By contrasting rhetoric and dialectic, Aristotle provided a solid foundation for understanding the methodical character of rhetorical thinking. Rhetoric is a method for framing popular arguments intended to be persuasive. It is a method that can be used on any subject; it has no subject matter of its own. It begins with the opinions of the audience and builds arguments to support a partisan proposition. Because it is a method that relies on opinions, it gives us conclusions that are likelihoods, not certainties. This is not a weakness of rhetorical thinking. Its strength is as a method of reasoning suited to the contingent and uncertain character of practical affairs.

These methodological features of dialectical and rhetorical thinking are illustrated in the antitrust case involving the computer software giant, Microsoft. Microsoft's operating system, Windows, had been integral to the mass use of personal computers in the workplace and by private individuals. Since most laypeople lack technical programming knowledge, Windows provided a simple system for mastering the powerful information-processing capacity of the computer. Meanwhile, Microsoft had expanded the reach of desktop computer applications by developing new features, including its version of an Internet browser, and bundling them with each new edition of its operating system. That meant the person who purchased a computer with a Microsoft operating system also got its Internet browser.

The capitalist economic system argues that fair competition is necessary to spur innovation and to provide consumers with the lowest price. Microsoft's bundling of its browser with its Windows operating system posed a problem for its competitors. Consumers already had a browser once they bought Windows, so why should they buy a second one? Since by the end of the twentieth century 85 percent of all personal computers were using the Windows operating system, competitors in the Internet browser software industry complained that Microsoft had an unfair advantage. The government agreed, and the U.S. attorney general brought a suit that alleged Microsoft was a monopoly in violation of U.S. antitrust laws. The initial ruling was against Microsoft. The case was still under appeal in 2002, and legal experts expect it will take years before it is finally resolved. Regardless of the outcome, the rapid proliferation of desktop computers that work in a Windows environment has given the general public considerable experience with Microsoft products and those of its competitors. In addition to legal deliberations, there has been public discussion.

From the legal point of view, arguments of attorneys representing the government and Microsoft have had to satisfy the conditions and definitions of acceptable and unacceptable practices as set forth by U.S. antitrust laws. The courts must determine whether Microsoft engaged in business practices that suppressed innovation, drove competitors from the marketplace, and denied consumers the best product for the cheapest price. These are technical legal questions and require technical legal answers. They require expert knowledge of the relevant laws and judicial precedents, technical testimony by computer scientists about computer logic and the relation of software to a computer's operating system, and business analysis from accountants about real and potential profits and losses resulting from Microsoft's business practices. As the Microsoft case works its way through the appellate process, lawyers who are experts on antitrust law will make more technical arguments to other legal experts who sit as judges. At the appeals level, these will involve questions of precedent, actual wording of the law, and technical accounting evidence about the actual harms caused by Microsoft's business practices and harms to Microsoft by the original decision.

In these instances the lawyers won't have scientific proofs to determine the outcomes, they will have arguments from opinion. But the opinions that matter will be legal and expert opinions. Whether the executives of Microsoft believe they have been treated unfairly is not a relevant opinion on which to base a legal decision. Past antitrust cases, on the other hand, offer a font of relevant opinions to help the courts find a proper resolution.

From the layperson's point of view, arguments that address the likely implications of the court's decision are extremely relevant and invite response. For example, Microsoft's lawyers have argued that the marketplace benefits from its practice of protecting its proprietary rights. This means it assumes that innovation advances faster, and therefore the consumer benefits more, from a practice of patenting innovations to prevent other firms from copying them and/or to require payment of royalties to Microsoft for using them. The proprietary rights model holds that protection of intellectual property provides an incentive to develop high quality software as expeditiously as possible: the first one to the patent office earns the profit. The opposite view holds that innovation proceeds more rapidly and with higher quality on an open-source model. In an open-source model, firms share their innovations with one another. This theory holds that when firms can access the latest innovation without paying royalties or penalties for its use, their profits will increase and innovation will proceed faster. Without knowing much about business law or economics, the average person is able to understand the implications of policies that foster selfishness or cooperation and can offer an opinion on which of these alternatives the laws should encourage.

Reading the newspapers and Internet responses to the initial ruling indicates that people other than the litigants had an interest in the case and drew inferences about the implications of the judge's ruling. Judge Jackson used nontechnical reasoning (**logos**, argument based on reason) to support his decision. He chastised Microsoft for continuing a business-as-usual mentality in the face of a guilty verdict. He took this as a sign of Microsoft's failure to recognize that it had engaged in illegal practices and used the behavior as justification for the government's harsh plan for dividing Microsoft's assets. Some disputed his reasoning with the counterargument (more *logos*) that his ruling was likely to divert innovation, since it punished innovation and success. Others hailed the judge's decision as promoting competition. Some denounced the decision as a travesty (**pathos** or appeal based on emotion)—we have a system of laws, not of justice, while others praised it as a sign that the system works. Meanwhile, other newspaper articles analyzed the influence of the decision on Microsoft stock and that of its competitors. They offered real and potential investors nontechnical arguments to buy or sell based on what a cross-section of analysts believed (**ethos**, argument based on authority). These arguments rest on opinions, they are made in layperson's language, and they support inferences about policy and the likelihood of future conduct. They exhibit the method of rhetoric in soliciting opinion in support of or opposition to the ruling and its likely consequences.

☙

Summary

We began this chapter by discussing language as inherently persuasive. It invites us to perceive and respond to the world in a particular way. Individually, our rhetorical actions relative to a given issue are eventful, each occurring at a specific time and each being of interest as an episode or part of an episode that contributes to the event's final resolution. Because there is dynamic interaction among these discursive acts, they constitute a dialogue. They are a mode of thinking that is visible, one hopes, in the symbolic acts themselves. In this chapter we have tried to clarify the nature of rhetorical thinking by considering rhetoric as a social practice and as a method.

We saw that as a social practice, rhetorical thinking deals with what is expressed or expressible. Its domain is the discourse itself. Thoughts and feelings that are inexpressible are not dealt with in rhetorical thinking. Rhetorical thinking is joint thinking that arrives at conclusions through transactions between the audience and the communicator. It is particularized thinking that is marked by immediacy. It addresses situations that are real or purported to be real. It is, finally, holistic and necessarily partisan because it brings rationally defensible propositions into contact with existence and human experience. It necessarily involves interests, values, beliefs, and feelings, as well as more objective and dispassionate reasoning in a complex pattern of response.

We saw that as a method rhetorical thinking is concerned with finding things to say that will advance our purpose with an audience. It is a method that cuts across subjects; it is universally available in any area where people are addressed for purposes of coordinating social action. It is thinking based on shared opinions and aims to persuade by building arguments that show the likelihood of a conclusion. It is not inferior to science or technical reasoning. It differs from those modes of thinking because it deals with subjects of practical conduct where the best we can do is frame a likely solution. The method of rhetorical thinking helps us determine how best to communicate to an audience for a given objective. It is essential for the management of our social affairs. In the next chapter, we will extend this line of analysis to consider how rhetorical thinking is modified by the situation in which discourse is generated.

3

Rhetorical Opportunities

In August 1998, then President Clinton was deposed via closed circuit television before a grand jury impaneled by Special Prosecutor Kenneth Starr. The nation was in an uproar over the president's testimony about his relationship with Monica Lewinsky, a former White House intern, and its implications for his presidency. That night, the president addressed the nation to explain the essence of his testimony and to answer questions his previous denials had raised about his character. Was it mandatory that he speak? What should he have spoken about? What did he need to say for himself? Was it a public or private matter? What was the role of the audience? What were the consequences that followed from his choices in the speech?

These questions about the Clinton speech pose some of the most basic concerns of rhetoric. They highlight the role of the environment in prompting rhetoric to address the problems and questions that concern us and the role of rhetoric in influencing the shape of the human world. One approach to the questions in the first paragraph is to consider rhetoric in functional terms. This is not the only approach to rhetoric, but it is one of the fundamental approaches we can take toward the subject. Lloyd Bitzer, in essays dealing with the concept of the **rhetorical situation**,[1] has contributed some of the most influential statements about this approach. In this chapter we will consider a functional orientation to rhetoric through an examination of the situational perspective.

࢙

Defining the Situation

Have you ever heard someone summarize a set of circumstances by exclaiming, "That was a situation!"? The exclamation is an attempt to set off a unique experience from the mundane occurrences of everyday life. The remark implies "This was unusual. There were novelties involved, choices to be made: I wasn't sure how it would turn out."

We can find situations of all types that would merit such a characterization: Confronted in the wild by a crazed moose, how will we escape injury? Just before a social gathering we discover that our supply of refreshments is low and the stores are closed: how will we avoid embarrassment? Out for a mountain hike, the weather suddenly turns foul and we can't make out the trail markers: how will we get to safety? Granted an interview for an article we are writing for the student newspaper, the interview threatens to go beyond our editor's deadline: how will we end it diplomatically? The list of such situations, real and imagined, could go on indefinitely with each of us supplying our own examples. The significance of these cases depends on how we define them. Indeed, the very fact that we regard each as a situation, in the sense of something out of the ordinary, is a product of the meaning we attach to the event.

Clearly, situations occur in space and time, but these are rarely the coordinates that make a set of circumstances the object of conscious reflection. E-mail messages exchanged on specific dates and times between Seattle-based officers of Microsoft are unremarkable. E-mail messages about the advantages of bundling software tools with an operating system are very significant within a complex of circumstances labeled "The Microsoft Anti-trust Case." Within that context, messages can reveal intent to create a monopoly. Conceivably, the e-mail could have been exchanged from officials located anywhere, and the exchange could have occurred a week earlier or later, without altering the transaction as a significant situation. But it is not conceivable that we could alter the meaning of the Microsoft exchange from "conspiring to gain unfair marketplace advantage" to "seeking a marketplace niche" without changing the characterization of the circumstances.

Although situations have a spatio-temporal definition, their relevance to symbol-using animals requires that *chronological time* and *physical space* be translated into *psychological time* and *social space*. This transformation is marked by two characteristics: **emergence** and **relativity**.[2]

Emergence refers to the meaning of an event across time. Events occur in chronological time: they have a past, present, and future. But these distinct temporal sequences are muted by the meanings we ascribe to an event. We draw on our memory of the event in the past and our anticipation of it into the future to find its meaning for the present. Because meanings develop in relationship to their contexts, they are dynamic and shift as the context changes. This means we are always recasting the past and, consequently, changing the meaning of the present and future. Why? Because unanticipated changes in the present require reassessment of the past and future. We change our understanding of an event and its meaning to adapt to a dynamic and changing environment. The meanings we ascribe rely more on this psychological use of time than a fixed chronology.

Relativity refers to the meaning of an event based on the perspective of the individual. Relativity indicates the absence of a static standpoint. The meaning of an event will depend on an individual's perspective. The more people involved in a situation, the more likely there will be multiple interpretations. In addition, individual perspectives are not fixed. They change over time as our experience grows and our role changes. As our orientation changes, so does our definition of the situation. This poses a significant problem for social life, since we constantly face the challenge of trying to forge unique points of view into a unified approach in order to engage in collective activity. Rhetoric provides the path to shared social space. It bridges the divide between our individual perspectives.

For example, suppose that you are about to graduate and job prospects seem slim. You find a position that is sort of related to what you'd like to do, but the wages are minimal. Still, you don't have other prospects, so you accept it. Your family is distressed, and your friends question your sanity. When they ask you why you accepted, you answer by stressing positive, mostly future-oriented aspects of your new position: It's providing good experience, this is a growing firm, there are opportunities for advancement, the contacts are valuable, and so on. A year later, suppose your salary increases and your responsibilities grow. Now the positive aspects of your position are easier to accentuate. If this continues throughout your career, the meaning of your first job will **emerge** as a very shrewd move on your part.

On the other hand, suppose nothing improves after a year. Job-wise, you are unhappy. Unless your employer provides some aspect of job satisfaction beyond remuneration and responsibility, that positive story about your job becomes difficult to maintain. In fact, you are looking for another job. Things get worse; you are unsuccessful in your job hunt, and your position doesn't improve. A negative meaning of your job will **emerge**. You probably are thinking that accepting this job was a dreadful mistake. The meaning of the job at time 1 is not the same as at time 2. Its meaning emerges as factors change or remain the same; its meaning is dynamic.

Moreover, meanings are **relative** to the perspective and role of the perceiver. Our perspective is influenced by such factors as level of involvement, ability to create emotional distance, strength of commitment, ethical beliefs, and level of information and knowledge. Our role will influence what we see as the imperatives and consequences relative to our role demands, what we see as our relevant modes of involvement, what we expect of others, and the like. For example, your boss thinks she is paying you a fair wage for an entry-level position but seeks to motivate you by giving you assignments that require you to learn new skills. This requires time outside work to "do your homework." From her perspective this is a fair test of your future prospects. Meanwhile, although you like the firm and your boss, you have doubts about her assignments. You have studied rhetoric and think you could be a stronger asset to the company if she gave you more opportunities to deal with clients and to create public messages. From your perspective, her assignments are not well suited to your skills. You have a hard time getting motivated for unpaid extra work you aren't confident you can master. Meanwhile, your family thinks you have a "loser" job and keeps asking you about your future plans, as if it's a foregone conclusion you will be moving on soon.

Because each person in this vignette has a different role, they each ascribe a different meaning to the same objective elements of the situation. Your boss may be miffed because she has given you what she regards as a golden opportunity and you seem unenthused. You are confused because you thought you were hired on the basis of your college preparation in rhetoric, which your boss seems to ignore. Your family is anxious because it thinks you are making poor career decisions. As each of you interact, there will be attempts through management of symbolic resources to bring about a common understanding of the situation that will foster coordinated action: "take up the new challenge," "give me more rhetorically oriented assignments," "get a new job."

In defining any situation, then, we are confronted with the reality of **dynamics** and **flux**. *Meanings emerge and are relative.* It is important not to lose sight of this, for *humans act on the basis of how they define the situation.* Our situational definitions evoke basic response patterns of approach and avoidance, of territoriality and self-preservation, as well as more sophisticated responses of a symbolic nature. If we are unable to define a situation, we are unable to act because it lacks meaning for us.

ॐ
Rhetorical Situations

So far we have been emphasizing the idea that situations are meaningful combinations of events, objects, and people and that they call for action. Without action, the dynamics of the interacting factors would continue unchecked, leading to undesirable results (hence, the motivation to act). The action chosen depends on the definition of the situation. We define some situations in ways that call for physical effort as the appropriate action: we define others in ways that call for symbolic action to address, either partially or completely, the concern at hand.

For example, if you want to grow vegetables, you can't just scatter seeds and expect a garden to sprout. Before you can harvest a crop, you must till the soil, plant the seeds, water the garden, thin the seedlings, mulch the garden, pick the weeds, fertilize the plants, and so forth. Your efforts are dictated by nature: If there is sufficient rain, you won't have to water the garden; if not, you will. If you don't hoe and mulch the garden, weeds will grow and compete with the plants for nutrients from the soil. If you let the weeds grow unchecked, they eventually will overtake the garden, diminishing the yield from some plants, destroying others. To prevent this from happening, active intervention is required. But your intervention in this case is likely to be physical effort, not symbolic. Talking about the ravages of drought or strangulation by weeds will not nurture the plants; only regular watering and weeding will accomplish that goal. Such problems call for non-rhetorical action.

On the other hand, we also confront problems that only discourse can partially or completely resolve. These are **rhetorical situations**. They call for functional uses of discourse to adjust people, objects, events, relations, and thoughts. Rhetorical situations are ones in which either we must change people directly by persuading them to think, feel, believe, understand, or act in a particular manner, or we must change the physical environment indirectly through the intervention of human cooperation. Rhetorical situations, then, are ones that appear uniquely suited to the instrumental uses of language.

In his pioneer essay on this topic, Lloyd Bitzer defined a rhetorical situation as:

> a complex of persons, events, objects, and relations presenting an actual or potential exigence which can be completely or partially removed if discourse, introduced into the situation, can so constrain human decision or action as to bring about the significant modification of the exigence.[3]

At first reading, this may seem like a complicated definition, but it thoughtfully presents all the components for our understanding of rhetoric, as the example that follows illustrates.

In the fall of 1999, an illness called the West Nile virus was spreading across the New York City area. This was a new virus; there was no public knowledge of its nature, causes, or cure. People infected with the virus were becoming gravely ill. Even though the number of deaths was small, people in the New York area were very uneasy, and reports of new cases prompted public alarm: what is causing this disease? is there an effective treatment? are there preventive measures individuals should take? what are our officials (local, state, federal) doing to prevent its spread? When the National Centers for Disease Control announced that mosquitoes carried the virus, folks became more strident in their calls for action. Officials first offered assurances that the small number of cases suggested that the disease was not spreading rapidly and that localized spraying in areas where cases were reported was a sound strategy. Later, when tests of dead birds revealed that the virus was more widespread than had been believed, officials made an abrupt change of tactics and began preventive spraying of all locales. In the words of Thomas S. Gulotta, Nassau County Executive, the decision was made to launch "a pre-emptive strike" in order to stop the virus from spreading further.[4] This tactic seemed to work. As the spread halted, public alarm subsided.

Bitzer's definition holds that rhetorical situations are "complexes," or situations that contain multiple features. These features include the persons involved, the events that involve them, the object of their conscious attention within the context of the salient events, and the relations among the persons, events, and objects. In this case a "complex," or group of interrelated factors, interacted to give the West Nile virus multiple meanings and provoked responses that were sometimes volatile. The disease itself, public awareness, and official responses of medical, preventative, and informational natures all were part of this complex. We might be tempted to think that this complex wouldn't exist without the physical fact of the disease. But what if folks were unaware of the disease? In that case there would be no reason, in their minds, for discourse. And what if the official responses weren't given? How would laypeople form a sense of what was happening and its meaning? In this case all three of these features (perhaps you can think of others) are basic to the meaning of the situation and the responses that it evoked.

The first signs of a new disease raised information-seeking questions out of fear of the unknown. As the agent spreading the disease became known, people who were not infected focused on measures to prevent its spread before it was too late. The West Nile virus situation included both its meaning as immanent health threat and its meaning in terms of responsible official response. For the medical community it represented a possible epidemic to be halted. For public officials, it meant an emergency of both public health and of public panic.

Bitzer goes on to state that this complex of factors presents "an actual or potential exigence." By this he means that these interacting features give rise to a problem of some sort: either in an actual way, where the problem is immediate and requires our attention, or in a potential way, where we face a likely difficulty if we do not act now. The fact that people were getting sick and dying was, itself, not unusual. That happens every day. What made this case unusual, however, was that people who had contracted the virus went to the hospital and the doctors couldn't figure out what was wrong. As the mysterious illness caused deaths, a greater sense of public urgency arose that had to be addressed. People wanted information and appropriate courses of action to be taken. Significantly, the problems of infection, grave illness, the need for explanation and action, or "exigencies," were ones that could be modified to some extent—"completely or partially"—through "discourse," they were *rhetorical* in nature. The disease itself and its mode of transmission were not directly resolvable through discourse, but the public's need to know what was going on and the question of whether or not officials were taking appropriate action were.

Rhetorical situations, in other words, are situations that present problems that can be resolved meaningfully through speech and writing. Problems that require changes of belief or attitude or that require cooperation are typically ones in which skill in the management of language can make a difference. In this case, getting people to recognize symptoms and to seek immediate medical care plus restoring public confidence in attempts to keep the disease from spreading could be and were addressed through discourse.

Bitzer's definition suggests that the skillful management of language tends to "constrain human decision or action"—to make human agents aware of the opportunities and limitations present in a situation, so that audiences respond in ways that alter the original problem in some significant way. Certainly it appears that Nassau County Executive Gulotta regarded public anxiety as an urgency that he had to address. Calling the aerial spraying "a pre-emptive strike" conveyed a sense that the county meant business in trying to stop the virus from spreading. Insofar as restoring public confidence was possible through discourse, his situation was rhetorical. In brief, rhetorical situations are ones that present problems we can resolve completely or partially through effective use of language.

We can say more than this, however. Our previous discussion established that the way we define a situation is significant because this provides our parameters for appropriate behavior. When we define a situation as rhetorical, we are not merely saying that it is a situation in which discourse can be of some consequence; we are saying also that it calls for a deliberate communicative response. As our definition of a situation emerges as rhetorical—one presenting a problem that calls for discourse—we frame expectations of appropriate responses for the people who have an interest in the problem. We expect certain individuals, by virtue of their role, to address the problem (County Executive Gulotta, in our example). We expect other individuals, by virtue of their role, to be addressed (the citizens of Nassau County). We expect the ensuing discourse to be functionally relevant to the problem. (Mr. Gulotta has to address the concerns on people's minds; he has to inform them of what the county is doing to stop the virus from spreading and to insure public health.) We anticipate that functionally relevant discourse from appropriate sources addressed to appropriate audiences will so engage thoughts and feelings as to alter the environment.

Moreover we anticipate that the environment will be altered partially or completely to resolve the compelling urgency that called for communication. Conversely, we anticipate that in the absence of such discourse, the pressing demands of the situation will become critical, lead to a crisis of some sort, and eventually deteriorate beyond the point of human repair.

Remember we mentioned earlier that people respond to their definition of the situation. In the West Nile virus case, even though the county took aggressive action to exterminate its mosquito population, if citizens thought nothing was being done and that their lives were endangered, the meaning of the situation to them would be "life threatening." Had Mr. Gulotta said nothing about the county taking aggressive action, but instead used the press conference to praise the Mets' attempt to win the National League pennant, people were likely to think, "He's avoiding the issue because he has something to hide; maybe the virus can't be checked." Their perception that they were in danger could have deepened, and public panic might have followed. Even though the danger had been removed, if the public was unaware the threat had been lifted their behavior would reflect their unchecked fears.

In short, a rhetorical situation will not resolve itself, nor can it be satisfactorily resolved through wholly nonsymbolic means (such as the aerial spraying of the mosquito infestation). Once we define a situation as rhetorical, the *emergent* meaning of the situation *relative* to the actors involved calls for discourse as the appropriate mode of human action. Unless a person could claim ignorance of the situation or silence as a strategic choice, failure to respond to a rhetorical situation when in a position to do so would be foolish at best, perhaps even irresponsible.

Finally, by maintaining that rhetoric can "bring about the significant modification of the exigence," Bitzer adopts an explicitly functional view of rhetoric. While this is not the only view one may take, it has utility for analyzing the pragmatic uses of communication. Prior to Bitzer's essay, rhetors were advised to analyze their audience, the occasion, and the possibilities of subject matter. Then, on the basis of these analyses, they were instructed to select the options best suited to their goals. This view was most memorably expressed by Donald C. Bryant, who spoke of the function of rhetoric as "adjusting ideas to people and . . . people to ideas."[5] Bitzer's theory of a rhetorical situation does not contradict this view, but it captures better the complex interaction of factors that bring rhetoric into being and shape its development and outcomes. In a later essay, in which he enlarged upon his conception, Bitzer summarized the functional nature of a situational perspective toward rhetoric in these words:

> The situational view of rhetoric takes as its starting point the observable fact that human beings interact functionally with their environment. This is not an inevitable starting point. Typically, stylistic rhetorics commence with the relation between the nature and resources of language on the one hand and the intentions or meanings of the speaker on the other. The scientific rhetorics of the eighteenth century commenced with the relation between natural psychological processes and communicative intentions and activities. These and similar approaches either dismiss the relations of persons and their messages to environment, or regard this relation as secondary. The situational view, however, seeks to discover the fundamental conditions of rhetoric—of pragmatic communication—in the interaction of man with environment. This inquiry therefore looks toward a starting point similar to that examined by Kenneth Burke, who observed that

experience presents divisions that can be bridged through identification and remarked, "Out of the division and the community arises the 'universal' rhetorical situation."[6]

This brings us to the constituent elements that provide the basic conditions for rhetoric.

Constituent Elements of Rhetorical Situations

According to Bitzer, every rhetorical situation is composed of three elements: an **exigence**, an **audience**, and **constraints**. Analysis of these features helps to determine the definition of a given rhetorical situation and further serves to indicate what is required to make a **fitting response**.

Exigence

Bitzer defines an exigence as "an imperfection marked by urgency." Any undesirable element in a situation can satisfy the demands of this definition. Sometimes an exigence may be as common as our mundane interactions to negotiate our way through everyday life: We utter cordial and supportive words to roommates, coworkers, friends; we make pleas for cooperation in performing group activities; we request favors; we offer arguments for particular ways of solving our social problems, and so forth. At other times an exigence may take on importance of greater magnitude: senators deliberate on legislative matters, lawyers plead legal cases, trustees make arguments establishing policies for complex organizations in both the private and public sectors. Whenever there is a defect that can be remedied in meaningful ways through speech or writing, the exigence becomes the focus of rhetoric.

A rhetorical situation may be marked by a number of exigencies, making analysis sometimes complex and the framing of a fitting response a matter of judgment. For example, as the United States Congress deliberated on giving military aid to Bosnia, there were a number of exigencies to be addressed. Rival ethnic groups were claiming rights to self-determination over the same territory. Given the historically complex politics of this region, should the United States choose sides? Bosnian Serb soldiers were engaging in genocidal practices of ethnic cleansing (killing Bosnian Muslims), and women of all indigenous ethnicities were being sexually assaulted by soldiers of opposing ethnicities. Against compelling evidence of human rights abuses and genocide, does the United States have a moral responsibility to intervene? Serbia was accused of providing covert support to Bosnian Serbs and was threatening military involvement if the United States provided military aid. Should the United States risk becoming involved in an expanded war over principle or confine its activity to peacekeeping efforts while innocent women, children, and the elderly were being raped and slaughtered? Polls showed American citizens were not supportive of unilateral American involvement. What role should opinion polls play in setting national policy? Senators were unconvinced that Bosnian civil war was a matter of U.S. national interest, and many elected representatives and commentators questioned the long-range consequences of any involvement that included U.S. troops. How should our policy makers balance overwhelming evidence of human rights abuse against national interest?

Each of these conditions exists in observable ways; they are not the products of imagination. Each is a condition that may be regarded as an imperfection marked by urgency and could, of itself, be a sufficient call to bring rhetoric into existence. Yet in this situation there is one exigence that will eventually serve as the **controlling exigence** in the minds of the participants, giving definition to the situation and demarcating the range of viable responses. If the controlling exigence is seen as the threat of genocide, we will be compelled to provide assistance. If the controlling exigence is seen as national interests, we will be compelled to withhold aid. Significantly, as Congress deliberated this very matter in the mid-1990s, its eventual course of action was to combine these concerns by participating in a U.N. peacekeeping force that imposed a military presence designed to halt the conflict while political negotiations to resolve the conflict took place. Moreover, the exigence posed by Bosnia's tragedy remained an active topic of discussion within the United States and throughout the world. Consequently later in the decade, when Serbia's President Milosovic embarked on a program of ethnic cleansing against Kosovo's Albanian residents, President Clinton, with congressional support, responded with U.S. air attacks against Serbia until its army withdrew.

The exigence, then, is the imperfection in the environment that calls rhetoric into being. It may be simple or complex. For rhetoric to be fitting, it must address this imperfection in meaningful ways.

Audience

A second defining feature of a rhetorical situation is the audience. A common misunderstanding of audience is to include in it anyone who has access to the message. That understanding ignores two very important features. First, rhetorical discourse is addressed communication. It speaks to some individual or group in particular. Second, it seeks a specifiable response from the audience. Bitzer attempts to include these features by eliminating mere hearers or readers from this set. He says, "Properly speaking, a rhetorical audience consists only of those persons who are capable of being influenced by discourse and of being mediators of change."[7]

This definition includes two salient features. *Audiences consist only of the individuals who are capable of being influenced.* Such individuals have an interest in an exigence and its resolution. What would be the marks of such interest? Factual knowledge, experiential knowledge, concern about the outcome, proximity in time, proximity of place, a sense of responsibility for the exigence, and the magnitude of the imperfection all contribute to audience interest and, thereby, their capability to respond in meaningful ways to the exigence. In addition, *the people in the audience must be capable of mediating change.* When people think they cannot influence the outcome, they are less likely to respond to messages; they become excluded from the audience.

Thus, for example, if our alma mater launches a campaign to boost the arts and sets $500 as the minimum donation, thousands of potential contributors stop listening to the message. Most students do not have $500 to spare. Most assistant professors do not either. Both groups may strongly believe the arts are important to college life, but they have been defined out of the audience by virtue of the situation's requirement for meaningful response. Such an appeal may be sensibly constructed if the fund-raisers have reason to believe they are more likely to reach their goal by securing a small number of large gifts than through mass donations of small amounts and if they know that donors of large gifts are more generous if their philanthropy places them among an exclusive group.

The point to bear in mind is that every rhetorical situation requires the mediating action of an audience. Speakers and writers must make careful choices in determining who is, in fact, within their audience and how their readiness to respond can be maximized.

We need to exercise caution, however, not to treat audience as if it were concretely present in the world as a preexisting group with a fixed identity waiting to receive the rhetor's appeals. Such an approach would place the rhetor at the center of rhetoric and would treat the audience as if it were passively molded by a rhetorical engagement. Since Bitzer's essay first appeared, rhetoricians have embraced the concept of rhetoric as a constitutive power. By this they mean that the rhetorical event brings identities into existence.[8]

In our earlier discussion of emergence and relativity we established that situations are dynamic. They have multiple meanings that reflect changing contexts across time and the multiple perspectives of participants. There is no essential situation, only our individual and collective understandings of it. Moreover, these elements are interactive, which means the meaning is constantly in flux. In the same way, there is no essential audience defined by a pregiven set of beliefs and attitudes, even though those who construct appeals based on audience demographics proceed as if there were. Were they correct, human behavior would be entirely predictable and change would be nearly impossible. Rather, whatever meaning a situation may have for us as individuals or groups is a construction; it is provisional and subject to change. Rhetoric is the process by which we attempt to overcome the apparent "given" status of an objective situation and the multiplicity of individual perspectives to constitute a shared meaning and a sense of shared power to do something about it.

This line of thought leads to a significant modification of Bitzer's original formulation of audience. It suggests that discourse itself is the constituting agency of the audience. That means an audience understands a situation and its power to act based on the way it is addressed and how it interacts with the discourse. The merging of multiple perspectives into one capable of making sense of the imperfection presented, responding to it, and acting in ways that make a difference constitute the audience.[9] This also means that the exigence is a product of how we have been addressed and how we have interacted with the discourse. Rhetoric seeks to place us in relation not only to factual conditions in the world but to our interpretations of the relevance of those conditions to us in ways that give them urgency and invite us to do something about them.

Constraints

A third constituent factor of all rhetorical situations is its salient constraints. These are both the limitations and the opportunities present in a situation that bear on what may or may not be said to the audience about the imperfection they are being asked to remedy. Constraints may be physical, such as time of day, place where the message is presented, occasion for the presentation, medium of transmission, and similar material conditions of the environment. Constraints also may be psychological. Psychological constraints frequently are the more important ones a rhetor must acknowledge. Such constraints include persons involved in the situation, who they are and what the audience thinks of them; events surrounding the exigence and their bearing on audience dispositions at the time of performance; relations among the rhetor, the audience, and the exigence that can color an audience's receptiveness to an appeal; rules that govern what a body may or may not do; facts known or unknown that can inhibit or encourage readiness to believe and act; principles to which a rhetor or an audience is committed; laws that limit or make possible certain modes of conduct in resolving an exigence; images that audiences and rhetors have of each other; interests that are enhanced or threatened by resolving the exigence in certain ways; emotions that aid or hinder recognition of the exigence; and myriad similar considerations that occur to parties engaged in rhetorical transactions. These factors have the power to influence decisions because they shape what an audience is ready to believe and the actions it is prepared to take.

For example, when Bill Clinton was subpoenaed to give testimony to the grand jury regarding his relationship with Monica Lewinsky, the fact that he was a sitting president affected the venue in which the testimony would take place. Should he go to the courthouse, thereby giving the appearance that the courts can dictate the movements of a sitting president? Or should he agree to be interrogated only if it was in the White House, thereby preserving the appearance that the president is equal to the judiciary? The President's lawyers convinced him that going to the courthouse would make him appear as if he were a criminal, whereas testifying from the White House would make him appear presidential. The setting for the discourse influenced the shape and texture of the situation.

Constraints contribute to the emergent and relative meaning of the situation. Clinton's choice to be deposed from the White House required a closed circuit video feed. This meant that the testimony would be on videotape, making it possible for the closed proceedings of the grand jury to be made public. Indeed, the Republican leadership in the House of Representatives chose to do just that, and placed the unedited testimony on TV and the Web for the entire world to see. Citizens witnessed their president being cross-examined, saw for themselves how he engaged in verbal swordplay with the prosecutors, and were able to judge the consistency of his answers. Later, the video testimony was introduced as evidence that he had committed perjury. Thus, the impeachment situation *emerged* from the grand jury situation.

This example alerts us to how challenging it can be to identify constraints and whether those limitations will help or hurt the effort to influence the audience's judgment through discourse. The strategy to determine the physical place where it is best to present your message intersects with the psychological perceptions of role definition. In this case it led to an unintended enlargement of the exigence itself.

Bitzer depicted the rhetorical situation as a complex of a controlling exigence, an audience, and a collection of constraints that come together to call for a rhetorical response. His theory holds that a rhetor's appeals must be suited to these factors for them to remedy the prevailing imperfection. We have modified his position to recognize the fluidity of these three defining conditions as interacting variables that are mutually constitutive. This modification reflects the diverse character of the social landscape and how a rhetorical situation and its constituent elements are themselves constituted by the multiple ways in which rhetorical acts are performed. Ideally, analysis of the constituents of a rhetorical situation will bring forth a fitting response.

༃

Life Cycles and Fitting Responses

Up to this point, our discussion has emphasized how contemporary rhetoricians have modified the theory to reflect its emergent and relative qualities. This modification reflects a turn from the instrumentalism in Bitzer's original formulation to an emphasis on rhetoric's constitutive power. Rhetorical situations are not only complex; they are dynamic. Their emergent and relative meaning, which is the basis for how we respond, develops out of the interplay between context, message, messenger, and audience. Their flux is not just a product of changing conditions; it is the consequence of our human capacity to articulate ideas and emotions that signify meaning for audiences. Through speaking, writing, filmmaking, etc. we do more than reference material reality, we constitute our own identity as meaningful subjects in relation to conditions in the world, including the meanings of those conditions.[10] We conclude this chapter by considering this dynamic interplay in terms of the life cycle of rhetorical situations, the relationship of responses to these stages, and the intentions of rhetors.

Life Cycles

According to Bitzer, a rhetorical situation comes into being, evolves to maturity, decays, and eventually dies. Along the way, this cycle may be retarded or hastened as new dimensions of a situation are perceived, new issues emerge to consciousness, and new voices are heard.

Eventually, however, every rhetorical situation passes from the scene into a newly defined situation with its own controlling exigence. Situations change because they are resolved, or because people lose interest, or because they are transformed. Their changes may be mapped as a cycle of situational development with four stages: origin, maturity, deterioration, and disintegration. The following example provides a vehicle for discussing these stages.

On November 22, 1999, a group of 14 Cubans left their homeland in a motorboat headed for the United States; the boat capsized. Three days later on Thanksgiving Day two Americans found a survivor, a six-year-old child named Elián González, clinging to an inner tube. Elián's mother, Elisabeth Brotons, died at sea. The next day, the Immigration and Naturalization Service (INS) released Elián to his great-uncle Lazaro González of Miami, while it deliberated his immigration status. On November 27, Elián's father, Juan Miguel González, demanded the return of his son to Cuba. The saga of Elián was catapulted to the front pages of U.S. newspapers and was the lead story of network television news, as the Cuban-American community embarked on a fervent seven-month struggle with the United States government.

Miami's Cuban-American community mobilized to demonstrate a show of solidarity with Elián's relatives for keeping him in the United States. They protested that his mother, who was divorced from his father, had left Cuba to seek asylum in the United States. Returning Elián to communist Cuba would mean that his mother had died in vain. Her wish was for him to be free. On that basis, Lazaro applied for asylum for Elián.

On January 5, 2000, INS Commissioner Doris Meissner decided that Elián belonged with his father and should be returned to Cuba by January 14. The decision sparked protests in Miami and celebrations in Cuba. Elián's Miami relatives asked Attorney General Janet Reno to reconsider. Meanwhile, television viewers and newspaper readers saw pictures of little Elián being walked to school, playing with other children, and interacting playfully with his Miami relatives, especially his cousin Marisleysis González who acted as his surrogate mother, juxtaposed with images of agitated supporters milling about with placards pleading for his right to asylum.

A series of legal maneuvers followed as the Miami relatives sought to retain custody of the child and to secure his asylum in the United States. Outside the courts, a raging debate occurred on television talk shows, on editorial pages, in front of Lazaro González's residence, on the presidential primary campaign trail, and among a wide spectrum of U.S. citizens over the priority of a father's custody rights versus the well-being of a child whose mother died while in flight for political asylum. After the U.S. district court dismissed Lazaro's petition to set aside the INS ruling and Attorney General Reno insisted on the father's right to custody, arrangements were made for Elián's father, Juan Miguel, his wife, and their son to come to the United States.

Reno met with Elián's Miami relatives on April 12–13 to negotiate his return to his father while the case continued to work its way through the courts. She ordered the relatives to surrender the boy. They defied her order and responded by securing a court order to keep the child in the United States. Reno responded on April 22 by authorizing federal agents to seize the boy. In a pre-dawn raid, 151 armed federal agents stormed the González domicile in Miami's Little Havana, took the boy, and reunited him with his father in Washington.

In the wake of the raid, the emotional distress of Elián's Miami relatives was widely covered. Television reports showed armed federal agents dressed in combat fatigues breaking through the front door, emerging with Elián in the arms of a female agent, then the caravan of armed agents backing out of the neighborhood at high speed. There also was a disturbing photo of an armed agent who appeared to be pointing his rifle in the direction of Elián and a family friend who was holding him. The boy seemed frightened. The relatives' emotional distress over their loss of Elián was compounded by the government's overwhelming show of force.

The relatives flew to Washington in an abortive attempt to join Juan Miguel—whom they had earlier spurned—and the child. They gave interviews denouncing the government's forceful breach of their home and alleged that the agents threatened them with assault rifles and spewed profanity while seizing the boy. Demonstrations occurred in Washington in support of their position. Significantly, the demonstrators included a broad cross-section of Americans, suggesting that more than the Cuban-American community was influenced by the appeals. Meanwhile, Little Havana's Cuban-American community was seething over the government's use of force and the prospect that the child would be returned to Fidel Castro's communist Cuba. It staged protests and a general strike on April 25.

The government released photographs of Elián hugging Juan Miguel to counter the negative impression generated by the forceful removal of the boy from Miami. Stories reported that he was adjusting well to his "new" family, which included a half-brother who was born after he left

Cuba with his mother, how the family was spending its time, and little Elián's continued innocence.

Finally, on June 28, with the court order blocking Elián's return to Cuba having expired, the Supreme Court rejected the appeals of Lazaro González to keep the boy in the United States. Elián and his family returned to Cuba. News accounts covered his return, his reunion with his relatives on the island, national celebrations in Havana staged by the Castro government, expressions of joy and gratitude by his father, and his return to his hometown and playful gathering with old classmates. Apart from his return, coverage of these episodes moved toward the bottom of the news agenda, and after a few weeks the hotly debated issue of Elián's fate faded from national center stage, although it remained alive in the courts.

Clearly the Elián saga was a rhetorical situation. His citizenship was an imperfection marked by urgency, which gave rise to multiple other exigencies. Appeals were made to every conceivable body that might mediate change—government officials, the courts, and the American people. Each participant had to work within constraints of cultural beliefs about parental custody rights, political ideology, and the laws of the land. In addition, the saga had multiple meanings that emerged as the struggle unfolded relative to the positions of the participants and those who were engaged as an audience forming a judgment.

The case also illustrates the power of rhetoric to constitute audiences and identities. Elián was the picture of childhood's innocence. Some fused his innocence with nationalist aspirations, legal and moral rights, images of power, and family feuds. Collectively these combinations created an understanding of his identity as representative of larger geopolitical issues and actors. The rhetoric that brought this story to consciousness and engaged national attention in the United States and Cuba illustrates the life cycle of a rhetorical situation: origin, maturity, deterioration, and disintegration.

Origin. When the INS placed Elián in Lazaro's custody following his rescue, it is a safe guess that it was not seeking to cause a national furor. It was likely seeking to place him in a safe and caring environment while it determined his immigration status. The boy's fate would not have become a national *cause célèbre* had his great uncle not determined to keep him here. At this stage, Lazaro perceived an exigence to exist, but the audience and the constraints were still unformed. Those who might form an audience—the INS, the Department of Justice, the courts, the media, the American citizens, and the Cuban-American community of Little Havana, among others—were largely unaware of conditions marked by imperfection and urgency. It fell to Lazaro and his emissaries (his lawyers and Little Havana's Cuban-American leadership) to awaken these possible audiences to the imperfection at hand and to heighten their awareness of how this situation bore on their interests. *The rhetor position involves defining the situation as rhetorical and salient to those s/he would have act as mediators of change.*

Clearly not all situations survive their birth. Some may be wrongly perceived as rhetorical, some may be miscast and fail to gain notice, and others are directed to people who are incapable of responding to the issues as cast. Some do hit their mark and generate continued attention, as Elián's clearly plight did.

Maturity. By December 10, the Elián situation reached maturity with the filing for asylum. This gave a clear definition to the overriding exigence of the case—whether a mother's flight for political asylum should carry forward to define her son's status as a political refugee, or whether this was a simple case of custody in which a father's rights precede those of his relatives. Rhetors could address this issue in meaningful ways. Meaningful discourse in this case came from a number of fronts, as both sides fashioned appeals designed to sway beliefs and induce actions capable of altering the environment.

Lazaro, his attorneys, the mayor of Miami, Catholic clergy, and presidential hopeful Senator John McCain, among others, made the argument that Elisabeth Brotons lost her life during political flight and therefore her wish for Elián to have freedom in the United States should take precedence. The street demonstrators in front of Lazaro's home—a form of vernacular rhetoric—reinforced the message. Equally, Elián's own photogenic appeal supported this cause. Nightly newscasts featured images of this seemingly happy, playful, and affectionate child engaging other children and his relatives with innocence and wonder at all the fuss. And the relatives, especially Marisleysis González, displayed love and care for the child. The news reports may have been about that day's actions in court, but TV images told the story of a family of modest means taking on the monolith of the U.S. government because they were completely in love with and committed to this child. Nonetheless, linking the warm and fuzzy feeling of these images to political asylum was not an easy rhetorical accomplishment.

On the other side, the argument was simple: children should not be made political pawns; Elián belongs with his father. In addition to INS Commissioner Meissner, Attorney General Reno, and President Clinton, this was the message of countless nonpolitical spokespersons such as child psychologists appearing on talk shows, of Cuban-American counterdemonstrators at the González residence, of newspaper editorial pages, and of expert opinion offered by lawyers versed in family law. Soon there were television shots of Juan Miguel pleading for the return of his son, thereby humanizing the boy's father with a publicly recognizable face.

Audiences were equally matched in their concern about the situation, their receptiveness to discourse, and their willingness to mediate change. Some of these audiences were pregiven: the INS commissioner rules about immigration status, the attorney general enforces federal laws, respective judges determine whether a legal right has been violated. Elián's fate was in the legal system and, in terms of Bitzer's theory, these were the audiences that were capable of mediating change. However, the montage of public messages from Lazaro González, his lawyers, Juan Miguel and his spokespersons, political candidates, talk show guests, the mayor of Miami, Cuban-American leaders, and the footage that accompanied newscasts called a larger national (and possibly international) audience into being. Although their judgments would not decide Elián's legal fate, they engaged in a national dialogue that covered the range of topics noted earlier and contributed to the weight of public opinion for both sides in this struggle.

The constraints of the legal system were clearly at work. For instance, the court calendar dictated the time frame in which decisions would be reached and provided the Miami relatives the opportunity to take their case to the people. That case was largely built through use of the media and its lust for images with a strong story line. Those in favor of keeping Elián here took full advantage of TV's propensity for covering drama by providing it: supporters were on constant vigil outside the González home, they clashed with counterdemonstrators when they appeared, and adoring family members typically accompanied Elián when he ventured outdoors. These situational constraints provided means of persuasion with the potential to modify the exigence in the court of public opinion.

Appropriate responses at this point could have brought the situation to a resolution. In part the Miami relatives miscalculated the willingness of Reno to use force to regain the child. From their perspective stalling tactics in negotiations were a sensible strategy for keeping the child until the court decision on his immigration status had been made. Reno seized on their strategy as a failure of rhetoric to bring about a satisfactory resolution and responded accordingly. Her response essentially negated the relevance of the family's public-opinion campaign. By returning Elián to his father, the only judgment that then mattered was the court's. Further, the government engaged in its own public-opinion campaign with pictures and accounts that showed Elián was doing well since being reunited with his father. Once the court made its decision to uphold the INS decision that the boy should be in his father's custody, the resolved situation naturally passed from the scene. At some future time, however, the issues of returning the child to his father and their return to Cuba, the INS decision on who qualifies for asylum, the sense of alienation among the still seething Cuban-American community, or the tactics authorized for taking the boy from Lazaro's home may resurface as part of new issues that give rise to future rhetorical situations.

Deterioration. Had the government's or the Miami relatives' rhetorical efforts failed to seize the moment of maturity, the situation may have moved into a third stage where the modifying potential of rhetoric is diminished. At this stage, the exigence becomes more difficult to remedy. When a rhetorical situation deteriorates, other factors may complicate the situation. Attitudes may harden, making audiences less capable of being influenced by people who disagree with them; interest may weaken as the novelty wears thin, and audiences may shift attention to other matters that appear more urgent. At this stage, actions or attitudes or both have begun to move the definition of the situation out of the rhetorical realm. Without some extraordinary intervening circumstance or inspired rhetorical performance, the situation will pass to its final stage. Certainly there is room to argue that Reno's ultimatum to release the child or have him taken by federal marshals marked an end to the situation as the relatives had defined it.

Disintegration. At this point, the imperfection is no longer perceived as modifiable in whole or in part by rhetoric. Once a decision had been made by Reno to seize the child, the audience attending to the street rhetoric in Little Havana was still capable of being influenced, but it was no longer capable of mediating change. Attempts at rhetorical discourse addressed to its members became futile since they no longer served any functional purpose. Conditions in the environment that were open to modification through the instrumentality of discourse now were focused exclusively in the courts.

Fitting Response

When we view rhetoric situationally, we are concerned with how our speech and writing are functioning in our environment. Hence we assess rhetorical efforts in terms of whether or not they are suited to modify other people's opinions and actions in order to effect change. Appropriate rhetorical efforts in this regard are *fitting responses*. A fitting response is not necessarily a successful one but one that is *addressed to resolving the complex of factors that define the situation*. We may lose an issue and even a decision but still have responded in a fitting way. Determining whether any response is fitting requires that we understand how the rhetor's discourse reflects his or her definition of the situation and meshes with that of the audience.

We may ask if a speaker has communicated in a way that is capable of correcting a real or potential problem in the environment. For example, in the Elián case the relatives exercised every legal option to retain custody of the boy. Since the courts would be the ultimate arbiters of his fate, legal rhetoric was a fitting response. At the same time, their attempts to sway public opinion also were fitting in that pressure from a supportive public may have led government officials to take a more sympathetic stance to their cause.

One approach to rhetor-audience interaction that permits a degree of objectivity in considering the audience's role is to evaluate whether rhetoric is fitting in terms of its potential to remedy an imperfection and whether it is fitting in its constitution of the audience it addresses. Because audiences are marked by interest and ability to mediate change, there are four possibilities for assessing the fit of a rhetorical response:

1. Audience has an interest and is capable of mediating change.
2. Audience lacks an interest but is capable of mediating change.

  3. Audience has an interest but is incapable of mediating change.

  4. Audience lacks an interest and is incapable of mediating change.

Rhetoric addressed to audience 1 is fitting. Rhetoric to audience 2 is fitting only if it is geared toward kindling an interest. Rhetoric addressed to audience 3 is fitting only if it is focused on potential exigencies in the future, when impediments to mediating change may not exist. Rhetoric to audience 4 is futile and therefore unfitting. In each of these cases, a fitting response is one that is potentially corrective of the imperfection in the environment.

  In the Elián case, we might assess appeals to the courts, administration, Cuban-American community, and the general public differently. Fitting responses to judges and administrators who were decision makers should take into account their official responsibilities in the case. Arguments to them would have to recognize these constraints and those of the law, since these conditions defined the judges' authority to act. Residents of Little Havana are predisposed to mobilize for anti-Castro demonstrations. Framing the child's custody in political terms awoke support in this audience, resulting in demonstrations for granting Elián asylum. There were others in South Florida and the nation, meanwhile, who followed developments in this matter but regarded it as an issue for the courts, not public opinion, and concluded they lacked effective means for action. Finally, discourse addressed to the world community would probably have been misdirected, since those outside the United States did not have an interest in its immigration laws (unless they themselves were candidates for asylum), nor was their opinion sought on such matters.

  Saying this, we must bear in mind that fitting responses will be influenced by the stage in the situation's life cycle and, in turn, will influence how the life cycle develops. Appeals for public support were fitting only while there was a chance for a political solution to the exigence. Once Reno declared her decision that the boy had to be returned to his father while the courts decided his fate, public support became irrelevant. After that, the custody issue belonged exclusively to the judicial system.

☙

Rhetor's Intentions

  Finally, we should consider the role of the rhetor's intentions in shaping rhetorical situations. The major criticism against a situational perspective is that it appears to rest on a deterministic assumption. The theory seems to suggest that discourse is called into being because the situation exists and that the discourse called into being is shaped by the demands of the situation in ways that are beyond the rhetor's control. In part this appearance of determinism reflects a process of analysis that stops rhetorical situations at any given moment to account for the elements that are present. Analysts often freeze situations in order to better understand and assess their components. In part it also reflects a functional approach's tendency to privilege the question: "What is to be done?" This question emphasizes rhetoric as a means to an end, or as an instrumental mode of communication. When rhetoric is understood in purely instrumental terms, the focus becomes the rhetor's intended outcome with respect to some set of circumstances, as she understands them.

In actual practice, however, we experience rhetorical situations in the activity of their life cycle. Significantly, this dynamic is one in which messages that are "fitting responses" constantly realign exigencies, audiences, and constraints. These messages reflect the situational demands, the interpretive responses of rhetors engaged in intentional acts designed to alter them, and the responses of audiences that emerge through their discursive encounter with the situation. Once messages and messengers enter the situation and interact with receivers, they alter the situation—its meanings are emergent and relative.

Situational changes are not the result of natural forces (except in rare cases where some event so alters a situation as to eliminate the need for further rhetoric: if the bridge falls down, the debate over repairs is over). They are the result of symbolic actions that are purposive and have consequences for listener perceptions. Consequently, rhetors' intentions play a role in shaping and resolving situations as they are defined in the minds of listeners. Clearly, what speakers and writers say to listeners and readers cannot ignore situational demands as they are understood by the audience. Obviously, the objective circumstances to be addressed influence the rhetor's goals (Lazaro had the boy, INS Commissioner Meissner had the authority to return him to his father). In this respect, intentions are shaped by the demands of the situation. Such demands cannot be ignored without violating the audience's propriety rules (*prepon*): what they regard as appropriate and meaningful discourse in the situation as they understand it. At the same time, it would be absurd to suppose that rhetors are without purposes that may require redefining the situation as opportunity arises (*kairos*).

When Cuban-American spokespersons declared that Elián was a political refugee because he was in his mother's care when she fled from Cuba to seek asylum in the United States, they sought to shift the focus from a legal to political struggle. For the fervently anti-communist community of Little Havana, such a change was in keeping with its long-standing anti-Castro sentiment. Whether the mother's intent in fleeing Cuba was relevant to her son's *legal* status is dubious at best. But in the political arena, which has greater latitude for the role of emotion in crafting judgment than does a bureaucracy like the INS, this shift offered a base for rallying support in a symbolic war with Cuba. Supporters of this view held that it was a matter of principle to protest so that Elisabeth Brotons did not die in vain. Cuban-American rhetors, as all rhetors, saw some resolutions more desirable than others and tried to define and remake the situation in ways that would accommodate the solution they proposed. The Cuban-American argument was intended to court public opinion and put the government on the defensive.

In sum, the life cycle of a rhetorical situation and the fitting responses to each stage are not solely products of the environment to be remedied. The rhetor's intentions also play a significant role in shaping and advancing the ongoing dynamic of rhetorical situations as they work their way toward resolution.

ॐ
Summary

In this chapter, we have been concerned with a functional view of rhetoric. This view emphasizes the instrumental role of rhetoric in changing the environment. Since the environment of our minds, our social relations, and our physical surroundings are significantly influenced by beliefs and ultimately by actions, rhetoric is a major source of influence in shaping the world we inhabit. For rhetoric to function as a source of modification, it must interact with the definition of the situation that exists in the minds of its audience. Simply put, action is guided by our definition of a situation. Lacking a definition, we would be unable to respond.

We saw that rhetorical situations are ones that can be modified through discourse. They have three constituent elements: an exigence, an audience, and constraints. Moreover, we saw that the specific situation addressed acquires its definition through the interplay of these constitutive elements. This interplay of elements creates the possibility for rhetoric to occur and to have functional consequences for resolving problems of social action.

Finally, we saw that rhetorical situations have a life cycle. As they pass from origin to disintegration, fitting responses are ones that accommodate audience interests the and ability to mediate change while addressing the controlling exigence. We need to bear in mind, however, that these responses are not mechanical; they are the products of human insight and intuition in response to the problems people face together. Ultimately, for a fitting response to be a satisfying one, it must intersect with the values, ethics, and personal commitments of both rhetor and audience. This is the mark of responsible rhetoric, a concern we will address in chapter 4.

❧ 4 ❧

Making Commitments through Rhetoric

In his 1988 acceptance speech at the Republican National Convention, George H. Bush dramatically proclaimed to the delegates who had just nominated him as their candidate, "Read my lips: No new taxes!" As President, when Bush found it necessary to raise selected taxes, a general howl of protest swept the nation. Long after the cheers of the RNC had faded, the citizens (and the Democratic Party) remembered his pledge and voted him out of office in 1992, in part for having violated his promise. The people's objections that Bush hadn't kept his word indicate the seriousness with which we regard what people say. Rhetoric makes commitments.

Our practice of forming expectations of persons in public life based on their public statements is no less true in our private relations. We all know individuals whose habit is to say what they think others want to hear. We may find ourselves unusually skeptical of their statements about matters where there are differences of opinion because we question their sincerity. To have a serious discussion we must be able to count on our conversational partners to speak the truth and to follow through with deeds that support their words. Our daily lives are filled with significant but often unnoticed rhetorical transactions that require the same ingredients for success as any event enacted in the full glare of publicity: mutual understanding and commitment.

As we saw in chapter 3, we can develop a functional perspective on rhetoric as a means for altering the environment, a very important role. But a functional viewpoint alone can overlook another important aspect of

61

rhetoric. Functionalism usually depicts the environment and the modifications we seek as "out there," external to our personal selves. From this we may form the false impression that rhetoric is a unidirectional practice—rhetors acting on the world as change agents but immune from being transformed themselves. Nothing could be further from the truth; every rhetorical transaction involves personal stakes for all participants.

Rhetoric arises in contexts open to choice. It flourishes in an environment in which these choices are made freely. Our need to choose makes rhetoric important as a means for handling our private and public affairs. Responsible rhetoric must be based on the truth, as best we can know it, and serve moral ends. Our choices reflect our commitments in this regard. When we make choices through rhetoric, we share our commitments to truth and moral conduct with others. In short, rhetoric makes commitments: to the self, to others, to the truth of our ideas, and to our view of what is required for humane social relations.

In this chapter we will explore the proposition that rhetoric makes commitments: What is the type of world we commit to when we choose to alter the environment through discourse rather than through force? What are the risks inherent in adopting discourse as a means for creating opportunities, resolving problems, and expressing thoughts and feelings that are important to us? This chapter considers the very personal stakes we accept when we decide to practice rhetoric responsibly and to face the consequences of our decisions.

∞

Expressive versus Other-Directed Talk

One useful distinction between rhetorical discourse and other forms is the ends or purposes they serve. Rhetoric, generally and basically, is a mode of discourse that serves the purpose of reaching agreement. Aristotle viewed its purpose as judgment; those who are more strategically minded see it as persuasion; some, as reflected in our initial definition, focus on the end of coordinating social action; others focus on evoking a particular state of conscious awareness in the audience. Each of these definitions is other-directed: each understands rhetoric as a mode of discourse addressed to others in order to influence their thinking so that they will make a sound judgment, behave in ways the rhetor desires, coordinate their actions to achieve common goals, or become conscious of conditions that require their attention.

Not all communication is intended to influence others. Sometimes we engage in **expressive communication**, speaking or writing primarily to vent our feelings. For example, upon striking our thumb with a hammer we may utter a blasphemous expression. Our words are not intended to alter the environment of prevailing opinion on nail striking nor to persuade the Almighty to punish the errant hammer for eternity. Our utterance is purely expressive, venting frustration and anger at ourselves and at an inanimate object.

Sometimes expressive language is used in more public ways. For example, when we receive a poor grade, we may say things to let off steam. We may express ire, frustration, even outrage to a friend about our instructor's grading. Our purpose in venting these emotions is to "get them off our chest," presumably because expressing internal feelings helps to relieve them—not because the expression will change the behavior that angered us. Such communication is self-directed in the sense that it is more concerned with giving expression to our feelings than to changing another's opinion.

Can expressive communication serve rhetorical ends? Absolutely. Witnessing expression of powerful feelings can produce a greater awareness of a problem, may lead us to sympathize with the other person's feelings, and may lead us to discover we share those feelings. Witnessing the spontaneous expressions of sadness by British subjects over the sudden death of Princess Diana, for example, paved the way for an international television audience to share the grief and to question why Queen Elizabeth was so slow to lead her subjects in public acts of mourning.

The important point here is that rhetorical communication, unlike expressive communication, is designed to achieve its goal by use of appeals that are other-directed. Were we interested in changing our poor grade, we would have to speak to the instructor, not to a friend. Though giving the instructor a piece of our mind might be an effective mode of catharsis, it is not likely secure the desired change. Remarks specifically calculated to influence her thinking would put our frustration and even anger aside. We would focus instead on leading her to appreciate why our answers were stronger than the grade reflected or how the questions posed were ambiguous and could be answered in more than one way. Rather than communication uttered for its own sake we would consider our utterance as a means to an end—namely, persuading the instructor to raise our grade.

Rhetorical communication is typically concerned with bringing about agreement, often with the further goal of eliciting action. When we decide to alter or to maintain our environment through rhetorical means, we have made a commitment to communicate purposively with an audience in mind. Audience-oriented communication involves us in the continual effort to adjust ideas and people to one another. The adjustive function of rhetoric, however, gives rise to two problems. The first is the problem of being true to our own ideas while adapting them to the audience's readiness to respond. The second grows from the obvious possibility that persuasive communication may encourage actions that are not necessarily in the audience's best interest. It is possible to use language to deceive audiences.

ଓ
Argument and Self-Risk

The process of adjusting ideas to people and people to ideas places heavy stock in arguments. Rhetorical theory uses "**argument**" as a techni-

cal term. It does not refer to the activity of people squabbling. Arguments
are reasoned appeals based on evidence of fact and opinion that lead to a
conclusion. Through arguments, rhetors attempt to provide an audience
with a solid basis for holding a belief and coordinating actions with that
belief. Without arguments, rhetoric would degenerate into the excesses of
unsupported emotional or authoritarian appeals or become limited exclusively to matters of style. Arguments are the superstructure on which all
responsible rhetoric depends.

Since an argument consists of reasons supported by data that lead to a
specific conclusion, we can test its value by asking whether it can support
its expressed outcome. This means that an argument's strength is not mea-
sured merely by its acceptability to a set of listeners. Telling people what
they want to hear, even if false, could pass that test. While common acceptance may be a point of departure, arguments are tested through the give
and take of refutation and rebuttal. Strong ideas can withstand objections;
weak ones cannot. Thus in seeking to adjust ideas to an audience, we are
seeking expressions that will be meaningful to our listeners, appeals that
rely on audience opinions, and arguments that can withstand scrutiny.

Philosopher Henry Johnstone cautions that we must fulfill certain conditions for our arguments to be genuine.[1] First, we must assume that *the
audience to whom we offer arguments is beyond our control.* Its members
can think and articulate their own thoughts; they can reflect on what we
say and offer reasoned assessments of our discourse; if they respond positively, it is because we have secured their agreement. They are not like ro-
bots or computers, who perform on appropriate command. They are not
small children, who can be told what to do. They cannot be regarded as
objects of manipulation through means of suggestion. When we engage in
argument we regard our audience as free to make its own choices. In
short, we must regard our audience as human.

A second condition of genuine arguments is that *the audience to whom
we offer arguments is free to ignore them, disbelieve them, or even refute
them.* Consequently, as Johnstone points out, choosing to offer arguments
in support of ideas runs the risk of having ideas defeated. At the same
time, an audience that is responsive to arguments also risks having its behavior or beliefs altered. If its members are unwilling to run this risk, they
cannot function as a genuine audience. In the terms of chapter 3, they are
incapable of being influenced and therefore fail to meet a necessary condition to be a rhetorical audience. We may characterize people willing to run
these risks as open-minded.

A third condition necessary for genuine arguments is that *both the arguer and those responding have an interest in the outcome of the argument.*
They are not considering mere possibilities but outcomes with consequences that affect both sides. There is risk because those involved have a
stake in the outcome; we do not have a stake in mere possibilities. The
specific risk is whether we will be able to maintain our system of beliefs

and values, the commitments of mind and spirit that define the self, or whether we will have to change a significant commitment, thereby reassessing the self. This tension between self-maintenance and change is essential for human growth, for getting beyond our individual and immediate experiences, and for inhabiting a common world with others who share our interests.

For example, most students have discussions with their parents about their college major. Sometimes parents question why their child has chosen to specialize in, say, communication rather than accounting. These discussions can become tense, with father telling son that he must major in something practical and son telling father that he's old enough to make his own decisions. At this stage, effective rhetoric has left the scene. Neither party is using other-directed talk designed to persuade or evoke awareness; instead, both are resorting to assertions and counterassertions that don't take the other's views seriously. Neither is offering compelling reasons to support expressed beliefs.

Should father and son wish to deal with their problem more productively, they must first change their approach toward each other. They must treat each other as capable of reasoning and responding to reason, and they must take each other's views seriously. Further, each must be open to the possibility that he may be mistaken, that his reasons will not withstand objections, and that he may have to change his views on a proper major. Finally, each must recognize that his interest in the matter involves important elements of his belief structure: about education, about careers, about motivations regarding this issue, and probably about the father-and-son relationship.

Arguments that meet these requirements make the outcomes of rhetorical transactions highly personal. Rhetorical exchanges in which we respect the audience's freedom to choose, accept the possibility of being wrong, and have an interest in the outcome can increase self-awareness when we confront the risk of having to reassess our beliefs, values, and commitments, all of which define us as unique individuals. Without arguments that force us to consider contradictory views and impulses, we would lack consciousness of a self. *Consciousness of our contradictory impulses and potential resolution on the basis of arguments tell the self who it is and where it stands.*

With respect to the first problem of how far we may go in adapting ideas to audiences without sacrificing the integrity of our ideas, Johnstone's discussion of arguments provides useful guidelines. In every rhetorical transaction, the purpose or goal is to evoke conscious awareness of the commitments embedded in our assumptions and, quite possibly, to persuade listeners to our point of view. We address arguments to our audience in ways that are likely to facilitate these objectives. Consequently the rhetor whose mode of argument sacrifices personal opinions is engaged in an insincere practice. The arguments are insincere because they do not articulate self-interests; they do not represent views in which the rhetor has a stake. Pandering to the sentiments of the crowd may result in popularity or power, but they misuse rhetoric as an instrumental act by misrepresenting the rhetor's views. Responsible rhetorical arguments are always cast with the listener in mind, but such arguments must also reflect the essential views of the rhetor.

ॐ

Unilateral and Bilateral Arguments

The second problem we raised earlier was the contrast between the use of language to communicate with audiences and the use of language to deceive audiences. Again, we can find guidance on this problem from Johnstone, specifically in the distinction he draws between **unilateral** and **bilateral** arguments.[2]

A bilateral argument is guided by the principle that "the arguer must use no device of argument he could not in principle permit his interlocutor to use."[3] In essence, bilateral arguments are ones that avoid tricks, deception, and falsehoods—they observe the Golden Rule, so to speak. In contrast a unilateral argument is one in which the arguer uses devices of argument not available for the interlocutor's use. These may include not only gambits and ploys that attempt to elude critical inspection but also role-specific communication, such as directives from superiors to subordinates. Unilateral arguments frequently advance claims in false or misleading ways, although we can imagine situations where unilateral arguments would be essential to avoid chaos.

The concepts of bilateral and unilateral arguments can be extended to characterize a rhetor's mode of communication. Working from the definitions just offered, *bilateral communication* may be defined as *"the transmission of messages to another in such a way that it is clear that both participants are entitled to transmit messages in the same way* (emphasis added)."[4] This would include such features as opportunity for questions and refutation, common access to information, reasoned arguments supported by data, avoidance of devices that would impose unilateral restrictions (such as an unqualified appeal to one's authority or refusing to discuss concerns other than one's own). Unilateral communication denies the other party equal opportunity of response. Techniques such as authoritative pronouncements, suggestion, hypnosis, brainwashing, and heavy reliance on presence and personality to carry the message are examples of a unilateral mode of transmission.[5]

For example, after the nuclear power plant accident at Three Mile Island in 1979, Metropolitan Edison, which operated the power plant, engaged in unilateral communication. It assumed it had no obligation to tell laypeople the truth about technical matters.[6] Thus, it told the citizens of the greater Harrisburg area that they were in no danger from nuclear radiation. Similarly, slowdown tactics by airline pilots to create flight delays as a means of forcing management to agree to a new labor agreement and management's unresponsiveness to the slowdowns represent assumptions that it is acceptable to create hardships on third parties (passengers, in this case) as a means of resolving a labor dispute. Both sides are banking on the pressure of irate customers who have had to suffer through delays and missed connections to coerce the other side to relent. Passengers, who lack comparable means to pressure the airline into getting them to their destination on time, often respond with rage vented at a ticket agent, who has had nothing to do with creating the inconvenience. Such communication techniques and modes are clearly unilateral; they rely on intimidation to succeed. If an instructor responds to student objections about certain course requirements by claiming to be personally devastated, he is using his position of authority to change the issue from problematic aspects of the course to his worth as a human being. Again, that's clearly a tactic of unilateral communication.

However, not all instances of unilateral communication are wicked. For example, requests for information, ordering from a menu, announcements of company policy, and directions to subordinates are pragmatic exchanges of the sort that usually do not invite or require reflection on the assertions advanced. The use of unilateral communication in such situations is not necessarily destructive and, in fact, may be essential for social coordination. When is unilateral communication harmful? If discussion is necessary for social coordination or if the issues involved require the mediation of reflection and deliberation, unilateral communication prevents the exploration of meaningful resolutions. When interacting parties have a mutual stake in the outcome, when conflicts abide, when confronting alternatives can give rise to consciousness, and when the points at issue are self-involving, unilateral communication is harmful.

We are not always aware of our stake in a rhetorical situation. Sometimes we must be brought to conscious awareness of this fact. For example, we may not engage in conscious reflection on the state's right to impose capital punishment. We may be oblivious to cases where this penalty is enacted until someone makes an argument questioning the death penalty and asks our view. At the moment that we become aware of our stake in the practice of capital punishment, there is a **wedge** between the state and the message its practices communicate. The wedge of bilateral communication is precisely this: *the separation of the rhetor from the message thereby allowing us to consider that the message may have to be revised.*

We make these active considerations whenever our previously unexamined assumptions are called into question. Any rhetoric that forces us to attend to ideas and practices that we normally take for granted or had previously ignored is forcing a wedge between the assumptions we have made and the beliefs based on those assumptions. It allows us to reflect on what we have accepted without question. For example, a rhetorical appeal challenging resumption of normal diplomatic relations with China because of its human rights violations forces us to think about our assumption that the internal affairs of a foreign nation are none of our business. An appeal challenging a previously unexamined assumption that all students benefit from intercollegiate athletics and therefore student fees must be maintained to support this benefit may force us to reflect on the legitimacy of the initial premise.

Unilateral communication typically fails to drive this wedge; it closes the spaces that might invite reflection by manipulating the audience's beliefs. When the mode of presentation uses devices of language and techniques of appeal that condense the reasoning implicit in the appeal, it disengages rhetor and audience from the mediating exercise of reflection. It fuses speaker, speech, and audience into a composite whole, often inviting acceptance on the basis of the speaker's or writer's authority. Conversely, bilateral communication uses language and appeals that explicitly welcome reflection on the message and the possibilities for its revision to improve its expression of a sound and shared opinion.

In rhetorical transactions, then, unilateral discourse uses devices not open to the audience, such as those of propaganda. Because it does not invite reflection on the validity of its premises, it avoids the evocation of consciousness and confrontation with the self. It represses self-aware action by encouraging compliant behavior. Bilateral rhetoric uncouples a message from the minds addressed, thereby inviting reflection. As Johnstone says:

> Before we can think about any issue, we must first attend to it. The rhetoric that forces it on our attention is the rhetoric of bilaterality, because no one can, in the nature of the case, have a monopoly on it. If I can point out your unnoticed assumptions, you can point out mine.[7]

✑
Rhetoric and the Self

In terms of our original question, the bilateral/unilateral distinction helps us to distinguish between rhetoric that humanizes and rhetoric that invites unreflective responses. Within this framework, let us now examine some scholarly findings that illustrate these techniques and their consequences for our self-awareness. We can point to four propositions concerning rhetoric and the self:

1. Rhetoric can reflect a self.

2. Rhetoric can evoke a self.

3. Rhetoric can maintain a self.

4. Rhetoric can destroy a self.

Reflecting a Self

Rhetoric can reflect a self through the types of arguments developed and the language used. Here we are concerned with the self of the rhetor as we perceive it in the way her appeals are developed and her invitation

to audiences to share in this view. With respect
amine the typical manner of reasoning employed
major contentions. A twentieth-century rhetorici
merates four possible modes for such argument.
cause and effect, and circumstance.[8]

Weaver, among others, has argued that patterns
in a sample of messages by a particular communica
the world. Individuals who believe that there are "truth
best when our conduct is guided by these truths tend to argue
tion. Definitional arguments assert the basic nature of their subjec.
Lincoln arguing that by definition, all humans are created equal) and base
policy on these definitions (thus slavery is wrong and must be abolished).

Next come arguments that are in search of "truths" that have not yet
been discovered. These arguments rely on the use of analogy to known or
accepted truths to find their way in novel situations. These are arguments
based on relationship or **similitude**. They reason to the probability of a
conclusion from the similarity of a new situation to a known one. One
might find arguments of this sort in appeals that take a more poetic or
nonliteral approach to their subject. For example, Swift's *Gulliver's Travels*,
Sinclair's *The Jungle*, and Miller's *The Crucible* are instances of fictional
messages that nonetheless were commentaries on real conditions of their
times. Their persuasion was wielded in terms of the relationships audiences could see between their imaginative worlds (the land of Lilliput, the
Chicago stockyards, Salem's witch trials) and the ones they actually popu-
lated. This technique is also employed when the rhetor perceives that an
indirect approach will be tactful or will best respect the audience's capacity for conscious reflection (as when Martin Luther King, Jr., in his "I Have
a Dream" speech, indicted the civil rights practices of the federal government by developing an elaborate analogy to banking: civil rights guarantees are like promissory notes).

A third type of appeal is to **cause and effect**. This view emphasizes
the developmental features of a situation rather than its essence. Political
arguments of a pragmatic sort urge us to respond because the consequences of a present policy are undesirable or the consequences of change
are an improvement. It does not focus on underlying principles that could
suggest that while pragmatically less satisfying, a course of action is preferable because it is the right thing to do. We can find this pattern in arguments to provide military aid to beleaguered governments friendly to the
United States because if we do not support the friendly governments, rebel
insurgents will take over. This ignores raising issues related to the types of
regimes we are supporting: Are they democracies or dictatorships? Are
they open to dissenting opinion, or are they repressive? Do they violate
human rights? A more extreme subversion of the cause-and-effect argument is argument from circumstances. Its appeal is to the force of immediate facts. It does not offer a cause-and-effect explanation of the facts but

as a given, commanding response. We may find this pattern in
ment that the United States should use deadly force as a means of
eeping in order to avoid a repeat of Mogadishu, Somalia, where the
es of Army Rangers were dragged through the streets after 18 were
ed in October 1998. The circumstances of "winning the peace" require
illingness to kill those we are to keep at bay. This mode of argument
leaves unasked the questions of what "winning" means other than "kill or
be killed." Whereas the first two modes reflect an awareness of self as
grounded in its knowledge of being, the second two emphasize the self in
relation to processes of change. Significantly, the final tactic of argument
does not drive the wedge of bilaterality that urges reflection. It argues that
we have no alternative but to respond or be crushed.

Another way in which a self is reflected is through our **uses of language**. Metaphors, images, descriptive adjectives, and the like reveal an
orientation that can be most illuminating. For example, in his essay, "Constitutive Rhetoric: The Case of the *Peuple Québécois*," rhetorical analyst
Maurice Charland explored the declaration of a unique national identity for
French-speaking citizens of Quebec. *Québécois* was an identity other than
Canadien Français, or French Canadian.[9] Those who promoted the secession of Quebec from Canada argued that their choice of self-reference signified a different cultural heritage from the rest of Canada. Secession was
the natural and necessary political choice to preserve the cultural identity
of the *Québécois*. Secession constituted an identity among French readers
and a sense of alienation among Quebec's English-speaking citizens. It was
a powerful wedging device. The subsequent and sometimes contentious deliberation over national identity and multiculturalism among the *Québécois*
and their English-speaking neighbors has included serious dialogue of bilateral communication on Quebec's self-identity. At other times when language has fused cultural uniqueness with national identity, the appeals for
and against secession have tended to exclude the cultural Other, and appeals have functioned as unilateral communication.

Evoking a Self

Rhetoric can evoke a self through arguments that force the individual
to reexamine assumptions and the self they define. Critical inspection of
issues, in other words, can be so profound in its consequences that it leads
the person to discover a new self. One of the very best illustrations of this
occurred during the new social movements of the 1980s and 1990s. Millions of Americans and Europeans found their traditional assumptions
about identity called into question. Traditional ways of speaking about
personal responsibility or agency, education, sex, gender roles, the body,
the family, ethnicity, cultural hegemony, and other questions of distinctiveness were challenged. As was true of social protests in the United States
during the 1930s and again in the 1960s and early 1970s, attending to this
rhetoric led substantial numbers of people to become "politicized" in that

they were suddenly awakened to their stake in political processes. One consequence was the emergence of cultural politics, which overtly challenged discourse and actions insensitive to social diversity. The rhetoric of new social movements has consciously challenged the basic assumptions on which Western European and U.S. society is based; it has called attention to inconsistencies between the cultural value of "inclusiveness" and policies that excluded certain segments of the population: women, welfare mothers, gays and lesbians, nontraditional families and ethnic minorities, to name some of the more prominent groups. By defining themselves as different from and put upon by "the system," their rhetoric urged a reconsideration of self.

Maintaining a Self

Not only can rhetoric bring us to a new self-awareness, but it can also support and sustain an existing self. In his much-cited study of protest rhetoric, rhetorician Richard Gregg[11] points out that one way protesters distinguish themselves from opponents is by labeling them as "oppressor groups." The oppressor groups identified are then subjected to rhetorical attacks. This mode of self-identification by means of differentiation allows protesters to enhance their own self-awareness, insulating them from attack by unworthy oppressors and maintaining their sense of self-worth.

Self-identity among dissidents is developed and maintained internally through the rhetorical transactions that accompany each phase in the life cycle of the protest group. Group unity, and the deliberation that manifests unity, provide a powerful experience of identity.

Equally important to the internal experience of "groupness" in maintaining a sense of self-identity is the rhetorical framing—propounding a view of the world that both legitimates and motivates actions—that proclaims a public identity. For example, sociologist Doug McAdam points out that while much is made of the Gandhian model of nonviolence as a cornerstone for Martin Luther King's leadership of the civil rights movement, the rapid emergence and spread of the struggle was more profoundly influenced by King's appropriation of powerful cultural themes, both the Southern Baptist tradition and that of the U.S. political culture more generally.[12] His observation echoes the comment by Robert Bellah and his associates on King's framing of the struggle in his "I Have a Dream" speech:

> Juxtaposing the poetry of the scriptural prophets—"I have a dream that every valley shall be exalted, every hill and mountain shall be made low"—with the lyrics of patriotic anthems—"This will be the day when all of God's children will be able to sing with new meaning, 'My country 'tis of thee, sweet land of liberty, of thee I sing' "—King's oration reappropriated that classic strand of the American tradition that understands the true meaning of freedom to lie in the affirmation of responsibility for uniting all of the diverse members of society into a just social order.[13]

By such juxtapositions, as McAdam notes, King was able to frame civil rights activities in a way that resonated with the culture of both the oppressed and the oppressor. This contributed a great deal to gaining sympathy among whites who shared in this identity.[14]

Destroying a Self

Finally, rhetoric that engages in scapegoating attempts to slay symbolically the selves of its target. That is, it can focus a public's discontent on a target group as the cause of its problems. Hitler used this tactic against the Jews; he blamed Germany's economic and social problems on them and denied their human dignity and worth. Administration officials and political activists employed similar rhetorical tactics in the attacks and counterattacks during the protests of the 1960s and 1970s. A less extreme but highly persuasive form of destroying a self is found in rhetoric that confronts an adversary with a contradiction that she seems unwilling to remedy. Such rhetoric frames the outsider's identity in a way that imputes an identity of insincerity, thereby undermining the opponent's claims. For example, during the Persian Gulf War, proponents challenged the patriotism of those who opposed the war. One female member of Nebraskans for Peace responded as follows to such a challenge that appeared in a letter published in the *Omaha World Herald*:

> This letter says that those demonstrating for peace are unpatriotic. It says we should be grateful that men are willing to die to guarantee our rights of free speech. It suggests that since we protest for peace, we aren't grateful and we shouldn't be allowed to exercise our right of free speech that those men died for. Make sense to you? Even though this idea of patriotism has some limits, we are patriotic. We love our country and want to do the right thing. I can't think of anything more patriotic than taking a despised position and making your voice heard so that your country will do the right thing.[15]

Imputing an "unpatriotic" motive to a group effectively rules it out of the national discussion. Challenging the reasoning of those who hurled the charge effectively questions their rationality and their sincerity in espousing values of "free speech." Both frames are equally destructive of the self.

In these four ways—reflecting, evoking, maintaining, and destroying a self—rhetorical appeals can confront the self with the possibility of reconsidering matters of self-interest or prohibit reflection and thereby risk manipulation. In each case the bilateral versus unilateral nature of the exchanges determines whether rhetorical transactions have the potential to enhance self-awareness. As we noted earlier, tension between self-maintenance and receptivity marks the open-minded person.

This tension is especially reflected in protest rhetoric. Gregg's discussion of protestors maintaining self-identity by attacking oppressor groups illustrates that the ego function of protest rhetoric preserves the self by not risking argument. The period he examined deployed rhetoric of markedly insular quality, in which disciples were reinforced and opponents vilified. Their "us versus them" view of the world encouraged separation from adversaries. By dividing the world into opposing camps, it became easier to define the situation as one that was threatening. This threatening definition, in turn, attracted attention to and sometimes evoked fear of protesters as aliens in society's midst. When this fear was coupled with the provocative scorn protesters showed for establishment ways, retaliation frequently resulted in the form of police brutalities. These counterreactions reinforced the perception among protesters that this was a nation divided—a final proof that the rhetoric of division was correct.[16] But this type of rhetoric is based on tactics of control. Nowhere do the protesters manifest the modes of bilateral rhetoric that would permit meaningful communication between opposing groups. These traits illustrate people behaving out of keen awareness of the risks of dealing with an adversary by engaging in argument and an equally keen awareness of the need to establish uniqueness.

Subsequent research on new social movements indicates that the tension between self maintenance and change is not confined to a particular period; it is generally found in struggles for social identity, which is to say in those movements that attempt to define and shape our society and influence the course of its policies. Whenever there is disagreement, this tension is present, including rhetorical encounters with others in the "movement." Some African-American students during the 1960s and 1970s rejected the appeals of black power advocates as Marxist extremism; some women then and now dismiss feminist appeals as based on assumptions of class and race that have no bearing on their lives; some Christians separate their personal religious convictions from civil rights as defined by law on questions of abortion rights. In the forums where persuasive appeals are open to question and refutation, dissidents and proponents of the status quo alike encounter the invitation to risk themselves.

ഔ

Summary

We have been considering the role of rhetoric as a source for greater understanding of who we are and what we might become. We have suggested that there are heavy personal stakes for a person who chooses to treat problematic matters in a rhetorical fashion because such a choice opens the possibility of self-discovery but also the possibility of change. In this respect, we focused on the importance of bilateral rhetoric in encouraging self-discovery and self-growth by communicating in ways that permitted a separation between a message and the persons involved in its delivery and reception. Rhetoric has the potential to reflect, evoke, maintain, or destroy a self. The choice between unilateral and bilateral rhetoric plays a significant role in achieving or thwarting these potentialities.

The ramifications of these considerations are profound for the type of world we inhabit. In an argument, both parties have something to lose—the comfort and security of currently held ideas and opinions. Rhetoric may expose us to the contradictions in our views, both logical and moral, making us painfully self-conscious by forcing us to reconsider the grounds for our beliefs. In existentialist terms, a person is his or her possibilities, his or her moral commitments. Thus rhetoric may help make men and women of us by forcing us to become more responsible for beliefs and actions.

Rhetoric also forces us to choose, and choice entails freedom. If rhetoric presents us with alternatives, and if we are compelled to choose, rhetoric is the judge or condemning agency that makes us face up to what we are and what we could be. Rhetoric makes us take on the burden of freedom.

Finally, because of the risk of identity and security involved, rhetoric gives experience a deeper meaning and significance. It amplifies the importance of certain acts, ideas, or beliefs and thus presents the potential of another mode of being through the proposition being championed. Rhetoric throws the audience back on themselves, putting them face to face with their basic assumptions and offering the possibilities for growth or stagnation.

❦ 5 ❧

Public Judgment

When democracy was still in its infancy, Aristotle observed that the **telos** (purpose) of rhetoric was judgment. His insight still applies. When the dust settles and all sides have had their say, a democracy expects and requires its citizens to make decisions. Participating in public decision making is the basic right and duty we share as citizens of a free society. A primary value of rhetoric lies in helping us arrive at sound decisions. Although we may explore the nature of practical discourse in more complicated terms, the fundamental relationship between public discourse and judgment remains the core civic function of rhetoric.

In modern democracies, arriving at a judgment is complicated by the range of voices that engage in public deliberations, the number of people who sit as judges, differences between citizen voices and those of elected representatives who have the exclusive privilege of a vote, and the difficulty of gauging public opinion.

For example, in school districts across the United States the subject of primary and secondary education receives considerable public attention. Most school districts generate their budget through a property tax, so *property owners* are watchful of school programs, class size, teachers' salaries, and the physical plant of the school itself, since these elements translate into costs that influence how much property tax they will pay. *Parents and citizens* show general concern about the performance of students from grades 3 through 12 on standardized tests. Declining scores have been interpreted by some as a sign that teaching quality is not what it used to be. Some *state legislatures* have addressed these expressions of concern by grading schools based on their students' performance on state-mandated tests. These grades often are used to determine the school district's share of the state's appropriation based on how well its students perform. Some

75

teachers regard standardized test scores as a poor index of learning that encourages teaching to the test rather than to student needs. Meanwhile there are *parent groups* and *educators in the private sector* who have argued that a better solution is to allow parents to choose how their tax dollars are spent through a voucher system that follows the student, whether he or she attends a public school, a parochial or charter school, or is home schooled. *School boards* have strenuously objected that a voucher system would ring the death knell for public education because it would drain funds from already impoverished schools and privilege the affluent at the expense of children from low income families.

This list barely scratches the surface of concerns that citizens, educators, and public officials have raised about the quality of public education. Our judgments about how best to insure the quality of our children's education are among the most important we make as citizens. With so many active interests bearing on the problem, it is difficult to sort out the central issues and to decipher where these perspectives converge to form a public mandate.

The range of actively engaged voices indicates that the quality of public education is a *public problem*; it pertains to everyone in the community and is open to their inspection, knowledge, and judgment. It is unlike private matters, such as our choice of friends or college major, or our personal finances, which are the business of those involved, not the community. Public problems are different from private ones in that they are avowed as problems that affect all members of the community and, therefore, call for general attention and public solution.

Framing public problems in general terms pertaining to everyone and open to inspection by all can be misleading, however, since that suggests public problems are objectively present in the world. As we saw in our discussion of rhetorical situations, that is seldom the case. Certainly it may be true that, say, 57 percent of third graders at Brightness Elementary met or exceeded the state's minimal reading standard. That would be an objective fact. But whether the test was a good one, or the state's standard a reasonable one, or what the scores meant, or that the scores related to teaching quality are not objective facts; they are matters of inference and interpretation. Whether the scores are a problem is not an objective fact; that evaluation depends on our point of view.

Public problems are not problems in and of themselves but are deemed so within our cultural system of symbols by which we constitute and convey meaning.[1] Our culture provides us with a language for talking about the circumstances we encounter. Our symbol system influences why we regard a set of circumstances as problematic in the first place. Culture affects our understanding of the nature of a problem and the parameters for possible solutions. The Western world, for instance, tends to talk about public problems in scientific terms. We look for natural causes and solutions. Theistic cultures, on the other hand, tend to use religious language to discuss public problems, perhaps looking for sinful acts as their cause and establishing forms of spiritual atonement and divine intervention as solutions. Societies tend to have their own cultures of public problems. Regardless of their differences, however, every culture of public problems is a rhetorical construction. In this chapter we will explore how public problems are rhetorically constructed so that they become real for social actors—members of society who participate in a collective consciousness, which includes awareness of cultural traditions, values, mores and sanctions as they bear on the social construction of reality.[2] We will take up four sets of concerns: basic rhetorical characteristics of public problems, the rhetorical formation of publics that are engaged by these problems, the rhetorical characteristics of public spheres in which these problems are discussed and debated, and the rhetorical character of the public opinions that emerge from these deliberations.

Rhetorical Characteristics of Public Problems

How does a problem become a public problem? There is a significant body of evidence that indicates people are not typically engaged by public problems until they see some connection to their lives. For example, survey researcher Samuel Popkin, who studies how voters think about public issues, points out that people do not have incentives to gather information simply to be good citizens. We gather information as it is personally relevant. For instance, we gather a great deal of information to negotiate our daily lives. If we are planning a weekend hike, we are likely to monitor the weekend weather reports. In addition, sometimes we seek information of a more general nature that is relevant to our planning and future decisions. A student estimating his chances of being drafted studies draft board policies; a businessperson interested in developing an overseas sales strategy becomes knowledgeable about commercial regulations in other countries; senior citizens about to retire learn the social security regulations; prospective home buyers research mortgage rates. Unless a person is aware of how a policy, law, or existing practice directly affects her, at best she is conscious of these as addressing problems other people have, not ones facing her community or country. For her to become engaged by a public problem, she needs someone to make a link between her daily life and larger conditions affecting it.[3] When we are waiting in long gas lines and paying high prices for fuel, we are more aware of the precariousness of fossil fuel supply and the need for a sensible energy policy than in times when "the livin' is easy." Sometimes, of course, a cataclysmic event, such as the attacks of September 11, 2001, on the World Trade Center and the Pentagon, may awaken us to a public problem, such as airport security checks. More typically, however, the transition in conscious awareness of a problem from one that other people have to one that affects our country or community, and therefore affects us, is a rhetorical accomplishment.

A **public problem** is a matter of conflict and controversy that is (or should be) open to discussion in the arenas of public action by everyone with an interest in it. Not every problem belongs in a public arena. If a vegan and a carnivore become roommates, they can resolve their differences over diet among themselves. On the other hand, sometimes powerful individuals and groups successfully exclude problems that properly belong in public arenas from appearing there. Partner abuse, for example, usually occurs in private. Is it a private or public problem? For a long time it was treated as a private problem; the label "domestic dispute" implied a confinement of the problem to the privacy of a couple's home. Today most people regard it as a serious social problem and open to public discussion. As soon as we begin to discuss partner abuse as a public problem, differences of opinion will arise regarding its nature, who is responsible, and what is to be done.

These concerns of **definition, cause,** and **solution** are the basic elements of a public problem's rhetorical structure. Sociologist Joseph Gusfield provides us with a useful set of distinctions for understanding this structure. Gusfield conducted studies of public talk about automobile accidents in which the driver had some trace of alcohol in his or her system at the time of the mishap. The people he interviewed had a typical way of describing driving under the influence of alcohol that provided a fairly uniform view of the problem and what must be done. Here's what most people thought: Alcohol leads to impaired driving and increases the risk of accident, injury, and death. Since drinking coupled with driving "causes" auto accidents, solutions lie in strategies that diminish either drinking or driving after drinking. The available strategy is to persuade the drinker not to get behind the wheel of the car. Law enforcement and punishment, perhaps supplemented by education, are the most useful and acceptable means to diminish auto accidents due to drinking. Some people thought in longer-range terms and wanted impaired drivers screened for alcoholism and treated for their illness.[4]

Because Gusfield had conducted earlier studies of prohibition and the Temperance Movement, he was aware of a wider range of possible viewpoints toward issues of alcohol than those expressed by the people he interviewed. He was struck by how those he studied took auto safety and alcohol consumption uniformly to be the responsibility of the individual motorist. They did not consider institutions, such as the alcoholic beverage or hospitality industries, as part of the problem. Nor did they mention weather conditions, the safety of the roadway, or the driving behavior of the other motorist involved in an accident. Why did people respond so uniformly? Gusfield found his answer in the way public problems become contests over **ownership, causal responsibility** and **political responsibility.** Public problems are **agonistic** (i.e., oppositional) in character. Competing interests tend to vie for control of the problem. These three features are the areas in which groups focus their rhetorical strategies in order to influence how we define the problem and arrive at a judgment about what must be done and who is responsible.

Ownership of Public Problems

Every public problem involves a contest between competing groups trying to control the discourse on the problem: What is its nature? Who gets to advocate? Whom should we ignore? Where can we discuss this problem? When should we remain silent? Who counts as an authority? Which evidence is relevant? and so forth. *Ownership* refers to *the ability to create and influence the public definition of a problem.*

In the arenas where public problems are debated and public opinion is formed, some groups are more powerful than others. Some groups are called to testify before legislative bodies, have access to the media, or command an audience of interested readers, viewers, and listeners. Owners make claims and assertions that carry weight for our understanding and action. Members of the public attending to an issue look to them for information, definitions, analysis, arguments, and solutions to the problem. For those in the engaged public, owners have **ethos** (authority) on the subject, a concept we will consider in greater detail in chapter 8. Even though others may oppose them, owners remain among those whose views are taken seriously.

In the nineteenth century, for example, churches owned alcohol problems. Their ownership was expressed publicly in the form of the Temperance Movement. The most prominent group in this movement was the Women's Christian Temperance Union. The WCTU proclaimed the evils of alcohol and sought legislative bans and personal reform, which eventually resulted in prohibition, but when prohibition was repealed, the WCTU (and the churches) lost ownership of the alcohol issue. Today MADD (Mothers Against Drunk Driving), medicine/psychology experts, and 12-step groups own the drinking-driving issue. MADD, for example, lobbies legislatures, speaks at schools, organizes youth groups that support their cause among teenagers, places ads on TV, and contributes to an atmosphere of public intolerance for drinking and driving.

The changing ownership of drinking issues alerts us to ownership's emerging and unstable character. Like a property owner, groups that own a public problem seek to **control** its discussion and debate in the arenas of decision and public opinion. They try to fix the definition of the problem, identify the key issues, and determine what will be discussed and how it will be discussed. They also seek to become the **exclusive authority** on the problem, while diminishing the authority of opposing groups. Sometimes a group's primary mission may divert its energies from full attention to a problem, leading it to **transfer** ownership to another group, as illustrated by the transfer of drinking issues from the church to the WCTU. Finally, the balance of public opinion and action may turn against the group so that they **lose ownership** of the problem. When prohibition was repealed, for instance, the WCTU lost ownership of the alcohol issue. Although we still consider public problems related to alcohol consumption, they are no longer framed in religious terms.

Ownership implies its opposite, or **disownership**. Groups *disown* public problems *by acts of word and deed that distance them from the problem.* The concept of disownership alerts us to look for those who should be addressing a public problem but are not. According to Gusfield, disowners are interested in "avoiding the obligation to be involved in the problem-creating or problem-solving process. They deliberately seek to resist claims that the phenomenon is their problem."[5] For example, during the active periods of the Temperance Movement, the alcohol industry made little effort at counterarguments. "The fault is in the man, not the bottle" is a slogan that says "it's not our fault." Equally, the drinking and driving problem is part of the more general problem of auto safety. Until the late 1960s, however, the automobile industry spent very little time or money researching safety. It left this issue to departments of transportation, as if to say, "the fault is with the nut behind the wheel, not our cars."

In sum, ownership and disownership are matters of power and authority. A group's power to enter influential public spheres, to keep opponents out, or to avoid having to join the discussion will bear on its success in shaping our understanding of a problem. Debate makes differences of opinion and perspective evident. It elevates our conscious awareness of structures that, otherwise, we might take for granted, and it fosters critical understanding and informed choice. Owners also accrue authority. As their views influence a public's definition of a problem they shape the audience's perception of reality. Equally, the lack of conflict, which is a consequence of disownership, may hide aspects of social structures that, if brought to consciousness, we would want to change. Disownership is a rhetorical strategy that hides our alternatives when making political choices.

Responsibility: Causal and Political

In addition to defining the problem, owners seek to affix **responsibility**. The term is used here in two distinct senses. There is a difference between saying "a high fever was responsible for my poor performance on the midterm" and "I am responsible for turning in my work on time." The first refers to a condition that caused a particular outcome: my illness prevented me from doing as well as I might have on the test. The second refers to the person obliged to control the situation and make sure expectations are met: it's my job to meet the deadline. Both of these senses of responsibility are present in the rhetorical structure of public problems.

Owners make claims about who or what is responsible for **causing** the problem. The cause may take a variety of forms ranging from a condition in the environment to the practices of an individual or group. Those who are competing for ownership often disagree about who or what caused the problem. Those who act as judges resolve these disagreements. Sometimes they are literally a judge and jury, as when citizens joined in a class action suit against the tobacco industry. Sometimes elected officials act as judges, as when they hear testimony that influences the drafting of laws regulating automobile fuel emissions. Sometimes citizens are judges, as when British citizens were critical of their monarchy for its slow demonstration of public grief over the death of Princess Diana. In each of these instances the determination of causal responsibility depends on which owner's arguments are accepted by the relevant judges. *Causal responsibility* thus refers to *a shared belief about the sequence of occurrences that factually accounts for the existence of a problem.*

Determining causal responsibility is important because reaching agreement on the agent or agency responsible for bringing the problem into being will focus the discussion on how to fix the problem. Owners attempt to fix **political responsibility** on those who are accountable for insuring that the problem is corrected. They assert claims about who is responsible for finding a solution, establishing policies, enforcing laws, and the like. Political responsibility is often a matter of policy, sometimes of law, but also can be a domain of knowledge. Fixing *political responsibility* asserts that *some office or group is obligated to do something about the problem.* Here we should be cautious not to think of politics in the narrow sense of government. If you are suffering from migraine headaches, you don't expect your priest, astrologer, or rhetoric professor to be responsible for curing you. In our society we commonly place this responsibility with physicians (i.e., with a domain of knowledge—medicine).

The structure of public problems, in sum, involves groups and institutions, including governmental agencies, competing over ownership and disownership, the acceptance of causal theories for the problem, and the fixation of political responsibility for resolving it. This structure is rhetorical in character; a public problem is an arena of conflict that is constituted and resolved via the use of symbols in ways that will lead to coordinated social action.

The Organization of Public Consciousness

We began our discussion of public problems by noting that until people see the link between conditions in the world or government policies and their lives, they have little conscious awareness of public problems. They frequently need someone to make the connection to their own circumstances for them to recognize the personal relevance of the problem, to go from seeing it as a problem other people have to a problem that affects their lives. This transformation in conscious awareness requires that our personal knowledge about a problem, which is often fragmented, uncertain, and inconsistent, be sculpted into a public system of certain and consistent knowledge. How is this shared knowledge formed?

Gusfield's investigation of the discourse on drinking and driving uncovered some patterns that help us answer this question. In order to develop policy actions with support from a public that often has limited and flawed knowledge, owners must engage in rhetorical efforts that heighten the believability of their claims about responsibility and the awareness of the problem's impact. One very potent source of believable argument in our society is science. Science garners its authority through rhetorical claims to rigor, objectivity, consistency, and adherence to prescribed conventions and protocols in collecting data and drawing inferences of causation. This rhetoric says the scientist offers an unbiased window to objective reality. Thus we may expect that owners will seek to establish a scientific basis for their claims. They will try to find empirical evidence that supports their assertions and refutes those of their opponents. By laying claim to a scientific basis for their analysis of a public problem, owners heighten the believability of their position.

Although scientific arguments provide a strong basis for rational belief, they do not necessarily carry high dramatic impact. Public action, by contrast, is extremely high in dramatic effect. **Public performances** can call attention to a problem and define its issues in memorable ways. Demonstrations, strikes, and favorable media coverage of public deeds can dramatize an owner's views. We may expect owners to seek opportunities or engage in practices to publicize their causes. This rhetoric says there is a problem that is serious and is being ignored. It suggests that those in power are deeply opposed to recognizing the troubling nature of existing conditions. Dramatic publicity heightens our sense of awareness of a problem and conveys a sense of the activists' deep commitment to a particular definition of its character and relevance to the community.

Cultural metaphors that organize and provide orientation are another potent means for structuring public knowledge. In his drinking driver studies, for example, Gusfield found that cultural metaphors were used to transform the offender into either a "social drinker" or a "problem drinker." Each system advanced a set of cultural associations that organized public understanding. Calling a person a social drinker emphasized action that was normal. Occasionally a social drinker slipped and drank too much, but did not have a serious drinking problem and was not a bad person. The problem drinker, by contrast, suffered a pathology and needed intervention and treatment. The terms "social drinker" and "problem drinker" are metaphors with cultural resonance; they recall familiar images. These contrasting images establish a culture of what is permissible and what is prohibited. Their wide acceptance gives them exceptional rhetorical force, which can drive policy decisions. Calling a drinking driver a problem drinker, for instance, turns the act into a pathology. By extension, if this is a sickness, it can't be controlled by law because it is a medical problem. The drinking driver isn't a lawbreaker, rather a sick person who needs help.

When issues become public, the very fact that we're talking about them gives them a degree of legitimacy. The way we talk about them conveys an understanding of the shape of our social world, what is causing disorder in it, and how we might return order to it. Our sense that a particular condition or practice is a problem, what caused it, and who should be responsible for fixing it are rhetorical constructions. Consequently, struggles over ownership of the problem, attempts at disownership, definition of key issues, and fixing of causal and political responsibilities bear directly on the central activity we are called upon to perform as citizens: to engage in public judgment.

෯

Publics Theory

Thus far we have stressed the rhetorical structure of public problems. We have emphasized the discourse of owners, who are typically the leaders of activist groups. Now we will examine in greater detail the role of citizen voices in the ongoing social dialogue on public problems and their remedies.

During the last quarter of the twentieth century, scholars in a number of disciplines awakened to the ways in which knowledge and power shape our social and political practices and how both are formed through discourse. This recognition of rhetoric's constitutive character contributed to the development of a new strand in rhetorical theory called **publics theory**. Publics theory is addressed to understanding and critiquing how the rhetorical characteristics of public problems shape the publics that form around them and the opinions they form.

Like all rhetorical theory, publics theory shares the central insight that practical discourse is addressed to an audience. However, this theory also recognizes that frequently in mass societies those who receive a message and respond to it are scattered to all corners of the community, nation, or even planet. We receive messages through a variety of media, engage issues in varying degrees, have opportunities to interact with strangers, and have more say on issues than our distant ancestors, many of whom were subject to the rule of a king. On the other hand, citizens today seldom have direct authority to determine the outcome of an issue. Their role is to convey a sense of **public opinion** to those with authority to act and to legitimate the actions of those in authority by support of their actions.

A liberal democracy, such as exists in most Western nations, rests on the assumption that for democracy to work citizens must form as a public and express a public opinion that should inform public policy. This assumption gives publics theory both a **descriptive** and a **normative** dimension. It is descriptive in that it explains how rhetorical conditions influence the ways in which democracy today actually works. It is normative in that it assumes certain ideals of communicative practice as tests for the quality of actual practice. Publics theory is developing around three key concepts: **publics, public sphere,** and **public opinion**.

Publics

Shortly after World War I, the distinguished American journalist Walter Lippmann and the distinguished American philosopher John Dewey had an important exchange of views on whether citizens were able to play a meaningful role in public decision making.[6] Their concerns arose from the complexity of public problems generated by the technical, economic, political, and social developments of their era. These problems, many of which were manifested in the destruction that occurred in World War I as a result of such inventions as chemical warfare, were beyond the comprehension of the average person. The question facing society, they agreed, was whether citizens who lacked technical knowledge could have an informed opinion with any relevance to the problems being decided. Lippmann thought they could not without assistance, and the assistance he proposed was a cadre of journalists who would become expert on an issue and inform the general public of its best interests and how it should act to protect them. Dewey was horrified by this proposal because it had citizens relinquishing their active role in shaping public policies to an expert elite that would lead them like sheep. It missed the more basic issue, Dewey thought, of reforming the way issues are raised and discussed so that citizens can participate in the process. "The essential need, in other words, is the improvement of the methods and conditions of debate, discussion, and persuasion. This is *the* problem of the public."[7]

The problem debated by Lippmann and Dewey is still with us. John F. Kennedy, for example, posed the problem of decision making during his presidency this way:

> Most of us are conditioned for many years to have a political viewpoint—Republican or democratic, liberal, conservative, or moderate. The fact of the matter is that most of the problems . . . that we now face are technical problems. They are very sophisticated judgments, which do not lend themselves to the great sort of passionate movements which have stirred this country so often in the past. [They] deal with questions which are now beyond the comprehension of most men.[8]

Kennedy's statement suggests that he thought common sense language was no longer able to express "sophisticated judgments" on public issues. But if he was correct, his assessment carries serious consequences.

Unquestionably some dimensions of public problems do present technical difficulties and do require a specialist's knowledge to resolve. We can hardly imagine finding a remedy to pollution of our drinking water, for example, without drawing on the knowledge of chemists and civil engineers. Were Lippmann and Kennedy justified in advocating the transfer of deliberation on public problems from citizen forums to technically educated elites? When participation in public discussions requires competence in information sciences plus technical expertise, the average citizen is reduced to a silent and often befuddled observer. Decision making on public prob-

lems that privileges experts and uses technical language moves policy issues from public arenas accessible to citizen participation into technical
arenas reserved for experts.[9]

Why should we care? Isn't it better to resolve public problems on the
basis of technical knowledge? Do we want an ignorant public influencing
public policy? This is a false dichotomy. Clearly no one wants ignoramuses
making policy decisions. But citizens do not have to be expert ecologists,
say, to form an intelligent opinion on whether tax dollars should be spent
on reclaiming endangered wetlands. They need a clear explanation of the
relation of wetlands to the cycles of nature and to the quality of the air we
breathe and the water we drink. And they need public debate in order to
sort through the available options and the trade-offs involved before deciding how to spend scarce tax dollars.

We should care because as citizens we bear the consequences of pub-
lic-policy decisions. Public deliberative processes allow citizens to discover
their interests, form a sense of the issues that bear on them, develop an informed opinion about public problems and their solutions, and convey
their views with the expectation that they will be taken seriously. Publics
are important in a democracy because their opinions certify the legitimacy
of the state's actions.[10] Our need to participate in the deliberative process
is no less real today than for our forbearers in the Athenian democracy of
2,500 years ago. Without opportunities to participate in discussion and debate that influence the formation of public opinion, we cannot form as a
public—as a body whose views matter on the public issues that confront
us. Instead, we become spectators to political spectacle, estranged from
the decision-making processes that influence the quality of our lives.

Because today few citizens actually participate in the formal debates
of the bodies that make and enforce our laws and policies, forming and
communicating the people's will is more complicated than for our ancient
ancestors. Mass media can disseminate messages to the entire populace
and pollsters can report survey results drawn from the entire populace.
But not everyone pays attention to all public questions nor has an opinion,
much less an informed opinion, on each of them. The concept of a public
therefore needs careful definition. Rhetoricians usually refer to *a public* as
*that portion of the populace engaged in evolving shared opinion on a particu-
lar issue, with the intent of influencing its resolution.* Publics are not fixed,
they are not idealized constructs; they are **emergences** that arise from
rhetorical experience.[11]

Developed societies are montages of publics. Any given public is activated as its members become aware of issues that intersect with the conditions of their lives and require their attention. These multiple publics are
composed of members of a community (or even the entire society) who
have a stake in an issue but do not necessarily hold the same opinion on it.
The current debate on social security, for example, spans the generations.
Those nearing retirement and Gen-Xers have an equal stake in the out-

come of this debate, but from very different points of view. Because financing the social security system is their mutual problem, interactions across the generational divide try to influence opposing viewpoints and to use these exchanges to reach solutions that all parties can accept.

Publics can be described with greater specificity than the populace, since the populace includes all citizens regardless of whether they are interested in a problem, are engaged in discussions of it, or are even receptive to sharing opinions. On the other hand, a public's members form a collective of engaged social actors, although often loosely organized at best. Their members exhibit three broad rhetorical characteristics.

First, publics are **active**. We recognize publics by the way they manifest their attention to public problems. Certainly this would include their voting behavior, but just as often we detect their presence by their use of buying power to send a message, demonstrations of sympathy or opposition, adornments of colored ribbons, debates in classrooms and on factory floors, speeches on library steps or letters to the editor, correspondence with public officials, and other expressions of stance and judgment.

Second, publics **emerge**; they are not pregiven. A public is not an interest group, such as people on a mailing list who send a check. It consists of those who are actively creating and attending to discussion of the problem. Their behavior both publicizes opinions and makes them felt by others. Publics emerge as people make, assess, and judge appeals that contribute to the evolution of a widely shared opinion on the problem.

Third, membership in a public requires **rhetorical competence**, or a capacity to participate in rhetorical experiences. Since the function of a public is to form an opinion on the basis of the arguments, it is difficult to imagine how a closed-minded group can perform its job. A public's members, on balance, must exhibit such traits as:

- **receptivity** to modes of expression other than and in addition to formal argumentation
- **critical listening** (reading, viewing) to understand what is being said and how it relates to them
- **open-mindedness** to other points of view, including openness to change
- **active** attempts to engage in bilateral communication and resistance to passive acceptance of unilateral communication
- **inventional skill** to discuss a public problem in ways that encompass and appreciate the views and needs of others
- **contingent thinking** in which the ongoing discussion opens all claims to amendment, qualification, and even contradiction and carries an understanding that even seeming bedrock agreements are, to some extent, provisional
- **inclusivity** of all relevant voices in the discussion

These are the traits of persons who are able to participate in rhetorical exchanges and who are open to the possibility of collective participation in rhetorical processes that might persuade them to change their beliefs. These traits set members of a public apart from interest-group members, who often proceed on closed-minded assumptions that only support one point of view. Whether attention to social exchange alters or reinforces personal views, collective participation in rhetorical processes *constitutes individuals as a public.*

Public Spheres

At the founding of the United States, James Madison wrote his famous Federalist Paper No. 10, in which he warned against the dangers of factions and the tyranny of the majority. Madison was aware of the enormous influence that well-organized groups of zealous advocates on a single issue or for an extreme point of view might have on the government. Today we share that concern with our fear of well-financed special-interest lobbies that can influence the shape of legislation for personal benefit without regard for the consequences this may have for the majority of citizens. Groups such as the tobacco, oil, or pharmaceutical lobbies come quickly to mind. At the other extreme, Madison also was leery of a political system in which a simple majority of decision makers could force its will on the minority without regard for the possible virtues of the minority position. Today we share his concern when Congress or our state's legislature or our local city council acts along strict party lines. Unless we share the views of the party in power, we probably are skeptical of such ideologically based decisions. A democracy relies on open deliberation to test the merits of a proposal.

Madison's concerns indicate the important link between informed opinion and democratic action. Although democratic procedures of open discussion and debate are not terribly efficient, we require them to insure that the full range of relevant perspectives are explored and that decisions reflect the will of the majority as expressed through public opinion. Open deliberation helps participants arrive at shared reasoning rather than shared prejudice as the basis for their judgments. Evidence gathered by political scientist James Fishkin shows that when people are exposed to relevant facts and different points of view on an issue, they often come to very different conclusions than those they expressed on survey questionnaires administered before discussion of the issue.[12] Informed discussion does make a difference.

Polls can't substitute for informed deliberation. They may give a convenient indication of what a representative aggregate of private individuals believe, and leaders may use poll results to suggest that the majority supports their actions, but without deliberation we have no assurance that these opinions are informed or that the poll results reflect what public judgment would look like if people were informed. The answer to Madison's and our fear of factions and of the tyranny of the majority lies in the quality of public discussion that shapes public judgment. The quality of public discussion, in turn, depends on the conditions under which it takes place. Publics theory addresses these conditions under the concept of the **public sphere.**

Any discursive arena in which rhetorical action contributes to shared opinion on a public problem can qualify as part of the public sphere for that problem. As social theorist Jürgen Habermas has argued, the public sphere arises to some degree whenever two or more people engage in serious discussion of a public issue.[13]

The spatial metaphor used for this concept may suggest that the public sphere is a particular physical place, such as the geographical location of a town hall or legislative assembly. Certainly there are institutional spaces such as these that serve as arenas for open deliberation, but properties of physical geography are less important than properties of "discursive" or rhetorical geography. A public sphere is a **discursive space.** It is constituted by our rhetorical exchanges, whether in informal conversation or formal debate, that contribute to shared sentiments on a public problem among a significant segment of a public. Usually, rhetoricians understand a *public sphere* as "*a discursive space in which individuals and groups associate to discuss matters of mutual interest and, where possible, reach a common judgment about them. It is the site of emergence for rhetorically salient meanings.*"[14]

How can you spot a public sphere when you come across one? Usually we spot one by the nature of the topic being discussed in relation to the people engaged in the communicative exchange. John Dewey made a distinction in *The Public and its Problems* that helps us. He differentiated public problems from private ones on the basis of who experiences the consequences of the decisions reached. A private problem is one where the resolution doesn't extend beyond those involved. A public problem is one where others suffer the *indirect consequences* of the decision makers' actions. A public sphere, then, would be any discursive space in which a problem bearing such indirect consequences was being considered.

For example, your decision to pursue a college education was a private matter. It may have involved your parents, friends, romantic partner, or children. It may have had implications for your finances, intimate relationships, plans to have children, and so forth. Still you had a direct say in the decision, and its consequences most likely will not be pronounced in a very specific way beyond your life and that of your immediate loved ones. On the other hand, individual colleges and universities set entrance requirements. You have no direct say about what they will be, but you bear the indirect consequences of whatever is decided. In this connection many professional schools set admission quotas to insure a certain mix of students. Starting in the 1960s, these schools adopted a widespread practice of reserving spaces for underrepresented groups. When Medical School applicant James Bakke was denied admission to the University of California, he brought a lawsuit against the University for unfair discrimination.

Bakke's decision to pursue a medical degree was a private one, but the Medical School's admission criteria designed to increase minority representation in the medical profession produced a negative indirect consequence that some applicants regarded as unjust.

The Bakke suit instigated a spirited national debate on affirmative action that continues today. Partly that debate has occurred in our courts, going as far as the Supreme Court, which ruled (*Bakke v. Regents of University of California*) that universities may consider race in admission decisions in order to maintain diverse enrollment and to remedy past discrimination. The legal debate continues, as owners who disagree with the court continue to test the decision with new cases, as the recent modification of that decision by the Hopwood decision in Texas illustrates.

In 1992, Cheryl Hopwood, who had been denied admission to the University of Texas Law School, and others sued the Law School claiming that it preferenced African-American and Mexican-American applicants. U.S. District Judge Sam Sparks followed the Bakke ruling and held that the University could consider race in making admission decisions. However, the Fifth U.S. Circuit Court of Appeals held that such practices were unconstitutional. When the U.S. Supreme Court refused to review the decision, all affirmative action admissions were halted in Texas's public universities. Other states were in a quandary concerning their own affirmative action policies, since they believed the ruling made them vulnerable to lawsuits if they continued to use race as an admission consideration, and some ceased to do so. The University of Washington continued its past practice and was sued. However, when the Supreme Court also allowed the University of Washington to continue using race as one factor in admissions by declining to review a Ninth U.S. Circuit Court decision in favor of the University's affirmative action policy, the Court left the legal status of affirmative action open to further interpretation. Consequently, the public concerned with affirmative action will continue to debate the issue through the courts.

The debate on affirmative action will occur in many places other than the courts. On campuses across the United States spirited debate occurred in student governments, faculty assemblies, student and local newspapers, countless student organization meetings, and the executive suite. Equally, citizens, city councils, and members of institutions and organizations other than colleges and universities continued to consider whether affirmative action is just. You and your immediate circle can privately decide whether you should pursue a college education; we require a public sphere to resolve the question of whether affirmative action is fair and should be a public policy.

Democracies have multiple arenas in which people communicate about issues such as these. Some are formal ones, such as the op-ed pages of newspapers, while others are of the more informal "water cooler" variety. Some arenas form around specific issues, such as global warming, while others are more general, such as the economy. Some are more inclusive in who they admit, such as the town hall, while others are more resistant to the voice and views of "outsiders," such as a political party. Rather than a single public sphere, in reality we have multiple spheres.

Regardless of their multiplicity, these arenas share the trait of forming something approaching common understanding and shared judgment through the give and take of discussion and debate. Going back to the problem Madison addressed in Federalist 10, since public spheres are the places where informed public opinion emerges, the rhetorical characteristics of these spheres will have a direct bearing on the quality of the opinions that form there.

Obviously, for a deliberative process to inspire confidence, the communication conditions that underwrite the **publicity principle**—the right to make your views known—must be present. Everyone with a legitimate interest or stake in the problem should have the **right to participate** in the public dialogue. They should have **access to relevant information** so that they can make informed arguments. They should have **access to the relevant media of dissemination** so that they can share their point of view with others in the public. And their **rights of free speech** must be guaranteed; they must be free to assemble, associate with whomever they choose, express and defend their views, and challenge the views of others without fear of penalty or imprisonment.

These conditions are **normative standards** we use to assess the actual rhetorical conditions of a particular public sphere. Whenever these conditions are compromised or absent, they are likely to produce one-sided discussion, unexamined assertions, and uninformed judgments. For example, the government's legal action against the tobacco industry revealed evidence that the large tobacco companies deliberately deceived the American people. Internal industry memos showed that firms had conducted studies on the addictive properties of tobacco and used this information to increase the addictive power of cigarettes. Meanwhile, during the public debate over the dangers of tobacco products, the industry denied these facts about smoking and their manufacturing practices. An important part of the government's case rested on the industry's deliberate attempts at deception. In effect, it argued that the industry deliberately tried to undermine the public sphere in which Americans were trying to reach an important judgment about a deadly health issue.

Public spheres take a variety of forms that are influenced by whether they are **institutional** or **preinstitutional forums** and by their recognition by agents with power as bearing on public problems. Institutional forums, such as legislative assemblies, have limited access and strict rules on speaking privileges. Legislators are agents with power; their exchanges bear directly on public decisions. Preinstitutional arenas, such as ongoing public discussion over whether to boycott products made in Third-World sweat shops, have much looser rules of access and accommodate a wider range of expression. Their focus is not on making official policy decisions but on deciding whether there is support for, say, discouraging the purchase of sweatshop products. Their output may be a movement to communicate public judgment in a way that those with decision-making power—manufacturers, financiers, your school's administration, legislators—will have to take seriously, such as a boycott.

Sometimes the dominant public sphere will be inclusive, giving opportunities for all legitimate views to be heard. But more exclusionary spheres also form, with restricted access and a limited range of viewpoints and problems it will acknowledge. In large measure the women's movement, for example, addressed gaining access to public spheres and recognizing women's issues as public problems. The movement formed a **counterpublic sphere**, a discursive arena in which women (and sometimes men) deliberated on problems, including how best to gain access to arenas where expression of opinion influenced those with the power to act.

Regardless of its institutional status and recognition by those with authority, participation in a public sphere and the opinions that emerge there will be shaped by the **rhetorical ecology** of the sphere. Of course, for any rhetorical exchange to contribute to a sound public judgment, participants must be able to support and publicize their positions, as we noted before. But beyond that set of conditions, there are traits of the sphere's rhetorical environment that influence the degree to which it accommodates full and open exchange of ideas. These traits may be expressed as a set of six principles.

Inclusion.   Every public sphere has *discursive borders*. You might think of these as you do geographic borders, some of which are shared and some of which are not, some of which are easy to cross and some of which are more impenetrable. As issues develop, a sphere's border conditions may change. Its operating rules of exclusion and inclusion will indicate the breadth of participants in the sphere and the range of opinions that are likely to be expressed.

These rules are seldom spelled out formally, as in an organization's membership requirements and by-laws. Mostly they are implicit. A political party, for example, is open to anyone in theory. But in practice if you do not share its values, you will be excluded from serious discussion as soon as party members discover your true sentiments lie elsewhere, and they probably will discourage you from attending further meetings. More commonly, a public sphere may exclude consideration of selected issues as public problems. In 1992, for example, the citizens of Colorado passed a state constitutional amendment that denied explicit mention of sexual orientation as entitled to legal protection. Some argued that sexual orientation was not a civil right; others argued that there was no need to make such protections explicit because they were implicit in existing laws. But the gay and lesbian community thought the amendment created a license for hostile behavior toward them by denying them explicit protection. The amendment, in effect, excluded gay and lesbian concerns as a public problem appropriate to the state's political public sphere. Subsequent ruling by the U.S. Supreme Court proved their concern valid, and the amendment was struck down.

Range of appeals.   Closely related to inclusion is the range of permissible appeals in a public sphere. The range of permissible appeals is an index of the openness of the sphere to diverse perspectives. Certainly not all perspectives have equal merit. But the point of a serious discussion is to let ideas stand or fall on their own merits, not on the basis of prevailing prejudices. Excluding legitimate arguments is a sign that the sphere is less focused on using *critical publicity* to generate public judgment than in advancing a particular point of view.

Believable appearance.   Being admitted to a sphere does not necessarily mean your participation will have credibility. Credibility requires, among other things, the ability to make a *believable appearance.* Public spheres often will have implicit rules that privilege certain voices or that require demonstration of certain qualities before opinions will be taken seriously. Adhering to these rules can convey authority. For example, Martin Luther King's "Letter From Birmingham Jail" was addressed to the white ministers of Birmingham who had opposed his civil rights activities in their city. He counted on their Christian beliefs to provide a salient frame for the issues of social justice for which he was campaigning. Conversely, in the 1996 presidential campaign, Ross Perot addressed the national meeting of the NAACP to solicit its support. In the process of outlining his thoughts on fostering economic development of African-American communities, he referred to his African-American audience as "you people." His remark so distanced him from his audience—from their rules of believable appearance—that they created a furor over his attitudes rather than a discussion of his proposals.

Rhetorically salient meaning.   The rhetoric of a public sphere is significantly influenced by the language it admits and privileges. Public spheres are our *sites of emergence for rhetorically salient meaning.* These meanings constitute our understanding of a public problem and influence our thinking and acting on it. These meanings also are specific to an issue, a context, a rhetor, or audience. Consequently, they may be unstable. As a vocabulary gains salience, it provides orientation, value, and even a telos that defines the issue and our role as a public. For example, during the first three-quarters of the twentieth century, rhetors constructed the meaning of the United States through rhetorical imagery of a "melting pot." We may have arrived here with different ethnicities, but as Americans we were to melt into a homogenous whole. Today that imagery is contested by the more fragmented imagery of "quilt" and "rainbow." Our job is not to eliminate our differences but to sew them together to make a whole that retains its sense of diverse parts.

Rhetorically salient meanings depend on at least two qualities of language use. For everyone with a stake in the problem to share a meaningful discussion, participants must use *contextualized language*. Since rhetorical discourse is framed by a specific set of considerations of issue, time, place and audience, the first requirement of language is that it be tied to the specific problem under consideration. Speaking or writing in generalities or relying on euphemisms are two traits we might detect in discourse that violates this requirement. The second requirement is that the language be *intelligible to all the participants*. This can be a difficult challenge to meet. Contemporary problems often involve technical components and legal or bureaucratic regulations. As specialists enter a public sphere they can usurp the possibilities for vernacular exchange by substituting technical language as the coin of the rhetorical realm. Controlling the language in which issues are discussed determines how they are expressed, relevance of experience, and expertise in adjudicating the issues they raise.

Tolerance. Complex societies are constituted by difference rather than identity, by diversity rather than unity. Contact with alternative ideas and traditions and relations of mutual dependency are inevitable. Presupposing conformity of values and ends or imposing a preordained orientation weakens a public sphere. It excludes those who are different from us but who also have a stake in whatever gets decided. We cannot expect cooperation in solutions that affect everyone if we do not encourage and promote full participation in forming those solutions.

The implication of this observation can be unsettling. Tolerance is easy when we do not have relations of mutual dependency with those who are different from us or disagree with us; we can adopt a live-and-let-live attitude. However, most public problems involve participants who are interdependent. They need each other's cooperation to accomplish goals. In this case tolerance means very little if it does not produce mutual cooperation. Because radically divergent perspectives are unlikely to reach consensus on their ideological presuppositions, we cannot expect one side to adopt the other's point of view. Instead, they must find grounds for cooperation that both can accept. Since these grounds typically are mutually acceptable outcomes, we can gauge the quality of a public sphere by its prevailing language and salient meanings. In general, well functioning inclusive spheres express solutions that interdependent partners regard as acceptable for their own reasons. Unlike a rhetoric that justifies acceptable action on the basis of shared reason, tolerance uses *cooperation* as the test of public judgments.

Empowerment of its public. Well functioning public spheres invite their participants to weigh and choose among their alternatives. In this respect their dominant rhetoric does not attempt to control audience responses (unlike much of the discourse of powerful factions in mass societies) or to treat audiences as passive by asking them only to purchase and to applaud. Publics, unlike audiences of spectators, are presumed to have a guiding interest for which they have the potential to become active. We can detect the extent to which rhetoric is empowering its public by the way the dominant discourse of a sphere asks for its opinions. Publics are empowered to engage in their primary activity—forming a public judgment—whenever they engage diverse viewpoints and interests that intersect on common problems and that interact in creating policies and evaluating deeds. Put differently, an active society hears and speaks to the multiple interests that converge on any issue. When individuals talk to a closed enclave, they become powerless to effect change. Their choices are essentially limited to subscribing to a point of view that strips them of their autonomy or becoming insulated from and insensitive to perspectives of others whose cooperation is essential for resolving problems. Social actors must hear multiple voices to realize that they can do more than respond—they can choose. A diverse and empowered public is more likely than its mass counterpart to differentiate between the glitz of public relations satisfied with images and competent rhetoric seeking to articulate shared reality.

Public Opinion

Today there is widespread understanding of public opinion as the results of an opinion poll. Polls report how a sample of individuals responded to questions posed by a survey researcher, a news organization, a political party, or a private enterprise. The distinguishing feature of opinion polls is their inference of public opinion from the selections made by respondents to structured questions (e.g., How would you rate the president's performance? Excellent, Good, Fair, Poor, or No Opinion?). But opinion polls do not tell us whether the participants in the survey were engaged by the issues in the questions asked, whether they had little or a great deal of knowledge on the subject, whether they were actively engaged in expressing their opinions to others or preferred keeping them to themselves, or even whether they told the researcher the truth. This does not mean that opinion polls are without value; they are an important but limited source of information. The specific limitation of most concern to publics theory is the inability of polls to capture discourse. Why is that a limitation? Because public opinion without discourse loses the sense of context and reasoning that provides the basis for holding an opinion in the first place, for interpreting its meaning to those who hold it, and for future courses of action.

As an alternative to opinion polls, rhetoricians understand *public opinion* as referring to *a discursive expression of civil judgment that reflects a common understanding among the members of a public.*[15] It is the expression of meaning and preference by the active members of society through assertions of affirmation, rejection, concern, or hope that frame the public experience of their common interests and how they should be protected. The qualifier "civil" may seem a strange prefix in this discussion. Its use is similar to other uses in our society, such as "civil disobedience," "civil rights," and "civil society." "Civil" in these expressions suggests a society marked by diversity and difference, but also by regard for others and tolerance of differences when confronting public problems and the conflict over them that is essential for a democracy to function.[16]

Since antiquity, Western civilization has proclaimed its reliance on the voice of the people—*vox populi*—on the assumption that the laws and policies of a democracy reflect the will of the governed. In the representative democracies of contemporary mass societies, the difficulty with this conviction lies in detecting the people's voice. One way has been to use numerical measures. Counting noses is a very old and useful method for getting a sense of where people's sentiments lie on an issue at a given moment. Rhetorical approaches tend to seek other indicators found in actual discourses. Consequently, publics theory does not rely exclusively on polls as an indicator of public opinion. It also places weight on the prevailing tendency of views that *emerge from people deliberating* (i.e., discussing and sometimes debating) the merits of ideas and actions. It regards public opinion as a rhetorically formed understanding that conveys more than a bottom line summary; it includes a public's shared sense of reality and its members' reasons for holding that view.

Each of us, without the aid of a personal pollster, has a sense of the prevailing views within our own community.[17] Just as our physical skin detects the condition of the physical atmosphere, from which we infer whether we need to dress for warmth or coolness, our social skin, so to speak, provides us with basic data on our rhetorical environment. It detects the views we are expected to share, what views are safe or dangerous to express, and whether we are in the majority or minority on an issue. We know what most people think by monitoring our rhetorical ecology.

This detective work is conducted through our local surveillance of **vernacular rhetoric**, such as everyday interactions, cultural artifacts, local events, demonstrations and their size, signs of affiliation, and so forth. These everyday transactions provide us with information about what is going on, who is involved, and how many seem to be in support. They also tell us what people think and why; they invite us to become aware of issues and to entertain alternative points of view on them. Monitoring the rhetorical ecology also includes the formal messages of leaders, such as elected officials, persons in positions of authority and influence, and spokespersons for groups.

If we are keen observers of our rhetorical environment, we will notice that, contrary to what opinion polls suggest, not everyone has an opinion and not all opinions count equally. People pay attention to matters that concern them, especially in their everyday lives, as we noted earlier. Unlike pollsters, who seek to gather a random sample of opinions, our personal surveillance tends to discriminate among opinion sources by making rhetorical assessments. We place more **weight** on the opinions of those who are actively engaged. While sheer quantity of shared or similar opinion is important, we also pay attention to the **intensity** with which an opinion is held. A group that has strong commitment to its opinion may exercise greater influence on official action because it exerts greater effort to publicize its view and is more tenacious in arguing its case to decision makers. We also notice that there is a difference in **duration**, or persistence across time, between popular moods and deeply held opinions. The former are what the ancient Greeks called **doxa**, strongly held but weakly grounded preferences. These are frequently what opinion polls report. The latter are a form of public knowledge, based on communal experience and reflective discussion, that support civil judgment. Finally, since we lack a personal pollster, we don't look for standardized responses but for rhetorical messages to locate salient opinions.

Public opinion is therefore not the same as majority opinion or popular opinion. It is marked by weight, intensity, and duration, as are exhibited by those whose common ends, purposes, and rules of procedure form a community. Public opinion of this sort is a form of **public judgment**. Its "public" character emerges through the constitutive spirit of deliberation that seeks consensus on the common good. Public judgment reflects convergence among the diverse perspectives represented in pluralistic politics. We cannot form it without integrating that judgment into the community to which it applies. It makes participation in the public sphere "the vehicle for transporting us from our private and subjective existence into the common realm of shared reality."[18]

Summary

The cornerstone of a democracy is the conviction that the people reign. For this reason, democracies depend on citizens to have the necessary competencies for participation in the ongoing deliberations that identify and resolve public concerns. This chapter has discussed how rhetoric shapes public problems and the rhetorical features of discursive arenas in which public problems are addressed and resolved. Public problems are matters of conflict and controversy that affect a significant segment of society. We expect those whose interests are at stake to be engaged in the rhetorical process of exploring and resolving these problems. This is to say that public problems are rhetorically constituted. Consequently, their discursive development and resolution is significant for the quality of our communal lives. The area of rhetoric that addresses this concern is called publics theory.

The rhetorical development of public problems is conducted by owners—those who seek to define the critical issues—to influence the salient meanings of the issues and to assign responsibilities related to them. We saw that public problems carry two types of responsibility: causal responsibility, which assigns the reason for the problem's existence, and political responsibility, which assigns the obligation to solve the problem to a specific person or group. Through the dramatic character of public performances and the use of salient cultural metaphors, owner rhetoric brings problems to conscious awareness and structures public knowledge of them.

While owners play a leading role in publicizing and defining public problems, their trajectory is significantly influenced by the way in which public participation is encouraged and factored into the decision-making process. In this regard, publics theory considers the role of citizens under three overarching concepts: publics, public spheres, and public opinion. We saw that the rhetorical understanding of a public makes it specific to a domain of concern. Publics emerge from rhetorical experiences. Their members are active in weighing and shaping public issues. Their activity requires that they be rhetorically competent. For a public to participate actively in the deliberative process by which public problems develop and are resolved, they must be receptive to a variety of modes of expression, be capable of listening critically to all sides and considering them with an open mind, engage other members with bilateral communication that exhibits inventional skill, employ contingent thinking, and strive for inclusive participation of all who have an interest in the outcome. These ideal traits of rhetorical competence serve as benchmarks for assessing the quality of actual publics that do form.

Publics surface in public spheres—discursive spaces in which individuals and groups associate to discuss matters of mutual interest and, where possible, reach a common judgment about them. These spheres are defined by various qualities that make it possible for them to utilize the publicity principle, such as having the right to participate, to access relevant information, to access relevant media of dissemination, and to exercise free speech. In addition, their rhetoric has defining characteristics that influence the qualities of the actual discourse they accommodate, such as an inclusive range of positions and appeals, rules of believable appearance, rhetorically salient meanings particular to the sphere's deliberative conversations, tolerance for alternative points of view, and empowerment of activity. Again, these normative traits are benchmarks for assessing the quality of a public sphere. The degree to which they are present will bear upon the confidence we can have in the public opinion that emerges from the discursive exchanges in these arenas.

Finally, we saw that a rhetorical construction of public opinion goes beyond polling data to examine the interactions between vernacular and formal rhetoric in order to gauge the civil judgment of those actively considering an issue. To have a sense of public reasoning that will lead to prevailing tendencies of shared sentiment requires more than a numerical count. In the next two chapters, we will explore specific rhetorical characteristics of reasoned appeals that surface in public judgments.

๑ 6 ๑

Finding Ideas

In the preceding chapters we have been considering different perspectives toward rhetoric. The various theories we have examined thus far indicate that *rhetoric* is a term with multiple meanings. Some use it to refer to a set of rules for composing a competent set of remarks addressed to an audience of competent listeners or readers. Some use it to refer to a social practice of public deliberation and decision making. Some use it to refer to instrumental discourse, or as a means to an end. Some refer to rhetoric as communication that evokes the conscious awareness necessary for us to engage in reasoned reflection and action. Some consider it to have a constitutive capacity, or the power to construct social reality by inducing collective consciousness of public problems and collective identity of groups in relation to them.

Their differences notwithstanding, these perspectives share some basic premises about rhetoric as a mode of discourse and as a social practice. They agree that rhetoric is occasioned discourse; that it is addressed to an audience; that it is practical discourse concerned with issues of the day as they intersect with the concerns of the audience; that it is a mode of thinking suited to inducing and coordinating social action on contingent problems. These points of agreement indicate rhetoric's overriding concern with the realities faced in civic life and the cultural world. This chapter explores creativity in rhetorical communication. It considers the basic method for generating ideas to address a rhetorical situation. The next three chapters build on this base to consider the appeals or arguments and other modes of persuasion based on observed principles of discourse—appeals that attempt to induce cooperation—developed in the message. These include the reasons offered to support a contention, how these appeals engage audience feelings, and the influence of the rhetor's character on an audience's judgment. In each case our concern is to find materials

99

that will energize our ideas in relevant ways for our audience. In rhetoric, the activity of finding things to say is called **invention**.

୬

The Problem of Invention

We hear a lot these days about "thinking outside the box." Although this expression is becoming clichéd, it points to a perennial problem. The human world is one of contingencies. We lack certainties on most things, and for that reason most of our human problems don't have evident answers. We have to devise solutions by reasoning about our problems and seeking the best solution possible in light of all the information available to us. Our approach to problems will reflect our analytic skills. Our past experiences inform our understanding about what worked or failed in similar situations. Experience is an invaluable resource, but if that is all we rely on, we risk applying habitual responses to problems instead of thinking them through. A habitual response is not necessarily bad if it effectively solves a problem. When our tooth aches, we see a dentist. On the other hand, when our customary understanding proves ineffectual and the problem persists, we need a fresh perspective to resolve it. Being liberated from the constraints of what we take for granted often helps us to gain fresh insight—a new perspective from which novel solutions flow. Thinking "outside the box" requires that we suspend our conventional assumptions in order to think creatively.

Consider, for example, the problem of poverty in the Third World. Despite foreign aid or loans from the World Bank, Third-World nations have remained poor. Often their leaders have redirected foreign aid to their own pockets, their workers have been exploited as a source of cheap labor, and political interests of more powerful nations often have thwarted the development of a sustainable industrial base by policies that support leaders more interested in protecting their power than in advancing the welfare of their people. As an alternative to foreign aid, loans, or investment by multinational corporations, reformers hoping to break the cycle of poverty in the Third World often have focused on the wealth of an elite few. Following Karl Marx's thought, they have argued for redistribution of their wealth, but that hasn't worked much better. This approach often has created political instability, precipitated civil war, frightened foreign investors, and created political obstacles to foreign trade.

Peruvian economist Hernando de Soto proposed a different solution.[1] De Soto does not deny the inequitable distribution of wealth, but his focus is on the absence of property rights. Except for the elite, few in the Third World hold official title to the land they live on or the homes they occupy, even if they have been there for decades. This poses a problem, since owning property is a basic means for leveraging existing wealth into new wealth. Say, for instance, you want to open a small boutique. If you own property, you can use it as collateral for a small business loan to start your new venture. But because Third-World nations do not share the Western conception of private property, their citizens lack a basic means for improving their economic condition.

De Soto argues that instead of designing economic reform with socialist proposals, we should start with a basic capitalist assumption: the cornerstone of wealth is private ownership of property. De Soto explains his idea by referring to an everyday experience in Bali. Bali lacks formal property deeds. So how do you know when you cross one person's property and enter another's? You know you have crossed the line when a different dog barks. The dogs know. If the dogs know, de Soto reasons, it must be because they learned the boundaries from their masters, who recognize and observe property lines even though there are no documents codifying ownership.

De Soto estimates that the world's poor have accumulated assets worth $9 trillion through extralegal means—46 times what the World Bank has lent them in the last three decades. However, since they don't hold titles, they don't have collateral to borrow money, and their trading activity is limited to a small circle in which they are known and trusted. De Soto proposes we end this cycle by recognizing squatter's rights, similar to how the United States settled land claims established during the nineteenth-century gold rush. He proposes the same be done for the untitled masses of the Third World. Although academic economists have debunked his theory as simplistic, Third-World leaders take him seriously and call him for advice. By challenging conventional modes of analysis, de Soto invented a new way of thinking about a serious economic problem.

What has this to do with rhetoric? The ingenuity called for by persistent economic problems is a subset of the general need for ingenious approaches to public problems, including the need for inventing appeals that actively engage an audience in the process of analyzing and understanding the relevance of problems and in finding effective solutions. Perhaps we can see how this need surfaces in rhetoric by considering a case where inventiveness seemed to be absent.

In the early part of 2001, Representative Joe Moakley, whose congressional district was in Boston, learned he had terminal leukemia. His death would create the need for a special election; because it was imminent, the Democratic Party began searching for possible successors. Attention quickly turned to Max Kennedy, the youngest child of Robert and Ethel Kennedy, who had indicated a desire to serve in the House of Representatives. Kennedy had to make a number of preparations if he was to run for Moakley's seat, including enlisting advisers to help him prepare his campaign speeches and to deliver them effectively. He recruited media consultant Doug Hattaway and speechwriter Bob Schrum, both of whom had worked for the Gore presidential campaign in 2000. Kennedy eventually decided not to run for office, and the following incident gives insight into his change of heart.

Every candidate for Congress has a stump speech—a basic speech that sets out the candidate's vision and goals as the people's representative. This speech is delivered to various audiences throughout the campaign. As Kennedy was nearing announcement of his candidacy, he was rehearsing his stump speech in Hattaway's Boston office. Kennedy was upset that Schrum's speech made him sound like Al Gore, whose speeches had been characterized as boring. Hattaway asked Kennedy to deliver the speech from a lectern in the corner. Kennedy did so, mechanically intoning its cli-chéd phrases: "I want to fight for all of you," "I'll commit myself heart and soul to be the kind of congressman who cares about you," "I'll dedicate myself to fighting for working families to have a fair chance," and the con-cluding promise, "I'll make this one pledge: I will always be there for you."

If the speech was lame, it was not because Schrum did not know how to write stump rhetoric. If he wanted the speech to be more suited to his personality and ideas, he would have think about what he stood for and the public concerns that most mattered to him. Toward this end, Hattaway tried to coax Kennedy into the composing process by pressing him on the reasons he wanted to run:

> "What's the take-away message to the speech?"

> "Huh?"

> "What do you want people to take away from it? When Mabel goes back outside and sees her neighbor on the street, she says, 'I saw Max Kennedy.' 'Oh, really? And what did he say?'"

> [Pause] "He's a really nice guy, and he cares about me. He'll work harder than anyone else."

> "But what's the take-away message?"

> "That I'm a nice guy. . . . And I care about health care, jobs, education, environment [the four pillars of his speech]."

> "O.K., but what will you say? What's the one thing that people will hear?"

> [With a shrug of despair] "I don't know. Whatever it has to be."[2]

What's wrong with this picture? On the face of it, the prospective can-didate doesn't seem to have a clear reason for seeking office. But his frus-tration also reflects the difficulty he has in thinking creatively about how to communicate his concerns for health care, jobs, education, and the en-vironment. He isn't thinking about how to express these to "Mabel" in a way that she'll remember so that she can tell her friends that Kennedy is the right person to represent them. Because Kennedy is missing from the speech, the only content is the liberal clichés he found so boring in the original draft.

Kennedy was not thinking outside the box. He was caught inside his speechwriter's words, which lacked a spark from Kennedy's own motiva-tions for his candidacy. By contrast, de Soto's flash of insight was generated by an experience that defied his everyday assumptions and got him thinking about property in a new way: the barking dogs of Bali. From that insight, he built an argument that framed Third-World poverty in new terms and captured the attention of Third-World leaders.

Novel thought may spring from the most unlikely sources, which raises the question of how we might direct our thinking to explore our resources for invention and expression. This chapter discusses **topical reasoning** as a method to generate fresh ideas suited to the rhetor, the topic, the audience, and the occasion. To set this method in context, we will begin with a general discussion of creativity. From there we will consider the specific need for creativity in goal-oriented communication. Then we will elaborate the method of topical reasoning and its relevance to resolving rhetorical situations.

ॐ
Creativity and Inventiveness

The subject of creativity has a long and rich history. From antiquity to the present, humans have attempted to explain how thoughts and feelings are born and expressed. Why should this be such an attractive topic? Partly, our interest grows from the important relationship between creativity and art. More basically, however, we continue to speculate about creativity because it plays a necessary role in every human's life. Each of us must create in order to give meaning to our experiences. Without creativity, the data of experience would be merely brute facts. We would be no different from other animals, responding to the events of nature and our biological needs as stimuli with sign value at best. Like animals, our senses would command us to eat! avoid! run! The data of nature would lack symbolic meaning. An infant nestled asleep in her mother's arms would be merely an organism at rest. The seepage of dioxin into the soil would be no more than one chemical mixing with another chemical composition. The light-headed giddiness of new lovers would be merely a set of physiological conditions. Through creativity, we transform the brute data of experience into expressions of thoughts and feelings.

Creativity is an act of symbolic expression. As an act, it is eventful because it occurs at a particular time and place. Since it is an event, it has temporality, which reflects the historical past and the anticipated future. Because it is symbolic, it is referential, drawing on the resources of the world to illuminate the meaning of inner experiences. As an expression, others may respond to it and interpret it through previous individual experiences. The only limitations to creativity are our personal limitations, for the thinkable offers a limitless source of meaning and the world an inexhaustible supply of references.

Symbolic expressions can take a variety of forms. Whether the medium of expression is words, music, painting, or dance, it must place the data of experience in relationship to the self, to one another, and to the world. Each relationship is a manifestation of our uniquely human capacity to create meanings out of nature and its life forms, to share those meanings with others, and through symbolic sharing to create a self and a world. The painter's depiction of an infant asleep in her mother's arms may become an expression of vulnerability and innocence, of love and protection; it may become a statement that infants are to be cherished and mothers revered; in a political context, it may serve as an exhortation against abortion. The question is never whether symbols will evoke responses of thought, emotion, sentiment, or action, since they are naturally evocative and humans are inherently capable of using and responding to them. Rather, the question is which specific thoughts, emotions, sentiments, or actions they are likely to evoke.

Symbols provide labels to the data of experience—such as the physiological reactions experienced when we fall in love or the environmental effects of chemical products—that connote thoughts and feelings beyond their data-level meanings. As associated thoughts and feelings become part of what the data mean, the language by which we refer to them creates realities for us. Moreover, because symbols are arbitrary inventions, they can express data in a variety of modes. Our word choice can place data in a multitude of contexts that establish relationships, each distinct in some way from any other. They can reveal alternative interpretations of data and offer a framework for thought and emotion, even to the point of becoming an "-ism" with implications for understanding and action.

Each rhetorical transaction is a creative act. It is an act of construction through which maker and audience interact to determine what they know, believe, value, and feel about a common world. Whenever human expression occurs, the possibility for creativity of some sort exists.

Having said this, some qualifications have doubtless come to your mind. Are banal expressions such as clichés creative? Obviously, they are not very creative. If they are thoughtless utterances of stock expressions, they may be no more creative than those of a parrot triggered by an appropriate cue. Parrots can speak, not converse. Remember, we have maintained that creativity is an act of symbolic expression. That does not mean that all acts of symbolic expression realize their creative potential.

Are we always creative? Aren't there times when the use of symbols doesn't involve creativity? Certainly. Each day we engage in hundreds of routine transactions of speech and writing where symbols are used to express the ordinary. For example, our friends and acquaintances know we are still on speaking terms because we use the clichés of speech and writing that signal this fact. These acts are called *phatic communion*, a type of communication in which the act of speaking or writing in a particular form is more important than the literal meanings of the words used. We will discuss this concept at greater length in chapter 12. Here our point is that we say "hello" to acquaintances, we wish people "a good day," we thank a salesclerk at the close of a transaction, we request the salt at dinner with words that say nothing original but are essential for maintaining cordial relations. Or, for example, at work we may have to log vital weights and measures. Since this is valuable information to the firm, the form in which the data are recorded is specified by the technical purposes for which they will be used. Though these recordings are no test of our creative powers, they serve a vital function for maintaining accurate files for future reference and decision making. Once we learn the appropriate social clichés and the relevant information to record we can execute these communication transactions automatically, without engaging in conscious reflection on what we are experiencing or what it means.

The key question is: When do we require creativity to manage our environment beyond these routine acts? While all symbolic acts express meanings, we are most acutely aware of our need to create in situations that are out of the ordinary in some respect. Creativity is necessary when standard interpretations and standard responses are not available, when ordinary solutions to problems are not obvious. For example, if your car is out of gas, you have to put fuel in the tank for it to run. You have no choice because the car won't function otherwise. On the other hand, if your town is suffering unemployment, it is not as obvious what must be done to correct the situation. This is not an ordinary situation with an obvious solution but a problematic one lacking a common interpretation and determined solution. Unemployment problems have a variety of causes, making each one unique. Simply saying, "Well, let's attract new industry to create jobs" won't do. That's a clichéd response, not an analysis. In brief, such a situation is indeterminate in some important respect that only human creativity can remove. It requires expressions that give the situation meaning.

To bring clarity and resolution to an unusual situation, we must first locate the likely sources of uncertainty that inhibit understanding and action. Typically, problematic situations are marked by tension of some sort: by **conflict**, where competing interests pull us in opposite directions; by **novelty**, where the circumstances confronting us are outside our frames of reference; or by **ambiguity**, where meanings aren't clearly established but must be selected and developed. Conflict, novelty, and ambiguity heighten our awareness that experiences may be interpreted in a variety of ways, with each alternative projecting a different view of the world and what it might become. Conflict, novelty, and ambiguity also require that we select from among alternative interpretations, with our choices palpably evident in the symbols we select to create meanings for others and ourselves.

The need to select from among alternatives in order to interpret our experiences is evident in every human activity: in work and in play, in public life and in private, in the sciences, the professions, the arts, and in business. This need is manifested not only in our discovery of new thoughts and interpretations but also in reformulating old ones. We find interpretive selection evident in a Beethoven composition inspired by the sight of a beautiful young woman, in a Ramsey Lewis jazz improvisation on a traditional ballad, and in an André Previn lecture on a musical genre. We find it in Cornel West's scholarly treatment of race relations in the United States, *Race Matters*, in the irreverent treatment of the same subject by Chris Rock, and in a Jesse Jackson speech appealing for redress of racial inequities. We find it in an I. M. Pei design of space intended to encourage people to congregate and in a conversationalist's management of topics for the same end.

Each of these circumstances lacks certainty of meaning and outcome. In each case choices must be made. Each choice will create meanings by virtue of selecting one symbol over another to express an experience. Lacking true, correct, or sometimes even effective precedents, we nonetheless must resort to symbol selection if we are to make any sense of our experiences. Our symbol choices reflect our interpretations of our experience and provide **frames** for further analysis and interpretation. That is, they impose a framework on ambiguous, novel, and conflicting experiences. Frames help us resolve tension by placing what is novel or uncertain in relation to the known—albeit this "knowing" is itself an interpretation that carries its own biases.

While our creations reflect the meanings we attach to our experiences, their symbolic character permits others to share them. In this sense creativity is a social activity, and creations are meaningful as social constructs. They bring to others a symbolic structure that is open to appreciation, discussion, modification, action, and a multitude of possible responses in symbolic exchanges. Because human creations can be shared, they can give meaning to the experiences of whoever encounters them, even if their experiences are not the same as those of the creator. A good example of this is comedy.

Black and white Americans, considered as aggregates, have differing experiences of economic opportunities, political power, cultural expression, family structure, and a host of other indicators documented by sociological research. How blacks and whites interpret these differences and what responses they find appropriate vary greatly between and within the groups. Some group members are consumed by anger and resort to violence, some persist in bigotry and repression, some experience differences as threats to be feared and avoided, some find diversity an opportunity and cause for celebration, some resort to pragmatic action, and some drop out. The facts of experience may be the same, but their meanings are different.

During the 1960s and early 1970s, comedian Flip Wilson was one of America's most popular entertainers. His creative response to the racial tensions of his day was to exalt his blackness with characters who reflected the stereotypes of white America—the sexual predator; the assertive brassy female; the jive-talking, high-living storefront minister. Wilson dealt with these stereotypes by portraying them in the outrageous and hilarious antics of his characters. The fantasies were not sanitized for home consumption; they were not softened to do social work by presenting the black experience as just a deeper shade of pale. None of his routines tried to demonstrate identity with whites or equality with whites or subservience or superiority to whites. Indeed, these issues and questions were never raised. Wilson's routines hurled white stereotypes into absurd situations that, at a time of racial unrest, used laughter to create new meanings for white experiences of black people. As TV critic John Leonard observed at the time, Wilson's genius lay in his insights into our vulnerabilities, black or white; to our hopes, black or white; to our needs, black or white. He was black and he was likable, approachable, and unequivocating in celebrating his blackness.[3]

Thirty years later Chris Rock (hailed at the turn of the millennium by *Time* as "the funniest man in America") commands a similar national audience. Rock made his name with a stint on *Saturday Night Live,* as the voice of the animated Penny character of TV commercial fame, but mostly as a stand-up comedian on HBO and other television venues. On stage his signature delivery is a loud, gravelly yell that gives unexpected emphasis to topics you wouldn't normally consider funny—such as pork chops or crack cocaine. He also is controversial because he takes up racial issues and speaks as an African American about stereotypes of African Americans in ways and with language that can make audiences cringe.

The most notorious of these is his "Niggas vs. Black People" routine from the *Bring the Pain* HBO special in 1996. The politically incorrect bent of Rock's humor was, to some African Americans, over the top in this routine. Its gist is captured in this excerpt:

> Every time black people want to have a good time, ign'ant-ass niggas f--- it up! . . . Can't do nothing! Can't keep a disco open more than three weeks! Grand opening! Grand closing! Can't go to a movie the first week it comes out! Why? Cause niggas are shooting at the screen! . . . I love black people, but I hate niggas, brother. Oh, I hate niggas!

Some African Americans think his use of what white America refers to as "the N word" and his ridiculing of stereotyped African-American behavior, as in the excerpt above, reinforces racist prejudices and behaviors. But there's more to Rock's humor. In the words of TV critic Bruce Handy:

> As with all great comedians—which is to say, as with all original thinkers—Rock's insights are beyond tidy labels such as "black," "white," "left," "right," "offensive" or "as harmlessly amusing as 'Friends.'" . . . Unlike many of today's allegedly political comics, whose insights go no deeper than poking knee-jerk fun at Bill Clinton's appetites or George W. Bush's intellectual dullness, Rock at his best lays bare society's underlying fault lines. . . . Rock knows the most cathartic laughter springs from a masochistic impulse. (Sadistic laughter, on the other hand, is the junk food of mirth.) Bring the pain—please.[4]

The "cathartic laughter" Rock evokes through the insights of his creative genius graphically illustrates how the imaginative expression of experience can influence others. But the illustration reveals another point as well: The socially shared aspect of creativity is capable of making commentary, of exerting influence, of changing attitudes, beliefs, and opinions. Creativity can lead us to insight and to action. It can function aesthetically and rhetorically. Rock is not only a comedic artist who entertains, but he is also a rhetor whose specialty is to confront us with our own shortcomings in ways that not only get us to laugh at ourselves but help us to discover how foolish we have been and to provoke us to consider change. This discovery process is invention.

࿇

Invention in Purposive Discourse

Invention is the branch of rhetoric concerned with discovering what might be communicated on a subject to persuade an audience. It was the first of **five canons** of rhetoric developed and discussed in classical antiquity; the others were **disposition** (or structure), **style, memory,** and **delivery.** The canons organized the discussion of rhetorical principles in Greek and Roman handbooks and were seen as the natural process followed in developing a speech from the inception of ideas to actual presentation. As the first canon, invention received extended treatment, especially by those who were concerned with the content of rhetoric. It was, and remains, an area of study and instruction concerned with creating arguments.

As we have seen in previous chapters, rhetorical events arise when human experiences are subject to changing circumstances and are open to interpretation. The ancient Greeks referred to realities that were determined by human conventions as **nomos.** They distinguished *nomos* realties from those of *physis*, things that were real by nature. As Protagoras said, "Man is the measure of all things." Reality for the community was what its members agreed to regard as reality. For example, in the city where I live, it is illegal to smoke in any public building. Consequently, when we dine in a restaurant, there is no "smoking" section. A neighboring city, only 15 miles away, does not prohibit smoking in restaurants. There the host will ask whether you would prefer to sit in the "smoking" or "nonsmoking" section of the restaurant. The difference between the two communities is arbitrary; it is a matter of convention.

As a social practice, rhetoric is occasioned discourse. It is specific to a time, place, and an audience of interested others. It is concerned with inventing appeals that suit the needs of the occasion and the audience to solve an exigence. The presence of an imperfection marked by urgency is a sign that novelty, conflict, or ambiguity is a defining feature of the problem. There is no certain answer about what to do nor, perhaps, even a common understanding of the circumstances at hand. For this reason, whatever sense we make of our experiences to resolve a rhetorical exigence is a human construction. Consequently, rhetorical situations are typified by their concern with *nomos* because speaking or writing can alter opinions, feelings, or actions. Rhetorically constituted realities are social inventions or constructions, which means they are indeterminate and subject to human convention and change. Rhetorical inventions provide frameworks that aid us in interpreting novel, conflicting, or ambiguous data by employing lines of thought or arguments that interpret experiences in a particular way.

The question facing every communicator at the outset of developing a message is what determination he or she wishes the audience to make of its circumstances. Rhetorical appeals are intent on influencing someone to accept a particular point of view as correct and to act with respect to that point of view. Hence we need to bear in mind that rhetorical discourse is goal-oriented. Rhetors seek general goals—to entertain, to instruct, to persuade, to motivate to action—as well as specific goals—support the NAACP, vote for Jesse Ventura, buy a Chrysler product, think of the accused as a loving father and devoted husband. Goals are established in line with the outcomes a rhetor desires and the perceived readiness of the audience to respond. Rhetoric, as we have considered it thus far, is intentional discourse addressed to somebody; it is adapted to what we want to accomplish in light of what we think somebody is ready to understand.

The specificity of rhetoric to occasion, audience, and situation gives rhetoric a practicality and immediacy not typical of other modes of communication. One would be foolhardy to address the American Council of Catholic Bishops, say, on the topic of birth control and advocate that the church change its restrictions. Because Catholic bishops may be presumed to have opinions and beliefs that support the doctrines of their religion, they probably have strong opposition to birth control and are unlikely to be moved by such an appeal. More modest objectives, such as tolerance for alternative systems of beliefs, are better suited to their readiness to respond. Closer to home, it would be foolhardy to tell your professor that you missed his test because you were studying for a test in another course. The rhetor who succeeds at opening her audience to her point of view will do so because the appeals presented were intentionally designed to influence her specific audience in a particular way. In sum, rhetorical discourse is designed to encourage an audience to think and feel along a particular bias.

The rhetor's means for achieving his intentions are most responsibly present when he relies on arguments that provide reasons for believing and acting. Thus rhetors, regardless of setting, always have to find a means of persuasion that will gain an advantageous hearing or reading for their ideas. They seek to present ideas as they intersect with audience experiences because these intersections determine a matter in the audience's mind. This activity of seeking effective ways to present ideas is called invention. Thus we may define *invention* as *the method of finding "sayables" (symbols) with the potential to transform some matter or question of an indeterminate nature into one that is determinate in the mind of the audience.*

The transformation of an indeterminate matter or question into one that is determinate requires discoveries by both the speaker or writer and the audience. The rhetor must know the audience's level of tolerance.

"What do they know?" and "What do they believe?" are dominant questions. They aid the rhetor in discovering what may be communicated effectively to this audience on this subject at this time for this end. The audience members must sense what the rhetor wants from them and what the rhetor is prepared to give in exchange. This helps the audience to relate the ideas presented to its own experiences and to gain new insights that help to form a considered judgment. Both rhetor and audience must discover how to interpret the events under consideration in a way that will permit an appropriate and effective response.

In actual practice, these respective modes of discovery can be found in the arguments by which a proposition is advanced. The arguments stand as an index to the rhetor's discovery of means of persuasion. The arguments also serve as the stimuli for discoveries, thoughts, and feelings that inevitably accompany an audience's internalizing of a message.[5]

⚘
Topical Thinking

Aristotle, who provides the first extensive discussion of invention, was aware of this relationship between modes of discovery and argument. In fact, he devoted the first two books of his treatise on rhetoric to the ways in which arguments are found and developed. His approach is still useful and can help us understand how to employ the method of rhetorical invention.

Aristotle argued that at the heart of every persuasive appeal was the argument supporting the statements or claims advanced. Arguments were of two basic sorts. There were deductive arguments, called **enthymemes**, and inductive arguments, called **examples**. We will develop each in greater detail in chapter 7. For now, the important point is that these two types of arguments employ distinct reasoning patterns. Each requires premises that support a claim the rhetor wishes to advance. The problem facing every rhetor, as Aristotle noted, is finding premises that link the advocate's claims with the views of the audience. If these linking premises can be found, the audience is more likely to assent to the argument.

Aristotle tells us that we find the premises from which to build arguments through a method called **topical thinking**. Topical thinking is akin to what you may know as brainstorming. In brainstorming you try to imagine or recall everything that is possibly relevant to a subject. Topical thinking tries to do the same. The differences are that topical thinking is systematic and that it uses a specific device of thought called a **topos** to help generate ideas. We need to consider this device in some detail, for it is at the heart of rhetorical invention.

Topos is a Greek word for "place." As used in rhetoric, it refers to the place one goes to find arguments. By place we do not mean an actual physical location; it is a metaphor that refers to places in your mind where you would find arguments. That probably sounds obscure. Let's try to make it clearer with some analogies.

First, think of place as a physical location. Imagine, for example, that we are tourists visiting Niagara Falls. Our interest as tourists is to view this natural wonder in as many ways as possible. We might stand next to the Horseshoe Falls and watch the water cascade over the edge. We might ride in the "Maid of the Mist" tour boat to see the falls from below. We might walk along the Canadian shore to see the American Falls at a distance. We might travel down into the Cave of the Winds to see the American Falls up close. We might ride in a touring helicopter to see the spectacle from above. In each case we are occupying a different place to look at Niagara Falls. Each place gives us a unique view, reveals an aspect all its own, and gives us a different perspective on the whole.

A topical place is like a physical place in that it, too, gives a unique perspective or way of looking at matters. The difference, of course, is that a topical place is conceptual; it exists in our mind. Its function is to help us think about a subject to discover what, if anything, may be said about it from the perspective of the place. So the first thing we can say about a *topos* or topic is that it provides a mental perspective from which we can analyze a subject. It is **analytic**.

There is a second aspect to topical thinking suggested by the metaphor of place: a location where something can be put. To use another analogy, suppose that you had a jug in which you stored liquids. Sometimes you may use it to store water, sometimes wine, sometimes olive oil, sometimes broth. Regardless of what you store in it, the jug retains its shape, size, and chemical composition. As a place, it is not affected by its content. So if you put water in at one time and olive oil at another, you still have the same jug. The jug may be said to have no content of its own but can hold any liquid you care to store in it.

A place for topical reasoning is like a jug in that it also has no content of its own. It is able to accommodate some contents better than others; those it accommodates well conform to its unique dimensions. But the material placed in it does not change the place. For this reason it can give shape to a variety of materials without being consumed in the process. It can be used again and again. So a second feature of *topoi* (the plural of *topos*), or places, is that they are **contentless** and therefore can be applied to any material we choose. For this reason, *topoi* are sometimes referred to as **commonplaces** because they are locations for ideas that are shared by or common to a great variety of subjects—in fact, without restriction to any subject whatsoever.

Finally, the place metaphor suggests a sense of discovery. We sometimes use the term place to refer to the spot where an object or a person belongs, as in "put it in its place" or "I feel out of place." Suppose we were to observe a young man in different places. We would see him with his parents, his friends, his teachers, his employer; at a sporting event, the opera, a symphony, a rock concert, the home of a wealthy patrician, the shanty of a beggar, and so on. In each of these places, we would discover different aspects of this fellow's personality, talents, self-awareness, insecurities—where he seemed to feel "in place" and "out of place." Each of these place scenes would be **heuristic**, that is, it would generate some additional bit of information to characterize our subject. This is the third attribute of *topoi*. By considering a subject in terms of a *topos*, we discover new things we might say. A *topos* has heuristic value because it helps us to discover what can be said about anything put in its place.

Topoi, to summarize, are mental locations that we use to discover what may be said about anything whatsoever. They are **contentless** in that they have no proper subject that is their own. They can be applied to any subject we choose. They are **analytic** in that they help us to discover the numerous dimensions of a subject. Finally, they are **heuristic** in that they lead us to discover new things to say. Rhetorical invention consists in the act of finding suasive sayables by thinking of a subject in terms of *topoi*. Having said that, let us try to make the concept more concrete by discussing the ways in which topical thinking is actually employed.

ॐ
Topical Reasoning and Relevant Discourse

There is a big difference between thinking about a topic for your own understanding and thinking about that same topic in order to communicate relevant ideas to an audience. Thinking about something for your own purposes—say, the costs of a college education—can lead you to form an opinion that makes sense to you but not necessarily to anyone else. Merely thinking about rising college costs does not require you to act, nor does it provide reasons for others to act. However, when you think about communicating these thoughts, new dimensions are added. For one thing, you probably think about communicating because you experience some tension that can be relieved by sharing your thoughts and feelings with others. That tension is in you, not in your environment. The impulse comes from within. For another, you probably think about communication when you have an expectation that communication can get results. It is a choice you've made from among nonsymbolic alternatives, such as applying mechanical force, and other possible symbolic responses, such as oaths or screams. When you think about communication, you usually expect that those you are addressing are able to respond to your message in appropriate ways and, moreover, that their response is essential to relieving the tensions that impel you to communicate in the first place. Finally, thinking about communicating is other-directed thought, since the reasons in support of a proposition must satisfy your listeners or readers.

Thus thinking about communicating is not the same as thinking in general. It reflects a commitment to reach someone, to affect that person in some way, and to bring about action through the mediation of symbols.

This kind of thinking focuses on determining what to say. Blurting out our first thoughts or initial feelings is not likely to be as effective as remarks specially chosen to fit the dynamics of the rhetorical situation. For this reason, Aristotle defined rhetoric as "the faculty of discovering the available means of persuasion in the given case." His emphasis was not on persuasion but on discovering the means of persuasion. When we search for "sayables" of this sort, we are thinking communicatively. This type of thinking is always about finding the alternatives best suited to the particular case, about what is most likely to influence our audience.

Having said that rhetorical thinking was about the means of persuasion with greatest promise in the given case, Aristotle went on to discuss how we discover these means. He developed this analysis in terms of the three types of speaking contexts that dominated public life in ancient Athens. First he considered the kinds of speeches given in the courts. These speeches, called **forensic** speeches, were concerned with justice or injustice, guilt or innocence. These were not speeches by lawyers, because ancient Athens did not have professional lawyers, as we know them. If you were in legal trouble, you (or someone more gifted at argumentation) had to speak on your behalf. So Aristotle had in mind the kinds of nontechnical appeals average people would make on their own behalf. Speeches and essays concerned with justice and injustice, innocence and guilt, can appear in places other than courts, but they are fashioned after the courtroom speeches of Aristotle's day. Whenever people accuse or defend actions in terms of justice or injustice, they make forensic appeals.

Next Aristotle considered the kinds of speeches given in the legislative assembly. These were called **deliberative** speeches, and they were concerned with expedience and inexpedience, advantage and injury. These were not speeches by elected representatives, because ancient Athens was a democracy where every citizen could participate in making laws. If you felt that something should be done, you had to advocate it yourself. Aristotle once more had in mind the kinds of nontechnical appeals average people would make to protect their interests. Speeches and essays concerned with expedience and inexpedience are not restricted to legislative chambers, but they follow the pattern of legislative speaking as Aristotle observed it. Whenever people exhort or dissuade others about the wisdom of some course of action, about its benefits or disadvantages, they make deliberative appeals.

Finally, Aristotle considered the kinds of speeches given on ceremonial occasions. These were called **epideictic** speeches, and they were concerned with praiseworthy or condemnable actions, virtue or vice. They were speeches given by leaders when some event made it important that the community acknowledge or disparage what was done. Leaders were sometimes the people who administered the city or who led the army, but they could also be the head of a family or a person whose wisdom had earned respect. Aristotle had in mind the kinds of nontechnical appeals that deal with the basic values we embrace in our families and communities and that form our bonds to one another. Speeches and essays concerned with virtue and vice can be presented in a variety of places and are very important for establishing and maintaining our sense of community. Whenever people praise or blame actions—of individuals or groups, of the moment or a lifetime—by acknowledging excellence and disparaging meanness, they make epideictic appeals.

Taken in a literal sense, Aristotle imposed an incomplete frame of official state functions on rhetoric. For instance, Aristotle's three types of speeches are limited to his experience and do not include the genres of commerce and religion or ends such as instructing or inquiring, although these modes of discourse were present in his day. Moreover, his concerns were limited to official speech making. They did not address the exchanges of conversation, such as Plato depicts in his *Symposium*, in which informed men and women in Athens engaged in the important business of exploring ideas and forming opinions about the issues of the day. Because Aristotle neglected these arenas, we confront a distorted historical picture in which women play no role. One of the ironies of the Athenian democracy was that as the political franchise was extended to more of its citizens, it increasingly required participation in public forums of deliberative assemblies and law courts—which increasingly excluded women from the official political processes.[6] On the other hand, we know that women, such as Aspasia and Diotima, did participate with men in discussions. According to Plato's *Menexenus*, Socrates credits Aspasia with teaching him rhetoric and with assisting Pericles, who was her companion, in composing his "Funeral Oration." In Plato's *Symposium*, Diotima is depicted as an active participant in the discussion of love.[7] And we know that women played active roles (including that of priestess) in religious observances, in which women were equivalent to men.[8]

Although students of rhetoric should be aware of these limitations to Aristotle's discussion of invention, the important point for our purposes is the way in which he thought about communication. Aristotle analyzed each of the three genres because he believed that successful orators had to know their subject matter in order to present relevant propositions and to organize those propositions in some manageable way. In other words, if you knew about justice and injustice, you would have resources at the ready to make appropriate arguments on matters of law. By reviewing the things that could be said to prove the justness or unjustness of an act, you develop a defense or bring an accusation by selecting and using evidence relevant to the given case, or your rhetorical situation. By the same token, if a person knew about marketplace conditions, she would have resources for making appropriate arguments about commerce.

Aristotle's discussion of this matter in Book I of his *Rhetoric* gives us good leads for how to be systematic in inventing arguments—and also how to be systematic in dissecting arguments for purposes of analyzing their inventional strengths and weaknesses: Did the rhetor seize the kairotic moment? Did *prepon* guide what was said or left unspoken? Were issues framed with lines of reasoning that maximized the likelihood of the rhetor's advocacy within a context of contingencies? Were these arguments fitting responses? and so forth. Aristotle developed his theory of invention in terms of the places where one searched to find arguments. He discussed two types of places. First there were general places, called **konoi topoi** (common topics), that applied to any subject matter and provided overall patterns of inclusive thought: Was something *possible* (or *impossible*)? Were there *past facts* that provided the guidance of precedence? Were there predictable *future facts* whose consequences could be judged desirable or undesirable? Could we estimate the degrees of *more and less* or magnitude?

We find *konoi topoi* exhibited today in virtually every rhetorical situation. For example, in the world of mass culture, "hype"—a form of the *topos* of magnitude—is dominant. Advertisers proclaim that their products make us sexier or healthier or happier or wealthier. Pop stars like Britney Spears market themselves to teens and young adults through commercials, Web sites, MTV, and albums. But as broad and inclusive patterns, *konoi topoi* do not provide specific propositions to have handy for given cases.

Special or material topics, called **idia**, generated specific premises peculiar to a subject. One had to master the particular aspects of an issue in order to make knowledgeable claims that stood a chance of being taken seriously by an audience. For example, if you were discussing political matters, you would be expected to deliberate about specific topics such as ways and means, war and peace, constitutional forms, and the like. Today if you were talking about maritime issues, you would have to know about fish and fishing rights, trading lanes, industrial sites, pollution dangers, recreational uses, and so forth. No serious persuasion about our waterways and their uses could ignore these topics particular to maritime issues.

In summary, Aristotle's advice for thinking creatively about communication is to review systematically the possible things that might be said or written. Examining general themes (*konoi topoi*) that are especially relevant to the specific issue in combination with the specific topics (*idia*) that indicate thorough knowledge about an issue will produce a multitude of specific premises. By thinking in these terms, we can select the appropriate lines of reasoning with the greatest promise. Thinking about communicating is superior to merely imitating what others have said or delivering adaptations of standard or stock themes. It is creative thinking capable of investing experience with new meaning and of opening audiences to new possibilities for action.

Still, Aristotle's system remains unclear in its precise method of execution. Though interesting work on *topoi* has been done recently, it has not eliminated the unwieldy aspects of Aristotle's particular system. We can retain his notion for general topics and his notion that rhetoric becomes more precise and persuasive as we use the topics special to a given subject area. At the same time, we can search for a more precise and usable method of topical review suited to our needs today.

One such method was developed by John Wilson and Carroll Arnold.[9] Basing their idea on Roget's *Thesaurus*, they developed a 16-item system of **review topics** applicable to all subjects. Their list is as follows.

A. Attributes commonly discussed

    1. Existence or nonexistence of things

    2. Degree or quantity of things, forces, etc.

    3. Spatial attributes, including adjacency, distribution, place

    4. Attributes of time

    5. Motion or activity

    6. Form, either physical or abstract

    7. Substance: physical, abstract, or psychophysical

    8. Capacity to change, including predictability

    9. Potency: power or energy, including capacity to further or hinder anything

    10. Desirability in terms of rewards or punishments

    11. Feasibility: workability or practicability

B. Basic relationships commonly asserted or argued

    1. Causality: the relations of causes to effects, effects to causes, effects to effects, adequacy of causes, etc.

    2. Correlation: coexistence or coordination of things, forces, etc.

    3. Genus/species relationships

    4. Similarity or dissimilarity

    5. Possibility or impossibility

This list of topics is not intended to apply to specific subjects, as do the *idia* or material topics; it is intended to apply to all subjects. We employ it by asking if anything useful can be said about the subject that will support our cause and gain audience assent. By proceeding through each attribute and relationship, speakers and writers attempt to generate a substantial list of possible lines of reasoning from which the most promising ones may be selected. Here's how these topics might work. Suppose you were to write an op-ed essay urging a job placement center on campus.

> Existence: "We don't have a job placement center. Other schools have such centers. Seniors have a need for this service."

> Degree: "It is easier to find a job with the aid of a placement center. Schools that provide this service have a higher percentage of seniors who graduate with a job than schools without this service."

> Spatial: "The remoteness of our school from major employment centers puts our students at a disadvantage for finding jobs."

Time: "Many employers recruit new employees during the spring. Having a center on campus will minimize time taken from study for a job search."

Motion: "It is important for us to be active in shaping employer perceptions of our graduates. They will be impressed when they discover the forward-looking momentum of our curriculum."

Form: "Such a center should be modeled so as to take advantage of online information about employers, our majors, and our students."

Substance: Nothing comes immediately to mind. Move on to the next topic.

Capacity to change: "Several years ago, we changed our admission procedures to recruit new students. We can change our counseling procedures to place our graduates better."

Potency: "Our school's potential to influence life in our state is advanced or hindered by the occupations of its graduates."

Desirability: "Better jobs mean bigger alumni donations. Bringing recruiters on campus can provide valuable information about the fit between technical education here and needs out there."

Feasibility: "We already possess a counseling service; no elaborate new administration is required. Overhead costs would be marginal, since staff needs are small and existing facilities can be used for interviews."

Causality: "In specialized fields, firms seek prospects. Bringing them on campus will get them to think of our students as ones they should pursue."

Correlation: "Job placement success correlates with recruitment success."

Genus/species: "A placement center would be in keeping with the administrative reorganization last year to improve student services. We have an active placement program to place students in graduate schools. We invite interviewers from medical schools to campus."

Similarity/dissimilarity: "A job placement center is not like an employment agency because the essential features of professional-client relationship and fee structure are absent."

Possibility/impossibility: "Though it is impossible to place everyone, it is possible to improve our placement record."

This list of possible arguments was composed in approximately 30 minutes. Obviously not everything listed is something that should or could be developed in your essay. Variables of exigence, audience, rhetor, and goal will influence which of our generated items will be retained and which discarded. There is also the obvious need to buttress the items that are retained with evidence of fact and expert opinion to establish the reasonableness of each statement. Moreover, as you read through this list, other thoughts worth developing may have occurred to you. By reflecting on the subject of job placement in terms of Wilson and Arnold's review topics, we can generate numerous specific lines of thought, which can then be developed into actual appeals suited to the demands of a specific rhetorical situation.

৯০

Summary

In this chapter we discussed the ways in which speakers and writers find ideas. We search for the thoughts and words that will give meaning to events and allow us to share this meaning with others. Our search for meaning is essentially an act of creativity; it is as much a necessary part of each of our lives as providing for our physical needs. Our creativity allows us to go beyond reacting to signs. We can invent symbolic significance that allows us to mold our human realities. As much as the painter and poet, each language user is necessarily a creative being.

Our capacity and our need to create have a special relevance for rhetorical communication. Since rhetoric arises in situations where alternatives exist, it becomes a means for defining realities and fostering choices. It accomplishes this through arguments that people believe and feel. Thus all rhetorical communicators need a method to help find effective arguments. In short, they need an art of invention. We have discussed this art as one of thinking communicatively through the use of topical reasoning.

In each of the three types of topical systems we have considered—the general topics of *konoi topoi*, the specialized topics of *idia*, and the review topics that stimulate our thinking about possible lines of reasoning—the object has been to discover ways to invent messages that provoke shared meaning in the minds of listeners and readers. The method of topical thinking is the cornerstone of rhetorical thinking. It is the method for creating the materials from which appeals are fashioned. It involves us in the creative process of discovering what may be argued to some end or goal. For this reason, the topical method is essential to rhetoric's function as a means to resolving problems. Ultimately, topical thinking becomes a reciprocal process between rhetor and audience, regardless of setting. It is not just what the rhetor makes but what the audience remakes that emerges as the meaning of a rhetorical transaction. It is not just what a rhetor-artist like Chris Rock invents but what we do with what he invents—in our heads and hearts and actions—that is at the core of rhetorical arguments. In the next chapter we will consider this process further as it applies to the type of reasoning that underwrites the integrity of rhetorical arguments.

7

Using Good Reasons to Persuade

Karl Wallace, a noted scholar of rhetoric, published an essay in the early 1960s in which he argued that rhetoric was an art of providing **good reasons**.[1] By that he meant that rhetoric's business was to find and present the types of reasons that would move interested and reasonable people to assent to a point of view. They would be "good" reasons for holding or altering beliefs and actions.

Wallace's essay highlights a still important but frequently ignored point about rhetorical communication. As we negotiate our way through a rhetorical event, audience and rhetor transact a reasoning process. When we seek a project extension, argue for a raise, interview for a job, justify our actions, advise a friend, write an op-ed on issues of the day, or attend as an audience to any of these, we are involved in acts that require good reasons. Good reasons allow us to find a shared and presumably intersubjectively valid basis for acting. They permit us collectively to draw inferences that can withstand critical inspection, as blind prejudice cannot. In speaking and writing, we may use marvelous language, tell great stories, provide exciting metaphors, speak in enthralling tones, and even use our reputation to advantage, but in the final analysis we must communicate with reasons an audience will understand. A message is most influential when it provides its audience with good reasons to believe and to act. In rhetorical theory the process of reasoning with the audience is called **logos**, the subject of this chapter.

༄

Internal and External Appeals

Perhaps the clearest statement on the essential technical considerations in constructing rhetorical appeals is found in Aristotle's *Rhetoric*. As we learned in chapter 2, he regarded rhetoric as both a practical and a productive art. As a practical art, it was especially suited to doing things in the world—bringing about persuasion. As a productive art, it was well suited to making things—an art of finding and making **pisteis.** This Greek term is difficult to translate into English. Some translators have rendered it as "proof," but we must be careful to distinguish this use from scientific proof and mathematical deduction. As we have seen, rhetorical reasoning is concerned with questions of a distinctly uncertain character. These questions are often decided by the values and beliefs that prevail in the community. As an alternative to "proof," we may refer to the modes of persuasion invented through the creative powers of the rhetor as "arguments." Aristotle used the term **internal** (often translated as *artistic*) to describe this type of persuasion. Rhetoric as an art was concerned only with developing internal arguments.

Aristotle recognized that in matters of dispute, arguments are not the only means of resolution. Sometimes, for example, the evidence itself can be so compelling that rhetorically invented arguments are secondary. He called the modes of persuasion that were given by the situation and its facts **external** (sometimes rendered as *nonartistic*). For example, if you think you have received the wrong change at the drugstore, it is a simple matter for you to demonstrate that this is so. Add the change you received to the total bill. That should equal the money you originally gave the clerk. If it is less, you were shortchanged. A bit of simple arithmetic makes the point. If an accused thief pleads guilty, there is no need for rhetorical appeals to show there was motive, opportunity, ability, and the like. It is not necessary to invent an argument.

Whenever the facts "speak for themselves," we have sufficient grounds to make a decision without rhetoric. The facts do not require artistry when they are clear and compelling. Yet they can be persuasive nonetheless. Rhetoric is needed at times when the facts don't speak for themselves. When cases are ambiguous, conflicting, incomplete, inconclusive, and yet a decision or action is required, we turn to rhetoric to devise premises that will allow us to form a judgment. Discovery and development of internal arguments are the proper concern of rhetoric.

Aristotle made an additional point that is important for understanding what rhetorical modes of persuasion do and do not include. He recognized that in a given case factors other than the rhetor's message might influence the audience. For the most part these are the **constraints** present in a rhetorical situation. The rhetor should make every attempt to take them into account. Rhetors sometimes overlook constraints or fail to discover the means to compensate for or to exploit them. Consequently, the constraints may act as external influences on an audience's assessment. While external factors can be influential, Aristotle's point is that they are not part of the **techné** or art of rhetoric. The *techné* of rhetoric is focused on those modes of persuasion *internal to the message itself* that bring listeners and readers to the point where they are ready to form a judgment.

Even though we may disagree that the facts speak entirely for themselves, Aristotle has made a valid point. There is no denying that our age of science often regards factual data as compelling. Responsible rhetorical practice requires that the facts be known and be used as evidence to support our claims. But at the same time, we must remember that rhetoric does not invent the facts; it invents arguments that interpret the facts to give them meaning. This inventing of arguments and their articulation in a rhetorical transaction is the proper subject of the art.

ℒ

Paradigms and Enthymemes

Each of us regularly draws conclusions from observations. Sometimes we add up individual observations to reach a general conclusion. For example: I have observed Jeff, Barbara, Don, and Molly in the Engineering College. They are all well versed in calculus. I conclude from this that competence in calculus is required of engineers. The observations and details about Jeff, Barbara, Don, and Molly are referred to as data. The process of putting them together to form a conclusion is called **inductive** reasoning.

At other times a general observation is applied to individual data to reach a particular conclusion. For instance: All the student athletes I've met have been competitive individuals. I was just speaking with my student, Galen, and found out that he's on the lacrosse team. From this I conclude that Galen is probably motivated by competition. The observation about student athletes is a generalization. The process of applying a generalization to a datum to form a particular conclusion about it is called **deduction**.

Induction and deduction are the basic patterns of reasoning followed in rhetorical arguments. Arguments that follow inductive patterns are called **paradigms** (sometimes also referred to as argument from **examples**); those that follow deductive patterns are called **enthymemes**. These are technical terms that we need to consider in some detail, because they provide us with basic patterns that arguments take and insight into the ways in which an internal argument persuades.

Paradigms

Aristotle originally defined paradigms as "rhetorical inductions." We still use that definition today. They are the form inductive reasoning takes when we make nontechnical or popular arguments to persuade. *Induction is a pattern of reasoning that goes from particular cases to a generalization.* For instance, when scientists pose a research question—say, the effects of cigarette smoking on the lungs—they run the same test over and over to see if they get the same results. If they do, they form a generalization, such as "smoking cigarettes causes emphysema." We follow the same patterns in everyday life. You observe, for instance, that your roommate becomes irritable before taking an exam. The pattern repeats itself throughout the semester. As finals approach, you have an expectation of your roommate's disposition. On the basis of recurrent experiences of the same pattern, you abstract a general observation: Nancy gets testy when studying for an exam.

In a strictly logical sense, such a pattern of reasoning requires controlled observation and extensive enumeration to yield a strong conclusion. Were the cases alike in all salient respects? Was the relationship observed an essential one? Were there sufficient cases to warrant any conclusion at all? Are there countercases in fact? Are countercases conceivable? In technical areas of investigation, such questions are commonly used for testing hypotheses that an audience of experts will agree support valid conclusions. But the requirements for technical arguments addressed to experts are not the same as those for arguments on contingent matters addressed to an intelligent but not technically trained audience. The subject matter of rhetorical arguments does not permit the same control of variables or the same level of certainty for its conclusions as technical ones. Rhetorical issues are not decided by general rules of knowledge but by specific decisions of conduct. The judges of rhetorical appeals usually are not technically trained in subject matter and may not be trained in formal modes of reasoning. They are generally laypeople with an interest in how an issue is resolved and a say in its resolution. These considerations were apparently as true in Aristotle's day as in our own and led him to define a rhetorical induction in a unique way.

Aristotle maintained that *argument from paradigm* did not go from particular to general but *from particular to particular*. In other words, because the given case asks for a decision of a particular nature, the goals of rhetorical arguments are always particular. Paradigms provide **parallel cases**. These permit the audience to infer what it should do in the present case based on what occurred under similar circumstances in the past. For instance, we inquire of a friend whether now is the time to invest in a high-definition television. Our friend reminds us that when color televisions were first marketed their price was high, but after the novelty wore off their prices became more reasonable. Without expressing it, our friend told us that better prices are likely to be available later. We have been invited to draw an inference from a concrete case in the past to the concrete case under discussion.

There has been scholarly controversy over the nature of the inference involved in this type of reasoning.[3] Some have argued that it involves the logic of forming an unexpressed general rule (say, technological innovations tend to be more expensive when first marketed) and then the application of the rule to the particular case (HDTV is a newly marketed technological innovation; therefore, its price is higher now than it will be later). Others have argued that the reasoning is less like formal logic than a "psycho-logic"—an unmediated recognition of similarities without specifying the logical connections, sort of like mental shorthand (wait; a better price is sure to follow). Regardless of how one interprets the mental connections involved, the important point for our discussion is that only particulars are presented when constructing an argument from paradigm. It does not ask the audience to follow a train of formal reasoning but to reason from something known in its particularity to something novel in its particularity, from what happened in the past to what we should expect now or in the future.

Having said that the rhetorical form of induction asks an audience to reason from case to similar case, certain assumptions and implications should be noted.

1. Asking an audience to reason from something familiar to something unknown makes it an active partner in constructing the argument. The audience must understand the paradigm, must recognize its connection to the exemplified instance of the present case, and must infer what follows in the present case. Matters are not laid out in the meticulous fashion of a thorough scientific demonstration but in the shorthand of joined minds that share something in common but don't bother to express it: common experiences and interpretations of their meaning.

2. We should avoid presenting too many paradigms; otherwise, our argument will begin to resemble a formal technical argument and become difficult for laypeople to follow.

3. Paradigms are best suited to making inferences about the future, such as we do when deciding questions of policy, because they help us to frame expectations of the likely impact of our decisions on the basis of past experiences of a similar sort. They are less useful in settling questions of the past such as occur in judicial proceedings, where inferring guilt on the basis of a person's (or group's) record risks an unjust verdict.

4. Paradigms are best suited to audiences that have not yet formed general rules from which to reason, such as youths and novices. These audiences are much more likely to understand in terms of particular cases that fall within their frames of experience.

5. Paradigms do not permit the maximum amount of control over how an audience reasons. Paradigms may be interpreted in a number of ways, resulting in confusion or a missed point or even seeming to prove something unintended. Because they are not the most efficient mode of argument, they are to be used with caution.

6. For this reason, the preferred use of a paradigm is not as the main argument but as an illustration for an argument. Placing a well-cho-

sen illustrative example at the end of an appeal helps the rhetor to secure his reasoning in the audience's mind. The preferred mode of argument, then, is not inductive but deductive, the enthymeme.

Enthymemes

Aristotle maintained that the enthymeme was the very heart and soul of rhetoric. Today we still share his opinion; contemporary rhetoric also sees argument as the essential ingredient for responsible discourse. However, enthymeme refers to something more specific than arguments at large. It involves the form the argument takes—the mode of appeal through which audiences are persuaded and the mastery of which is essential to practicing rhetoric as an art.

Aristotle defined enthymeme as a "**rhetorical syllogism.**" Syllogism refers to the specific logical form of an argument consisting of two premises and a conclusion that follows from them. This form is used in logic to display the premises in a reasoned argument and test for whether the relation among them leads to a valid conclusion. In logic, an *enthymeme* is a truncated syllogism, or one with either a premise or a conclusion left unexpressed. Aristotle's meaning in calling rhetorical deduction an enthymeme is somewhat obscured by his use of this term drawn from logic. For example, a syllogistic argument would be as follows:

Major premise: Students of rhetoric are interested in persuasion.

Minor premise: I am a student of rhetoric.

Therefore, I am interested in persuasion.

Expressed enthymematically, with one of its premises suppressed, it may take one of these forms:

Students of rhetoric are interested in persuasion.

Therefore, I am interested in persuasion.

Or,

I am a student of rhetoric.

Therefore, I am interested in persuasion.

Or,

Students of rhetoric are interested in persuasion.

I am a student of rhetoric.

In each case, one statement has been suppressed. It is understood so well that it is unnecessary to express it for us to judge the validity of the argument. In logic, the essential feature emphasized is that enthymemes have suppressed premises.

Confusion arises when we take Aristotle to mean the same thing by "enthymeme" in rhetoric as he does in logic. Although premises often are suppressed in rhetorical syllogisms, Aristotle's discussion of *pisteis* suggests that this is not necessarily so in all cases, nor is it an enthymeme's essential feature. When a speaker says, "As a student of rhetoric, I am interested in persuasion," the essential feature of this statement is the way it involves the audience. An argument of this sort includes the audience in the active process of building a proof from what it already knows and believes or from what it can recognize with ease.

The first essential feature of an enthymeme is usually some point of **common ground** among rhetor and audience. It may be a belief (drug traffic threatens social welfare), a value (we should be generous to those less fortunate than ourselves), or a goal (we want to live in peace). If the argument is properly constructed, the audience will provide the common-ground premises without the rhetor expressing them.

The second essential feature of an enthymeme is a **linking premise** that joins the common ground of rhetor and audience to a conclusion. The linking premise is particular and targeted at the belief (the Colombians in South America are trafficking in drugs), value (millions of Rwandans live with the constant pain of hunger; malnutrition is rampant), or goal (controlling nuclear weapons will provide a secure future for our children) we wish to elicit.

The third essential feature is that enthymematic arguments are **coconstructed** by audience and rhetor. By linking the expressed with the unexpressed, enthymemes actively join the audience with the rhetor in the process of supplying premises that support their shared inferences. Providing premises needed to complete the enthymeme helps build the appeal. In effect, the audience cocreates arguments to itself. In this way, the enthymeme works as a self-persuasive appeal.[4] When audiences participate in constructing the argument, they provide their own good reasons for believing and acting. This is why enthymemes are such strong persuasive devices.

✐
Enthymemes and Good Reasons

The three essential features of the enthymeme create a necessity for the rhetor. It is important to know what the audience believes about the possible ways of presenting and arguing for ideas in order to know which enthymemes will be most effective. We have to analyze our audience to know in advance the types of premises they are likely to provide. Otherwise, our contentions are at risk of misfiring—leading to misunderstanding or refutation or flat rejection of the message. For this reason, as we saw in chapter 6, knowledge of *idia* is a great help because these topics provide specific "sayables" that are unique to a subject area. People interested in the subject are likely to recognize the relationship of certain premises to beliefs and values implicit in a message. Similarly, review topics provide an index to what might be said or avoided in terms of the likelihood of involving audiences in the active process of remaking proofs along desired lines.

The type of reasoning found in advertising in the United States provides a convenient illustration of how this reasoning process works. Advertising attempts to link a product or service with attributes we value. A product is good because it makes us socially acceptable or because it has scientifically advanced features, and the like. Such reasoning relies on our acceptance of such values, eliciting them to complete the appeal as a good reason for buying or supporting the product or service.

Several decades ago, two researchers conducted simultaneous but independent studies of U.S. value premises. They came to surprisingly similar conclusions and reported their findings in a joint publication.[5] Their findings still provide a handy index of basic values to which most Americans subscribe and to which advertisers may appeal. Here is a summary of the basic values they uncovered:

1. The Value of the Individual
2. Achievement and Success
3. Change and Progress
4. Ethical Equality
5. Equality of Opportunity
6. Effort and Optimism
7. Efficiency, Practicality, and Pragmatism
8. Rejection of Authority
9. Science and Secular Rationality
10. Sociality
11. Material Comfort
12. Quantification
13. External Conformity
14. Humor
15. Generosity and "Considerateness"
16. Patriotism[6]

Were we to examine public messages—commercial, political, legal, and so forth—such values would likely be premises understood and quite frequently supplied by the audience to complete arguments but seldom explicitly expressed. Several such values are enjoined in patterns of argument that conform to the lines of reasoning suggested by the review topics discussed in chapter 6 in the following two-page ad that appeared in the *New York Times Magazine* of March 11, 2001.

On the top of the right-hand page was the banner: "HELPING END DOMESTIC VIOLENCE." On the left-hand page and continuing onto the right-hand side was a picture of a thirty-something woman. Overimposed were the words, "I thought domestic violence only happened to other people. Then it happened to me."[1] On the right-hand page the copy read:

HELPING END DOMESTIC VIOLENCE

When Shari's "perfect" boyfriend turned violent, she felt trapped, alone, and worthless. [2]

Beyond the beatings and harassment, she was consumed with the fear that she would hurt her children if she tried to escape. [3]

Finally, Shari found SAFEHOME, a program for victims of domestic violence in Johnson County, Kansas that gave her counseling and support—and the courage to begin a better life. [4]

As a career woman and mother of two, Shari knows firsthand that domestic abuse is not the problem of "other" people. [5]

It affects millions of women, men, and children in every community, regardless of race or income. [6]

The time to stop violence is now. [7]

That's why we established *The Phillip Morris Campaign Against Domestic Violence.* [8]

Our support of SAFEHOME and similar organizations nationwide is just one of the ways we've been making a difference in communities in need for more than forty years. [9]

The advertisement ends with the address and contact information for those in need of help, followed by the statement "Supported by the Phillip Morris family of companies."

There are nine statements in the ad. Statement 7 is an imperative. The remaining eight offer reasoning in support of the imperative. As you read through the ad, the reasoning is extremely truncated, which is typical of advertisements and illustrates in a microcosm how enthymemes persuade.

The ostensible audience for this ad is women, quite possibly women with dependent children. By virtue of its placement in the *New York Times Magazine*, it is sure to be read by a substantial adult audience. Some will be individuals who have committed acts of domestic violence, and to them the copy may serve as a mild form of chastisement for their behavior. Some will be men and women who have had no direct experience of domestic violence, and they may find Phillip Morris (PM) acting responsibly by supporting organizations that assist victims of partner abuse. If nothing else, it may gain Phillip Morris a few PR points with this segment of the audience. Still others may read the ad and think it is a slick attempt at **image restoration**[7] by a company that made its fortune in the tobacco industry through the manufacture and marketing of products it knew were deadly. Regardless, we can see that an ad targeted explicitly for one audience reaches several and will have impacts on those audiences because it cannot help but engage values and beliefs that produce closure in conclusions about the message and the maker.

But what of its intended audience? Consider the reasons offered, the unexpressed values they enjoin, and the *topos* that advances this reasoning.

Statement 1 is a quotation from the victim. It reasons from existence/ nonexistence—domestic violence did not exist in Shari's world. It is an implied negative of *value of the individual* in that prior to her encounter with partner abuse, she had considered this as a social problem in general and not one that applied to her individually.

Statement 2 reasons from causality between domestic violence and its effects on Shari's sense of self. It implies *value of the individual*, since it attributes demeaning consequences to abusive behavior.

Statement 3 uses the topos of correlation: namely, her fears for her children accompany her sense of personal debasement. Again we see a negation of *value of the individual* and of *optimism*.

Statement 4 uses three topoi. Its claims about SAFEHOME use substance by listing its defining attributes. It also employs causality, linking

SAFEHOME counseling to Shari's "courage to begin a better life." Here the value is *ethical equality*. But it also makes statements about Shari that draw on capacity to *change* and invoke the value of *effort and optimism*.

Statement 5 returns to the topos of existence, first by stating attributes of Shari that encourage us to infer she is intelligent (career woman) and responsible (mother of two). Here the value of *secular rationality* is invoked: Shari is a paradigm from whom we can infer our own vulnerability. This pattern also resonates with *value of the individual*.

Statement 6 uses the topos of degree to argue that no one is exempt. Again, the implied value is *individuality*.

Statement 7 is the imperative claim that we must act now. It draws on the line of reasoning that society has the capacity to *change*, and it implies the value that *change* will bring *progress*.

Statement 8 uses the topos of correlation: PM's concern for victims of domestic violence correlates with its "campaign." It draws on the value *generosity and considerateness*.

Statement 9 relies on desirability for its line of reasoning. Its value is *achievement of success*, since PM claims it is "making a difference." Moreover, it has been addressing community needs "for more than forty years."

In an overall pattern of argument, this ad implies that we have the capacity to change patterns of domestic violence. Individuals who are victims can be helped by trained agencies that can assist them in reclaiming their lives. By particularizing its appeal in terms of Shari, it emphasizes the value of the individual rather than more general social norms regarding domestic abuse. The ad also challenges the public perception of Phillip Morris as a giant in the tobacco industry by casting it in the light of a socially enlightened and morally upright corporation.

Finally, this ad illustrates in capsule form the variety of reasoning and different invitations to complete thought patterns that are typical of enthymematic arguments. Well-adapted arguments involve audiences in argument construction without conscious reflection on their participatory role. They involve audience members in overall patterns of response that are typical for their group or culture. They provide lines of thinking and valuing that are honored as good reasons to accede to an appeal. Most important, as we have stressed throughout, the enthymematic structure gains assent by involving an audience in the actual construction of the argument. The audience actually helps to persuade itself.

❧
Good Reasons and Issues

Messages may have several persuasive dimensions. To some extent we usually are influenced by our perceptions of the speaker or writer (for instance, our admiration for Julia Roberts's acting ability may lead us to accept her views on the quality of contemporary films). At another level our emotional involvement in the topic may sway our judgment (our love for children leads us to fear the rise of drug consumption in schools as a threat to their welfare). Finally, we may find ourselves influenced above all by the reasoning of the arguments themselves (the data and reasoning presented lead us to conclude that downtown stores have lost trade due to congested traffic conditions). The argument of the discourse itself, considered quite apart from the emotional involvement of the listeners and their opinion of the rhetor, is our concern here.

The Greek term *logos* has a variety of meanings (some of which we encountered in chapter 2) and, like pisteis, is not easily rendered into English. Sometimes its reference to a mode of rhetorical appeal has been translated as "logical proof." But as our discussion of paradigm and enthymeme has indicated, the proofs of rhetoric are hardly "logical" in any rigorous sense. Formal validity is frequently violated in rhetorical appeals, though that does not diminish their persuasive or rational power. Rather than strictly logical appeals, paradigms and enthymemes exhibit reasoning more like a "psycho-logic" because they involve audience interests, values, and readiness to respond. These biases and commitments are important elements in rhetorical reasoning. The term "proof" also is a misleading rendition. The appeals of popular essays and public addresses certainly are not proofs in the same sense as scientific demonstrations. They are better thought of as arguments that urge assent but hardly compel it. Indeed, the art of rhetoric resides in the acquired skill of making arguments that show the likelihood of a claim on the basis of what listeners and readers take to be reasonable, even if not formally valid, grounds. So, for example, when world leaders threaten to retaliate against terrorist groups, such as al-Qaeda, they might have a difficult time proving that taking terrorist lives is logically necessary. At the same time, this extreme course may well be perceived as reasonable within their society's scheme of values, especially if it has been the victim of a terrorist attack that has cost civilian lives. After all, the objective of rhetorical arguments, the *logos* of the speech itself, is to reason with the audience to a common basis for assent. In short, through developing good reasons, the rhetor builds a persuasive case.

Detecting a Case

While individual arguments in a message may be more or less reasonable, we need to bear in mind that audiences tend to respond to messages in terms of broad and inclusive patterns of reasoning found in the discourse. For instance, the mayor may offer six reasons why we need a center-city parking ramp. Individually, these reasons may be unimpressive. However, if they complement one another to develop the overall message that a vibrant downtown benefits everyone, the mayor may have a winning appeal. Taken together, her arguments provide a most persuasive case for this project. The *logos* of the mayor's speech resides in the cumulative argument of her entire presentation. In rhetoric, the entire argumentation in a presentation is referred to as a **case**. *A case consists of the overall management of evidence and reasoning to support a proposition.*

The reasoning of the case is toward some end or purpose—the removal of certain tensions of novelty, ambiguity, or conflict that mark a situation as rhetorical. Such reasoning requires carefully chosen remarks, ones suited to the given circumstances or, in the language of situation theory, a fitting response. How do we select the most fitting remarks from among all the remarks that we might make? To answer that question we must determine the issues to be addressed in order to resolve the rhetorical situation.

In chapter 3 we discussed the concept of an exigence as the central feature of every rhetorical situation. An exigence was defined as an imperfection marked by urgency. We noted that imperfections might be of varying sorts, each requiring different types of responses. We now need to consider the way in which rhetors diagnose these exigencies in order to develop appropriate arguments. This method of analysis is called **stasis**.

Determining Issues

Stasis is a Greek term. It refers to a point of suspended animation. It was originally used in Greek physics to refer to the point at which two lines of force would collide and ricochet in a new direction. As figure 7.1 indicates, line of force A collides with line of force B at point C. The force and angle of their collision deflect them in new directions, A1 and B1. Point C represents the point of stasis: It is both a stopping point for lines of force A and B and a starting point for lines of force A1 and B1. Ancient rhetoricians borrowed this concept of simultaneous stopping and starting to describe what happens in the development of rhetorical issues. It remains descriptive of how issues are located and how we must persuade if we are to resolve them.

Imagine a contention as if it were a line of force (say, computer literacy should be required of all college graduates). The line of force would continue to infinity if it encountered no obstacle (since no one disagrees, it

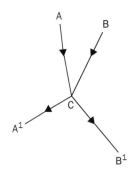

Figure 7.1   Diagram of Stasis

shall be a degree requirement). Now imagine a contrary contention as a line of force moving in the opposite direction (computer literacy should not be a degree requirement). When the two collide, their initial motion is stopped, and stasis is reached. But there is renewed motion as arguments in support of one view and against the other are developed and presented. Thus, as figure 7.2 indicates, contrary motions clash to produce stasis. Stasis in turn produces an **issue**. *An issue consists of the clash of ideas that differ about the same thing* (whether computer literacy should be a degree requirement). From this clash arises a **question** that must be decided.

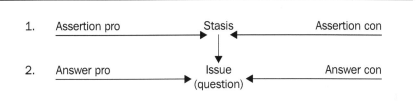

Figure 7.2 Diagram of Rhetorical Stasis

Consider, for example, the historical changes in the U.S. government's understanding of immigration. Dating from the Chinese Exclusion Act of 1882, the United States has barred the immigration of citizens from certain countries. At the same time it has welcomed or made exceptions for certain others. The groups in or out of favor have not always been the same. For instance, in 1921 the United States adopted a national origins quota system that limited immigrants from each European country to three percent of the foreign-born population here as of the 1910 census. This policy favored northern Europeans, Germans, Irish and Scandinavians, among others, over southern and eastern Europeans, such as Greeks and Italians. In 1997 the government made entry easier for Nicaraguans than for Salvadorans and Guatemalans, while Hondurans and Haitians were left out. Each of these groups was fleeing from the civil disorders of the 1980s, but U.S. policy favored those fleeing from former communist regimes. In 2000, the technology industries facing labor shortages lobbied Congress to double the annual quota for temporary high-skilled immigrants to 195,000. These workers were primarily from China and India. These examples show that U.S. policy has not been even-handed toward all peoples and that it has been guided by economic, political, and quite possibly racial considerations.

During the summer of 2001, President Bush proposed to grant permanent residency status (green cards) to three million undocumented Mexicans living and working in the United States. His proposal drew fire from a number of objectors. The extremes along this range of opinion might be expressed this way: "All undocumented workers in the United States illegally should be given permanent residency status over time" vs. "No undocumented workers in the United States should be given permanent residency status." These competing claims bump into each other; they **clash**. Since they advocate opposite and mutually exclusive positions, both can't be correct. Hence there is an **issue** because we have differing ideas about the same thing, and this **clash** gives rise to a **question** we must answer as judges: "Should a specific group of illegal aliens be given permanent residency in the United States?"

In terms of our concerns with logos, the presence of a question serves the useful function of focusing our understanding of the rhetorical situation and options for a fitting response. Only remarks that address the issue are fitting. For example, while the possibility that Latin nations governed by repressive regimes might impose severe penalties on political opponents, thereby threatening their survival, is distressing, it is not relevant to this particular issue because it doesn't address the question we must answer.

We determine what will answer our question by examining the essential grounds proposed to support each assertion. As we have reasons offered to support both points of view, an "answer pro" and an "answer con," the question is narrowed to specific points to be decided, as figure 7.3 illustrates. For example, "A policy of guest worker status limited to undocumented Mexican laborers currently in the United States and permitting new migrants to apply for green cards over time will move us closer to a broad-based accord with Mexico that links immigration to trade, energy, human rights, and the fight against drug trafficking." "Granting permanent status to any group of illegal aliens rewards those who have broken the law and undermines U.S. immigration law." In making the answer and response, a series of points become apparent as matters for us to address and resolve in reaching a decision. Can the United States and Mexico police their 1,984-mile border? Does the historical relation of the U.S. with Mexico make Mexico exceptional with respect to U.S. immigration law? Is the movement of workers across national borders a natural evolution of NAFTA, thereby calling for special immigration regulations in the case of Mexican workers? What are the implications for U.S.-Mexican joint policy in other areas if Mexican workers are given special U.S. immigration status? If illegal Mexican workers in the United States are granted amnesty

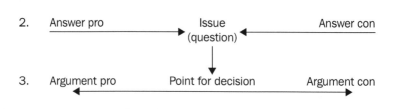

Figure 7.3   Narrowing the Question

and green cards, can other groups living illegally be overlooked without damaging U.S. foreign relations? What are the implications for U.S. workers of accepting guest workers who have gained illegal entry? What, in light of the 1.5 million arrests made annually of Mexicans attempting to gain illegal entry into the United States, will be an acceptable criterion for exclusion? And will any policy other than an open door bring an end to the tragic deaths resulting from attempts of Mexicans to gain illegal entry? The arguments developed in the deliberation of this matter—whether in discussion, partisan oratory, editorial opinion, government position paper, or formal debate—must address these concerns because given the way the question or issue has evolved, these are the points we must resolve before we can make a decision.

Before leaving this point, one more observation is in order. The point for decision is a product of the specific type of accusation and defense presented. One can imagine, for example, the anti-illegal alien proponent arguing simply, "Even if a massive amnesty is granted and those Mexicans here illegally are granted green cards, it will not solve the basic problem—stemming the flow of workers—legal and illegal—beyond the capacity of our economy to support them." This would narrow the discussion to the "carrying capacity" of the U.S. economy and the consequences of an unrestrained flow of guest workers on U.S. citizens in the short and long run. Rhetors have choices in how issues evolve and are guided by their understanding of what evidence and reasoning can be developed persuasively in the given case. Once the point for decision has been determined, rhetors build persuasive appeals designed to sway the judges in their direction. Thus the arrows in line 3 of figure 7.3 lead away from the point for decision, indicating that the rhetoric is clearly partisan, pro or con, in the attempt to secure a favorable hearing from the listeners or readers.

Classifying Issues

So far we have noted that the exigence of a rhetorical situation can be analyzed with some precision by thinking of it as an issue that arises from competing viewpoints. These clashing positions create a stasis that must be resolved through effective arguments. The rhetorical participants responding to each other make fitting responses as they address the issue in terms of the question it poses and the points for decision in resolving the question. Having noted this, we can take the model of stasis, or issue analysis, a step further.

Roman treatises on rhetoric have influenced much of our thinking on the character of stasis. A great deal of Roman discussion centered on legal oratory because in those times success in legal pleading was an avenue to public notice and an opportunity for entering a political career. But the schema they developed is usable elsewhere, with modification.

The Romans discovered four types of issues, each different from but related to the others, and each calling for different types of arguments:

1. **Conjectural issue**: an issue of fact (What happened?)
2. **Definitional issue**: an issue of definition or naming the fact (What shall we call it?)
3. **Qualitative issue**: an issue of causes and mitigating circumstances (What is the nature of the act?)
4. **Translative issue**: an issue of procedure (Are any rights or procedures violated?)

As a law case develops, it is first necessary to determine what happened—an issue of fact; then what law applies—an issue of definition; then the causes and mitigating circumstances—an issue of quality. These proceed in order, requiring that we argue from fact to definition to quality. The translative issue can be raised at any point, however. For example, at the beginning of the trial, the attorney for the defendant makes a motion to dismiss because the defendant's rights were violated (the evidence was collected from her apartment without a search warrant) or a motion for a change of venue because local publicity makes a fair trial unlikely (Timothy McVeigh could not be tried in Oklahoma City because local publicity and emotions attached to the crime for which he was charged made it impossible to empanel an open-minded jury). As the trial proceeds, motions and objections are raised concerning testimony believed to violate legal rules of evidence, and so on. In other words, matters of proper procedure can arise at any time.

The original purpose of this analysis was to locate the precise issue before the court so that pertinent arguments might be invented. We still find it useful for preparing arguments. For example, if the issue is *conjectural*—whether something did occur—we require evidence of observation, corroborating testimony, relevant artifacts, and the like. Was a person killed? We have the dead body; we have photos and testimony that it is Jones and that Jones is dead. We have a coroner's report that says Jones died of a bullet wound to the heart. We have the chemist's report that says the powder burns on Jones's clothing indicate a shot fired at close range. We have the ballistics report that says the bullet was fired from a .38 revolver. These are bits and pieces of evidence that help us resolve a question of fact—Was Jones killed? After all, Jones could be missing and not dead at all, or Jones could be dead of natural causes. Before the trial may proceed, this issue of fact must first be determined. It doesn't matter that Jones was an eccentric or a drug pusher or a regular churchgoer because, even if true, these points are irrelevant to the question we have to answer—was Jones killed?

Having determined that Jones was killed, the next question is *definitive*: What shall we call it? Is it murder? Here we have several possibilities. It could be a self-inflicted wound—either an accident or suicide—but the reports of the coroner and the chemist indicate that the distance from which the shot was fired and the angle of entry make it impossible for the wound to have been self-inflicted. Was it murder or self-defense? Arguments are directed to identifying the culprit, placing the gun in his possession, locating him at the scene, proving that he did the deed—all questions of fact. These facts help the prosecutor prove that this person had motive and opportunity and was not himself endangered, thereby eliminating the possibility of self-defense and allowing us to call it murder.

Finally, having resolved the *conjectural* issues (Jones was killed, Smith did it) and the *definitive* issue (Jones was murdered), *qualitative issues* surrounding the act may be at issue. The attorney may argue that the accused's wife was seriously ill and his children without food, and that he was out of work and needed money to care for his family. He was driven to the desperate act of robbery and panicked when his victim resisted. The court should be lenient because he never committed a crime before and because these mitigating family circumstances drove him to a tragic act. Again, relevant arguments here have to do with the quality of what was done. Appeals are fitting insofar as they are relevant to assessing this matter. By knowing the issue, the attorney can be more precise in the inventional process, selecting from among all those things that might be said— lines of argument that have the *most promise* for resolving the points for decision in the audience's mind.

Conjectural, definitive, qualitative, and translative issues are important in arenas other than legal pleadings. Questions of fact, definition, quality, and procedure arise as major areas of disagreement whenever there are exigencies to be resolved. Understanding how to apply the theory of stasis to find and assess relevant arguments is extremely significant for the way issues are resolved and the consequences that impact us and the communities in which we live.

For example, in the period of the Cold War, the United States developed a large nuclear arsenal. Each of these nuclear weapons required the manufacture of a plutonium trigger to detonate the bomb. Rocky Flats Nuclear Arsenal, located in the Denver metro area between Boulder and Golden, was one of the main sites where plutonium triggers were produced. Since plutonium is not located in the soil, it cannot be mined. It is produced from uranium in a process that leaves a byproduct of radioactive waste. This highly volatile and dangerous waste must be contained and stored in a manner that will not permit it to vent into the air or to seep into the water table, since its radioactivity constitutes a significant health hazard. The production of plutonium triggers at Rocky Flats created a significant amount of nuclear waste, which was stored in drums housed in warehouses on the arsenal site. The result of this practice left Rocky Flats a radioactive dump that endangers the 2.5 million inhabitants of the Denver metro region. Considerable public pressure exists to clean up the waste, which is the responsibility of the Department of Energy. As you might imagine, Coloradans living along the front range of the Rockies are uneasy about this project. Concerned citizen groups have become owners of the cleanup issue and use the publicity principle (the right to make your views known, as discussed in chapter 5) to maintain vital public awareness of potential health hazards from the waste site and the cleanup operation itself, which is an enormous undertaking because the volume of waste is so massive. The Department of Energy (DOE), which has political responsibility for the cleanup, also uses the publicity principle to address public fears. Public involvement via press coverage, Internet sources, and citizen advisory groups is relatively high, and there is ongoing deliberation regarding all aspects of the cleanup project.

Here is an excerpt from a question-and-answer session posted in 1996 on the PBS homepage:

> Gerald Foster of Denver, CO, asks:
> Where I live in Denver is about ten miles from Rocky Flats, which has been active in the past in the nuclear weapons program. We are told that removal and cleanup of the area is underway. What is the status of the program, especially the hazard reduction efforts for the surrounding area—at least ten miles worth?

> Tom Carpenter of the Government Accountability Project replies:
> They are just getting started on the cleanup, and it is going badly. The Department of Energy and its contractors have experienced several recent mishaps and problems, and face some very serious problems for the future. These include issues associated with the storage of plutonium in barrels that are becoming pressurized with hydrogen gases, loose plutonium in the ductworks, environmental cleanups of mind-boggling proportions, etc. I wouldn't live within ten miles of the plant, personally.

Foster has raised a question of fact: What's the status of the cleanup? He wants to know whether there has been a reduction in public danger from hazardous waste. Carpenter answers by pointing out certain conditions that suggest the cleanup is running into difficulty, and he specifies the areas of concern. Carpenter concludes by saying he wouldn't live within ten miles of the plant. From the evidence of fact, Carpenter draws a conclusion. Neither person has stated a premise such as "avoid obvious health hazards," or "act prudently to protect your health," but such a premise is functioning for them to form an enthymeme with this information relevant to Foster's question of whether it is safe to live within ten miles of Rocky Flats.

After reading Carpenter's rendition, you may say to yourself, "That poor fellow should move," or "I'm glad I don't live there," or something similar that defines the cleanup as a local problem for Coloradans to solve. But here's an excerpt from an article by Mark Obmascik that appeared on the front page of the *Denver Post* on June 25, 2000.

> With little public attention, the top-secret complex has trucked out an estimated 600 plutonium pits, key weapon parts that each carry the killing power of a Hiroshima bomb, down Interstate 25 in Denver to another government facility in Texas. . . . Now the U.S. government is pushing ahead to do something at Rocky Flats that has never been done anywhere: detoxify a nuclear bomb plant. Among the challenges:

. . . Trucking out dangerous materials. In the next two years, an estimated 16,000 pounds of high-grade plutonium must be moved
through metro Denver to South Carolina. On top of that, to meet the
planned 2006 cleanup completion date, Rocky Flats must ship out
more than three truckloads of radioactive waste each day; the plant
now moves only two truckloads a week.

The *Denver Post* article raises a new question about how to define the
Rocky Flats cleanup project: Is this a local issue or a national issue? The
waste is being trucked to Texas and South Carolina. Its route takes it
through downtown Denver and along I-25. To get to Texas or South Carolina waste sites, it has to pass through a number of states. And the material
each truck is carting has the explosive potential of a Hiroshima bomb. Notice that the author does not provide a dictionary definition of the scope of
the challenge. He describes the steps in the process. This is called an **oper-
ational** definition, in which a thing is defined by its performance traits.
Other types of definition include **stipulative** definitions, where a group
specifies the meaning it will assign a specific term, **ostensive** definitions,
in which we point to a referent for what a term means, or various uses of
language, such as defining something by its opposite (**negative** definition), similar terms (**synonyms**), **descriptions**, and the like. In this case,
whether the problem is defined as a local or national issue carries implications for who should have a say in the project and the extent of public risk
involved. It raises questions about public safety that extend beyond the
ten-mile radius of Foster's concern. If radioactive isotopes should leak from
the waste containers, which seems quite possible since Carpenter reports
that they are stored in barrels under exceptional pressure, additional questions of definition arise as we inquire into what kind of thing or event this
is: "If it is granted that some radioactive isotopes are released in a nuclear
waste cleanup, is this eventuality regulated by law? Is it considered dangerous? Is the waste considered a noncontaminant if below a certain
level?" and so on.

Finally, qualitative issues may surface. If leakage exists and has been
defined, how is the quality of the cleanup effort to be judged? Is DOE doing all it can to insure public safety? How competent is the cleanup company (Kaiser-Hill)? Can we have confidence in it? These are questions of
degree that must be resolved to affirm the level of confidence we may
have in the DOE. While we raise these concerns, the spokespersons for the
DOE and Kaiser-Hill will conduct their own persuasive campaign to reas-
sure the public that there is no danger. In all probability, their campaign
will attempt to redefine the issue as one of responsible action and safeguards to protect public health. The rhetoric of their responses often rest
on assumptions of degree. For example, the magnitude of the project requires patience. Or the magnitude of the effort makes it unreasonable to
expect there will be no accidents. Responses such as this attempt to keep
the focus on issues of quality.

An example of qualitative argument followed immediately after Carpenter's response to Foster. Jim Warner of the Department of Energy answered Foster's question in a way that argued for a different conclusion about his public safety concern.

> The workers at the Rocky Flats site have made tremendous progress on risk reduction and cleanup in the past couple of years. Perhaps the biggest news at the site is that in the last year we have cleaned up three of the top ten highest priority cleanup areas, shipped more waste offsite for disposal than in the past five years and decommissioned and demolished the first formerly radioactive production facility.
>
> The Department has also made substantial progress on reducing the urgent risks at Rocky Flats. The highly enriched uranium solutions have been removed from Rocky Flats, eliminating the single biggest worker risk on site. Also, we have safely vented more than 1,100 residue drums from Building 771, and we have completed all plutonium-related activities specified in the new Rocky Flats regulatory agreement.
>
> The Department has also laid the groundwork for accelerated cleanup and closure of Rocky Flats: We formed a Site Specific Advisory Board to provide an effective forum for community input into the cleanup process. We negotiated a regulatory agreement with EPA and the State of Colorado that spells out enforceable cleanup milestones and streamlines the regulatory process, and we have established an aggressive ten-year closure plan that would substantially eliminate the risks at Rocky Flats by 2006. To help get this work done, we selected (through competitive bidding) a new experienced environmental contractor—the Kaiser-Hill Company. We also changed the structure to a first of its kind performance-based contract that requires progress towards specific cleanup goals for the contractor to get paid.

Notice that Warner shifts the focus from the dangers to the work accomplished. Certainly he is offering facts, but he also has shifted the question from a conjectural issue or question of fact (Is it or is it not safe to live within ten miles of Rocky Flats?) to a qualitative issue (Is the Department of Energy acting *responsibly* to insure your safety?). He doesn't directly answer Foster's question; instead his arguments are directed more toward actions that demonstrate progress: There has been progress in cleaning up three of the top ten highest priority cleanup areas, in removing urgent risks from Rocky Flats, and in establishing measures to complete the cleanup in ten years. Warner treats safety as a relative condition to be inferred from conditions now versus conditions when the project began. Warner's enthymeme relies on the unexpressed premise that responsible actions will insure public safety.

We might extend the stasis analysis one final step, noting that in areas where policy is at stake, there are standard or stock issues that must be resolved. These are commonly listed as questions of **ill** (what is the problem?), **blame** (what is the cause?), **remedy** (what can be done?), and **cost** (what resources must be expended?). How persuasive appeals develop depends on where we are in policy determinations. Questions of ill require that we discuss the harm involved, the significance of the harm, whether it is persistent or passing, whether it is inherent or accidental. (Is the detoxification of nuclear contamination at Rocky Flats removing the public danger from exposure to radioactive waste?) Only after we have resolved that there is harm can we consider blame. This requires examination of the causes, whether they are somehow inherent in present policies and structures, and whether they can be reformed. We must resolve matters of this sort before we can persuasively and responsibly propose remedies. In advocating remedies, we examine whether they will be effective in removing the ill, whether they are technically feasible so that we may implement them, whether they are desirable because they remedy the ill without causing worse problems, whether one solution is preferable to the alternatives, and whether the solution is enforceable and compliance can be ensured. Finally, having selected a remedy, we ask about costs—financial, psychological, moral, and so forth—to determine whether the benefits derived are worth the price we must pay. (Personal safety within a ten-mile radius, personal safety along the routes to the Texas and South Carolina waste sites, health dangers to cleanup workers, etc.)

We can acquire calculated precision in analyzing exigencies, thinking about communicating and developing arguments fitting the rhetorical situation. If we know what we are to discuss—what is at issue and therefore what must be decided by our readers and listeners—it is much easier to craft a persuasive message than proceeding randomly. If listeners and readers are to find good reasons for believing and acting in our appeal, we must look for the messages we *must* express to be effective rather than simply speaking or writing remarks we *wish* to make.

ভ

Stasis in Everyday Life

Our discussion of rhetorical methods and logos has focused on communicating and developing good reasons to resolve public issues. Although the theory of rhetoric was developed to deal with the needs of public communicators, it would be a mistake to limit our rhetorical modes of thinking to the public arena. Before concluding this chapter, let's consider one way in which topoi, logos, and stasis relate to our everyday communication needs, namely, those times when we are asked by parents, teachers, friends, and lovers to account for our behavior. To make the connection between *accounts* and good reasons clear, however, we will use the following discussion to gain some perspective.

In the 1950s two sociologists, Gresham Sykes and David Matza,[8] conducted a study of juvenile delinquents. They were interested in how juvenile delinquents saw themselves in relation to social norms. The prevailing theory at that time held that delinquents rejected society and its norms, and their deviant behavior was a sign of that rejection. Sykes and Matza approached this question with uniquely rhetorical assumptions: people use language to coordinate diverse actions; motives are not private states but are present in the typical ways that we talk.[9] Working on these assumptions, they found evidence that juvenile delinquents were at least partially committed to the same values as everyone else. For one thing, juvenile delinquents frequently exhibited shame or guilt when they violated society's prescriptions. For another, juvenile delinquents gave approval to certain conforming persons, such as law-abiding people who were "really honest," or selected authority figures like a pious, humble mother or a forgiving priest. Furthermore, juvenile delinquents distinguished between appropriate and inappropriate targets for their deviance. Not everyone was a potential victim.

These signs led Sykes and Matza to hypothesize that delinquents actually subscribed to the prevailing social order and that they had adopted verbal techniques for neutralizing their deviance by supplying verbal justifications for their acts. In short, they could have it both ways: They could hold the same values as the dominant order and rationalize away any apparent violations of that order in deviant acts.

Sykes and Matza uncovered five such verbal techniques:

1. **Denial of responsibility**—"Outside forces caused my behavior" (e.g., social environment).
2. **Denial of injury**—"The harm is less than alleged."
3. **Denial of the victim**—"He had it coming, it was rightful retaliation."
4. **Condemnation of the condemners**—"What hypocrites, the things they do are worse than anything I do; focus on them, not me."
5. **Appeal to higher loyalties**—"Other norms, more pressing and involving a higher loyalty, take precedence" (for example, membership in a gang or friendship clique has higher demands than the larger society).[10]

These communicative behaviors of juvenile delinquents suggest how others respond when their actions are questioned as violating expectations. Juvenile delinquents aren't alone in explaining themselves. This realization prompted another pair of researchers, Marvin Scott and Stanford Lyman,[11] to develop a theory of **accounts** to cover these explanatory acts.

An *account* is "*a linguistic device employed whenever an action is subjected to valuative inquiry*"[12] (italics added). Scott and Lyman explain it as a statement made by a social actor to explain unanticipated or untoward behavior. Accounts are called for, in other words, when behaviors disrupt our expectations of amicable relations. When interpersonal communication functions smoothly, this is a sign that we have a background consensus of shared expectations with our interacting partner. This background consensus is important to defining relationships. It represents our mutual understandings and expectations of shared commitments, and it allows us to project behaviors that are permissible within the relationship. Because it is a background consensus, we feel no need to discuss it; we implicitly trust that the other party will behave in ways appropriate to the relationship. However, when the background consensus is violated by some untoward or unanticipated act, we are offended and may ask the offending party for an account. In other words, the violation of our background consensus and the call for an account create an issue. For the issue to be resolved—for the rupture in our relationship to be repaired—it is imperative that an account be given. If our partner refuses to give an account of herself, she is essentially saying that she sees the relationship differently than we do, that there is no background consensus on this relationship. Equally crucial, we must honor the offered account if the relationship is to continue unimpaired. If we do not honor the account, the background consensus remains disrupted.

The idea of accounts captures the way in which the rhetorical theory of stasis applies to interpersonal communication when relationships experience trouble. For friends and lovers, as much as for lawyers and politicians, disagreements arise, issues are formed, and the people involved must make intelligent rhetorical choices if their speech is to resolve their difficulties.

Scott and Lyman classify accounts into two types: **justifications** and **excuses**. *Justifications are accounts in which a person accepts responsibility for the act in question but denies the negative quality associated with it.* In essence, we justify ourselves when we argue that our act is really acceptable if viewed in the proper light. Interestingly, Scott and Lyman find that the justifications offered in everyday life match up with the justifications Sykes and Matza found juvenile delinquents using. Thus the forms of justifications include:

1. **Denial of injury** (No harm was done.)
2. **Denial of the victim** (That person had it coming.)
3. **Condemnation of the condemners** (They do worse; don't focus on me, focus on them.)
4. **Appeal to loyalties** (The act is OK because it serves those to whom I am loyal.)
5. **Sad tales** (My sad past justifies my present behavior.)
6. **Self-fulfillment** (I gotta be me!)

Excuses are accounts in which the person admits that the act in question is bad, wrong, or inappropriate but denies full responsibility. Like justifications, excuses take a variety of forms:

1. **Appeal to accidents** (Forces beyond my control brought this about; it wasn't intended.)
2. **Appeal to defeasibility**, involving some mental element (I didn't know . . . ; I was forced against my will.)
3. **Appeal to biological drives** (Boys will be boys; women are like that.)
4. **Scapegoating** (My behavior was really in response to the attitude or behavior of another—it's that person's fault.)[13]

Notice how the types of justifications and excuses found by these researchers function as lines of argument or special topics (*idia*) to develop the enthymemes necessary for giving accounts. Although the theory of topics and enthymeme was developed to account for the rhetoric of public communication, the use of accounts shows that they are equally at work in our private communication within relationships.

The topoi of public address are only as valuable as their effectiveness in reaching an audience. The audience judges whether good reasons have been offered. So it is with accounts. Once an account—a justification or an excuse—is offered, the offended party must **honor** the account. Scott and Lyman found two basic reasons why some accounts are not honored. First, if the offended party thinks the account is **illegitimate**, it is rejected. For example, the gravity of the event (say, standing up your date) might exceed the type of account provided ("I was helping my roommate with calculus"), or the motives offered as reasons aren't acceptable ("I would have felt guilty if I didn't help him, he's so poor in that subject"). Second, accounts are rejected if they are perceived as **unreasonable**. This happens when the stated grounds for the offense cannot be "normalized" in terms of what everybody knows ("Why did you give me the bum's rush on the phone last night?" "Someone was in my room." "So why didn't you say so?" "I didn't think it would be polite."); that is, normal people don't act for the reason given, and everybody knows it.

Jackson Toby[14] conducted research before the analysis of Scott and Lyman was published. He was interested in the same problem: how people restored disrupted social stability. Toby focused on how we follow acceptable language behaviors or rules to resolve role conflicts. Role conflicts may extend beyond the interpersonal level to group or even organizational relations. The finding is the same. When conflicts arise, there are set ways in which the issues are treated—topoi for offering accounts. Moreover, implicit in Toby's report of language rules are argument tactics social actors employ to resolve instability. The list of appeals he found, some of which overlap with Scott and Lyman's list, suggests the tactics used to control the development and resolution of an issue. Here is Toby's list of things to which we appeal to resolve role conflicts:

1. **Hierarchies of role obligations**—I had conflicting role obligations and had to place one over the other. Please understand.

2. **Appeal to accident**—This is regrettable, but matters were beyond my control. There was nothing I could do.

3. **Etiquette**—Excuse me!

4. **Tact**—Legitimate deception such as a white lie. I cannot go to the movie with you; I have a previous commitment.

5. **Segregation of roles**—My role as father is segregated from my role as teacher. If my daughter receives a poor grade, she has no complaint against me as her father.[15]

The findings of what people do in interpersonal situations correlates with the general theory of rhetorical invention and logos. We can see the correlations in four areas. First, when accounts are called for, they require knowledge of and appeal to shared expectations. An account provides a good reason only if it stems from our background consensus on how we should treat each other and reestablishes the disrupted consensus that has jeopardized a relationship. Accounts are basically enthymematic in their structure, therefore, because they argue from shared premises. Second, the language rules followed in accounting for our role violations reflect common behavior patterns our culture uses to avoid interpersonal glitches. They are, in effect, topoi that provide lines of reasoning for repairing sundered or questioned relationships. Third, justifications and excuses are good reasons offered to resolve an issue in a listener's mind. That a person has been called to account for an untoward behavior indicates that there is an issue in the offended party's mind and that appropriate reasons are required to resolve this issue. Justifications and excuses thus appeal to matters of fact, definition, quality, and even procedure to resolve interpersonal points of stasis. Finally, when we offer an account, we cannot help but accept the commitments of rhetorical action. To offer an account we must assume a role, with the assets and liabilities it implies. In account giving, as in all rhetoric, we are not just uttering words. We are creating a possible world and inviting others to share in it with us.

༄

Summary

From ancient times to the present, rhetoric has been severely criticized as empty talk or exaggeration; history has witnessed its fair share of such performances. As Aristotle noted in the *Rhetoric*, there is no way to prevent foolish, thoughtless, or wicked people from speaking in these ways. But such practices are not genuinely artful practices of rhetoric because they lack the one essential requirement—a substantive argument. In this chapter we have been concerned with how such appeals are formed in responsible rhetoric. We have argued that at the heart of such rhetoric are good reasons that can give confidence in the rational integrity of what is advocated. Reasons are good insofar as they can withstand critical inspection; insofar as they take the traditions, beliefs, and commitments of the listeners and readers seriously; insofar as they are pertinent to the issues and responsive to other points of view. These attributes of good reasons hold regardless of setting, audience size, or topic of deliberation. They are the essential requirement for trustworthy discourse. Moreover, as we will see in the next two chapters, these are the bases for responsibly invoking character and engaging emotions as means of persuasion.

❧ 8 ❧

Persuasiveness of Character

In an ideal world where everybody was a model of rationality and integrity, a book on rhetoric might have been complete with chapter 7. In such a world, the art of persuasion would begin and end with finding good reasons. But in the real world, we know that humans respond to more than the reasoning of orators, writers, conversationalists, and other communicators. Our world is the hurly-burly of reason and emotion, of ethical proprieties and conniving machinations. These are the realities from which rhetoric springs and which it addresses.

As the method of communication we use to deal collectively with our common problems, rhetorical theory must account for the influence of emotions, ethics, values, interests, and level of trust (or distrust) in addition to reason. So in accounting for what happens when A speaks for some purpose to B, the persona of the speaker or writer and the emotional states of the listeners must be considered. Since these may be sources of distorted messages or interpretation, we must be on our guard in making judgments. At the same time, we recognize that humans are not just rational beings. We have desires and feelings that influence our conduct. Our assessment of the rhetor's persona as well as our emotional disposition can aid in making wise decisions. In this chapter we will consider the rhetor's character as a source of persuasion. In the next we will take up the subject of emotional appeals.

ૐ

The Problem of Authority

In his book *Authority*, sociologist Richard Sennett recounts the experience of observing the noted conductor Pierre Monteux take command of an orchestra.[1] He describes Monteux as a conductor of subtle movements, his baton working in a rectangle of space measuring approximately 12 by 18 inches. A nod, an arched brow, a flick of his eye are the only cues he provides. Yet so commanding is his knowledge of the music and so self-assured is his manner of expression that these slight movements are all he requires. Their subtlety keeps the players on their toes. They have to watch his every move if they are to play the music to the maestro's taste. As the orchestra rehearsed, Sennett observed Monteux sustain a gentle but firm commentary on the performance of each section—perhaps greater energy here to capture force, perhaps more life there lest the beauty of the music escape, always with a simple but sure tone that said, "I know with confidence how this should be played; do as I direct and the music will sound beautiful."

Monteux did not use bully tactics to discipline the orchestra. Absent were the tirades of say, a Toscanini, designed to strike terror into every member's heart at the thought of making a mistake. Monteux acted toward each musician in a manner that indicated he knew each player's ability; he set the standard each player was to achieve. If perchance a mistake was made, no words of reprimand were needed. A silent glare conveyed the message: "You have not played up to your ability. You have disappointed me. You have disappointed yourself." His standards, not those of peers, were imposed, and Monteux insisted that each player live up to them. For members of the orchestra, Pierre Monteux had **authority**. He possessed superior judgment, could impose discipline, had the capacity to inspire fear, and was self-assured.

Each of us has experienced authority as a problem in our lives. Authority is a problem because it can affect us in positive or negative ways. An authority may impose the discipline necessary for us to grow and improve or may provide direction that steers us away from disaster and toward personal success. An authority also can dominate, exercising such power over our thoughts and actions that we abdicate our independence and become subjects to the authority's dominion. In both aspects, our thoughts and actions are influenced because someone has a degree of power over us.

Several disciplines study personal power. Political science, sociology, history, management science, and psychology come readily to mind. It is also pertinent to human communication. Whenever our decisions are made more on the basis of who is advising us than on the advice itself, we are recognizing the advice giver as an authority. In rhetorical transactions, this form of personal power is an important source of persuasion, commonly called **ethos**. Before we turn to ethos itself we should illustrate some problems in the way authority is understood in order to provide a context for understanding ethos.

Sennett points out that there are two major schools of thought on the nature of authority.[2] One school, led by the German sociologist Max Weber, argues that authority is based on how a figure is regarded by his or her subordinates. If people view a figure as a legitimate authority, they will voluntarily comply with that person's requests. Authority is imagined to be a personal attribute that legitimates acquiescence. A second school, based on the thought of Sigmund Freud, maintains that authority stems from the ability to satisfy the human need to believe something or someone is credible. The Freudians challenge Weber's emphasis on the perception of legitimacy of character as a ground for belief. They replace it with an emphasis on the process—historical, cultural, and psychological—by which people perceive strength in others. But notice that the Freudian view also imagines authority to be a personal attribute—the power to satisfy our needs—that elicits compliance.

Sennett makes a valuable criticism by pointing out that we make authority static and thing-like when we think of it as an attribute. Freezing authority in this way misses the dynamism that accompanies its birth and passage. Rather than a thing, Sennett suggests, authority is a **social construct**. We encountered this concept in chapter 2 when we were considering Protagoras's dictum: "Man is the measure of all things." Social constructs exist as events in social time and space. They are the products of interaction.[3]

Sennett's observation is important in our consideration of ethos; it reminds us that ethos has reality for us as a result of our discourse about it—rather than as a quality or an attribute that a person possesses, such as weight or height. As mentioned above, discussions of ethos under the heading of "source credibility" frequently treat it as resting on whether an audience believes the speaker legitimately possesses certain attributes of character.[4] Other accounts depict ethos as resting on the needs of the audience and its belief that the rhetor can satisfy audience needs.[5] These are ingredients of ethos, to be sure. But both views omit the most important aspect present in the original discussions of this subject. *Ethos* is not a thing or a quality but *an interpretation that is the product of speaker-audience interaction*. Because ethos is dynamic and eventful, its rhetorical presence depends on how arguments and appeals are managed—how the ingredients of needs and perceptions are included in interpreting a rhetor's character through the give-and-take of a rhetorical exchange.

&

Ethos Developed in Message

Not a day passes that we fail to make some judgment of character. The acts of public officials, employers, coworkers, peers, and friends each in their own way contribute to our experience and our assessment of moral, emotional, and intellectual dispositions. These judgments linger with us,

framing future expectations and coloring our interpretations of one another as social actors. It could not be otherwise, for experience provides us
with a guide to understand the events of each day and to frame responses
we deem appropriate for negotiating our way through our social contexts.

Every communicator who has spoken or written previously thus has a
reservoir of audience expectations that will be evoked as a matter of
course as soon as he or she speaks or publishes again. These expectations
cannot be ignored, and it would be foolish to do so. For example, if bell
hooks were invited to speak on our campus, her reputation as an author
and leading feminist intellectual would precede her presentation. We may
regard her as a spokesperson for equal rights for all Americans or as a pro-
tector of women's interests—outspoken in her criticism of a patriarchal
culture, sincere in her advocacy. Or we may regard her as overly zealous in
her pursuit of women's issues, misguided in her attacks on traditional gender roles, and prone to exaggeration. Ms. hooks will want to take these
views of her character into consideration, building on the positive aspects
and defusing the negative. She also can ignore items that are not audience
concerns in her case. Unlike some public figures, her private life is not
plastered all over the newspapers; she is not rumored to be connected
with private interests or partisan economic causes; she has not been impli-
cated in scandals; and she is not regarded as a lunatic. In short, she is not
a subject of gossip. Hence she does not have a tarnished reputation to be
defended before she can gain a serious hearing.

Factors of previous reputation stand as so many "facts," external arguments for accepting bell hooks as a woman of good character. They are not
themselves internal arguments or appeals unless and until they are in some
way incorporated into her speech and become an explicit factor in
rhetor-audience interaction. While a communicator's reputation may precede her, ethos as a means of persuasion is concerned with going beyond
the past. It is concerned with the interpretation of character formed
through the patterns of interaction that occur in the actual rhetorical event.

Ethos has two important features we should bear in mind. First, ethos
is **dynamic**. It is developed through the way we talk. It is not an attribute
but an interpretation based on the way a rhetor behaves in presenting an
appeal and the many reactions an audience has to those behaviors. Reactions change moment by moment as audiences receive with pleasure, uncertainty, amusement, fear, agreement, and so forth the specific reasoning
and exhortations that comprise the whole of a rhetorical transaction.[6] Only
by understanding this process of interactive engagement can we appreciate
the essential character of ethos as a social construct, as an interpretation
developed through give-and-take, as an event rather than an entity.

Second, ethos is a **caused response**. It is developed through rhetor
choices of inclusion and exclusion. How we appear to others depends on the
choices we make in presenting our message and ourselves. We can guide interpretations of our mental, emotional, and moral dispositions by the ways

we argue, including the language we select, the tone we take, and the non-verbal cues we present.[7] The moment-by-moment unfolding of the presentation brings the audience to one judgment after another about our character.

For these reasons, rhetoricians have largely endorsed Aristotle's belief that a positive assessment of a rhetor's character could well be the most potent of all the available means of persuasion. Aristotle put it well at the beginning of the *Rhetoric*:

> [There is persuasion] through character whenever the speech is spoken [i.e., its thought and content] in such a way as to make the speaker worthy of credence; for we believe fair-minded people to a greater extent and more quickly [than we do others] on all subjects in general and completely so in cases where there is not exact knowledge but room for doubt. And this should result from the speech, not from previous opinion that the speaker is a certain kind of person; for it is not the case, as some of the technical writers propose in their treatment of the art, that fair-mindedness [*epieikeia*] on the part of the speaker makes no contribution to persuasiveness; rather, character, is almost, so to speak, the controlling factor in persuasion.[8]

In sum, when we cause a positive impression of our character, we gain the great advantage of trust in the midst of conflicting interpretations of issues and evidence. In such cases, where there is no clearly superior argument or where we lack the background to judge which view is more likely, we tend to affirm the views of those whose character we hold in high esteem. So the question becomes: On what basis do we form a judgment that a rhetor is trustworthy? Knowing that, we might better understand both how to cause positive interpretations of character and how to detect when rhetors are behaving in a two-faced manner.

༄

Ethos and the Habits of Life

From antiquity to the present, audiences have confronted the recurring problem of deciding whom to believe. In some cases, the difficulty may be that we fear a speaker is lying or in some way attempting to deceive us. In many more cases, we may lack sufficient background to decide whether a rhetor is truly knowledgeable or merely glib. In still other instances, we must sort through conflicting advice without decisive evidence of fact or prevailing opinion with only our sense of each person's wisdom as a guide. These are determinations of ethos. What leads us to interpret a person's rhetorical appeals as an argument for good character? What counts as good character in matters settled through persuasive discourse?

Excellence and Habits

We can draw a bead on our target by remembering that rhetoric is a civic art we practice to create and maintain community. It is a communicative method for conducting our public business, a means for common people to have a say in decisions of policy that affect their lives. Though we may be egalitarians in permitting freedom of speech on these matters, when weighing points of view we most likely give our attention to those speakers and writers who show qualities of wisdom in analyzing practical affairs and recommending appropriate courses of action.

In antiquity such wisdom was a mark of **excellence** (*arête* in Greek, *virtu* in Latin). The Greeks, for example, were profoundly aware that living in the polis civilized them. They had to set aside the barbaric ways of tribal life and cultivate political skills to promote the well-being of the community. If they lived by the law of the wild, they'd end up killing one another. A citizen's growth in civic skills was regarded as evidence of enhanced excellence as a human. The Sophists regarded this relationship between the city and the citizen as reciprocal. As the life of the city improved, it elevated the level of each citizen's cultural awareness. As each citizen grew in civic virtue, the quality of city life elevated. Thus city and citizen reciprocally enhanced one another in an ever-ascending quality of life.[9] John Herman Randall provides a succinct summary of this process:

> Any function is well performed when it is performed in accordance with its own proper excellence or "virtue." Hence the good of man—human welfare—is the functioning of man's various powers under the guidance of intelligence, and in accordance with their own proper and respective excellence or "virtue." . . . Social organization, the polis, provides the means of training in these individual excellences, and it also furnishes the field in which they can operate: it provides the materials and conditions for training in, and for the exercise of, the good life. Ethics and politics are hence two aspects of the same "architectonic" science. The excellences or *arêtai* of the individual are formed in the polis, in society, and they can function only in the polis.[10]

Excellence was created through participation in the affairs of the city. It was not an attribute of a person but a judgment about the person conferred by other citizens on the basis of how well the individual performed public functions, such as mediating disputes or writing laws. Such virtuosity required the opportunity of public affairs to manifest itself in a way that citizens of the polis might affirm.[11]

Quite clearly, the Greeks had a special type of virtue in mind. It was unlike the Christian virtues of faith, hope, and charity, for example, which are best practiced beyond the glare of publicity. They had in mind **practical virtues** that would help in forming prudent public decisions. Practical virtues are still important for making sound practical choices. We recognize their value especially in matters that are emotionally involving and can lead to the volatile rhetoric that distorts good ideas into dogma. Someone observes, say, that waste from the local mill is seeping into the water table and polluting the water supply. This is a serious situation and requires a remedy. But before one can be found, extremists condemn the mill owner for lack of conscience and for exploiting the community. The community gets upset and clamors for the mill to be shut down and management to be tried on criminal charges. The next thing you know, the plant does close, 500 workers are without jobs, and no solution has been found for the pollution problem. In situations like this we need advice that avoids the deficiency of doing nothing and the excess of throwing out the baby with the bath water. Such advice is a form of wisdom called **practical wisdom (phronêsis)** by the Greeks. They referred to the rhetor who exhibited practical wisdom, especially the primary public virtue of **prudence**, as a **phronêmos**. We still seek rhetors who manifest *phronêsis* in their discourse; we interpret prudent deliberation as a sign of their sound character.

Aristotle provides us with a useful set of concepts for understanding how this interpretation is formed. We are called upon to make public judgments (**krisis**) about practical affairs. In public life more is at stake than our personal benefit, since the welfare of the community will be influenced by what we decide. Rhetoric is necessary for citizens to discharge their responsibility of *krisis*. Through thoughtful consideration of contingent affairs, we are able to develop informed public opinion about how we may best achieve the common good. Aristotle thought the purpose (*telos*) of human conduct was to achieve happiness (**eudaimonia**). The things that make one person happy will not necessarily satisfy another, and the outcomes that lead to *eudaimonia* are specific to the situation.

Practical reasoning in rhetoric involves making choices about the **preferable** and the **good** specific to our rhetorical situation that will lead to **public happiness**. There is no god's-eye view that offers a single account of what *eudaimonia* may be.[12] We locate this through deliberation tempered by the fortunes of our particular way of life. What may be good for Floridians is not necessarily so for Pennsylvanians. The good life cannot be achieved by a set of rules, as Aristotle points out in his *Nichomachean Ethics* (1140b1). Living well is not a scientific enterprise but "a true and reasoned state of capacity to act with respect to the things that are good or bad for a man" (1140b4–6).

We achieve *eudaimonia* from a variety of conditions, such as good health, respectful children, wealth, friends, love, and so forth, which may exist alone or in combination. Because the conditions are independent of one another, each is valuable in itself. They are said to be **incommensurable**, which means that we desire them for themselves and estimate their specific relevance and importance in light of changing circumstances. The point of deliberation is to arrive at *krisis* (public judgment) about how these conditions contribute to the communal definition of public happiness under specific circumstances. The person skilled in deliberation is successful in building enthymemes that link desired conditions to the course of action being advocated, such as: "This will make us happy because it will promote good health."

Aristotle thought that a person skilled in a particular activity possessed a habit (**hexis**) for appropriate conduct in that sphere. When, for example, NBA all-star center Shaquille O'Neal described himself as "the big Aristotle," he was alluding loosely to this principle. When asked what he meant, he explained that he had developed habits of excellence on the basketball court. Aristotle might have pointed out that he was more concerned with political and moral habits than athletic ones. In *Ethics* and *Poetics*, Aristotle indicates that persons with practical wisdom (*phronêsis*) possess a *hexis* to avoid extremes and counsel virtuous acts—just the sort of public virtues necessary for responsible rhetoric. This disposition consists of knowing rules of thumb for making appropriate ethical choices (*prepon*, remember, is not an absolute, but applies to the situational appropriateness of action) and acting prudently in practical affairs. Through experience the *phronê-mos* learns which of the constituents of happiness apply in different circumstances and how best to achieve *eudaimonia* through practical conduct. As we observe the public behavior of those with *phronêsis*, we see their habits of prudence revealed in the choices they make. From observing their habits, we draw inferences about their character, or ethos.

When we consider ethos as caused by the discourse, we look for how rhetors reveal their *hexis* by the interests they espouse, the values they endorse, and the actions they counsel.[13] These habits are evaluated by the audience in terms of their vision of the good life. The interaction between the rhetor's advice and the audience's understanding leads to an interpretation of the rhetor's character.

Consider, for example, the way Americans reflected on the *hexis* of Representative Gary Condit during the summer of 2001. In spring of that year, Chandra Levy, a twenty-four-year-old intern in the Federal Bureau of Prisons, was reported missing. She was last seen in Washington, D.C., on April 30. Levy's disappearance created a national stir when her family reported that she was having an affair with Representative Condit, a married man in his late 50s. Their disclosure immediately cast a cloud of suspicion over the congressman. Condit initially denied having a romantic relationship with Levy and reportedly did not volunteer to be interviewed by police. Eventually, the congressman did talk to police and in his third interview acknowledged an affair with Levy. The police source who revealed the information also said Condit was not a suspect in the disappearance.

The news media, on the other hand, were in a feeding frenzy over the story for the balance of that summer. While Condit professed his innocence and denied knowledge of Levy's whereabouts or circumstances leading to her disappearance, he also refused to face the press. This left the field open for media speculation about what had happened and about Condit's conduct. The cable networks, CNN and Fox, along with NBC and its cable affiliates CNBC and MSNBC, were consumed with talk-show discussions and news reports that focused on Condit, his possible role in Levy's disappearance, and his conduct since the time she had disappeared. Why had Condit

not reported her disappearance to the police? Why had he steadfastly denied having an intimate relationship with Levy? And why was he not forthcoming about his contacts with her just prior to her disappearance?

Most commentators and talk-show panelists had their hackles raised
by his refusal to answer questions about the case. They regarded Condit's
uncooperative attitude as a basis for questioning his character. For example, on CNN's *Larry King Live*, former federal prosecutor Barbara Olson, alluding to recent TV footage of Condit, remarked, "If somebody you knew
was missing and no one knew what happened, why would you always be
having this big grin on your face?" King added: "Come on. It doesn't look
good."[14] Their questioning of Condit's character was bolstered when California's senior senator, Dianne Feinstein, was quoted in *USA Today* as saying Condit lied to her and had irreparably lost his credibility as a
politician. Feinstein, who said she questioned Condit several weeks earlier
about his relationship with Levy, stated, "He said he did not have a romantic relationship with her. . . . He lied to me, and that's something I just
can't forgive." She offered the view that there is nothing "(Condit) can do
to regain his credibility."[15]

Finally, Condit decided to go public. On August 22, he appeared in an
exclusive television interview with ABC's Connie Chung. Millions of Americans tuned in, making this the most watched TV interview since Barbara
Walters interviewed Monica Lewinsky about her relationship with Bill
Clinton. Americans were expecting to get his side of the story, but Condit's
performance seemed oblivious to the nature of his rhetorical situation.

There were a number of influences any competent communicator
would have recognized: statements by the police and the parents of Chandra Levy about the affair; subsequent disclosures by other women about
intimate relationships with Condit; public knowledge that he had betrayed
the trust of his wife of 34 years and his children; and the seeming similarity of his conduct to Bill Clinton's behavior with Monica Lewinsky, also a
government intern, and the public's disapproval of such behavior. One
could almost script what Condit should have done to restore his public image as a responsible and sensitive individual.[16] He needed to admit that he
had an inappropriate relationship with Chandra Levy, to acknowledge that
he had caused great pain to his family and shame to himself. He needed to
explain that his failure to be forthcoming was not an attempt to protect
himself but an effort to spare his family further embarrassment. He
needed to frame his participation in the interview as motivated to help the
Levys and to share whatever he knew that might be helpful in finding
Chandra—the person who deserved our attention and concern.

Instead, he refused to answer questions about the nature of his relationship with Levy under the pretext that he was honoring a request of the
Levys and out of respect for his family, a claim the Levys later denied. He
portrayed himself as a happily married family man who had made mis-
takes, although none he was willing to discuss. He denied police stories

that he refused to be interviewed. He branded as liars the other women who claimed to have had intimate relations with him. His demeanor remained detached, and he indicated no remorse about his conduct or empathy for the Levys' pain. In a high stakes rhetorical situation, Condit did nothing to quell the concerns about his character harbored by his constituents, the press, his party, and the general public—which ultimately questioned his fitness to continue serving in Congress.

When our loved ones are in danger, we fear for their safety and beseech those with authority to act on their behalf (like the family of Chandra Levy). We rely on their integrity to remove a danger or right a wrong. We rely on the honesty of those with whom we work closely (like Diane Feinstein). We are angered at and find it difficult to maintain positive relations with those who betray our confidence. We examine public demeanor to assess character (like Barbara Olson). When words and deeds seem insensitive to a situation, we question that person's moral compass. When we examine Condit's habits against this backdrop, his practices seem to be evasive and uncooperative regarding the search for Chandra, insensitive to the Levys' pain over their daughter's disappearance, hypocritical and lacking integrity regarding his marriage vows, and cowardly when faced with a moral decision. By stonewalling in the Chung interview, Condit compounded his problems by adding to the perception that he was impeding the effort to find Chandra and, perhaps, was lying because he had something to hide. In each of these ways, Condit's actions supported an inference about his *hexis*, his habits of moral conduct that allowed us to gauge his character.

Attributes of Character

Audiences consider three types of habits when assessing the character of a rhetor exhibited in her discourse; each is relevant to the rhetorical construction of ethos. First we gauge a person's **mental habits**. We trust individuals who are intelligent. If we believe the person is well informed, has studied a question thoroughly, is clearheaded and reasonable in her beliefs, is able to provide reasons and evidence in response to objections, does not utter exaggerated or banal opinions, is her own person and not easily misled, or has a special expertise through training or experience, we are likely to have confidence in her advice. Conversely, if a person is a sloppy reasoner, slow-witted, uninformed, given to extreme claims, or is easily duped, our guard is raised to be cautious of her advice because it may not be reliable.

For example, most Americans regard former president Bill Clinton as very intelligent. The fact that he was a Rhodes Scholar contributes to this perception, but that is an external source of ethos. What are the traits of his rhetoric, the internal sources? First, he has a great capacity for retaining and using facts; he seems unusually well informed. Second, he is particularly adroit in his use of clear examples to relate program proposals to the probable consequences for the average citizen. Making difficult ideas clear, the primary virtue of well-chosen examples, suggests analytic skill—the habit of a thinking person. Third, Clinton is fast on his feet. He can turn a loaded question back on his interrogator with ease, charm, and wit. He can make a joke out of an absurd question that dismisses the question without attacking the person of the questioner. Clinton treats interviews as opportunities to relate the distant process of governance to the lives of average citizens. His habit of mind is apparent in the way he handles himself and encourages repeated interpretations of himself as intelligent.

By way of contrast, former vice-president Dan Quayle committed political suicide through repeated public statements that seemed inane. Such comments as the following were reported in the press, shared via e-mail, and made available to the general public on the Internet:

- "I was recently on a tour of Latin America, and the only regret I have was that I didn't study Latin harder in school so I could converse with those people."
- "What a waste it is to lose one's mind. Or not to have a mind is being very wasteful. How true that is."
- "The Holocaust was an obscene period in our nation's history. I mean in this century's history. But we all lived in this century. I didn't live in this century."
- "It isn't pollution that's harming the environment. It's impurities in our air and water that are doing it."
- "When I have been asked during these last weeks who caused the riots and the killing in L.A., my answer has been direct and simple: Who is to blame for the riots? The rioters are to blame. Who is to blame for the killings? The killers are to blame."[17]

After the laughter subsided, voters had to ask themselves about the thinking ability of a person who made such whopping errors of expression and exhibited such shallow understanding of topics he had chosen to address. Did such a person have the intelligence to lead the nation, not to mention the world? In the 1996 primaries, Republican voters indicated they thought not.

The second assessment pertinent to ethos is of a person's **moral habits**. We trust people who speak with integrity, who make virtuous decisions, and whose actions inspire confidence that they know what is right and have the courage of their convictions. We trust these people to be truthful with us and to offer advice that will not harm others or make us regret our support. In assessing moral habits, we are especially concerned with the virtues of public life. Such virtues include the following:

1. **Justice**: Is there concern that people have what belongs to them? What equity principle is used? Is it used consistently? Are the community's laws respected and followed? Or is there blindness to, tolerance of, or even advocacy of injustices where people take what rightfully belongs to others?

2. **Courage**: Is concern for the right or the noble or the just a higher priority than the convenient? Is it pursued in the face of peril? Is there a habit of doing what is right regardless of its popularity? Or is there cowardice, caving in under pressure, or backsliding from principles that are not popular?

3. **Temperance**: Is there self-restraint in conduct and advice? Is there moderation between deficiency and excess? Is there control of emotions and appetites? Or is there a tendency to self-indulgence in opinions and excesses in advice?

4. **Generosity**: Is there a spirit of giving to others what they need to succeed? Are benefits conferred on others? Is a selfless spirit revealed? Or is there a stingy, selfish habit of conduct?

5. **Magnanimity**: Is there a nobility of thought and outlook? Is there a forgiving spirit? Are insults and injuries overlooked and opportunities to confer benefits sought? Is there a tendency to avoid or rise above pettiness or meanness? Or is the person mean-spirited in thought and deed?

6. **Magnificence**: Is there a sense for the exalted and the grand? Is there a vision of what elevates the human spirit? Is there commitment to the highest quality of life? Are the majestic and stately aspects of humanity advocated? Or does the rhetor exhibit a lowly opinion of humanity and a shabby vision of what we are and what we might become?

7. **Prudence**: Is there sound judgment in practical matters that allows for sound advice on how to act in ways that will accord with public virtues and will avoid the vices of their opposites?[18]

These virtues should be exhibited by the manner in which the rhetor argues a cause. In other words, virtue is not demonstrated by arguing that we are morally upright. It is demonstrated by arguing in a morally responsible way. We infer the moral habits of rhetors from the causes they espouse and the reasons they offer to support their beliefs and conduct, not from explicitly egocentric appeals. Our judgment is based on our sense of the moral habits the rhetor reveals in his practical reasoning.

For example, at the 1980 Democratic convention, Senator Edward Kennedy was in an unusual rhetorical situation. He had challenged President Carter for the Democratic presidential nomination and had lost, in his opinion as well as that of his many supporters, on the technicality that restricted the votes of delegates at the Democratic convention to the results of the primaries on a winner-take-all basis. When asked who they would support if freed to vote their conscience at the time of the convention, a majority appeared to favor Kennedy over Carter, whose political fortunes were mired in his ill-fated attempt to free Americans held hostage by revolutionaries in Iran. Kennedy challenged the rules of the convention, seeking to free the delegates to vote their own conscience, but he lost. The party then allowed him to address the convention, under the pretext of speaking for certain planks in the party's platform. Kennedy used this occasion to defend political liberalism, the cause he saw at risk as a result of his defeat, as an option that was still a viable alternative to the more conservative practices of the Carter administration. He also wished to reassert his position as a leading figure (even the preeminent one) among American liberals. At one point he made these remarks:

> The commitment I seek is not to outworn views but to old values that will never wear out. Programs may sometimes become obsolete, but the ideal of fairness always endures. Circumstances may change, but the work of compassion must continue. It is surely correct that we cannot solve problems by throwing money at them, but it is also correct that we dare not throw national problems onto a scrap heap of inattention and indifference.[19]

Kennedy does not claim that he is a morally virtuous man, but his pleading reveals his values and encourages us to see him as such. Moreover, notice the variety and rapidity with which we are taken through his moral register, as each sentence reveals a different ethical disposition. First we have an appeal resting on magnificence: "old values that will never wear out." Next we are urged to act with justice: "the ideal of fairness always endures." Then our generosity is enjoined: "the work of compassion must continue." Finally, temperance is urged: avoid the moral deficiency of "a scrap heap of inattention and indifference." For an audience ready to hear his appeals, the way these ideas unfold provide strong encouragement to interpret Kennedy as a man of good character and to place trust in what he said.

Finally, we gauge character by a person's **emotional habits**, especially as they reveal a disposition of good or ill will toward us as an audience. People show goodwill by their concern for our best interests. Do they share our fear of impending dangers? Are they joyful at our successes? Do they show anger toward those who insult or harm us? We further test the sincerity of their feelings in terms of the personal stakes they might have in the outcomes of their own advice. We know people are well disposed if they support our best interests, even when their advice is not necessarily in their own best interests. On the other hand, we distrust speakers or writers who appear not to offer the best advice, who manage information to their own advantage, or who use suspect reasoning to advance their propositions.

Dissimulation or lying is difficult to detect, of course. It would be impossible, and unjust, to dismiss every partisan pleader as ill-disposed. Partisanship cannot be avoided in rhetorical situations because it is a part of life. Humans have beliefs, isms, and causes they champion and try to get others to affirm and join. The problem is not with partisan rhetoric but with insincere rhetoric. Insincere appeals deliberately distort the facts and true feelings and in this way deceive audiences into beliefs and actions that benefit the rhetor in ways that are never disclosed.

Examples of deceptive rhetoric are everywhere; we find them in all walks of life. On television, ministers of the "electronic church" promise salvation and prosperity to those with the right kind of faith. The contributions of viewers who subscribe to this "give to get" message put millions of dollars in the coffers of these preachers and afford them secular power that many clergy find contrary to the teachings of Jesus.[20] In business, the Mansville Corporation separated its asbestos-producing division from the rest of its divisions. That done, it filed for bankruptcy, even though earning a profit, in order to avoid paying the damage claims of workers who contracted asbestosis from Mansville products. In advertising, the Phillip Morris Company engages in image construction by associating itself with programs of civic responsibility, while making substantial profits from its sales of hazardous tobacco products. This type of deception may be difficult to detect, but once perceived it earns our contempt.

Interpreting Ethos

Our assessments of mental, moral, and emotional habits are not infallible; misjudgments of character may occur in any given case. Remembering that the central issue that rhetoric addresses is what transpires during the speaking-listening or writing-reading transaction, we have focused on the ethos of the rhetor as an interpretation rather than as an existential attribute. We can draw *three conclusions* about how ethos as an interpretation is formed in rhetoric.

First, ethos grows from arguments and exhortations that are relevant to the subject. Except in rare cases when an individual speaks about himself, as when President Clinton spoke about his relationship with Monica Lewinsky, ethos is not established through direct appeal. Ethos is established by inference. We get a reputation for good reasoning and prudent judgment by demonstrating the appropriate mental, moral, and emotional habits in the types of appeals we make.

Second, ethos is the product of the interaction between our disposition to respond, as we reveal it in our speaking and writing, and the special needs of our audience. Audiences evaluate habits in terms of their own views of the good life. That is why it is important to address topics from our audience's point of view. Our rhetoric directs audience members to see us in a particular way, but at the same time they bring their own agenda of concerns to bear in forming their responses. If we become an authority for our audience, it is because our mutual interaction has led to a pattern of interpretation appropriate in the given case.

Finally, a rhetorical analysis of ethos avoids trait ascriptions as qualities that communicators actually possess. A rhetorical analysis focuses on ethos as a judgment that is caused by the speech itself. If we regularly meet our audience's needs by being informed, interesting, succinct, and focused on its concerns, we will encourage members to perceive us as someone whose views should be taken seriously. Their impression of us is an interpretation, a social construct, not an entity. Ethos is eventful in this respect, as is all rhetoric, occurring in the context of a response to a rhetorical demand. It is time-bound, confined to the configuration of speaker, speech, and audience in a given case. Each new situation calls anew for each rhetor to re-establish ethos through discourse.

૭

Ethos and Ethical Appeal

At the beginning of this chapter we noted that the experience of authority is problematic because authority figures can lead us to grow in knowledge and self-reliance, or they can dominate us and keep us subject to their wills. No less can be said about communicators who are accorded ethos. Their authority over our judgment can lead us toward wise decisions, but following any leader on the basis of that person's apparent habits can lead us into errors as well.

Determining whether a person is appealing in morally correct ways is never easy. Quite apart from the ethics of a person's views, there is always the question of whether the persuading agent is treating the audience with moral integrity. Consequently, we need to distinguish between **ethos** and **ethical appeals**. Questions of *ethos* focus on *the perceptions of the speaker caused by his rhetoric*. Questions of *ethical appeals* focus on *the issues raised (or suppressed) and the quality of arguments addressed to them*. We need a concept of ethical appeal, quite apart from ethos, as a guide for testing the moral quality of rhetorical arguments.

Some philosophers have objected to all rhetorical practices as unethical because rhetoric seeks endorsement of a partisan opinion rather than the truth. But that objection is specious because it reduces all matters to issues of true and false. The vast majority of human decisions are ones in which there are no true or false answers, only better and worse. The fascinating aspect of the human world is that we have choices. This is the very ground of our freedom, our morality, and our humanity. Choice always reflects values, beliefs, opinions, desires, and interests; it is inherently partisan activity. Objecting to rhetoric because persuaders seek endorsement of opinions amounts to objecting to the very condition of human existence. This complaint is difficult to sustain because it ignores two important elements: human reality is a social construction, and we constitute it with rhetorical discourse.

Partisanship is not the culprit so much as are the tactics to which partisans sometimes resort. In the give-and-take of deliberations, the partisan appeals of advocates should balance one another. Where matters are presented on their merits, advocates may be expected to emphasize what they find attractive on their side of the issue. But the question is whether these presentations are truthful and sincere or whether they are attempted seductions.

There is no easy way to ensure that our evaluations of moral character are correct, but we can follow some general guidelines that help in evaluating the ethics of a rhetorical appeal. As an overarching guideline, we may adapt Johnstone's rule of **bilateral argument** (discussed in chapter 4) to rhetoric: *A rhetor may use no device of persuasion that he could not in principle permit others to use on him.*[21] This rule judges any practice that distorts our choices as unethical, since it undermines our freedom and our humanity.

The bilaterality principle gives us the basic "sauce for the goose, sauce for the gander" rule in rhetorical communication. Rhetoric, considered as an art concerned with all the means of persuasion, can be practiced by any person. Presumably, people trained in rhetorical principles will be more skillful in crafting persuasive appeals than those who are not. It is a power (Aristotle's *dynamis*[22]) denied to no one. Further, the power of crafting persuasive appeals can be enhanced by anyone who undertakes training in rhetorical practice. Each of us can acquire skills in the use of persuasive appeals, but there are ethical limits on how we use those skills. We must always remember that others can use the same skills to persuade us.

We must be mindful of this last fact so that those who violate the rule of bilaterality do not trick us. The bilateral rule is especially helpful because it gives us a way to think about what is being said and the manner in which it is presented. Though a checklist of forbidden practices, such as "Don't lie," might be comforting, the problem would be to spot such instances when they occur. There is no easy way to do that. But we can examine how a rhetor treats an audience and ask whether we could generalize that treatment so that it would be acceptable in principle for everyone to persuade in that fashion.

For instance, when we seek agreement, the bilateral principle requires that we not hide or misrepresent our thinking. We allow our audience access to our beliefs and reasons so that they may form an accurate assessment of their value. Helpful guidelines for making this assessment are provided in a study by philosopher George Yoos concerning ethical appeals.[23] Yoos suggests four rules for audiences to use as tests.[24]

1. **A factor**: "The quality displaying the speaker as seeking mutual agreement with his audience." This factor requires that the reasons we give to our audience are our real reasons for what we believe. If we seek agreement, it is unethical to tell the audience only what it wants to believe. When we pander to our audience, we deny its members the chance to reach agreement because we only pretend to share common ground. The A factor also prohibits us from having a hidden agenda, whereby we try to confuse our audience about our true goals. As listeners and readers, we should be suspicious if there are inconsistencies in the rhetor's commitments to the reasons offered for mutual agreement.

2. **R factor**: "The quality displaying the speaker as recognizing the rational autonomy of his audience." Every rhetor who seeks agreement has an ethical responsibility to honor his audience's right to decide. This means that she may not brush aside the audience's criteria for judging. She shouldn't substitute her own criteria without justification. The audience has a right to set its own standards for decision. If she disagrees, she must provide arguments that demonstrate why her standards are better. As listeners, we should be suspicious if the rhetor abuses the common or shared sense of the audience.

3. **E factor**: "The quality displaying the speaker as recognizing the equality of the listener with himself." The only time that a rhetor may speak or write as one superior to his audience is when there is mutual acceptance of his authority by the audience. It is unethical to act like an authority (to make claims that we expect others to accept simply because we made them) unless the audience recognizes his expertise or the rhetor demonstrates it. As audience members, we should be on our guard when someone tries to gain our acceptance of his views on the basis of his word without giving us good reasons to accept him as specially qualified with superior knowledge. We can usually spot such rhetors because typically they address their audience as inferior to them.

4. **V factor**: "The quality displaying the speaker as recognizing that the ends of the audience have an intrinsic value for him." Speakers and writers show that they respect the audience's ends by only committing themselves to the ends they share and want to help become realities. At the same time, they are explicit in presenting their disagreements with the ends they don't share and in accepting the burden of proof for why those ends are inappropriate. Rhetors do not show respect when they pander to their audiences by giving them what they want. As audience members, we must be cautious of rhetors who disapprove of or dismiss audience goals without offering reasons for not taking them into account. Equally, we must keep an eye on those who seek goals that seem contrary to the audience's but offer no rationale for their choices.

When we seek agreement, bilaterality emphasizes open communication. However, there are a great many rhetorical situations in which communicators are likely to conceal some aspects of their views while emphasizing others. These are situations of advocacy, where persuasion and victory are the goals. Typically, we find these where interests are at stake, as in business, politics, law, and even interpersonal relations. Cultural norms regulate what are permissible omissions. For instance, before a big game, the coach may lament about his team's injuries and what a bad week it has had in practice. The other team will be praised as if it were an all-star squad. Few who follow sports take any of this seriously. It's permissible for the coach to bluff in this way. It is not, however, permissible for him to falsify records to play an ineligible student. Similarly, when we deal with salespersons, politicians, and star-struck lovers, we expect the things they say to be extravagant. We don't expect them deliberately to misrepresent the fact that they're partisan advocates.

Thus, in advocacy there is a permissible level of deception that is guided by the bilaterality principle. It requires our honesty about being artisans and our adherence to the norms that are conventions for our context.[25] To illustrate how we may use the bilateral rule as a test for ethical appeals, consider the advocacy of Eva Peron as portrayed in the play *Evita*. In its noted song "Don't Cry for Me, Argentina," Eva appeals to the people of Buenos Aires. The song is reintroduced at several places and adapted to the issues of the moment. But always the manner of her appeal is the same. After Juan Peron is inaugurated as president, she appears before the crowd. Her appeal, in part, is as follows:

[1]   And as for fortune, and as for fame
       I never invited them in
       Though it seemed to the world they were all I desired

[2]   They are illusions,
       They are not the solutions they promised to be
       The answer was here all the time
       I love you and hope you love me

[3]   Don't cry for me Argentina.
       (Eva breaks down; the CROWD takes up her tune)

[4]   Don't cry for me Argentina
       The truth is I never left you
       All through my wild days
       My mad existence
       I kept my promise
       Don't keep your distance
       Have I said too much? There's nothing more I can think
       of to say to you
       But all you have to do is look at me to know that
       every word is true.[26]

1. Eva, the poor backwater girl, now a woman of power and wealth, tells the poor workers of Buenos Aires to ignore the facts that she is now rich and famous. Can we generalize the appeal to ignore conflicts between our words and deeds?

2. Common people who are suffering the slings and arrows of an unstable economy are advised that financial well-being is an illusion, that the true answer to their problems is love. Can we generalize the appeal that denies the legitimacy of the audience's goals, which shifts attention from a problem by offering a laudable but irrelevant goal as an answer?

3. Eva says, "Don't cry for me, Argentina" and then cries herself. Can we generalize a practice that invites affirmation through sympathy rather than critical appraisal?

4. Eva concludes her appeal by asserting that we will know she is telling the truth just by looking at her. Can we generalize a practice that emphasizes presence and appearance as warrants for belief?

When we examine the appeals of a rhetor, just as when we examine these lines from the song, the bilaterality principle helps us to reflect critically on what we are hearing and reading. While it doesn't identify specific practices that should cause concern, it does help us to determine for ourselves whether we should be concerned. When assessing the ethos of communicators, the bilaterality principle can alert us to practices that are symptoms of seduction rather than of intellectual, moral, and emotional virtues and thereby help us to make better choices about the world we live in.

ॐ
Summary

The advances in knowledge and in technologies that put knowledge into practice have radically transformed contemporary societies. We are entwined in a complex network of production and services essential to our survival. Most of us have little firsthand knowledge of the whys and wherefores that are the pulse of the new millennium. We rely on others to possess this knowledge and on our good judgment to determine whose advice to believe. Aristotle's claim that our impressions of a person's character may be the most important factor influencing belief is even truer today than in Greek antiquity. We seek individuals with superior knowledge or ability and frequently give them authority in our lives.

In this chapter we have discussed the nature of this authority in rhetoric—ethos—and how it is established. Our emphasis has been on the dynamic interaction between a communicator and an audience. Through their transactions within a rhetorical event, the audience forms a judgment—a social construct—that this speaker or writer is trustworthy. Ethos is not an inherent quality a person possesses. It is an interpretation of that person's character based on how the person behaves in light of a specific audience's readiness to respond. Though many factors may influence the trust we place in a person, the strictly rhetorical factors are those internal to the message itself: the manifested intellectual, moral, and emotional qualities that we find admirable. Thus ethos is a dynamic attribution that is caused by the rhetorical choices a person makes.

By the same token, though we recognize that rhetor choices may cause a favorable impression, it is not necessarily the case that these appeals are themselves ethical. That judgment depends on the measure of respect extended to the integrity of the people addressed. We test this respect through the bilateral rule, which requires that no mode or means of persuasion be used on others that in principle we would not permit others to use on us. In a world where we seek authorities and invest them with powers that may dominate our lives, the force of ethos is crucial to shaping our private and public realities. Bilaterality as a test of ethos helps to safeguard the quality of our choices about whom to believe and what visions to pursue.

❧ 9 ❧

The Passions

Thus far we have focused on rhetoric as a form of thinking that occurs in communication dealing with contingent affairs. We have seen how essential it is to arrive at shared judgments as a basis for inducing and coordinating social action, and we have seen how such judgments are typically about matters of opinion. We require coordination of social action when there are differences of opinion and certainty about the best course of action is unlikely—at least not before we must act. The constant question in assessing rhetorical appeals—appeals that attempt to persuade us to a belief or action—is whether they lead us to a sound opinion, which is, after all, the *telos* of civic rhetoric. This is not an easy assessment to make, particularly when we are passionate about our interests. At those moments we experience strong emotions and sometimes, in retrospect, we fear they may have distorted our judgment. On the other hand, emotions are not entirely extraneous to arriving at sound public judgment about matters in which we have a stake. A central problem for rhetorical theory, therefore, is sorting out the role emotions play in responsible discourse. Moreover, we cannot avoid emotions influencing our judgments or our emotions being influenced by the language in which arguments are couched.

As evidence in support of the claim that our emotions inevitably enter into public judgment, consider the controversy surrounding stem cell research. In the summer of 2001 President Bush indicated he would decide whether he would permit federal support for stem cell research. Prior to his decision, he consulted with scientists, physicians, various leaders of world health organizations, and the Pope. On August 9 he announced he would allow using federal taxpayer money to support stem cell research. In the weeks that followed a flurry of articles and op-ed pieces appeared in the various news media concerning the decision, and the engaged public received a lesson in the microbiology of stem cell research.

The public's engagement on this issue grew from two primary, and often conflicting, interests. Stem cells taken from embryos are uncoded or blank. This permits scientists to develop cell strands capable of being coded in ways that make them useful for therapeutic purposes. The hope of medical science is that stem cell research will produce cures for diseases such as Alzheimer's, Parkinson's and diabetes—and possibly foster cell regeneration to reverse spinal cord trauma. For individuals who are victims of these afflictions and their loved ones, this line of research offers a beacon of hope. On the other hand, stem cell research requires that the embryo be destroyed, which raises the question of whether it involves destroying human life and the difficult moral and scientific question of when human life begins. Those on both sides of this question have reasoned analyses to support their positions. The choices between obstructing possible cures for debilitating and deadly diseases and destroying what some regard as life evoke strong feelings that influence the judgments we reach. Thus the debate often employed language such as that used by citizens who wrote to the *New York Times* in response to President Bush's decision and an op-ed piece he had published in the *Times* on August 12, 2001:[1]

> To the Editor:
> President Bush (Op-Ed, Aug. 12) declares that "life, including early life, is biologically human, genetically distinct and valuable." If this is the case, could he kindly explain his enthusiastic support for the death penalty? Certain forms of human life, it seems, are less "valuable" than others.
> STEVE GOLD
> Monmouth Junction, N.J., Aug. 12, 2001
>
> To the Editor:
> I am disappointed that President Bush broke his campaign pledge by announcing that he would allow federal financing to be used to experiment on murdered human embryos (Op-Ed, Aug. 12). Mr. Bush is rewarding those who have already killed by granting cash to their continued efforts. He is giving a monetary reward to them, while speaking noble words about being pro-life. He had the chance to say no and he did not. He had asserted that he would do what is right rather than follow public opinion polls. Instead, he has shown his willingness to bow to political pressure, and he caved in. If anything can be learned from the cruel atrocities committed against human beings in the last century and a half, it is the lesson that the utilitarian devaluation of one group of human beings for the alleged benefit of others is a price we simply cannot afford to pay.
> MARY T. CONVERSE
> Clinton, N.Y., Aug. 12, 2001
> The writer is chairwoman, Oneida County Right to Life Committee.

To the Editor:
Re "William Jefferson Bush" (editorial, Aug. 12), concerning President Bush's speech about stem cell research:
You were correct to point out how fascinated Bill Clinton and George W. Bush are with triangulation and the extremely fine balancing of differences between political constituencies. Theirs is nothing if not a very clever generation. But will it ever produce a president who is sometimes a little more than just clever? Trying to please everyone all the time is not leadership. This hand-wringing and chopping the baby up into a thousand pieces is just a way to avoid making decisions. It may be a clever generation, but it sure doesn't like pain. Our generation's presidents so far have been, in the old-fashioned words of our parents, small men.
JAMES DAY
Berkeley, Calif., Aug. 12, 2001

These writers find Bush's policy statement declaring all life valuable hypocritical in light of his support of the death penalty, in supporting research based on "murdered embryos," and in resembling former president Clinton in balancing one constituency's concerns against another's for political gain. They reflect the individual writers' fear, disappointment, and anger at the president's policy. These emotional states are involved to some degree in the writers' encouragement to share a public judgment. These are assertions likely to arouse reader emotions.

The fact that a rhetor can whip an audience into an emotional frenzy has been a reason for some to condemn rhetoric. How can communication that leads people to make emotion-based decisions be to their advantage? Reason, not emotion, should be our guide. This celebration of reason over the passions is not just the stuff from which intellectuals make assertions about how to tell fair arguments from foul. In a commonsense way, most people adopt this as a stated view in everyday life. We tend to express distrust of our emotions or, at the very least, imply that we value reason over emotion, such as when we explain untoward behavior as the result of being emotionally overwrought.

The celebration of reason over the passions has a history that goes back at least to Plato. In more modern times it has been advanced by the rationalism of Descartes and the objectivism of science. In essence, the passions are distrusted as the base impulses, desires, or feelings of the flesh. Without the control of reason, located in the mind, we fear that these base impulses will lead us into acts that are primitive or based on deception. This separation of reason and the passions is frequently referred to as a **mind-body dualism**. Contemporary philosophy questions this split. Present views consider humans to be more than aggregates of anatomic parts. In the holistic view of humans, what we call "reason" and what we call "emotion" are integrated.

The philosophers are not alone in finding evidence for the holistic character of human action. Psychologists, for example, have devoted considerable study to emotions, attempting to locate them, define them, and use them to construct a basic framework from which a scientific theory of human behavior would emerge. However, findings vary greatly about what an emotion is or what physiological responses distinguish one emotion from another. In other words, the findings illustrate that even though we can name feelings and describe them, this does not mean that they are discrete entities within us. Emotions aren't things; they are something else—patterns of response. These patterns are conditioned by a number of factors, but chief among them are our thoughts, which are connected to language. As behaviorist John Watson observed many years ago, "'Thinking' is largely 'subvocal talking.'"[2]

Once we abandon the split between mind and body, the argument that rhetoric is evil because it inflames the emotions seems unconvincing. All thinking involves language; all thinking engages emotional responses. Emotions aren't evil or untrustworthy. They are a necessary part of the holistic pattern by which we process and respond to the experiences of life. The issue is not whether our emotions are engaged but whether *appropriate* emotions are engaged so that we make wise decisions. In this chapter we will be concerned with how rhetoric addresses the whole person and how to test the emotional responses it elicits. Although we will list some of the more common emotions that are part of rhetorical situations, we will not focus on describing these emotions. Since emotions are products of language, they tend to be unique. The important issue for rhetorical theory is how emotions are brought about through the use of language.

Pathos as a Pattern of Response

As we saw earlier, rhetoricians since Aristotle have contended that there are three major sources of influence on audience judgment: the argument of the case itself, logos; the perception of the rhetor's character, ethos; and the audience's emotional engagement, pathos. To hear or read something and judge it requires that we think simultaneously about what is being expressed, who is saying it, and our feelings on the matter. When we think communicatively, each of these factors must be taken into account, as they must when we try to assess and understand what occurred when A communicated for a purpose with B.

The Aristotelian trilogy of logos, ethos, and pathos established a very important point: An understanding of rhetorical effects requires an understanding of the bases for human responses in general. Aristotle had developed a cognitive framework for discussing this subject. Contemporary thinkers have revived this cognitive perspective on emotions and provide us with a sensible approach to explain the integration of the three modes of persuasion as they address the whole person.[3] This pattern is called practical reasoning.

Practical matters are not solved entirely on their intellectual merits. Though some people may consider whether the propositions advanced are supported by fact and related in a logically valid fashion, such tight inspection is rare. First, a rhetorical argument comes in bits and pieces, requiring us to fill in the blank spaces with common knowledge, ideological commitments, values and goals, and the like. Second, our preferences, needs, desires, and values enter into our evaluation in important ways.

For example, we go to a party and find ourselves feeling "turned on" by some people, "turned off" by others. People who "turn us on" are fun, they're interesting, and they make us feel good about ourselves. People who "turn us off" are the opposite. For some of us, an exciting personality may be attractive; for others, a person of gentle sensitivity may fit the bill. Our responses are subjective and depend on our needs in the contexts in which we find ourselves rather than on objective discriminators of what produces a "good connection."

Practical decisions are much the same. They depend on the needs, goals, ideology, and desires of individuals in the contexts in which decisions are made. These personal "attributes" express themselves in terms of our physical needs (food, shelter, sexual release), our psychological needs (love, security, self-esteem), and our values. For example, when young couples fall in love, they face a series of practical decisions: Do we live together? Do we marry? Do we live together and if things work out then marry? Do we value the ceremony? If we want to marry, will it be a civil ceremony or a religious one? If a religious one, whose religion? Are we doing this for us or for our parents? All of these are practical decisions, decisions of action, and they are based on values. If your values were different, your outlook would change, and so might your practical choices.

As our desires, needs, values, and appetites are satisfied or frustrated, our disposition to respond is influenced. We seek to remove obstacles, avoid pain, acquire what brings pleasure, act in ways that will make us happy, and stop doing things that make us miserable. All of these can be expressed in a brief but handy form called a **practical syllogism**. This form contains a premise about **the agent**, a premise about **the conditions**, and a conclusion that results in **action**. "I'm the type of person who avoids people who make me envious. Professor Smart's lavish praise of Rosa's work has me drooling with envy. I don't want to have pizza with her this evening."

From the perspective of developing rhetorical appeals, it is important that the appeal establish a "proper" relationship between the audience and the point of discussion. If it is to the rhetor's advantage that the audience dislike an issue, it must be presented in a way that allows the audience to experience it as repelling. The converse is true when we hope the points receive an affirmative response. With these thoughts in mind, let us consider how the emotions are engaged in rhetoric.

ॐ
Pathos and Persuasive Reasoning

Common Misconceptions

A moment ago we noted that emotions are not things, and we need to return to that point now to get a better idea of what emotions are. There is a common way of talking that suggests a "commodities" view toward emotions, as if each human had storage bins and accountant's ledgers to inventory what's in stock. We speak of storing up resentment or having pent-up anger. We use metaphors like "our inner feelings," again suggesting an entity inside us. But if emotions were things and could be stored and released, why can't the millions of unhappy souls who lament that they have so much love just waiting to be shared make themselves ecstatic by releasing their love? The fact is that these metaphors mislead, portraying our emotions as something quite apart from our nature and our bodies as mere vessels for their storage. Emotions aren't "things" one has but actions of a particular sort, as we soon shall see.

Conversely, another common problem with the way we talk about emotions is to view ourselves as passive receivers of the emotional tides of life. Philosopher Robert Solomon maintains that our talking and thinking are riddled with this myth:

> We "fall in" love, much as one might fall into a tiger trap or a swamp. We find ourselves "paralyzed" with fear, as if we had been inoculated with a powerful drug. We are "plagued" with remorse, as if by flies or mosquitoes. We are "struck" by jealousy, as if by a Buick; "felled by shame" as a tree by an ax; "distracted" by grief, as if by a trombone in the kitchen; "haunted" by guilt, as if by a ghost; and "driven" by anger as if pushed by a prod.[4]

These expressions place emotions outside the self, which suggest the individual is a home of reason fighting off alien forces from outside. This myth denies us a sense of integrity with regard to our deepest feelings and commitments about life.

In place of these perspectives, rhetoric generally holds an **active** view of emotions and of the audiences who experience them. Indeed, by embracing the view that audiences are able to form sound judgments, rhetoric separates itself from other persuasive forms (like propaganda) that treat their receivers as malleable clumps to be molded or whipped into a particular behavioral state.

Emotions Reflect Judgments

Rather than viewing emotions as things or as passively received states, a rhetorical perspective views them as interpretations or judgments. Emotions obviously involve feelings such as helplessness, impotence, honor, power, euphoria, and the like. But when we experience an emotion, our feelings are not general; they are about something or someone. We don't feel love in general. We love Dad; we love Kirsten; we love our dear friends who have shared so many rich experiences with us. Because emotions are feelings about some object, they represent judgments: The proposal to remove speed bumps from my street is risky; Timothy McVeigh's bombing of the Oklahoma City Federal Office Building was cowardly; studying rhetoric is pleasurable; justice was served when Slobodan Milosovic was delivered to the Hague on charges of war crimes.

The concept of the practical syllogism helps us clarify the type of judgment emotion involves. Suppose a developer proposes to build a shopping mall on a tract of land that has poor drainage. The geologists tell us that the runoff from rain and melting snow won't be absorbed by the ground, so a retaining wall will have to be built to keep the water from cascading down onto the school at the bottom of the hill. One form of practical syllogism leads us to decide objectively that this development is not a sound idea. "If we cover the ground with pavement, there has to be suitable drainage for the water runoff. The Jones farm site does not have suitable drainage. We ought not to build the mall there." But the same set of facts could be construed in a different way: "I'm the type of person who believes children should not be endangered. This mall will endanger our children. I'm angered by this proposal." This syllogism implies a rejection of the proposed mall, but the rejection is couched in a subjective judgment about the proposal. The practical syllogism formed **puts the object in relationship to the self**, and the resulting judgment involves the self. Though not all judgments involve emotions, all emotions are expressions of judgments. Their particular character is that they are **self-involving judgments**.[5]

When we say that an emotion is the expression of a judgment, several important features are implied. For one thing, all judgments are **normative** in character. This means that we require criteria to make them. For example, if a friend tells us, "The steak at Louie's is good," we have a judgment. "But what do you mean by 'good'?" we ask. "I'm talking substantial steak—fourteen to sixteen ounces and at least an inch thick. Lean on the outside, marbled in the center. So tender you barely need a knife. They have that real charcoal-grilled flavor, and they're cooked just right—seared on the outside and red and juicy in the middle. Yum!" Then again, if your friend is partial to Middle Eastern cooking, you might be told, "These steaks really assault your taste buds. They are sliced thin and cooked to well done, embedded with pepper and covered with the wildest sauce of spices and sautéed vegetables. Yum!"

These judgments, like all judgments, reflect criteria. Sometimes, as in the case of what constitutes "good food," the criteria may be cultural and widespread. But not all judgments require intersubjective agreement, especially ones involving emotions. The whole of humanity may speak as one in telling you that you should not feel anxious or depressed or angry, but that does not alter the fact that you may actually experience those emotions despite assurances to the contrary.

Where emotions are involved, the judgments about subject-object relationship are based on criteria related to self-esteem. These criteria involve our images of what is and what we think should be—the present and a projected future. Thus we consider the interaction between what event is transpiring, our self-image, the impact of present events on our self-image, and the implied projection of that relationship into the future. Anxiety may not be a concern now but it can exist as a fear that the future will be undesirable in some way if events continue as we project them. Love is not a judgment isolated to the present but projects itself to the imagined ecstasy of a future that keeps in touch with love's mystery.

A second feature implied by conceptualizing emotions as judgments is that each emotional experience is **unique**, as we mentioned earlier. We do not have a single emotion called "love." Every time we feel love, it is different, depending on whom we love, the circumstances of the experience, our own subjective state of development, and the relationship's special features. These features impregnate our emotions as they are experienced because they alter the self-object relationship in terms of its specific circumstances and our projected futures from these circumstances. Emotions, in other words, may have generic labels, but they are unique to the given case.

A third dimension that emerges from our claim that emotions are judgments is their **dependence on language**. Without language, we would have sensations and could make sign responses, as do other animals. Beaten by a stick, a dog senses danger at the sign of a raised stick and flees—a point not lost on savvy joggers who need to keep the neighborhood beasts at bay. Lacking language, there is no way for dogs to get beyond their primitive sign response. They can't ask or even wonder, "Say, pal, are you engaged in gratuitous thrusting or do you mean to use that thing on me?" But with humans it is different. Language makes it possible for us to create relationships, to create and express the meanings of our experiences, and to alter their meanings by altering the relationships expressed.

You can observe the arbitrary and personal nature of emotional expression by watching the differences in parental responses to the predictable behaviors of their youngsters at the local supersaver department store. To children, the supersaver is the toy department, plain and simple. Their instinct is to bolt for the toys. Not all parents share in this delight. Some find a child's mad dash an inconvenience at best, even a sign of incorrigible misbehavior, but other parents seem to have a more serene perspective on matters. They watch as if in a state of grace. They gush in harmonious exclamations with their tykes and ask questions that help their youngsters express their fantasies. Doubtless they have joined in the children's safari spirit that makes the toy department a source of adventure. Emotions accompany both reactions, but the experiences are different: one parent aggravated at the inconvenience, the other enraptured by a child's sense of adventure. The differences stem from the symbolic configuration placed on the experience, altering its meaning and the self-involved judgment encouraged.

Finally, emotions are experienced in **eventful** ways. They occur in time, they are felt with respect to a referent, they are unique to the configuration of elements in the given case, they are judgments given meaning in language, and they culminate in acts that express these judgments and may terminate the episode. They are, in short, interpretive evaluations about some state that exists in terms of how we think things ought to be and the further actions to which these expectations lead. This is not to deny that we may experience the love of our mother throughout our lives as a process of care and affection affirming our worth. It is rather to assert that our consciousness of our mother's love or of any other emotion is tied to a given case, an episode of interaction, a configuration of circumstances, and in this sense is eventful.

The patterns of response we call "emotions" play an obvious and important role in communication. Since these patterns reflect judgments, emotions are not capricious but are tied to the active and ongoing self-involving interpretations we make of our experiences. Knowing that these judgments are normative, unique to their context, language-dependent, and eventful, we may understand more clearly how they are evoked and their propriety in the given case. Ideally, their role is to involve our selves in such ways as facilitate responsible action. If we return to the Aristotelian observation noted earlier regarding logos, ethos, and pathos as sources of persuasion, we may modernize Aristotle's expression as follows: *Rhetoric is the act of interpreting our experiences through symbols for the purpose of making sound practical choices.* In any communication, we are moved to such choices by interpretations of experience that are subject-involved (logos), source-involved (ethos), and self-involved (pathos).

Evoking Emotions

Our discussion of rhetoric has emphasized its design characteristics, or its dimension as an art of producing discourse intended to induce social action. Its search for persuasive appeals will take into account the complex of factors that define the given case as a unique rhetorical situation. In understanding how emotions are experienced in a rhetorical situation, we must be mindful of how the interpretive character of emotions interact.

Our discussion outlined three factors that seem to be a part of every emotion considered as a thought. First, we noted that the thought has a **referent**. This can be any object of experience: a thing, a person, an event, or another thought. Emotions are not free-floating; rather, they are thoughts with a referent. Second, an emotion is a self-involving judgment called a **feeling**. Feelings can be directed to oneself (as in the case of duty), toward another (such as we experience with envy), or toward a relationship (for instance, love). Again, feelings are not free-floating but directed. Third, the judgments we make in experiencing an emotion are toward the **future**. This means that emotions are experienced as **telic** (goal-oriented) states. The goal is an act appropriate to the self-involvement experienced. Thus, the experiencing of emotions includes thoughts about something that arouse feelings of self-involvement and lead to projections of appropriate actions that naturally follow.

You overhear someone gossiping about your friend. In general, loose talk is an annoyance, but this loose talk is about a friend. The thought makes a specific coupling of an act (gossip) with a referent (my friend). More than likely, you feel angry. Your friend has been slighted. This is unjust. Your thought is self-involving since you care about your friend and her welfare. In a state of anger, you act in ways that are appropriate. You interrupt the gossiper, telling the person to mind her own business.

The variables that will make these appeals effective will be the same as for all rhetorical appeals: speaker, speech, and audience, as they are related in the given case. The essentials for arousing emotions in persuasive appeals are arguments that engage audiences in terms of their experiences. *Pathos*, properly developed, does not refer to employing loaded language or wild-eyed harangues. It *refers to the self-evoking aspects of our total response to the arguments brought before us for our active consideration.* Pathos grows from the way in which the enthymemes of the discourse are developed.

Returning to our model of the practical syllogism, each argument developed needs to be evaluated in terms of how it will invite an audience to respond and whether the audience is ready to offer this response. For instance, feminist author Andrea Dworkin delivered a speech in October 1992 at a symposium entitled "Prostitution: From Academia to Activism," sponsored by the *Michigan Journal of Gender and Law* at the University of Michigan Law School. Her speech had as its central claim that you cannot understand prostitution in abstract terms. Its reality is that men reduce women to dirt. As part of her attempt to get academicians to see prostitution in concrete terms, she compares it to gang rape.

> Oh, you say, gang rape is completely different. An innocent woman is walking down the street and she is taken by surprise. Every woman is that same innocent woman. Every woman is taken by surprise. In a prostitute's life, she is taken by surprise over and over and over and over and over again. The gang rape is punctuated by a money exchange. That's all. That's the only difference. But money has a magical quality, doesn't it? You give a woman money and whatever it is that you did to her she wanted, she deserved. Now, we understand about male labor. We understand that men do things they do not like to do in order to earn a wage. When men do alienating labor in a factory we do not say that the money transforms the experience for them such that they loved it, had a good time, and in fact, aspired to nothing else. We look at the boredom, the dead-endedness; we say, surely the quality of a man's life should be better than that.[6]

She invites several responses from the audience: See the prostitute as a victim taken by surprise; see the exchange of money as punctuating prostitution's reality as gang rape—a difference of degree rather than kind; see money paid a prostitute in the same way as money paid to a male laborer alienated from his work; see the double standard we impose.

These responses are what she asks of her audience. However, the persuasive success of her appeal depends largely on how these responses are courted. Notice two features: the heavy stress on the woman as a nonvoluntary participant in her prostitution and the recognition that money can't change a demeaning experience. All of the responses invited are tied to the unalterable character of a demeaning experience. Because we place such high cultural value on human dignity, endorsement of demeaning acts is a morally unacceptable position. The role of human dignity in the reasoning process we are asked to share might be cast this way:

> I'm the type of person who feels shame when I act in ways that are blind to a person's human dignity.
> Unless I treat the prostitute as a human first, I strip her of her dignity in a shameful way.
> Therefore, I must rethink how I interpret her situation through the filter of money.

Dworkin's appeal associates human dignity with matters that are extremely important: recognizing prostitution as victimage, recognizing our gendered interpretation of receiving money for services, acknowledging the prostitute's humanity, and acknowledging our own culpability in perpetuating prostitution. These matters are highly self-involving. Consequently, joining or rejecting the plea for acknowledging the prostitute's human dignity is made to seem an affirmation or denial of matters that are crucial to our standing as morally responsible individuals. Such emotions as pity, anger, shame, fear, and hope come into play as relevant responses. If we wish to be morally responsible, the argument seems to say, we must engage in socially corrective action. Our emotion-engaging thoughts might be displayed this way:

> I'm the type of person whose self-respect depends on acting responsibly.
> Unless I oppose acts that degrade another human, I won't be acting responsibly.
> Therefore, I must oppose these acts of degradation.

For listeners already predisposed to her message, Dworkin's task is relatively straightforward. By highlighting thoughts they already accept, she encourages both reasoned assent and emotional reinforcement of this assent.

Whether Dworkin's listeners and subsequent readers are ready to give this response depends on several factors: Do they believe the analogy to gang rape was accurate? Are they able to subordinate their definition of solicitation to the depiction of prostitutes as caught by surprise? Do they believe that "money for services" necessarily carries a gendered interpretation? Do they think males who work on assembly lines are exploited? Do they view absence of intervention as a form of culpability? Those who disagree in these respects probably will resist the analysis she offers and thus experience the emotions invited by her appeal to a lesser extent or not at all.

When audiences are not positively predisposed, emotional support depends on first gaining acceptance of new ideas. Unless an audience can be brought to accept a claim, it cannot experience emotional rapport with the rhetor to act on the claim. The introduction of new thoughts, the placement of existing thoughts in new contexts, or the refutation and removal of thoughts are ways to change the emotional barometer of audiences. Persuaded to change their thinking, their emotional judgments are simultaneously altered.

Shortly after Dworkin's speech was published, Sallie Tisdale, who also identifies herself as a feminist, published a book, *Talk Dirty to Me*. In it she argues that we make much of sex and find it something we need to worry about because we don't see it for what it is. Included in her volume is a chapter on prostitution, which includes comments from interviews with prostitutes. We learn that COYOTE (Call Off Your Old Tired Ethics), the oldest prostitute's union in the United States, is the only group that attempts to collect accurate data on prostitution. Its data indicate that most prostitutes are not from backgrounds of poverty and that most choose to become prostitutes in their twenties and thirties. Most are white, contrary to police arrests that disproportionately target black and Latino women. We also learn that COYOTE thinks prostitution is more widespread, more underground, and includes a larger population of men than most people realize. Women who self-identify as prostitutes are seldom engaging in sex because they are down and out, contrary to the images portrayed by the media. Members of COYOTE, who refer to their profession as "sex work," do not regard prostitution as the problem but rather the legal system that passes laws designed to keep women powerless. COYOTE and the other organizations that represent prostitutes—ICPR (International Committee for Prostitutes Rights) and PONY (Prostitutes of New York)—along with the National Task Force on Prostitution are working to protect prostitutes by seeking decriminalization. Tisdale argues:

> Decriminalization puts the power of prostitution in the prostitutes' hands. All these labor organizations are concerned with and actively work against forced prostitution and any exploitation of young, poor, or addicted women and men. This particular liberation movement has several sectors of agreement and disagreement, but it sees itself as feminist at heart. It *must* be feminist, it seems to me, can't be anything but feminist, to support the right of women to control the use of their bodies. Work for prostitutes' rights is at one with work against poverty, lack of education, addiction, sexual inequality, and every other condition that limits the freedom of men and women both to choose for themselves.[7]

Tisdale's account brings a new set of thoughts onto the horizon of our consciousness. Like Dworkin, she believes the role of money is central to our understanding of prostitution. Unlike Dworkin, who locates the problem of male domination in the abuse of women, Tisdale invites us to see the problem of male domination perpetuated in manmade statutes that attempt to regulate women's use of their bodies by making prostitution a crime. Here, the individual's right to control her own body is at the heart of the issue. The issue of personal freedoms makes the Tisdale approval highly self-involving and rife with potential for strong emotional response. As in the case of Dworkin's appeal, anger, fear, shame and hope are likely responses, but they are associated with the opposite idea. If we want to support individual rights and remove exploitation, this argument seems to say, we must maximize our freedom to control our own bodies. The reasoning would go like this:

> I'm the type of person who requires confidence that our laws lead to just outcomes.
> The laws regulating prostitution do not lead to just outcomes.
> Therefore, I must support changing these laws.

The Dworkin and Tisdale examples illustrate how each thought brought before an audience has the potential to evoke an emotion. To succeed, it must intersect with the audience's experience and must be self-involving in some way.

᪣

Basic Emotions

So far our analysis of emotions has focused on them as cognitive responses. We have seen that a rhetorical view of emotions considers them to be self-involving judgments concerning our feelings about the objects of our experience. When we communicate, we constantly present others with ideas for their approval or rejection. These ideas are presented in appeals that provide reasons for assent or dissent and simultaneously engage receivers in interpretive acts in which they see the implications of these ideas or thoughts for themselves. Emotions in rhetoric are the products of these interpretations. We also considered how this cognitive model could be portrayed in the form of a practical syllogism. Emotional judgments are experiences of seeing oneself as the type of person who exhibits certain behavior when confronted by an object of a specific sort: "I'm the type of person who defends friends"; "I'm the type of person who seeks revenge when slighted"; "I'm the type of person who is embarrassed when I feel markedly inferior"; and so forth.

Each culture has typical response patterns specific to its members and their times. In Greek antiquity, Aristotle provided a list of 14 basic emotions (table 9.1) common to public life in the Athenian polis. Our culture experiences and expresses emotions particular to our place in time. Robert Solomon has assembled a dictionary of such emotions (table 9.2).[8] While these inventories are useful for initial understanding of the emotional possibilities we might attempt to explore, it is important to remember that emotions are argued responses specific to our culture and our times. They are not determined responses but interpretive responses. Thus for any analysis of a rhetorical situation, the basic emotions available are the ones that listeners and readers may provide by virtue of their acculturation.

Parents, teachers, playmates, and social networks offer us instruction about ourselves and about appropriate interpretations of our experiences. Mother teaches us to be courageous: "You have to go to school today, even though you dread your math exam"; "Be brave and don't cry when you get your shots." Father instructs us in duty: "Mow the lawn before you go swimming"; "Practice your instrument, then we'll watch TV." Many of our emotions (maybe all) are guided by such instruction, whereby we learn the rules for forming self-involving judgments about our experiences. At first we may learn these by rote, but eventually we are on our own to figure out which acts are loving, courageous, generous, and the like, in a given case.

Rhetorical engagements always bring our criteria for assessment to the surface. We bring values to bear throughout a rhetorical encounter according to the rules we have learned for their application to our experiences.

Table 9.1 Aristotle's List of Basic Emotions

Anger	Mildness
Love	Enmity (hatred)
Fear	Confidence
Shame	Shamelessness
Benevolence	Pity
Indignation	Envy
Emulation	Contempt

Table 9.2 Solomon's List of Basic Emotions

Angst, anguish, and anxiety	Frustration	Pride
Depression	Gratitude	Regret and remorse
Despair	Guilt	Respect
Dread	Hope	Sadness
Duty	Indifference	Self-respect
Embarrassment	Innocence	Vanity
Faith	Joy	Worship
Friendship		

Each of these standards is a thought with implications for our self-esteem. Audiences cannot offer responses other than the ones that are within their cultural experience. That is why the basic list of emotions is of less use than knowing the typical ways in which the given audience views the events to be considered, the values available to be tapped, the typical ways these values are used by them, and the ones best suited to the present circumstances. Considerations like these guide our judgments of attraction or repulsion. They are the available sources of emotion in the given case.

ॐ
Summary

From earliest times, emotions have been a source of suspicion about rhetoric. When people talk about matters they find important, they become personally involved, and they show it. However, Western societies have tended to value reason over emotion as the proper guide to sound conclusions. By extension, this bias has made us leery of the persuader skilled at inflaming our passions. We fear acting without deliberating a matter on its reasoned merits. Part of the negative associations people have for rhetorical communication stems from this fear. Persuaders are suspected of clouding our reason by playing on our emotions. Emotions that have no reasons behind them can be dangerous, leading to rash and even harmful deeds.

The point of this chapter has not been to dispel a cautious approach to emotional appeals. History contains too many examples of harm from actions guided by passions while lacking in common sense. Rather, we have been concerned with understanding the proper place of emotions in guiding our actions and how this understanding leads to a responsible rhetoric addressed to the whole person—a being that feels as well as thinks.

Emotions are patterns of response; they are specific, directed toward objects of our experience. Their directed character means that our emotions are subjective judgments that we express as feelings. We cannot help but form these judgments whenever the thoughts we entertain involve our selves in some way. We interpret such experiences in terms of what is, what we hope will, and how they relate to our self-esteem. The key to all of this, then, is the basis on which these judgments are formed. If they rest on good reasons—the logos of an appeal—our emotions are likely to be appropriate responses, essential for considered action. When a speaker or writer encourages our emotional responses without good reasons, we can be manipulated and need to exercise caution. A responsible rhetoric does not separate our thoughts from our feelings; it unites them by addressing the whole person in terms of that person's experiences and the judgments they support. Thus the question is not whether rhetoric engages our feelings—it cannot avoid doing so—but whether our feelings are appropriate in making wise decisions.

✎ 10 ✐

Narrative

On the morning of September 11, 2001, Americans were plunged into a state of shock, fear, sadness, anger, and uncertainty. Television coverage repeatedly showed Boeing 757 and 767 commercial airliners slamming into the twin towers of the World Trade Center in New York and detonating. The 1.2 kilotons of fuel carried by each plane created an explosion equal to one-tenth the nuclear bomb dropped on Hiroshima in 1945. The terrifying images more resembled a scene from a Hollywood action film than anything the mind could comprehend as real. Soon the Pentagon was ablaze from a similar attack. The surreal images against the background of a bright blue sky were soon replaced by equally horrifying visuals. One of the 110-story towers imploded into rubble, followed a half-hour later by its twin, and hours later by an adjoining 46-story skyscraper. Television viewers witnessed the mushroom of dust and debris billowing in the skyscraper canyons of lower Manhattan and the looks of terror and confusion as people ran for cover. The president addressed the nation three times that day. Commentators interviewed military and civilian leaders and authorities. That night Mayor Rudolph Giuliani of New York held a news conference at which he indicated that while the number of those who died in the calamity would not be known for several days, the number would be greater than we could bear. Later that night, when reporters asked firefighters what was left of the WTC, they responded, "Nothing."

The television news coverage on September 11 did not include much that could be regarded as reasoned argument. President Bush's evening address to the nation did not offer arguments so much as depictions of what had occurred, the characterization of the terrorist assault as an act of war, and the expression of his resolve to make a strong response. By the next morning shock had given way to widespread anger; an NBC/*Wall Street*

Journal poll reported that 92 percent of Americans favored armed aggression against the responsible party, should it turn out to be a sponsoring state.

Soon Americans were told the U.S. government believed the attack was sponsored by Osama bin Laden, a wealthy Saudi militant who was leader of al-Qaeda, a terrorist group of Muslim extremists. The president called world leaders to assemble a united international front against terrorists and to declare war on them. Airports were closed for the remainder of the week; the New York Stock Exchange also was closed for the week, the longest interruption in Wall Street trading since the Great Depression. The economic losses suffered by the airplane industry led to massive layoffs, the stock market tumbled, increased security changed freedom of access and movement at the nation's airports, and the president committed the country to a long-term and unconventional war against terrorists. Missile attacks on October 7 against military sites of Afghanistan's Taliban regime received widespread support from the international community; polls the next morning reported that 90 percent of Americans supported it, only 4 percent were opposed, and 6 percent were undecided. On the afternoon of October 7, U.S. news coverage included a videotaped statement by bin Laden, apparently made before the raid, which contrasted starkly with the perspective of most Westerners:

> Here is America struck by God Almighty in one of its vital organs, so that its greatest buildings are destroyed. Grace and gratitude to God. America has been filled with horror from north to south and east to west, and thanks be to God that what America is tasting now is only a copy of we have tasted [sic].
>
> Our Islamic nation has been tasting the same for more 80 years [sic], of humiliation and disgrace, its sons killed and their blood spilled, its sanctities desecrated.
>
> God has blessed a group of vanguard Muslims, the forefront of Islam, to destroy America. May God bless them and allot them a supreme place in heaven, for He is the only one capable and entitled to do so. When those have stood in defense of their weak children, their brothers and sisters in Palestine and other Muslim nations, the whole world went into an uproar, the infidels followed by the hypocrites.
>
> A million innocent children are dying at this time as we speak, killed in Iraq without any guilt. We hear no denunciation, we hear no edict from the hereditary rulers. In these days, Israeli tanks rampage across Palestine, in Ramallah, Rafah and Beit Jala and many other parts of the land of Islam, and we do not hear anyone raising his voice or reacting. But when the sword fell upon America after 80 years, hypocrisy raised its head up high bemoaning those killers who toyed with the blood, honour and sanctities of Muslims.
>
> The least that can be said about those hypocrites is that they are apostates who followed the wrong path. They backed the butcher against the victim, the oppressor against the innocent child. I seek refuge in God against them and ask Him to let us see them in what they deserve.

I say that the matter is very clear. Every Muslim after this event [should fight for their religion], after the senior officials in the United States of America starting with the head of international infidels, [U.S. President George W.] Bush and his staff who went on a display of vanity with their men and horses, those who turned even the countries that believe in Islam against us—the group that resorted to God, the Almighty, the group that refuses to be subdued in its religion.

They [America] have been telling the world falsehoods that they are fighting terrorism. In a nation at the far end of the world, Japan, hundreds of thousands, young and old, were killed and [they say] this is not a world crime. To them it is not a clear issue. A million children [were killed] in Iraq, to them this is not a clear issue.

But when a few more than 10 were killed in Nairobi and Dar es Salaam, Afghanistan and Iraq were bombed and hypocrisy stood behind the head of international infidels, the modern world's symbol of paganism, America, and its allies.

I tell them that these events have divided the world into two camps, the camp of the faithful and the camp of infidels. May God shield us and you from them.

Every Muslim must rise to defend his religion. The wind of faith is blowing and the wind of change is blowing to remove evil from the Peninsula of Mohammed, peace be upon him.

As to America, I say to it and its people a few words: I swear to God that America will not live in peace before peace reigns in Palestine, and before all the army of infidels depart the land of Mohammed, peace be upon him.

God is the Greatest and glory be to Islam.[1]

Bin Laden characterized the attacks and the response of the U.S. government and citizens in quite different terms than the U.S. government and news media. His portrayal of the United States as grieving for its own dead while insensitive to the deaths of innocents in the Middle East who were casualties of the Palestinian struggle struck a resonant cord with millions of Muslims who had experienced the pains of which he spoke. His claims that this attack had divided the world into two camps—the infidels and the Muslim faithful—and that the people of America would have no rest until there was a Palestinian state, its holy sites returned to their control, and U.S. troops retreated from outposts in Muslim lands were rallying points for young and disaffected Muslims, who took to the streets the next day in a number of Arab and Asian subcontinent countries.

In the United States in the four-week period from September 11 to October 7, partisan differences were set aside and national consensus was forged in a way that had seldom existed since World War II. There was very little public debate. Most of the discourse came in other forms: television images, characterizations of the effects of the attacks on the lives of its victims, the ongoing investigation that linked the hijackers to bin Laden, the unanimous support of international leaders, and the characterization of bin Laden as a Muslim extremist who did not represent the true character of Islam. Although there was heated debate in Internet chat groups, this was not the dominant medium in which public understanding was being formed. Americans were participants in a story that portrayed them and their institutions as under attack. Its rhetorical force was evident in the unanimity with which they endorsed it. Bin Laden's story was diametrically opposed. It held little credence with U.S. citizens, but it was extremely powerful among many Muslims in the Middle East.

The power of stories to shape public perceptions is not a new development. The ancient rhetoricians admired the power of winged words through which speakers could bring a scene before the audience in such a way that they could witness the deeds of which the orator spoke and, by extension, participate in judging the consequences. In fact, Plato thought stories so powerful that in his *Republic* he banned poets from his ideal state. However, as we saw in chapters 6–9, the emphasis of classical theory was less on stories than on the modes of making rhetorical appeals: logos, ethos, and pathos. Our discussion in those chapters considered the contents of these appeals. Our main interest was the method for finding good reasons to support the rhetor's cause. This included the modes of appeals that persuade and the ways in which audiences understand those appeals. The topic of language kept appearing throughout our discussion, as we might expect in a treatment of discourse intended for use. Now we will treat this topic in a more systematic fashion. The earlier discussion was heavily influenced by classical treatments of rhetoric because the ancients provided a particularly rich consideration of the techniques for rhetorical arguments. From here on, our perspective will be much more contemporary, drawing heavily on the work of rhetoricians, philosophers, and critics who have broadened the concerns of rhetoric. As a transition into this change of focus, we will consider narrative as a major source of rhetorical influence. We discussed narrative in chapter 2, as a mode of communication and social influence in Greek antiquity. That discussion was limited, however, to the role of poets in pre-alphabetic Greece. In this chapter we will be concerned with how narratives involve the audience in patterns of perception that organize and give meaning to rhetorical situations and suggest appropriate ways to respond.

ॐ
Narrative Framing

Our consideration of logos included a discussion of twentieth-century rhetoric's extension of the ancient canon in terms of audience-based arguments called good reasons. There we saw that theorists such as Karl Wallace maintained that rhetoric is unlike logic in the standards it applies for assessing the strength of an argument. Good reasons theory repositions the test of an argument's strength from formal standards to audience-based standards. It holds that audiences judge public arguments by the standard of **reasonableness**, not logical validity. Whereas logical validity relies on formal rules of inference, rhetorical validity takes into account the norms and standards of the audience to certify an argument's claims. Audiences determine these standards based on such variables as their cultural perspectives, community norms, relevant value systems, class, power, gender, ethnicity, and so forth. These defining features play a significant role in determining whether an audience assigns weight to a rhetorical argument. What one group regards as a good reason for believing or acting may be less compelling to another.

The Aristotelian presentation of logos has been interpreted by some to imply a relation between rhetorical validity and a logic-based understanding of rationality. A logic-based understanding of rationality holds that a relationship among premises is valid if it meets the formal requirements of inference within the logical system. The enthymematic argument, which Aristotle regarded as the central means for establishing logos, is both a rhetorical and logical argument form. Within the predicate logic of syllogistic reasoning, Aristotle defined an enthymeme as an argument with one premise missing. His discussion of it as a rhetorical argument suggests it derives its persuasive force from the fact that the audience supplies this missing premise. This act of completing the reasoning process makes enthymemes self-persuasive. Because audience members actively participate in constructing arguments, they essentially convince themselves. Certainly there is considerable merit to the theory that persuasive arguments typically draw on premises the audience already holds and that arguments become more persuasive when audience members actively participate in the reasoning process. However, the relationship of enthymemes to syllogistic form may mislead us to anticipate that arguments addressed to lay audiences will take a traditional logical form and resemble syllogisms. This is seldom the case, as few of us frame everyday arguments in a formal or quasi-formal structure. Rather, popular reasoning on public issues most frequently develops within narrative structures and follows narrative logic. Philosopher Donald Verene provides the reason for this. "Arguments," he writes, "are not very interesting in themselves; they are only interesting for the role they play in some narrative."[2]

A variety of scholars in such diverse disciplines as literature, philosophy, psychology, sociology, and rhetoric have pointed out that we make sense of the episodes and events of our lives by situating them within our respective value systems. This act of sense making commonly involves placing occurrences within a context of our individual lived histories and those of our group. Our understanding of these contexts typically takes the form of narratives. Narratives are not just stories of what happened; their very structure is shaped by our narrative histories. They color our perceptions, understanding, and reasoning about the settings in which we act and are acted upon. Their contexts provide us with sense-making perspectives that we invoke to make connections among events and draw inferences that follow from them about what is reasonable in our lives. This placement of specific occurrences, problems, and even persons and thoughts within a storyline is a communicative activity, an act of rhetorical invention, sometimes called **framing**. Framing is an inherent element of all narratives and of narratival logic.

A frame provides a context for ordering the elements of an episode and interpreting its meaning. A good example of how different frames lead to different interpretations of an event is the Rodney King trial and its aftermath. In the early 1990s King, a young and burly black man, was arrested by the LAPD after a high-speed chase. A citizen who happened to be at the scene captured King's arrest on videotape. It showed the police trying to immobilize and restrain King, police using a stun gun and batons to subdue him, four or five police wrestling him to the ground and finally handcuffing him. The citizen videographer, disturbed by what he saw and recorded, turned the videotape over to a local television station, which aired it. The dramatic footage was picked up by the networks and broadcast nationally. The images raised considerable questions and criticism of the LAPD and its chief, Daryl Gates. The arresting officers were charged with criminal assault and brought to trial. Public emotion in Los Angeles ran so high that the trial venue was changed to neighboring Orange County, which had a distinctly different economic, racial, and political profile from Los Angeles. When the Orange County jury found the officers not guilty, a shockwave of disbelief and anger surged through Los Angeles and the nation. Distraught youths in the black community of South LA took to the streets and vented their outrage in a rampage of resentment that resulted in considerable property damage within the black community and personal injury to people of all races who were unfortunate enough to be in the wrong place at the wrong time. As South LA was in turmoil, the LAPD was so slow to respond that it appeared to be standing on the sideline.

Each of the audiences that witnessed the events on the videotape created individual frames for the ensuing discussions of what they had seen— the trials of the police, the verdict, the aftermath in South LA, and the absent police response. Seemingly interminable talk shows became shouting matches dissecting all aspects of the event according to individual interpretations. The personal frames chosen to explain the Rodney King event dictated the meaning assigned. For those who framed the event as the police doing their job, the perception of police wrongdoing was the result of media hype and the marauding youths were hoodlums looking for an excuse to create public havoc. For those who framed it as racial stereotyping, the verdict was a case of the white community's insensitivity to police brutality inflicted on a black man. For those who framed it as a question for the courts, it was a case of the black community's unwillingness to accept a verdict with which it disagreed. For those who framed it as a case of distraught youths inflicting harm on their own community, the LAPD's slow response to the outbreak of street violence was further evidence of rampant racism.

Each of these perspectives provides a different frame for the narration and interpretation of what took place. For the event to make sense, it must conform to the assumptions of the frame: the police were using reasonable force; the police were bringing excessive force on a minority member; the jury system worked even if the verdict was not popular; the police response to the riot reflects deliberate neglect. Where do these frames come from and how do they bear on narrative form?

~

Lived Experience as Story

Narrative theory has been a major area of intellectual work since about the middle of the twentieth century. The unifying feature is a recognition that narratives and narrative structures are fundamentally concerned with stories. Scholars have engaged in serious debates with deep differences of opinion over what counts as a narrative and what its defining features are. They are not in agreement that all stories can be accounted for in terms of the aesthetic creations of poets and novelists. In most disciplines outside literary studies, in fact, narratives are interesting quite apart from their aesthetic dimensions as a literary form. The more common interest is with their relation to how humans understand lived experiences and relate them to others. With the exception of fiction, American philosopher Alisdair MacIntyre argues, we live these tales before we tell them.[3] By this he means that we can think of our lives as having a narrative structure, although not all of us are equally gifted at relating this structure in an interesting way. I am reminded of a former student who observed of a friend that although both of them often shared the same experience, his version often seemed mundane and hardly worth sharing while hers always came off as an exciting adventure.

More significant than our skill as a narrator for our understanding of what happens to and around us is the narrative structure we bring to our experiences in order to make sense of them. Psychologist Jerome Bruner has argued that we live our lives in terms of stories that make sense of who we are and what we do. These narratives are the means we use to engage in "world making," which he regards as a principal function of the human mind.[4] Our lives are not explained, he argues, in terms of propositions or abstractions about our identity but by the self-narratives of our autobiographies. We must use **lived time** to construct an autobiography. We cannot tell the story of our life with calendar time, or with serial or cyclical time forms. Lived time can only be related in the form of a narrative. Lived time is structured by the episodic development of events. We disclose very little about ourselves by relating that we were alive on September 11, 2001. We disclose a great deal about ourselves when we relate the lived sequence of episodes that account for what we were doing, thinking, and feeling on that date because this account of lived time informs others of how we construct ourselves as persons.

Bruner extends his argument about the impact of narrative. Not only do we use story form to reflect our lives, but our lives are in a mimetic, or imitative relationship, with the stories we construct of them. Here's how Bruner puts it:

> Narrative imitates life, life imitates narrative. "Life" in this sense is the same kind of construction of the human imagination as "a narrative" is. It is constructed by human beings through active ratiocination, by the same kind of ratiocination through which we construct narratives. When somebody tells you his life . . . it is always a cognitive achievement rather than a through-the-clear-crystal recital of something univocally given. In the end it is a narrative achievement. There is no such thing as "life itself." At very least, it is a selective achievement of memory recall; beyond that, recounting one's life is an interpretive feat.[5]

The kind of meaning we use to make sense of our human world—human actions and events that affect humans—is primarily narrative. Of course as the teller of our life's story, we are vulnerable to offering accounts that may be gross rationalizations of what we did and why we did it. Regardless of these suspicions, it also is the case that not any story will do. I cannot tell a story of my participation in high school sports as if I were an Olympian. Standards of **rightness** apply to my life story as much as my account of last Saturday's football game. These standards are not just of conformity to externally verifiable facts, they also apply to internal states of what I was thinking and feeling at the time, which give the story depth and provide insight into conduct.

Bruner makes the point that these culturally influenced cognitive and linguistic processes that shape the telling of our life story also condition the way we perceptually experience, remember, organize, and ascribe purpose to the events of a life. He illustrated the usefulness of the theory of life as narrative by examining the way a family of four used stories to give structure and continuity to the respective experiences of their lives. He was further interested in how the family formulated common rules for constructing these accounts. He found that family members narrated their lives in terms of a two-sided divide. First, one set of conditions was in play, then things changed and another set of conditions became the defining elements. Although parents and children used the same pattern, which suggests the family tended to make sense of shared experiences in the same way, the parents' stories were remarkably different from their children's. The parents narrated their lives in terms of a life of struggle and secret shame between unbearably capricious family settings and personhood that came with a good marriage (her) or accomplishments through hard work and helping others (him). In both cases they told their stories with a strong sense of their own agency. They did not portray themselves as victims of fate or beneficiaries of fortune but as actors whose choices influenced outcomes. They consciously structured an image of "home" for their children to shield them from the unhappiness the parents had experienced in their own childhoods. The children, on the other hand, told their stories in terms of having started out on the other side of the divide, existing in a world that was kindly but inert, entrenched, and "given" versus a "new" world that was their own. Things happened, but not always with a sense of their agency through conscious choices that have consequences.

Through such differences as these, Bruner provides some empirical verification for his theses that we internalize experiences in terms of our personal narratives about ourselves, that we interpret our experiences in ways that conform to the basic storyline by which we give meaning to our lives, and that as these experiences defy this storyline, we must make cognitive readjustments, such as reframing the event so it fits or altering the basic storyline. Moreover, Bruner's study suggests that our perceptions of events and the ways we connect them to our lives and make sense of them rely on **narrative structures** that influence our thoughts about and responses to them. Examining a narrative's basic structural features will help us better understand its rhetorical function.

Plot

We usually associate narratives with tales that are told, or stories. Sometimes these stories are inventions of imagination, such as a novel. But they also may be reports of actual events, as in the case of an historical account. Regardless of whether they are invented or not, narrative structures always involve **plot**. According to literary theorist Hayden White, *plot refers to "a structure of relationships by which the events contained in an account are endowed with a meaning by being identified as parts of an integrated whole"* (emphasis added).[6] Every story has more than a single occurrence. These occurrences must be placed in a sequence that relates them to one another in a meaningful whole. The sequence helps us to determine the meaning of the parts and also to form a sense of direction whereby we both understand and anticipate how one occurrence leads to the next, and the next, until it reaches its conclusion. The conclusion is not necessarily predictable; a good story seldom leads us to a forgone conclusion. But it must be acceptable; it must make sense in terms of what went before.

French philosopher Paul Ricoeur finds two aspects of sequencing that help develop plots into meaningful wholes that may be judged acceptable. He calls these the **episodic dimension** and the **configurational operation**.[7] The *episodic dimension* is chronological. It refers to the sequence of the story's contingent elements that allow us to follow its development as a coherent whole with anticipatory questions such as: and so? and then? what happened next? what was the outcome? and so forth. The *configurational operation* consists in extracting a pattern from the sequencing that allows us to join scattered episodes into a meaningful whole. It is our attempt to extract a sense of causality from the several episodic parts, which we accomplish by reflecting on the episodes and forming judgments on them individually and on the whole. This operation involves both our understanding of the logic of the plot—how its elements are related and whether this relationship makes sense—and whether the plot's causal sequence makes sense in our own world.

As these relationships become culturally inscribed and culturally transmitted, as say the story of the Hebrew people for members of Judaism or of westward expansion for citizens of the United States, they define a **nomos**—a normative universe. Such a universe contains an ordering of right and wrong, paradigms for action, a world to inhabit. This nomos is held together by the force of shared commitments—some small and private, others massive and public—that determine our laws, customs, politics, economics, and ultimately our traditions. They are captured in our mythos and borne to consciousness through narratives. Ricoeur, who has studied the relationship stories bear to cultural awareness, points out, "The historicity of human experience can be brought to language only as narrativity. . . . For historicity comes to language only insofar as we tell stories or tell history."[8]

By **historicity**, Ricoeur means more than our history; it refers to our sense of being a part of that history, of having a tradition that exerts an important defining force on our beliefs and values as a member of our clan or nation. German philosopher Hans Georg Gadamer, among others, has argued that historicity is constituted by a culture's stories, its narratives. He makes the point that we are born into a culture in which our cultural identity is pregiven by the language, customs, and institutions that we share. These are imbedded with affiliations, significant events, and dispositions to respond to the world in certain ways. They tell us who we are and why we believe as we do. Studies of American society by sociologist Robert Bellah[9] and of cultural patterns in American rhetoric by Richard Weaver[10] suggest that when a society ceases to share these bonds of common affiliation, ceases to be what Bellah and his associates refer to as a community of memory,[11] it becomes disoriented, begins to lose its capacity for common action, and its members find the meaning of their individual lives impoverished. To lose the capacity to respond to the culture's stories is to suffer a form of amnesia whose pathology eludes medical description, since it is not at all like the loss of a psychological faculty. Such amnesia is more profound, as Gadamer observes, because cultural memory is an essential element of the individual's and the culture's historical being.[12] Cultural memory places one inside a tradition in which past and present are constantly fused. A sense of history provides continuity of customs and traditions, of laws, and of accomplishments that fill temporal distance.[13] It also provides models with which to respond to the present and to shape the future.

These various scholarly studies in psychology, literary studies, philosophy, and sociology point to plot as an essential ingredient in the stories we construct to make sense of our experiences. Put differently, we understand the events of experience in terms of their emplotted character. Whereas Aristotle defined the human as a rational animal, contemporary rhetoric has begun to postulate that humans are more fundamentally story-telling animals. Since rhetoric is addressed to questions of action, the postulate that humans are story-telling animals—that they understand their lives in terms of plot—carries implications for discourse that induces action. MacIntyre helps us bring the macro-level relations of narrative to human conduct to a most basic level of everyday judgment and action. In his words, "I can answer the question 'What am I to do?' if I can answer the prior question 'Of what story do I find myself a part?'"[14] Knowing the story of which you are a part allows you to give the events you are encountering meaning because the story places them into a plot. Plot displays their significance in relation to one another, thereby suggesting your course of conduct.

MacIntyre is concerned with the judgments we make about right conduct, about what we should do, which brings us to the relation of narrative reasoning and rhetoric. Returning to the terrorist attacks recounted at the beginning of this chapter, the president and the Congress used the story of war to account for a variety of measures taken against the Taliban regime in Afghanistan and the al-Qaeda terrorist organization. The government sealed U.S. funds of organizations thought to support al-Qaeda, formed an international alliance against Osama bin Laden, launched air strikes against Taliban military installations, activated national guard units, and the secretaries of state and defense made trips overseas to talk to supporting nations. Bin Laden and other al-Qaeda leaders, on the other hand, constructed a story of a holy war or jihad against the U.S., accounted for the attacks on the World Trade Center and the Pentagon as a response to U.S. defilement of Islamic holy lands, the deaths of one million Iraqis, and U.S. deafness to the suffering of Palestinians at the hands of Israel.

These stories provided *accounts* for what each side was doing. They also served as the basis for *justifying* their actions. The U.S. accounted for its actions as self-defense. It was at war with an enemy that had attacked without provocation. Al-Qaeda accounted for its actions as morally justified since U.S. was an infidel nation guilty of sacrilege and mass murder. In their story, the attacks against the World Trade Center and Pentagon were proper and those who executed them deserved entry to paradise.

Finally, plots provided a *mode of reasoning* by which we *hold each other accountable*. This means that we become part of each other's stories whose internal logic links actions to consequences. For those in the U.S., members of al-Qaeda were cast as evildoers who had committed a senseless murder of thousands of innocent civilians. Muslim militants in the Middle East were portrayed as villains for condoning this act. Firefighters and police officers in New York were lionized as heroes for their rescue efforts at ground zero, while ordinary citizens were portrayed as patriots for displays of public support and spirit of public service and cooperation in the immediate aftermath of the attack. These same groups, and often the same acts, assumed quite different meanings when they became part of al-Qaeda's plot of jihad against infidels.

Narrative Quest

These differences remind us that stories do not exert influence in a vacuum. They are developed in the context of communities to which we belong: family, religion, locale, nation, profession, ethnicity, language, education, sexual orientation, gender, organization, and so forth. The stories of our lives are embedded in the stories of these communities. For stories to exert persuasive force, they must partake of the emplotted accounts that community members actively share. They are an important source of our identity and how it is manifested through words and deeds. By developing rhetorical appeals in ways that are sensitive to these elements, we influence how our audience's interests are engaged, emotions aroused, and thoughts channeled. The audience's use of narrative reasoning to make sense of novel situations is the primary way in which this is accomplished.

Our consideration of narrative reasoning has indicated that narratives are organized in terms of plots and that the plot of a story carries implications for those who participate in it. Narratives provide us with a sequence of actions or episodes that can be related to one another to make a unified whole, that lead to a conclusion. They involve the configurational operation of a sense of causality to join scattered episodes into a meaningful whole—extracting a pattern from the sequencing of actions. The pattern of narrative reasoning is a natural mode of reasoning and arguing we employ every day to arrive at judgments about what we believe and what we should do. Imagine, for example, that you have a package you promised you'd mail to a friend who lives in another part of the country. You should have mailed that package earlier in the week, but you've had a severe cold and the weather has been inclement. Finally you feel better and think you can go out. Before you venture forth you ask your roommate, who just came in, about the weather so you'll know how to dress. She says the wind has started to kick up and the temperature is dropping. The sky is lowering and it looks like it is going to rain or snow in the next half hour or so. As you imagine yourself in this picture, you project a series of actions: I go out, it starts to rain or snow, I get soaked and catch a chill, I have a relapse of my cold, the cold gets worse and turns into pneumonia, I end up in the hospital and possibly die! Conclusion: I think I'll wait till tomorrow to mail the package.

The sequence of this projection depends on a set of assumptions about the weather, health, and personal priorities that have implications. Each contributes to a coherent story whose conclusion will depend on the assumptions we emphasize as a narrative frame. In this case it was a health frame that led you to emphasize bad weather over personal obligation to mail the package. But you could have emphasized personal obligation, which would have supported a different conclusion. The significant point illustrated by this example, however, is that as we accept a particular plot as agreeing with our sense of reality, there are natural consequences and conclusions. Unless we are ready to act in ways that are inconsistent with our rendition of reality, the storyline makes a compelling argument for judgments we should draw and acts we should perform. This form of reasoning, what British philosopher Bernard Bosanquet writing at the early part of the twentieth century called **linear inference**,[15] depends on our participation in its narrative structure.

Narratives, however, are not complete or even accurate factual accounts. They are selective in the details they include or omit. They leave gaps a reader or listener must fill in order to find coherence. Your friend didn't mention your cold or your priorities. These were elements you had to bring in to complete the story of whether to walk to the post office. In this case, you had to decide which question to weight more heavily, "What is good for me?" or "What is good for my friend?" or "What is good for our friendship?" in order to decide whether to venture forth. Answering one question instead of the others allows you to take scattered elements and organize them into a coherent whole that indicates a course of action. This search for coherence is called **narrative quest**, and it is an important element of narrative reasoning.

A narrative quest seeks to bring closure to a story, to fill its gaps. Satisfying the narrative quest is essential for moving from the open-ended condition of a text, which is subject to multiple resolutions, to closure with a specific resolution. When we see a James Bond film, we expect there will be a secret weapon. Usually we are introduced to it at the beginning of the film, but we don't know how it will be used. Part of the narrative challenge of a James Bond movie is satisfying the audience's quest for Agent 007 using the secret weapon to make a death-defying escape that is nothing short of miraculous. We also have narrative quests in the more pragmatic nonfictional world of occupations, where we search for certain actions that go with the job and provide coherence to their narratives: students to graduation, soldiers to orders, professors to tenure, bakers to chocolate cakes. In each instance the quest is for closure. It seeks to fill in the story's gaps with an account that locates integrity in choices and supplies coherence to acts. If we set out to bake a chocolate cake but go to the fish market to purchase ingredients, our story better be a comedy because we've made an inappropriate choice with respect to the narrative quest. On the other hand, stories that provide closure with integrity and coherence gain authority. They provide us with accounts that both agree with our views of reality, of the way the world is, and answer the questions we pose as critical for knowing what we should do. How narratives move a story from being a text open to multiple interpretations to one that makes a particular appeal is the primary concern of rhetoricians who have studied narratives as a source of good reasons, since rhetorical appeals seek specific judgments about what should be done.

ช

Narrative Rationality

Since around 1980, rhetoricians have explored the relationship of these concerns to **public moral arguments**, or arguments that advance good reasons for public choices of judgment and conduct. Such arguments are moral in the sense that they involve value choices for responsible public conduct. Such choices place the public good ahead of individual benefits. The major theoretical model in this discussion is the **narrative paradigm** developed by rhetorician Walter Fisher.[16]

The narrative paradigm assumes that humans are valuing as much as reasoning creatures. Each of us belongs to a variety of communities with commitments of one sort or another. The commitments are embedded in the histories of their formation, experiences in pursuit of common goals, or interactions with other communities and cultures. All of these elements and others like them form the community's **public memory**. Stories, memorials, rituals, and the like are a community's cultural repository.[17] Oftentimes this repository includes narratives that refashion historical knowledge by mythologizing the past. Regardless of its historical accuracy, public memory is the dynamic and living part of our past and is part of our consciousness of identity as a people.[18] Whether George Washington chopped down the cherry tree or not, his story is one way our culture teaches the virtue of honesty.

In the larger society, public memory is, itself, a source of potent rhetorical invention and site of contention. The stories we tell of ourselves, of our past, of the themes that give meaning to action, are repositories of values that will be transmitted culturally and provide justification for public actions. For this reason, as historian John Bodnar has noted, "Public memory speaks primarily about the structure of power in society."[19] The story of who we are and the events and people who shape our identity are never given. They are always rhetorical achievements produced by communities of class and identity.[20] Further, these stories are not just about us. They include those outside our culture or group, often as "Others," aliens to our cultural world. For this reason we must be cautious not to romanticize the stories that transmit public memory. They always represent a point of view and often they construct a story that exercises power over the words, deeds, and events of which those it defines as foreigners are a part.

> So the question of public memory carries the questions of power into public life in at least two ways. Most obviously it raises concerns over how people find resources from their past to shape an account of their present and future. More vexingly it raises the problem of discovering the means to resist the subversive power of someone else's story to distort our own memories and appropriate our own experiences.[21]

Although some may use public memories as a resource for achieving and sustaining dominance, the stories are dynamic and subject to interpretation. They can serve a variety of inventional needs, including opening the way for mediating differences. Every rhetorical transaction, as Aristotle taught, is praxis created for the given case. Each rhetorical situation is marked by elements of novelty and possibility for refiguring the meaning of experience and human relations.

Narratives draw on the values inscribed in our cultural repository of public memory, Fisher argues, to structure words and deeds with sequence and meaning for those who live, create, or interpret them. They gain traction as rational structures for their audience to the extent that they satisfy two conditions: **narrative probability** and **narrative fidelity.**

Narrative Probability

Narrative probability refers to the coherence of the story. The test of narrative probability addresses whether the story holds together. Fisher points to three tests for narrative probability. First we may ask whether the narrative has **argumentative** or **structural coherence.** Earlier we considered the example of making a decision about walking to the post office in light of impending bad weather. Given what you know about your state of health, about weather conditions, about the distance you'd have to travel, and about possible consequences should you get drenched, there is a conclusion that naturally follows provided you see these events within a health frame. The parts fit together in an internally consistent way that leads you to the conclusion "stay home." And they also provide a set of internal relations that would give your conclusion coherence in the eyes of others. Should you be thinking in terms of a different frame, say your obligation to get this package in today's mail, this afternoon's impending weather does not establish a set of relationships that give coherence to the conclusion "meet your obligations, mail the package." That would require a different narrative frame.

The second test is **material coherence.** By that, Fisher means testing the narrative in relation to other narratives told in other discourses to see whether they agree. Have important facts been omitted, counterarguments ignored, and relevant issues overlooked? In the case of American rhetoric on the terrorist attack, for instance, there was a systematic denial of any attempt by administration spokespersons and other U.S. officials to dismiss claims from Middle East speakers that pointed to U.S. policies with respect to the aspirations of Palestinians as a contributing factor to anti-American sentiments in their part of the world. From an Arab point of view the U.S. story left out an important element. Arab states sympathetic to the United States could not afford to ignore strong feelings of alienation from the United States among their peoples. Without some recognition by the United States that these concerns must be addressed, agitation would likely continue and support of U.S. policies would have to be weighed in terms of the political realities in Arab states. The Bush administration countered the Arab story of omission with a narrative that portrayed the attack against innocent civilians, which could not be justified on grounds of Palestinian political aspirations and frustrations. A story of America at war could not accommodate a plot that accepted partial blame. If the general populace perceived that as true, then the justification for war would be undermined and the story would call for negotiation.

The third test of narrative probability is **characterological coherence**. This third test of coherence is concerned with the reliability of a character. Fisher maintains that we form a sense of a person's character based on his or her organized set of actional tendencies. We require people to act in ways that are characteristic of them in order to make predictions of future conduct on which trust, community, and rational human order rests. If individuals act erratically or in contradictory fashion, the coherence of the story in which they play a pivotal part is undermined. In the aftermath of the terrorist attack, for instance, President Bush repeatedly told the American people and world leaders that he was determined to pursue the war against terrorism to its conclusion. There were repeated attempts to assure everyone that he was following predictable tendencies of commitment on which they might base future expectations. It also required that he reframe his campaign promises regarding fiscal and social policies and priorities in light of a story of new realities.

Narrative Fidelity

Narrative fidelity refers to the extent to which the story rings true with the stories the audience members have known to be true in their lives. Narrative fidelity does not deny that there are traditional reasoning structures in specific argument forms, but it incorporates these into a larger framework that includes other structures as part of the reasoning process. Here Fisher returns to the good reasons position that had been advanced by rhetoricians such as Karl Wallace and Wayne Booth. Fisher found a problem with their respective positions on good reasons because they seemed circular. They seemed to assert "good reasons are what good people affirm and that good people know what is good." He proposes this revision, in which good reasons are conceived as *"those elements that provide warrants for accepting or adhering to the advice fostered by any form of communication that can be considered rhetorical."*[22]

The narrative paradigm contends that we provide good reasons through narrative structures that correspond with those patterns we have a predisposition to affirm because we have found them to be true in our own experience. Returning to the post office story, if from the recipient's perspective the package didn't arrive when expected, the sender's story would have narrative fidelity if it agreed with the recipient's experience of taking precautions when ill. Returning to the terrorist attacks, when bin Laden declared an Islamic holy war against the United States and militants in Muslim countries demonstrated in support by burning the American flag and effigies of George W. Bush, many Americans were mystified. This story line was outside the frame of public memory shared by most Americans. They saw themselves as providing relief and military assistance to Middle Eastern countries. Their general lack of knowledge about Islam made it difficult to interpret bin Laden's massage. Did he speak for the majority of Muslims? The story of continued threat to American lives bumped into the prevailing story of courage in the face of adversity. This story lacked narrative fidelity for an American audience—just as the American account of bin Laden as an evildoer lacked fidelity for many Muslims in the Middle East living under conditions of political and economic desperation.

☙

Voice

Fisher's narrative paradigm emphasizes the influence of an audience's background experience on narrative reasoning. Certainly individual and group experience is an invaluable resource for evaluating whether someone's claims make sense. However, experience is not seamless. We live in several narratives, and they do not always agree with one another. A married couple may practice birth control although their religion does not condone it, and they may oppose abortion on religious grounds but respect the right of the state to determine its legality. Moreover, Fisher's paradigm does not offer extensive treatment of the role narratives play in constituting social realities that go beyond our background experience. The variegated nature of experience and rhetoric's constitutive power require discussion of the relationship between rhetor and audience that privileges one set of experiences over another and that can constitute social reality. We will conclude our discussion of narrative by considering the relationship it forms between rhetor and audience through the narrator's **voice**.

Voice refers to the presentational quality of a narrative; it provides orientation through its point of view. Narrators don't just tell a story. If they are skilled, they provide us with guidance for understanding certain values and a code of conduct through the plot of the story. They guide our understanding of the world of human actions and events that affect humans revealed in their story. The way they offer this guidance is not, however, open-ended. The narrator's voice will be influenced by the genre of the discourse. For example, the narrator in a fiction speaks to us as the implied author. Although we know the narrator is not really the author, we are enticed by his or her voice to accept it *as if* s/he were the literal storyteller. Narrative theorists hold that this imagined literalness in fiction sidesteps the question of reading the actual author's mind and of lapsing into the intentional fallacy whereby we interpret the meaning of the fictive text on the basis of our perception of the author's intention. Of course the author's state of mind and intentions are not available to us. The only evidence we have for interpreting the meaning of the text is what is presented in the text itself.

The interpretive move of linking the narrator of a fiction with the author on the basis of what is actually presented allows the reader or listener of public discourse intended to persuade to share an interpretive stance with the rhetor. The evidence we have for interpreting what the rhetor means and whether we share in her analysis and commitments lies in what is said or written (a point we will develop in greater detail in chapter 11). For this reason we must pay special attention to the rhetor's voice—to the disposition it displays with respect to commitments of value and belief and to us as an audience.

We are assisted in performing this interpretive and evaluative act by monitoring narrative voice for qualities that make it **reliable**. The narrator's reliability, like the quality of ethos, encourages us to have faith in his claims. Unlike the narrator in fiction, the rhetor can establish reliability through material proofs developed to support a point. Reliability also comes from a narrative that speaks in an authoritative way within our culture's tradition of beliefs and values. A third way to establish reliability is through a voice consistent with audience expectations. For example, Polish political dissident Adam Michnik, writing from his cell in Bialoleka prison, explained to his fellow Poles why they should not sign a loyalty oath to the communist government that had declared Solidarity (the Polish trade union opposed to the government) illegal and thrown 10,000 of its members in jail.[23] His reasons were developed in a narrative of the tainted relationship between the Polish state and the people. It portrayed Poland's leaders as untrustworthy stooges of Moscow who had nothing Polish about them. They were outside the nation's traditions. His voice was trustworthy to his readers in its knowledge of their traditions, in his knowledge of common experiences that had alienated the common citizen from the state, and by employing a rhetorical convention of addressing his readers in familiar tones of "you" that suggested they knew each other well.[24]

On the other side of the coin, an absence of these qualities can make the narrator **unreliable**. Certainly the unreliability of unsupported claims, ignorance, and internal inconsistencies that violate plot and lack narratival probability and fidelity can confuse the audience and undermine the narrative. However, there are modes of unreliability that may give a voice exceptional power. For example, the voice of irony violates expectations in a way that forces a wedge between the reader or listener's mind and the assumptions it normally makes. The voice of metaphor also violates expectations by assimilating ideas, actions, objects, or qualities that are normally distant into a whole. Equally important, the advocate of fundamental change often must violate the narrative structure that supports the status quo in order to move readers and listeners to consider a different social plot and the relations it would foster.

Violation of expectations, in short, may serve important rhetorical ends. For instance, from the early 1960s until the early 1990s, South Africa's black political dissidents (convicted of crimes growing out of their opposition to apartheid) were sent to the prison on Robben Island. The guards, who perceived these prisoners from a racist narrative of white superiority, subjected the political prisoners to extreme forms of physical and psychological cruelty. The guards expected that torture would lead the prisoners to obey their every command, much like a trained animal, in order to escape further pain. This, of course, would have reinforced their perception of these prisoners as less than human. The prisoners recognized the reinforcing nature of the prison's narrative and sought to change it by responding to the guards' incivility with a voice of civility, such as addressing the guards politely, cooperating whenever possible without demeaning themselves, never challenging the guards' authority except when it might compromise their human dignity, and volunteering acts of kindness such as tutoring guards who were having difficulty with high school and college courses they were compelled to take. Their prison voice violated the guards' expectations and eventually opened them to a new narrative in which the prisoners were seen as humans deserving of humane treatment.[25]

A rhetor's voice is animated by a vision of the world and presents it to us as an exhortation to share its vision. Through voice the rhetor establishes a relationship with audience members, involving them in the narrative's depiction of reality, identifying with it (a topic we will develop further in chapter 11), and eliciting their cooperation in its quest. Narrative probability and fidelity require that we share this vision. For that reason, audiences must be aware that the rhetor's narrative is a constructed reality of an *as if* world that has meaning and reality only insofar as it is shared as the basis for collective action.

Adding the concept of voice to the narrative paradigm underscores the power of language to display a vision of reality—to make an *as if* world visible through verbal portrayal. The visual possibilities of verbal display go beyond metaphoric reasoning (to be discussed in chapter 12), which portrays apparent differences as assimilated into a unity, and irony, which portrays apparent unities as distanced from one another. Narrative situates us in a story through the point of view of the rhetor's voice. From its perspective, the *as if* quality of what we see is easily confused with *believing what we are seeing*. This illusion is present in all social constructions of reality insofar as they are rhetorically induced. *Holding as true* what the rhetor's voice defines as present means the audience succumbs, as Ricoeur has pointed out, "to the hallucination of presence."[26] We respond *as if* we were present to the scene of the story and participating in it. For this reason, the *reliability/unreliability* tension of voice imposes on us, as listeners and readers, the responsibility to think critically. It imposes the obligation to struggle with the rhetor's voice lest we unwittingly be seduced into an *as if* of someone else's imagination.

∾

Summary

In this chapter we have considered a language-based perspective on the ways in which rhetors make public arguments. Contemporary thought extends Aristotle's analysis and substitutes rhetorical validity for logical validity as the standard by which to test public argument. Rhetorical validity, in this respect, is established by the extent to which an appeal engaged the audience's value system.

Narrative logic develops from its most basic feature as a story form: it has plot. Humans live the story of their lives before they tell it. We make sense of the episodes of our lives by organizing them in terms of stories inherited from our culture—we are creatures of our tradition. Our stories situate episodes and help us decide what to do. The narrative paradigm broadens the theory of good reasons to include the tests of narrative probability and narrative fidelity for determining rhetorical validity of public arguments that urge us to action. This paradigm is extended by consideration of voice. Through voice we confront issues of reliability and the constructed character of the human world. We also encounter our own responsibility for critical examination of the narrator's world, lest we succumb to confusing its *as if* quality with that which is objectively true.

Acting with Language

The focus of classical rhetoric was persuasion as it occurred in public address, but the influence of language on our judgments is not limited to formal statements. Whenever symbols encourage us to share our attitudes, they are functioning rhetorically. This broader scope represents a new point of view. Contemporary rhetoricians have shifted their focus from persuasion to identification. Identification does not supersede our concerns with persuasive appeals; it incorporates them into a larger framework based on the unique uses made of language as the defining feature of our humanity.

In this chapter and the next we will consider persuasive uses of language—language as action. We will explain how language used in situated contexts exhibits our motives and encourages others to share them with us—what critic Kenneth Burke calls a rhetoric of motives.

Action and Motion

The moon is one of nature's majestic wonders. Set in its orbit, it circles the earth every 28 days. It is so regular that ever since our species started keeping track of time, the moon has provided an unfailing calendar. In addition, it regulates the ebb and flow of tides, offers mariners a reliable navigational aid, and provides the spectacle of a solar eclipse. Were there no humans to observe its cycle, the moon would still go through its phases, following a traceable path through the night sky. The moon, in this sense, is in the realm of **motion**. It is what it is, a clump of matter in orbit around another clump of matter.

In addition to these natural functions, the moon inspires the human imagination. It is the wellspring of romance, as lovers bathed in moonlight look heavenward in hopes that the mystery will never cease. It is the play-pen of science fiction come true, as astronauts hike and bike across its sur-face to play out the metaphor of America's destiny with the frontier. It is the culprit for lunacy, providing an excuse from responsibility for bizarre behavior. It is the mother lode for poets, songwriters, and wordsmiths who tinker with synecdochic possibilities to express the themes of life or at least tug at the heart. Left to human devices, the moon takes on symbolic significance and is thereby transferred from the realm of motion to the realm of **action**—the realm of our attitudes, where we attach interpreta-tions to the raw data of existence. It no longer is what it is; it is what we make of it.

All of nature is in the realm of motion—the earth, the universe, the trees, the fish in the river, the pumping of your heart. All of it is what it is. The term action indicates the realm of meaning in which humans use sym-bols: dance, painting, speech, writing, languages in general. Symbols give objects of nature transported to the realm of action meaning that goes be-yond their physical properties. Moreover, these symbolically created mean-ings cannot be reduced to physical properties. B. F. Skinner's[1] pigeons pecking away at their sources of reward are in the realm of motion: They are perfectly explainable in terms of their nonsymbolic or extrasymbolic operations of conditioned responses. But put a label on what those pigeons are doing—behaviorism—and soon you have controversy on your hands, as in "I ain't no pigeon, Jack!" Transferred into the symbolic realm of an ism, the pigeon becomes more than a pigeon; it is now a claim about the human condition. That statement can't be reduced to the bird pecking away. It is more than the bird, more than motion. Furthermore, the coun-terclaim makes no sense if taken to mean literally and exclusively that its human author is not a bird. Obviously not, since in the realm of motion there are only affirmatives—things are what they are. It makes sense only as a statement that rejects behaviorism.

Thus we can say that *motion refers to the **nonsymbolic** or the **extrasym-bolic** operations of nature*, as with the earth's rotation, the ebbing of tides, the growth and decay of vegetation, the breathing of mammals. *Action re-fers to the type of behavior that becomes possible with the use of symbols.* Rhe-torical theorist Kenneth Burke summarizes their relationship this way:

1. There can be no action without motion.

2. There can be motion without action.

3. Action is not reducible to terms of motion.[2]

✆
Humans Act with Language

A contemporary commonplace in the language arts holds that humans act with language. The claim is intriguing but ambiguous because it is used in a variety of ways. For instance, one school of thinkers has developed **speech act theory**. It maintains that each utterance has three components: what is said (**locution**); what is done in the saying (**illocution**); and the psychological impact of what was said (**perlocution**). This school focuses primarily on illocutions. Illocutions are speech acts uttered to communicate the speaker's intention; they can be promises, questions, warnings, commands, and so on—anything that reveals intention. For instance, when Chris says, "I'll bring the map of Michigan tomorrow," she has made a promise; when Shannon says, "Don't vote for him, he's a spendthrift," she has issued a warning. Both statements clearly communicate the speaker's intentions.

Another school of thinkers, started by anthropologist Bronislaw Malinowski, views humans as engaged in acts of communal joining when they speak. For instance, when you pass a friend on the street, what you say is less important than the fact that you offer a greeting. The **function** of the utterance is more important than its content. When you call out, "Larry, how're you doin'?" you are not likely asking for a medical update. If Larry starts complaining about his sinuses and insomnia, you may offer a sympathetic look, but behind this mask your mind is racing to find a graceful exit from this encounter. Your greeting really meant to convey your friendliness toward this person. It was an act of recognition. By the same token, were you to look him in the eye and pass in silence, he probably would interpret your act as a snub.

We will return to Malinowski's views in chapter 12, but for now we note that while these views illustrate that we act with language, they do not indicate how we do so. In order to answer that question, we need a functional perspective toward language. While most contemporary rhetoricians discuss their subject in functional terms, the most influential contemporary account in terms of acting with language is provided by Kenneth Burke. He develops an analysis of how humans act with language modeled after the dramatic action of the stage. This perspective is called **dramatism**.

Dramatistic Assumptions

Dramatism holds that people manage social situations through their uses of language or symbolic acts. Managing symbols is the principal means by which we coordinate our social actions. When we use symbols, our actions resemble those of a performer on a stage. Our acts are motivated, as are an actor's. We assume that our interlocutors are capable of sharing these motives, similar to an audience caught up in the ebb and flow of a play's dramatic action. When motives are shared, we feel and act as one. Our capacity to use and respond to language or symbols is at the heart of coordinating social action.

At first glance, this claim appears obvious. How else would we coordinate social action except through language? Indeed, we'd be lost otherwise. Less apparent is the reason why this is so. Burke, following the symbolic interactionist school of sociology, has suggested that we are able to coordinate our social lives only because we construct our social realities through symbols. In short, we are symbol-using animals. Burke's insight is captured in his definition of the human as

- the symbol-using (misusing) animal
- inventor of (or invented by) the negative
- separated from his natural condition by instruments of his own making
- goaded by a spirit of hierarchy
- rotten with perfection[3]

Each of these phrases deserves further inspection because each helps explain the basis for our human capacity to act with language. This capacity makes rhetorical analysis, when properly understood, among the most powerful tools available for illuminating social conduct.

Symbol User.   The first, and most basic, of Burke's assumptions is that humans are uniquely symbol-using animals. Whereas other animals can emit meaningful sounds or signals in the code of their species, only humans can reflect on this fact. As Burke says, "Cicero could both orate and write a treatise on oratory. A dog can bark but he can't bark a tract on barking."[4] Without the capacity to use symbols, we would be the same as all other animals. Because we can use symbols and reflect on our symbols, we are able to engage in the creative activity of making social realities with our symbols.

The implications of the capacity to use symbols are far-reaching. Humans can reflect on experience, abstract meaning from it, organize and communicate it to others for them to reflect in turn and to communicate back the thoughts they have in response. It enables us to create new understanding by inventing labels for unnamed experiences, especially through the use of metaphor. As symbol-using animals, we are also symbol-making animals. More than this, our symbols can separate us from the nonverbal realm to which they refer. Because symbols evoke responses to cognitive and emotional meanings rather than simple reference to material properties of existence they can create confusion (as when our isms lead to distorted views of those who practice other isms).

The Negative.   Our ability to use language permits us to engage in critical acts. This takes us beyond the implied criticism of an animal rejecting a particular food. As symbol-using animals, we can make choices that go beyond the factual "is—is not" to the moral realm of "shall—shall not." For example, formative childhood experiences, such as admonitions by our mother not to pull the cat's whiskers, or not to take coins off her dresser, or not to tease our sister taught us a basic moral code. It is not absurd to say that Mother's negatives invented us! As social actors, we possess an identity that has developed through symbolic acts of criticism and encouragement. "Shall—shall not" serves the hortatory or inciting function of urging us to make some choices and avoid others, but these choices themselves are open to criticism. The use of the negative to criticize choices anchors our morality as ethical creatures in our ability to use symbols.

Separation.   Choice also implies a condition somewhat removed from our primitive needs for food, shelter, and sexual release. All animals have these needs. Human inventions that take us beyond our primitive state create new possibilities—language inventions not the least among them. We can use language, like all tools, as an instrument to accomplish ends. Of course, the ends are higher-order abstract needs; they exist only because we have the tools at our disposal to accomplish them. For example, electronic communication creates the possibility for transmitting complex information across space in a matter of seconds. Interactive systems permit responses to flow back with lightning speed. There are efficiencies of time, human effort, and precision in data processing not conceivable by laypeople until about 1980. On the other hand, we risk becoming so reliant on our machines that should they fail us, we would be helpless. The panic that occurs in large metropolitan areas when the electricity goes out is a vivid example. So too is the international preparation that went into Y2K safeguards against massive computer failure at the turn of the millennium. Language can be an equally double-edged tool, creating the possibilities for survival (as when we are able to understand and manage the forces of nature because we can express them in symbolic ways) and the possibilities for extermination (as when we turn the forces of nature loose in a nuclear weapon).

Hierarchy.   Choice also involves order—determining what goes with what. Inherent in intelligible uses of symbols is organization, and organization introduces a principle of hierarchy. Symbols arrange referents in relationship to one another: similarity and difference, up and down. Up and down in turn introduce states, where what is up is guilty of not being down ("They think they're better than we are") and vice versa ("We wouldn't stoop to their level." or "They're not our kind."). In our uses of language we cannot avoid this, because language is riddled with valuing. All statements of more and less, better and worse, imply a hierarchical order. Sometimes we codify these in our laws or religious doctrines; sometimes we engage in social mystification, distrusting people who are different or turning them into deities to be worshiped. Regardless, as symbol-using animals, we are able to create social structures that impose status and place and that affect the condition of life as genuinely as any material force of nature.

Perfection.   As symbol-using (symbol-misusing) animals, we strive to perfect the logic of our forms and patterns. Aristotle believed the universe was **entelechial**, with all beings striving for perfection. Freud explored a negative corollary, the neurotic behavior of **compulsive repetition**. The neurotic conforms to a behavior pattern formed early in life, endlessly seeking the solution to an unresolved problem. In Burke's words, we are "rotten" with the spirit of perfection as we seek the logical extension of some principle, positive or negative. We can spend our whole lives perfecting our performance through symbols: perfection in work, in relationships, in performing a skill. Our expressions reflect our absorption with perfection, even in the ironic sense of the "perfect idiot" or "perfect fool." In this extension of symbol use, we have passed deep into the realm of action, where the forces at play are human motives as they are formed, exhibited, and managed in social intercourse.

Presentation versus Representation

Symbols have the power to alter our social world. By the selection and use of symbols, we create relationships (as when we make friends by speaking in terms of common interests) and change relationships (as when we embarrass a friend by revealing her secrets to others); we shape perceptions (say, by professing sincere interest) and alter perceptions (by grandstanding); we engage one set of motives impelling us to act for an idea ("I should do this because I'm obliged to"), then engage a contrary set of motives impelling us to act against an idea ("but I must be true to myself first"). Because we are symbol-using animals and because we are uniquely able to respond to symbols, we are able to act with symbols.

Sometimes we have a tendency to think and speak as if our language were only a symptom of some deeper reality hidden inside us. This view treats language as representational, a typically psychological view of language. It assumes that reality is under the surface; it lacks efficiency because it assumes that nothing is what it says it is. If we want to understand what any communication means, we have to act as detectives, assembling clues to support an inference. It is more efficient if we have a model for dealing with the data of communication in its own right.

More important, the tendency to think of communication as representing a hidden reality is not well grounded conceptually. Extending this view of communication leaves two choices. Either there is a basis for thought that is not symbolic (a very hard claim to prove), or all communication is inherently deceptive. But if it is deceptive, how will we get information that will permit valid inferences about the hidden reality? Except for Freudian slips, it is hard to imagine what this evidence would be. In the hidden reality scenario, all inferences from the evidence amassed in communication analysis would be about the past. This ignores the fact that people use communication to shape their futures. How could they do that if communication were nothing but a sign of some reality within the communicator?

A more direct route uses the perspective we have been developing. A rhetorical perspective regards communication as a **presentation** of reality. This view holds, first, that communication is the act of **inducing and coor-**

dinating social actions through the use of symbols. Symbolic forms express meanings. When we use expressive forms, we create meanings with others. For instance, does the appointment of Clarence Thomas to fill the Supreme Court seat previously held by Thurgood Marshall mean that African Americans have equal opportunity to fill the highest posts in the U.S. judiciary, or does it mean that the first Bush administration was cynical in making this appointment? Some viewed the appointment of Thomas as maintaining an African-American presence on the Supreme Court. Others countered that his lack of experience (compared to that of Marshall), his conservative interpretation of the U.S. Constitution, and his alleged sexual harassment of Anita Hill made his appointment a blatant form of tokenism without regard for qualifications or integrity. The meaning of his appointment was and is a social construct created by symbolic presentation of the appointment and the shared acceptance of those presentations by others. Rhetorical communication is, after all, addressed activity. It presents an image of reality that is responded to as it is presented. As speakers and listeners, we work together to form the cooperative measures necessary to meet our social objectives. In fact, even our social objectives are the products of our symbolicity.

Second, a rhetorical perspective views communication as presenting reality through the **organizing and projecting power** of symbols. Each of us has a personal history, but the meaning of our past depends on how it is constructed as a history or story with relationships to persons, places, episodes, and events. For example, the death of a classmate in an automobile accident is tragic, but its meaning is multidimensional. Life isn't fair; she had so much to live for; it is important to drive with special caution at night; you never know when it's your time, so treat everyone with love; and so forth. Symbols take past experiences and organize them in the present in ways that permit projections into the future. Communication is presentational because symbolic forms embody images of reality that invite actions of specifiable sorts. It does not simply represent a world that already exists (our dead classmate); it presents an image of the world as it is seen (this is a tragic loss) and as it might become (live each day as if it were your last).

Third, the presentational character of communication stems from the **situated context** in which communication occurs. Our motives for acting do not necessarily grow from within us but frequently from how we understand the situations in which we find ourselves.[5] These understandings are contained in the typical ways in which we present these scenes and the motives appropriate to them—a point we will develop shortly. Here the point is that humans act by presenting a scene in a way that delimits appropriate responses.

Dramatism

Understanding the presentational character of communication is valuable because it alerts us to the importance of a message's surface features, the basic connections between speakers or writers and their audiences as they bond in common solutions to common problems. But this insight in and of itself is not usable in a systematic fashion. To systematize it, a **model** is required. *A model is a conceptual structure that shows the interrelationships among relevant elements of some phenomenon of study.* We need a model that best shows the presentational character of communication as a symbolic action. This model is called **dramatism**. *Dramatism examines the ways in which we use language in the format of dramatic action.*

Dramatism is a functional perspective toward language; it is concerned with how people manage symbols for social coordination. Through analysis of how language is used, we gain insights into the motives that impel human actors to do what they do and to justify it to others. Burke's **dramatic pentad** formalizes the elements of dramatic presentation:

- **Act**: what was done; what communal moments were depicted

- **Scene**: where the act occurred; the context of interaction in time and place, including the conditions for interaction

- **Agent**: who performed the act; the individual or group engaged in some social function through the management of symbols

- **Agency**: the means of acting; how the deed was done, including the medium of enactment

- **Purpose**: the end or goal of the act; the communal values that were certified by engaging in an act.[6]

These five elements permit a complete description of the relevant aspects of a symbolic interaction. They are conceptual tools used to discover the facts about any communicative act and to put those facts in relationship to one another in a way that provides a plausible explanation for what happened, how it happened, and the motivational urges that account for why it happened.

This last point is important. As we watch a play, we are left unsatisfied if we do not know why the actors are doing what they are doing. We always search for motivations. Once we get a sense of motivations, we form expectations of what will happen next and why. Romeo loves Juliet, so we are not shocked to see him calling outside her balcony. Henry Higgins has a mission, so we do not find his treatment of Eliza Doolittle inexplicable. Burke maintains that the human arena is precisely the same. We act out of motives. More than that, we impute motives to other actors. We have to if we hope to understand why they are acting as they are. We use each element of the dramatic pentad in imputing motives. We examine how each contributes to or induces symbolic action. The patterns we discover allow us to draw inferences about a person's attitude. Burke says that when we think of communication as dramatic action, "the pattern is incipiently a hexad [the five elements of the pentad plus attitude], in connection with the different but complementary analysis of attitude (as an ambiguous term for incipient action)."[7]

By saying that "attitude is an incipient action," Burke means that every symbolic act conveys an attitude or disposition toward its referent. He maintains that attitudes are projections into the future of images from the past. For example, many learned about the tenacity of Erin Brockovich, the brash young legal secretary whose investigative persistence led to a record settlement of $333 million against Pacific Gas & Electric for poisoning the water in a small California desert town, through the movie that bore her name. If those moviegoers learned that Brockovich is now fighting the toxic effects of mold that has accumulated in her dream house, they might think, "Whoever built that house is in for it." Her single-mindedness in fighting for the welfare of others leads viewers to expect she will do no less when her health and that of her family has been threatened. "Whoever built that house is in for it," reflects an attitude, a projection into the future: "She will not take this lying down." Because they are projections into the future, attitudes are incipient acts—in their first stages, where their performance is just commencing. Attitudes are the first stage of the future we anticipate will occur.

At the beginning of this chapter we remarked that contemporary rhetorical thinking has expanded beyond public address to include all the ways and places in which language influences others. Contemporary rhetorical theory has extended its domain of interest beyond the concerns of formal presentations in institutional sites to include any use of symbols that encourages attitudes. In addition to its historical interest in the production of discourse (such as speeches and essays), it also is concerned with discourse as a social practice. Where does this leave us with respect to our original search for a functional account of how humans act with symbols?

With an expansion of rhetoric's boundaries to include all symbolic activity comes a corresponding need for a theory that is able to help us understand and interpret human symbolic behavior. Burke and other contemporary rhetoricians did not find the explanations they needed in science. Scientific constructs are designed for variables that are regular, predictable, and controllable. These are variables in the realm of motion; however, humans are more than machines in motion. Humans are intentional beings who can create meanings symbolically and who can act as well as move. At the heart of action is motive. When we focus on the motives for actions, we find ourselves investigating the mergers of individuals and groups: How do they merge? What are the reasons for these mergers? What forms do these mergers take? And what human "realities" do they delimit? This is the social realm of humans using symbolic forms as means for promoting cooperation.

ଙ

Motives and Action

If we took a representational view of communication, we would assume that motives are hidden within the individual and that we must engage in the detective's task of collecting data to permit an inference about this inner reality. But the type of inference this assumption requires can never satisfy Sherlock Holmes because there is no basis for confirming or denying the inference, since its referent is presumably hidden. By adopting a presentational view of communication, we assume that people reveal their motives by the ways they bond to one another. Motives are observable in the ways we use language and, therefore, are available to anyone who cares to look for them. Motives are also present in everyone's use of language and are the source material from which rhetoric develops.

The presentational view introduces this important shift: It changes motive from a psychological concept that must be inferred to a vocabulary concept that can be observed. A vocabulary concept allows us to listen or read to discover why people do and say what they do. In other words, a motive is contained in a term or set of terms that people use to explain what they are doing. Such terms have ascertainable functions for the individual and the group in promoting social cooperation. They are elements in vocabulary that permit interpretations of meaning and intent that are necessary for social action to proceed.

For example, consider this excerpt from a speech by union organizer Edward Keller:

> Our political action agenda must continue, because for public workers it goes hand in hand with the collective bargaining process!!! Let me tell you that our commitment to aggressive political action is as resolute as it ever was, because we have no other choice!! We have other options. We could give up the fight, and we could resign ourselves to second-class citizenship, or we could return to collective begging, and macing, and patronage, but, Brothers and Sisters, they are irresponsible choices. If we opted for them, we wouldn't deserve to be called a Union . . . and we wouldn't deserve to be called AFSCME![8]

Clearly, Mr. Keller wants his audience to continue political efforts, but notice how this language provides a justification for the union members' world. He depicts the union in a "fight." If it "gives up," the taboos of "collective begging, and macing, and patronage" follow. If it fights on, it is "responsible." How does it fight? Through political action. Why does it fight? For advantage in collective bargaining. Who are the fighters? "Brothers and Sisters" who earn their family status only through continued political efforts. All of this is presented to Keller's listeners by the language he chooses to motivate their collective action. His language provides them with an explanation of who they are and what they are doing. In short, he provides them with a meaningful vocabulary of motives.

All action, as we have noted, is situated action. The situations in which actions occur lend significance to those acts and are essential for understanding them. A priest walking to the altar of a church and genuflecting is showing reverence. The same priest instructing a college class and genuflecting toward the front of the room upon hearing a very confused student answer is showing despair. Situation provides us with the context for interpreting the symbolic actions that occur in them.

Not all situations are ones of conscious reflection, however. There are hundreds of acts we perform every day without reflecting on them. They are routine and not marked by conflict. We shut off our alarm and take a shower without thinking. We put on our jeans, the same leg first each day, without thinking. We walk to class without thinking about how to walk or which route to travel. Our minds are elsewhere, worrying about today's exam, determining whether we'll finish a project in time, recounting the stimulating events of last night, conversing with friends. Soon we're at the building, in the room listening to the lecturer. In the hour that passed, we were continuously situated but not consciously aware of that fact.

Consciousness arises in situations marked by conflict of some sort. Impulses pull us in different directions—approach this, avoid that. This is a bind; what shall I do? I can't do both; I'm faced with choice. In situations of conflicting impulses, choice is the essential ingredient. We have to decide what to do. When we decide what to do, we do so on the basis of a motive. We can offer an explanation. As Mother taught us, "just because" is ambiguous and not a very satisfactory explanation of our conduct. Thus consciousness is concerned with motives, because motives move us to choose one alternative over the others. Burke summarizes this point when he asks, "Would not such facts all converge to indicate that our introspective words for motives are rough, shorthand descriptions for certain typical patterns of conflicting stimuli?"[10]

For example, your friend asks you to go to her party on Saturday, but you still have work to do on a term project due Monday. This weekend is your best shot at meeting the deadline. You think of your professor, who has encouraged you in your work; you think of what a fine course it has been and all that you have gained from it; you think of the consequences for your grade if the project is rushed or turned in late. You decline the invitation. If your friend asks why, you might say, "I have an obligation to my course work first." Your statement conveys very clearly a motive for turning down her invitation, one that most of us would expect a friend to understand as a reasonable excuse, a proper motive.

On the other hand, suppose you think about how dull your life has been, how uninspired you are about this project, how much fun you'll have at the party, what a stimulating group of people will be there, how much better you'll feel on Sunday. You'll go. And if we ask you why, you might say, "I needed a change of pace." Again, your statement conveys a motive for attending the party, one most of us have experienced and can understand as a way to release tension and allow us to work more productively because we're refreshed. It would be odd, if sensible at all, to say you went to the party as an obligation. That would suggest an entirely different set of conflicts—between you and your friend—not between your desire to finish a quality report and your need to socialize. Similarly, we would find it odd if you said you didn't attend because you needed a change of pace. You mean you haven't been doing course work lately?

In this case, *obligation* and *change of pace* are shorthand expressions that are used to resolve patterns of conflicting impulses so recurrent in our society that we have special terms for them. They are shorthand for situations of conflict and the ways in which they are resolved. They are words that organize conflicting stimuli on the basis of images drawn from the past. They project an anticipated outcome from imposing this organization on the present.

Through the process of socialization, we learn a **vocabulary of motive terms**. In fact, we learn several vocabularies: of home, family, and neighborhood; of friends; of school; of subcultures. When we learn a vocabulary of motives, we have learned what counts as a legitimate way to resolve life's conflicts for people who use that vocabulary. In a sense, we learn to speak that language and, by speaking the language, to become a member of the group.

Our affiliation through a vocabulary of motives does more than provide us with group identity; it also provides us with an orientation toward the world. Through our use of symbols, we project images of reality. These projections are not of realities themselves as factually existing entities but of interpretations of realities. We know, for instance, as a matter of fact that the Protestants and Catholics of Northern Ireland live in a state of mutual animosity. We know that large numbers of these people are economically impoverished. We also know from listening to their rhetoric that they each act on their interpretations of reality, not on objective facts. Some vocabularies make Protestants the villains, some the Catholics. Some say it is really not a religious issue but an economic one. Some say it is a nationalistic issue at heart: The British are at fault, or the IRA is at fault. As confusing as this swarm of appeals may appear to an outsider, for those in the trenches of this conflict the vocabulary of motives they adopt makes all the difference in the world in determining their allegiances and targets of response.

Finally, we should observe that the concept of motive, when developed as the use of language to coordinate social functions, is quite similar to Aristotle's *idia* (special topics). Whereas special topics focused on the material premises that were common to a group, motives focus on the linguistic aspects of common orientation. Both provide the means from which rhetorical appeals are developed.

࿙

Rhetoric and Motives

Kenneth Burke tells us that rhetoric is not rooted in some magical power of primitive voodoo but "in an essential function of language itself, . . . the use of language as a symbolic means of inducing cooperation in beings that by nature respond to symbols."[11] Let us consider this definition as a summarizing statement for what we have thus far considered and as a transition to its rhetorical application.

First, we note that Burke thinks **rhetoric is an essential function of language.** By that he means that you could not have language without rhetoric being present in some way. We are reminded here of how the symbolic action perspective views all language as containing an attitude, which is an incipient act. All language, in other words, has bias in it, and that bias projects toward the future. It is an encouragement to perceive the world in a special way. Language sermonizes, much as a preachment, about our point of view, whether we intended to or not.[12]

Second, **rhetoric is a use of language.** So the study of rhetoric is concerned with the way language functions, with what people do with it. We are reminded that the contemporary study of language emphasizes the function it serves in coordinating social action and that in this respect people act with language. The uses of language are to form bonds between individuals and groups through their shared motives.

Third, **rhetoric is a symbolic means of inducing cooperation.** Consequently, a rhetorical perspective toward social action is not only concerned with the act of social bonding through cooperative exchange but also with how such acts are induced. People are encouraged to bond, not required to do so; they have choices. Moreover, these inducements are symbolic in character. They are not in the realm of motion as, for example, might be the case in the face of a natural emergency (your stove is on fire, so your roommate cooperates by throwing salt on the flames). Symbolic inducements are in the realm of action—human acts of selection, organization, and emphasis through intentional choices of symbols to interpret experiences.

Finally, **rhetoric is directed to beings that by nature respond to symbols.** As symbol-using animals, humans can be moved by symbols. They can use them, reflect on them, embellish or refute them, and act on them as interpretations of reality.

Identification

The primary rhetorical function of symbolic acts is to produce **identification.** This does not eliminate persuasion from rhetoric; it views persuasion as part of a larger, more general whole. Identification does not refer to *identification of* such as my identification of the picture before me as my son or the sounds outside my windows as birds chirping. It refers to *identification with,* whereby we find that our ways are the same. At the most basic level, identification occurs when we try to show that our ways are like the other person's: "I was once an undergraduate myself." At its most complex, it can go to the extreme of fusing rhetor and audience together in the cultural ideologies that mark us off as unique groups of people—nationally, religiously, economically, politically, philosophically. Regardless of its depth or sophistication, the basic principle of rhetoric, when examined dramatistically, is the act of identifying. Identification can occur through any symbolic means. It can come through speaking the same language, wearing similar clothing, exhibiting common tastes, espousing the same cause, buying into the same ideology and playing by its rules. Any mode of symbolic action can be the source of identification.

Identification is a **dialectical term**. *A dialectical term is one that implies its opposite.* Consequently, when we say that identification occurs, we simultaneously imply that **division** has occurred. To be attracted to one view implies that you forgo its opposing views. The rhetorical dimension of symbol use always involves the movement of identifying and dividing. But more than that, **rhetoric also overcomes or compensates for division.** We need rhetorical uses of language precisely because we are not united with each other. Rhetoric makes us one by showing us how our ways are joined, as when an older person says, "I can empathize with you; I was once a student." In this fashion rhetoric overcomes division. Thus the principle of identification creates an ongoing cycle of joining and dividing, creating the need for a new effort to join that will also divide us from something else.

You may witness yourself being tossed about in these rhetorical seas by listening to the types of speeches delivered as keynote addresses at national political conventions. The purpose of these speeches is to give the delegates a chance to shout and holler enthusiastically. How better to do this than to reaffirm what "we" stand for and denounce the folly of what "they" propose? Yet each party's speaker will try to hit themes that the average American believes. We believe that the nation should have defensive capabilities, that our dollars should be worth something, that federal expenditures should be controlled, that individual initiative should be encouraged. We know Republican keynoters will speak on these themes. Insofar as we assent, we may feel ourselves divided from the opposition. At the same time, we believe that the government should not adopt policies that create unemployment, that we have an obligation to ensure equal opportunity—economically, socially, and politically, that we should not reward people or regimes that suppress human rights—Democratic themes to be sure. We can identify with these appeals as surely as with the Republican speaker's. In both cases we identify and divide in an unceasing process of rhetorical exchanges.

Misidentification

Identification can also be misperceived. We may falsely believe that our ways and the rhetor's are one. In a word, we can **misidentify**. We may misidentify through the various ways in which misunderstanding and false interpretation can occur. We may think we stand for the same ideas, share common values, seek identical ends, only to discover that we have not heard correctly. Most frequently we will encounter this in conversations with strangers or new acquaintances. As our conversation progresses, we seek to understand what the other person says and how it relates to our beliefs and values. It is not uncommon for us to distort these messages toward symmetry of motives, lacking a history of behavior to help us interpret our newly acquired conversational partner's vocabulary of motives.

Misidentification may also occur through deceit and dissembling. Such occurrences require a deliberate management of symbols to create a false sense of unity. When a person engages in self-serving rhetoric or has ulterior motives in seeking our cooperation, misidentification is afoot.

Regardless of intention, we can look at misidentification as a perversion of identification. Whenever rhetoric leads us to change our perception, we identify with something new and divide from something old. In the act of dividing from a former perception, we have a tacit recognition that a former identification was a misidentification. Sometimes these divisions and simultaneous recognitions of misidentification are stark, as when a person experiences a religious conversion or becomes politically radicalized. At other times they are barely noticeable, as when a person adopts a modification of vocabulary to reformulate the expression of an experience. For example, the characterization of a military action as an "incursion" rather than an "invasion" may go unnoticed by most, but there is a clear difference in the perception each encourages of such an undertaking. Regardless of magnitude, identification and division are present whenever we use symbolic means to induce cooperation because all symbols express an attitude.

Vocabulary of Motives

The rhetorical objective of identification is advanced, therefore, by sharing a common vocabulary of motives. Such a vocabulary gives us a common framework in which to conceptualize our experiences. It provides a common rationale for our perceptions and interpretations of experiences, our expectations of future outcomes, and our confidence that we are bonded in a fashion that sees reality in ways that are essentially the same.

Each vocabulary of motives becomes an elaboration of a basic organizing principle that unites these symbols into a coherent whole. Take the vocabulary of "capitalism." The capitalist is concerned with the *acquisition of excess wealth* or *profits*. One acquires profits by providing something of value for *remuneration*. When the remuneration exceeds the costs, *profits* are *earned*. When costs exceed remuneration, *losses* are *suffered*. In order to know whether we are earning profits or suffering losses, we use methods of *accounting*. These will help us determine whether *costs* outweigh *benefits*. To account for costs and benefits, accountancy requires a *unit of measurement*. *Money* provides such a unit. Money is of value as a *medium of exchange*. *Work, time, creativity,* everything involved in a capitalist enterprise is of value insofar as it can be expressed in money. Money becomes the unit whereby we determine how we're doing. The more money we acquire as excess capital or wealth, the more *successful* we are.

Notice how easy it is now to slip into the social realm from the economic. If wealth is the measure of success, the only way anyone can measure my degree of success is by the amount of excess capital I have to spend. If I hoard my money, I do not use it for exchange value; it is not being put to use. If I spend money, I am using it for exchange value, but the exchange value is not just the material goods it purchases but also the social esteem it purchases. By subtle but traceable moves, we arrive at Thorsten Veblen's theory of conspicuous consumption, according to which the wealthy spend money lavishly to purchase recognition of their success.

But the matter does not stop there. Imagine that this vocabulary of economic exchange was used to discuss and make decisions about education. In the language of this vocabulary, we need a unit of exchange. If that unit is the student credit hour, then the more students we enroll in a course, the more valuable that course. Since the benefits of high enrollment outweigh the costs, we should encourage mass-enrollment courses and discourage low-enrollment courses. We will accord high status to departments that pack them in, low status to those with marginal enrollment. We will make decisions about which courses to offer and which departments to support on the basis of their popularity rather than on their merits as contributors to human knowledge. Students will not be considered in terms of their human potential to learn but in terms of their economic value in generating higher credit hours. Soon departments will make decisions based on the "draw potential" of a course rather than its intellectual merits. By adopting this vocabulary, it should be evident, we quickly lose sight of why students go to college in the first place, and we pervert the mission of higher education to discover, criticize, and disseminate knowledge.

The capitalist vocabulary illustrates how identification can involve a whole conceptual schema that articulates a coherent interpretation of reality. Moreover, such interpretations can be broad in scope, finding uses in more than one dimension of human experience. Capitalism provides a vocabulary of motives—a language for coordinating diverse social functions—not only in the economic realm. It can be applied to matters of social status, education, friendship, or politics, to mention a few. Each application may change the form that embodies the vocabulary, but it does not change the underlying principle of profitability.

Let us extend the contention that identification occurs through sharing a vocabulary of motives. Such vocabularies provide **conceptual patterns** for **interpreting reality**, and it is our conceptions of what is real that shape our responses. *When we identify, we become one in terms of a shared principle.* We cannot distinguish ourselves from one another in terms of that principle because we all adhere to it as essential to our orientation toward reality. This oneness in principle that underlies identification is called **con-**

substantiality, meaning that *there is an essential nature that is shared in common*. If we think of profits as the index of success, we are likely to adopt an instrumental (if not materialistic) orientation toward life. We are likely to identify with whatever embodies positive attitudes toward the means that will further our ends. We are likely to define value in terms of personal gain. We are not likely to identify with matters presented as worthy because they have intrinsic merit. We are likely to feel miserable if we don't achieve personal gains that exceed personal costs because we will have failed to achieve success.

By the same token, we can change the conceptual pattern we bring to experience and thereby change our interpretations of reality and the responses called for. If we think of success as, say, making a beautiful thing, we will shift the basic principle from the instrumental (and materialistic) concern with profit to the aesthetic (and spiritual) concern with creativity. We may find beauty in a task well done, in raising children to be caring and sensitive toward their neighbors, in living our lives in ways that bring out the virtues of the people we touch, in writing a poem that illuminates the predicaments of the human condition. We are likely to identify with appeals to creative virtues. We are not likely to identify with matters presented as worthy because they bring monetary rewards. We are likely to feel miserable if we don't experience imaginative release because we will have failed to achieve success.

Each act of identification implies some underlying principle that gives coherence and unity to our conceptions of reality. Because each conception is embodied in a vocabulary of motives, each set of motives also acts as a **terministic screen**, emphasizing some aspects while ignoring others. A terministic screen provides a partial perspective that serves as a mask concealing alternative interpretations we would make if we chose a different vocabulary emphasizing other conceptual possibilities. This uniquely human ability to make, use, and misuse symbols provides the basis for rhetorical acts to continue from event to event, with people identifying and dividing. Each rhetorical act is both an unmasking of the partial and negative aspects of our previous identifications and a creation of a new mask necessarily present in a new vocabulary of motives.

ɤ
Summary

The dramatistic perspective makes rhetoric central to the study of human action. Humans are symbol-using animals; consequently, we cannot understand human actions without studying uses of language. When we examine what humans do with language, we discover the primacy of attitude. All attitudes are incipient acts. They provide organization for our images from the past, and they project a future. All languages contain special terms that convey these projections, a vocabulary of motives. Rather than looking within to impute motives, we find people exhibiting motives in the typical ways they use language to facilitate social coordination and coop- eration. Motive terms provide inducements to cooperation. Thus all lan- guage is rhetorical. So when we examine the persuasive uses of language from a dramatistic perspective, we are really studying how the persuasive dynamics inherent in language allow humans to act cooperatively in con- structing interpretations of experience and social forms that define the hu- man world. At base we are essentially rhetorical creatures.

12

Experiencing Meaning in Rhetoric

In 1963 President Kennedy delivered a speech at the Berlin wall. The speech is remembered for its impact and for the statement, "Ich bin ein Berliner." Upon hearing these words, the crowd roared its sustained approval. As you listen to a recording of the address, you can sense the electricity of deep emotions flowing through the crowd. In the Cold War context of West Berlin's isolation and the symbolism of the physical barricade erected by East Germany, Kennedy's utterance became a commitment of continued American presence and of solidarity in the face of oppression. The meaning of his words existed not in their semantic content but in the act they performed. Kennedy identified himself as a citizen of the city. Although his status as a "Berliner" was more symbolically than materially true, his self-identification gave special meaning to the beleaguered citizens of West Berlin and to their relationship with the United States.

How any message acts as a source of meaning for its audience is a question of central importance to students of rhetoric. As producers and consumers of rhetoric, we need to understand the functional role symbols play in inducing social action. The topic of meaning is complex. We would require a volume of enormous proportions to deal with it in any complete way. Of necessity, our consideration will be partial and will focus on what is essential to an initial understanding of meaning in rhetoric.

When we ask about meaning from a rhetorical perspective, we are concerned with how people *act* with language to manage their affairs. How do the symbols of messages acquire their meaning for audiences? How do these meanings encourage perceptions of reality? How do these perceptions bear on salient variables in a rhetorical situation, including

219

language itself, to form relevant interpretations of experience? In sum, our questions ask, how should we understand the way language interacts with itself and with the experiences of audiences to create meanings that pertain to social cooperation?

These questions do not refer to the psychological processes of cognition. They are not about how the mind processes sensations or how the mind perceives patterns because neither of these gets at the concern for how meaning is formed in rhetorical exchanges. Nor are our questions of a linguistic nature. Clearly, utterances that violate the syntactic and semantic rules of the language system will also fail linguistically and rhetorically; they will be incoherent. But linguistic competence is not the same as communication competence; the rhetorician's concern is the *communicativeness* of the utterance.

৯৹

Meaning and Context

In the early part of the twentieth century, anthropologist Bronislaw Malinowski made an important breakthrough in how to study cultures. Malinowski was studying the Trobriand Islanders. He was attempting to form a lexicon of their language by recording what he thought each word meant. As he communicated with the natives, he discovered that his recorded meaning changed in actual usage. He was recording meanings as if they were fixed and static, much like an archeological shard; however, he soon learned that meanings depended on how words were used. This insight about language led to him to think about the Trobriand culture and cultures in general in a radically new way. Anthropologists before him had studied cultures as if they consisted of acts and artifacts. Malinowski's insight was that culture isn't these static things themselves but a process manifested in acts and artifacts. Puzzling over how to untangle the webs of culture if one did not find answers in the art and tools of a people, Malinowski's answer was to go into the culture to see what its members thought they were doing. In other words, one can untangle the web of cultural characteristics by taking the natives' point of view.

An important part of taking the natives' point of view involves studying their utterances. In an important essay,[1] Malinowski maintained that language has meaning only in terms of its context. To study language apart from the context in which it is situated gives us mere figments of meaning. Thus Malinowski proposed that students of language use and meaning should shift their attention from the derivation of words used in a general cultural context and focus instead on how language was used in actual practice. He called this type of situated study an **ethnographic** approach to language. Malinowski outlined two simple guidelines for ethnographic studies. First, you had to know about the culture you were studying. Were these farmers or hunters or industrial workers? Were they of a particular religion? What was their political structure, and how were they organized socially? In other words, one needed a baseline to anchor any claim about how users saw their contexts of utterance, including their relationships to one another as language users who shared a common culture. Second, he maintained that you had to determine the situation or circumstances of the utterance because language had no meaning apart from the contexts in which it was used.

When Malinowski examined the natives' uses of language from this perspective, he discovered that they did things or **acted with words**. In addition to signifying thoughts, language use was an action. Malinowski conjectured that the meaning of language usage was intertwined with its accompanying activity. Consequently, people cannot separate the two. *Meaning is embedded in an activity, and activity is enmeshed with the language used.*

We can find illustrations of Malinowski's point in our everyday lives. For example, when we pass friends on the street, we offer a greeting. The defining feature of phatic communion is not what we say to indicate acknowledgment of the other, as we noted in chapter 6, but the recognizable form we use to maintain cordial relationships. When we ask "how are you?" we are not asking for a medical or psychological bulletin; we are indicating that we acknowledge the other party as part of our social world. We have a variety of verbal and nonverbal ways to do this. People who believe they deserve our recognition would probably feel snubbed if we withheld signs of sociability. Similarly, when we visit with family members we haven't seen for awhile, we expect to offer and receive special attention. The patterns of inquiry and response that we inevitably adopt are not just to solicit and impart information; they are also symbolic acts that reaffirm our familial bonds.

Acts like these extend throughout our communication on practical matters, even to exchanges in which we are intent on communicating specific meanings. For example, we learn how to convey specific meanings to our family through the activity of managing practical matters with them (say, teaching the value of money by helping a child open and contribute periodically to a savings account). This is a participatory form of learning, not the type of knowledge acquired through abstract reflection. By the same measure, when we learn some specialized vocabulary (say, of music), we acquire it through some mode of active participation in that field (by study, practice, and discussion). When we discuss music, we are also acting as musicians (talking to musicians as peers), as musicologists, as critics, or simply as buffs. Malinowski's point would apply to any area where people manage practical matters with language. They learn to perform these tasks by participating in the activity of that domain in given contexts. Consequently, uses of language become bound to the activity. To use language in situated contexts is to act with language.

Rhetoricians understand "meaning" in a fashion similar to Malinowski's recommendations regarding language as "situated action." Rhetoricians understand the use of language in context. This means that they do not believe that words alone carry ideas but that meaning lies in an interaction of language and context. Thus, if we want to discover how meaning develops in rhetorical events, we must examine how writers and speakers use language.

✎
Dynamics of Meaning

Thus far we have claimed with Malinowski that the *meaning* of language depends on its *use*. Now we will advance that claim a step further to assert that *meanings develop through the interaction of symbols within contexts*. The following extended illustration will help us understand how meanings develop through the dynamic tensions among symbols, contexts, and symbol users.

Imagine hearing an instrumental tune for the first time. It is a simple piece with a romantic melody and a rhythm that is easy to detect. It is slow and not really the kind of music to which you tap your feet; you feel it someplace else. It is a duet played by a piano and a bass. The piano is played so that the individual notes of the melody seem accentuated over the chords. The bass is bowed with occasional finger plucking. Its sounds are deep, with an onomatopoeic quality to them. As you listen, the serenity of the piece makes you feel calm, even tranquil. You imagine scenes that fit the mood. One scene stands out—a meadow. You imagine it on a summer afternoon; the sun is high, but there is a cool and gentle breeze. You see patches of wildflowers painting the verdant setting with brilliant splashes of magenta, rust, violet, deep yellow, white, cranberry. You imagine hearing cows lowing in a distant field; birds chirping and insects humming lazily in the summer sun. In your mind's eye butterflies hover in the air and then zigzag in drowsy patterns of random flight. The scent of sweet grass perfumes the air. Puffy clouds float across the sky in rococo caricatures of creatures and things. The serene, imagined scene fits the music. You have interpreted the tune; your interpretation is forged from the interaction between the sounds you hear and the experiences you have lived. You interpret it as a song expressing tranquility. With only its sounds and rhythms as data, the meaning dictated by the song is not very specific. Consequently your own past experiences provide a context for constructing a pastoral scene.

You are curious to see whether your interpretation is on target, so you look at the song title: "Good Morning Heartache." Your interpretation does not fit that title at all! You play the song again, listening to it with the title in mind. Now you hear it differently. The deep and very slow bowing of the bass is not a musical imitation of cows lowing. It is the throbbing of a saddened heart. And the individual notes that stand out so clearly on the piano are not birds chirping or insects humming but emotions jabbing with piercing pain. The added information of the title brings to mind a different memory. This time it may not be a scene but a recollection of what it felt like to have a broken heart. As you think of sad times, you may recall the wrenching pain that greeted each morning—the feeling of despair at a profound loss, of helplessness because circumstances were beyond your control. You recall how slow your mind felt, how you sensed constriction in your chest that made it difficult to breathe. It is a very sad recollection, befitting the mood evoked by the song heard in this new way. The composer's title has altered your interpretation by giving you a context for listening. In turn, that context interacts dynamically with your experiential history. Still, since this is an instrumental rendition, you have great latitude in the meaning you construct from the music. The composer may have intended to express sadness, but you prefer your first interpretation. You listen to it in your own way and create your own meaning. Subsequently, you play the song to help yourself feel tranquil.

One day you discover a Billie Holiday recording of the song. The lyrics prevent you from interpreting it as you choose. The words speak thoughts and feelings that belong to one set of recollections (heartache) but not another (tranquility). You cannot imagine the bass as cows lowing or the piano as birds chirping. It is definitely a heart-wrenching ballad. If you are in the midst of personal trauma, the words may seem to express your feelings. Or you may find that the song recalls a past experience. If the specific event it recalls is distant, the song may give you ideas to help you find a pattern and to interpret what was previously a jumble of emotions. The song has helped you to perceive as a gestalt what you only perceived in its particular parts when you were actually in the saddened state. It has helped you frame your previous experience.

Six months later you may hear the lyrics again and have none of these thoughts. You may be ecstatically happy and so have the more general response of "that's sad" or "that's life" or "I know what she's singing about, I've been there." It makes no difference which of these is your response because the essential point is that the music plus the words are but a part of what the song actually does mean at any given moment. You bring your experiences to bear, and the relationships among sounds, words, past experiences, and present contexts interact to create meaning for you. You have a considerable and essential role to play in establishing the meanings that occur as you listen.

Let us extend our example one final step to make it completely contemporary. One day you are watching a music video channel and see a rendition of the song. This rendition translates the song into a visual narrative. A female singer acts out a scene that depicts the lyrics of "Good Morning Heartache." She confronts you with a different image again. You witness a particular setting, with a particular person enacting a scene from her life. The video image is so concrete that it obliterates your previously imagined scenarios for the song. In fact, it even obliterates you from the scene. It is not your story but that person's story. The potential for fantasy has been significantly reduced. The vividness of the visual depiction eliminates much of what you might have imagined as experiences to which the song alluded. In fact, you may be reduced now to the relative passivity of a spectator, invited to appreciate a scene played before you, rather than an active participant constructing the experiences that accompany the song's theme. To get yourself back into the scene, you have to struggle beyond the visual narrative. Perhaps you recoil in disgust, rejecting the video as a misrepresentation of "your" meaning of the song. For you, the video has destroyed the song as music and transformed it into spectacle.

What I have been describing is a process of meaning making. Stimulated by symbols, we interpret the song in various ways. Across time, as the symbols changed, the meaning changed. As your life changed, you responded differently because you heard and understood differently. These were changes of context, making it possible for some interpretations to flourish and others to wither. Further, these contextual changes suggest the multidimensional dynamics that are relevant to understanding how symbols create meanings for audiences.

Meanings Are Mediated

Formerly, theories of meaning held to the conviction that words had proper meanings and that communication was clearest when words were used precisely with respect to their proper meaning. As work like Malinowski's called proper meaning theories into question, a **mediation model** came to the fore. This model depicts meanings as the products of interaction between a thinking human and the stimuli of the environment. Its most recent versions in anthropology, psychology, neurophysiology, philosophy, and communication link meaning directly to the way language and experience are intertwined. This language-experience relationship is important to us because it explains meaning in a fashion that is directly applicable to rhetorical understanding.

Contemporary rhetorical theory generally adopts an experiential theory of meaning. It concentrates on how meanings emerge from utterances. The significance of individual isolated words is minimized, since rhetorical meaning derives from the larger thought units of propositions, arguments, and appeals intended to induce cooperation. Utterances indicate how people understand and share their experiences. So when we talk of "meaning" in rhetoric, we have in mind how symbols evoke meaning as **situated utterances**. We are interested in how we act with symbols to construct interpretations of our experiences and to forge social bonds through these constructions. For our purposes, let us define *meaning* as *the significance of an utterance as it emerges from a context of usage and the perceptions that it invites*. By *perception* we mean *the interpretive awareness of a referent*. Perception refers to how our minds grasp or understand something, as in these examples:

"I know that anthrax is a deadly bacteria. My perception is that the Department of Health and Human Welfare is unprepared for its use as a terrorist weapon."

"I know that Lauren expressed dissatisfaction with her courses this semester, but I perceive her to be happy with her overall program."

"George W. Bush wants us to perceive him as a leader."

"My perceptions of her basic values were mistaken."

In addition to being situated utterances, rhetorical production of meaning has the further characteristic of being specific to particular issues and audiences or publics. As we saw in chapter 5, rhetorically salient meanings are always specific to the situated and addressed character of our attempts to induce social action. Consequently, rhetorically salient meanings are unstable; they defy attempts to confine signification to a single grouping of referents. For instance, rhetorician Richard Weaver's study of early and mid-nineteenth century American public speakers found that a stable base of public understanding sustained their florid, spread-eagle oratory. These understandings were the mediating bridge, so to speak, that allowed audiences to connect lofty imagery and a common national identity without requiring further explanation.[2] By contrast, broadly shared visions of America's meaning are less available to contemporary audiences. Indeed, something as pervasive during the first three-quarters of the twentieth century as constructing America through rhetorical imagery of a "melting pot" is now contested by the more segmented imagery of "quilt" and "rainbow."

In our highly mobile and diverse society, traditions and relationships are less stable than in previous eras, which further adds to the instability of meaning across situations and groups. Indeed, scholars of new social movements or identity movements seem to agree that relational instability fosters a multiplicity of symbolic expressions and interpretations and inserts gaps between visions of order and reality. Efforts to snatch order from the flux of rhetorically salient meanings are frustrated by processes of signification that no one can completely control.[3] Thus, a rhetorical model of meaning must pay particular attention to the situated process or context wherein symbols acquire meaning and, thereby, induce social action.

With these thoughts in mind, let us advance our discussion by considering four propositions relative to meaning as it emerges in rhetoric:

1. Language usage is experientially based.

2. Perceptual patterns emerge from contexts of experience.

3. Language usage contains inherent frameworks for conceptualizing what we experience.

4. Meaning emerges from the interaction among symbols within their context of use.

Language Usage Is Experiential

The way our utterances present our experience is inextricably bound to the way we actually experience our environment, both physically and culturally.[4] At a very basic level, we experience ourselves directly in orientation to our environment. This is essentially an experience of spatial relationships: up—down, in—out, front—back, over—under, near—far, and so forth. We also have direct experience with existing objects in our environment. These are referred to as **ontological** experiences because they are of the *being* or *existence* of something. An ontological experience may be of an entity, like a train, or a substance, like food.

When we encounter our environment orientationally or ontologically, we simultaneously encounter the language of those experiences. Take *up—down*. We experience *up* as standing erect, as the position of the body in health, contrasted with *down*, the position assumed when ill. We are *up* when in a conscious state, whereas we are *down* when asleep. A person who is *up* is active, but *down* is the position of passivity. When we make comparisons, the greater quantity will be higher or *up* as contrasted with the lesser amount. The experience of *up* is positive—associated with power, health, activity, and progress toward a goal. The very way in which we experience *up* in our physical encounters (orientationally) with our environment gives us a basis for thinking in terms of *up* as an ontological concept.

The meaning of such basic experiences comes not just from our physical encounters with our environment but also from our cultural orientation. In our culture, we think of *up* as the top of something as seen from above. But this is a matter of perspective. For example, a ball literally has no top or bottom, no up or down. But our culture teaches us to orient to it as if it did. The bottom of the ball is the part closest to the ground, while the top is farthest away. Or take *front—back*. If we say, "Pam is hiding in back of the tree," we mean the tree is between Pam and the person from whom she is hiding. Trees do not have a front or back. Our culture makes an orientational assumption, however, that is present in the way we experience front and back. Other cultures may experience spatial orientation differently.

The ways in which we understand our world are conditioned by the interactions we have with our physical environment. But these interactions are themselves experienced in light of the cultural suppositions we share and the language we use. In other words, conceptual meanings that emerge from this interaction are experientially based. Researchers Lakoff and Johnson say that meanings that emerge this way are concepts we live by.[5]

Perceptual Patterns Emerge

When we say that meanings emerging in experience are concepts by which we live, we are not confining this claim to the direct experiences we may have of an entity or an orientation. Language acts have consequences, and indirect associations arise from the contexts in which we use language. These also are part of language's tie to experience. Any context of usage will contain a variety of salient factors that contribute in some measure to an utterance's meaning. Even more, contexts contribute to the development of perceptual patterns that are larger than the meaning of an utterance considered by itself.

Our usage occurs in contexts where knowledge of what is possible or impossible, fact or fiction, true or false interacts with values, emotions, social forces, and cultural conditions pertinent to the events and the other participants in which rhetoric transpires. Each of these interactive dimensions is individually meaningful, but their union provides a gestalt of meaning that includes not only the reference of symbols but also a pattern of the whole experience of which the utterance was a part. The Kennedy speech at the Berlin wall or the song "Good Morning Heartache" provides more than the memorable utterance "Ich bin ein Berliner" or the song title. The former provides us with an experience of a solemn commitment to defend the freedom of a beleaguered people, the latter an experience of the desolation that accompanies the loss of love. In both cases, the coherence among their constitutive elements provides a pattern for perceiving the experience.

As these gestalts recur in our culture, we develop culture-specific ways of speaking about and responding to experiences similar in kind. These recurrent patterns are contained in our motive terms and in the attitudes toward the future that they imply. As Lakoff and Johnson observe:

> Cultural assumptions, values, and attitudes are not a conceptual overlay that we may or may not place upon experience as we choose. It would be more correct to say that all experience is cultural through and through, that we experience our "world" in such a way that our culture is already present in the very experience itself.[6]

These patterns, inclusive and holistic, remain with us as acculturated individuals, to be called into play in our future language uses. They provide us with the stock of common assumptions, values, expectations, and motives that make it possible for us to share our perceptions of experience with others.

Language Usage Contains Inherent Frameworks

When we learn typical patterns for expressing ourselves, those patterns invariably provide conceptual frameworks that organize experience in a particular way. For example, we talk about our election campaigns as "races." The symbol of an election as a race expresses the following:

- Elections are contests.
- There will be a winner and a loser.

- Contestants need a sound strategy to race well.
- Those who are not in the race are observers.
- Contestants are expected to abide by the rules.
- Contestants must be in fit condition to race well.
- Observers who favor one of the contestants show support by partisan rooting and cheering.

This list could be extended, but the essential point is sufficiently illustrated. To talk about election campaigns as "races" invokes a framework that conceptualizes our political activity in terms of contests. We could also talk of campaigns as "trials" or "debates," in which case different conceptual frameworks would be involved. It is significantly different to talk about our politics as "games" where we sit as partisan fans, as "trials" where we sit as jurors, or as "referenda" where we sit as evaluators of issues and arguments. Further, notice how each frame organizes our thoughts in terms of a political process—the election campaign—rather than in terms of political policies that will have a direct bearing on our lives—what the candidates propose to implement once elected.

Our selection of symbols shapes the way we understand our experience. The selection creates a frame that highlights certain features and, necessarily, hides others. These frames are called **schemas**.[7] Schemas are mental models drawn from past experiences, which we use to organize new experiences and explain them. For instance, we may have schemas based on past experiences with conflict that we employ to think about war and peace. We may see conflicts as arising from competing interests (such as control of oil fields), in which case we organize war and peace in terms of self-protection. But we also could see conflict as arising from competing ideas (capitalism versus communism), in which case we would organize war and peace in terms of ideology.[8]

Every use of language is partial in the conceptual schema it advances. Nonetheless, it is the great power of language that these schemas provide the very ways in which we make sense out of what has occurred in our lives. Moreover, it provides the basis for sharing our experiences with others. Insofar as our utterances are within the cultural framework of our audience, its members may participate actively in reconceptualizing their experiences in terms that we provide. Language brings ideas, feelings, and values shared among speaker and audience into harmony.

Meaning Emerges from the Interaction of Symbols

We defined the meaning of an utterance as the significance that emerges from its context of usage and the perceptions that it invites. Thus far we have considered language usage in context and the patterns for perceiving and conceptualizing experience that are formed. Here we need to emphasize that language is dynamic in its interactions with other symbols and with its context. Meanings of utterances grow from the interactions of the words used in the utterance. I. A. Richards referred to this interactive character of words as interinanimation.[9] That is, words animate meanings in one another. The specific meanings they animate depend on the context of usage—both the external context of the situation and the internal contexts of the written phrase, sentence, paragraph, page, chapter, and book or of the spoken statement, contention, argument, case, and address. Richards summarized this process of interinanimation in his **context theorem of meaning**, which holds that *words are successfully meaningful in their contexts insofar as they animate and are animated.*

This interactive and interinanimating characteristic of language use contributes to rhetoric's capacity to constitute meaning and, therefore, social reality. Recent scholarship addressed to rhetoric's constitutive dimension has followed Richards by locating meaning in the symbolic interaction that occurs in language use. Legalist and critic James Boyd White has argued that during periods of political and social transformation, changing conditions can challenge shared understandings to the point where the words we use to express the social compact lose their meaning. He claims that "language is not stable but changing and that it is perpetually remade by its speakers, who are themselves remade, both as individuals and as communities, in what they say."[10] Rhetorician Steven Mailloux (1989) advances the equally strong thesis that because rhetorical exchanges establish our interpretive experiences, "there is no appeal outside rhetorical exchange."[11] Mailloux argues that rhetoric is the medium by which human reality is forged because the rhetoric of human communicative exchange establishes our interpretations of experience. Critic Maurice Charland (1987) illustrates the constitutive thesis, as we noted in chapter 3, through his analysis of the *Parti Québécois's* White Paper, which calls francophone Canadians of Quebec to answer their destiny as a separate people. The White Paper's internal and external contexts of usage amount to a rhetorical engagement of cultural relations that transform the identity of Canada's French speaking citizens from *Canadien Français* to *Peuple Québécois*. These works share Kenneth Burke's insight discussed in chapter 10 that the participatory dynamics of rhetorical acts lead to symbolically induced relations; rhetorically constituted meanings significantly shape social will.

The inclusion of everyday communication within context of usage is significant because it extends the context theorem of meaning beyond texts as objects of interpretation to include human interaction. Throughout our lives, we use words to label and to understand the events we experience. Our past experiences of situated usage form our knowledge of what words mean. Our contextual histories are projected into every utterance, guiding the specific meanings that emerge from the interinanimation process in each specific context. We must also be mindful of the role of audience or communication partner (with their own histories of usage) in the interinanimation process.

ↄ
Rhetorical Applications

Thus far we have been discussing the way meaning is developed in rhetoric. Our considerations have emphasized the link between a rhetorical understanding of meaning and the way people experience communication. We have borrowed two major sets of ideas to explain this linkage. We used Lakoff and Johnson's idea of concepts we live by to explain how our language shapes our experiences. Then we used Richards's idea of interinanimation of words to explain how meanings develop dynamically in context.

These considerations are important to students of rhetoric because they help us make wiser predictions about how our language choices will work in a given case. They also help us listen to and read more critically the choices of others. Finally, they allow us to reflect on and understand better why people experience a rhetorical transaction in a particular way. Our attention to theoretical concerns with meaning should help us make sounder practical language choices and judgments. We can see how this theory relates to practice in some clearly discernable ways.

Within an Utterance

First, there is the interaction of symbols within a single, meaningful utterance. In speech this consists of articulating a complete idea; in writing it consists of a sentence. Within an utterance, interaction occurs in terms of placement of words and phrases relative to one another. Manipulations of grammar, vocabulary choice, and imagery can alter meaning in significant ways.

Grammar. With respect to grammatical constructions, we can alter the strength of connection between ideas by **relative placement**, moving them closer together or farther apart:

I taught rhetoric to Nola.

I taught Nola rhetoric.

In the first sentence, *taught* is separated from *Nola*. It is not clear that Nola actually learned what she was taught. In the second sentence, the closeness of *Nola* to *taught* suggests that she learned her lessons. The placement of *rhetoric* immediately after *Nola* reinforces this suggestion because it implies that knowledge of the subject is something she possesses.

We can increase the emphasis on an idea through suggestions of **volume**. Sometimes we do this by *elongating a sound*, as in *h-u-u-u-u-g-e* to suggest something very large or *t-i-i-i-n-y* to suggest something very small. At other times the repetition of terms or *duplication* suggests volume:

1. David is a hunka hunka burnin' love!

2. Martha put a teeny tiny dent in Charles's fender.

3. Molly wrote and wrote and wrote until she had completed a 600-page manuscript.

The basic rule is that duplication increases the essential value of the referent. If the referent is one of *magnitude* (as in sentence 1), duplication increases the sense of size; if the referent is *diminutive* (sentence 2), duplication reduces the impact; if the duplicated term is an *active verb* (sentence 3), duplication intensifies the action.

Voice is another significant form for modifying meaning. By using *active voice*, the subject engages in action:

Bill hit the books last night.

Passive voice has the noun receiving the action, suggesting a shift in emphasis from the doer to the receiver of an action:

A lot of studying was going on last night at Bill's place.

In general, we perceive the first sentence to be about Bill and the second to be about studying. By increasing the use of active voice, we increase the sense of activity in our rhetoric; passive constructions do just the opposite.

Word order is another way to alter meaning. In general, we orient to placing the important or more desirable item first. It is more common for us to say "front to back" than "back to front," "up and down" than "down and up." Because our culture orders items in this way, we can alter suggestions of importance by the way we order items in a series. Word order also alters meaning through the use of **anterior shifters**, or those words that come before the term we are focused on and that modify its meaning. For example, in his study of the meanings of war and peace, political scientist Francis Beer constructs a partial list illustrating how the meanings of "war" are modified by an anterior shifter, e.g., "Academic War," "Genocidal War," "Just War," "Rhetorical War," "Urban War," "World War."[12]

We manipulate meanings by the way our grammatical constructions place ideas in relationship to one another. In other words, ideas are altered by the way we arrange the words describing them. These interactional variations influence meaning.

Vocabulary. Another obvious way in which meanings arise through interaction is by the **denotation** of word choice, or the specific meaning of a word, its literal sense. Dictionaries provide us with an inventory of the traditional meanings of words. They are context free and static. They are records of lexical meaning and provide a base of the heritage of a word, including its derivation from foreign roots. Consulting a dictionary is a wise starting place in your search for meanings. However, dictionaries alone encourage a proper meaning superstition, which holds that there is a right and wrong usage of a term, contingent on its dictionary meaning. When we examine how people use language we find that other variables of context enter into the meaning associated with any given term.

The terms we use carry a baggage train of meaning. As discussed earlier, in any utterance, nouns, verbs, and modifiers animate one another. They highlight selected aspects and hide others, modify one another, and create the unique meaning of that particular utterance. Even such mundane variations as

- Kacey is reading.
- Kacey is studying.
- Kacey is researching.
- Kacey is doing her homework.
- Kacey is hitting the books.

convey subtle differences in more than our sense of the distinctions among the actions described by the verbs.

Animation is achieved in vocabulary selection by tending to **connotation**, or the suggestions implied by usage, its associative sense. If Kacey is reading, she is occupied with a book, but we don't know why. If she is studying, we may assume that she is involved in some way with reading for scholarly purposes. She is also trying to understand and retain what she is reading. Her work is not a pastime but a serious pursuit. If she is researching, she probably has a specific project on which to focus her work. The questions she wants to answer are more controlling of her activity than the information on the printed pages she reads. We may see Kacey as a person who engages in specific intellectual pursuits if she conducts research. If her reading is homework, she is answering someone else's questions or fulfilling an assignment. Here we get a clearer sense of Kacey as a student. If she is hitting the books, she is engaged in an assault of sorts. This image of violence suggests the need for emergency measures, as when she is behind in her work or cramming for an exam.

In each of these cases, an interactive relationship is established between the gestalt of meaning we ascribe to Kacey and to the verb that presents her activity. The interaction between these two clusters of meaning brings certain senses of Kacey and her reading to the fore and suppresses others. The clusters animate each other in an utterance that has a sense for us, a sense that is unique.

Denotation and connotation are always at work in the interinanimation process. Both dimensions are important and both must be taken into account when we are examining discourse at the level of vocabulary. While connotation obviously depends on context, it is also the case that some uses of language rely more heavily than others on the connotative value of words to convey meaning. We may depict this phenomenon by thinking of denotation and connotation as forming a continuum. Usages that emphasize most heavily the specific meaning of a term fall at the denotative end, while usages that rely extensively on the associated suggestions of a term are at the connotative end. For example, medical lectures rely on specific, technical, denotative meanings of terms so that the audience can uniformly apply the scientific results presented in the lecture. At the other end of the continuum is a conversation between lifelong friends. They can use connotation as a conversational shorthand. Strangers overhearing the conversation would have no idea what the friends were discussing because they would not share the connotations established through years of interaction.

Denotation and connotation are two of the principal dimensions of word choice that contribute to meaning. Any term's connotative or denotative value is relative to the larger frame of the **textual narrative** in which it is used. For instance, as we saw in chapter 9, a term like "prostitution" can be used in opposing textual narratives dealing with issues of exploitation and of justice. Andrea Dworkin's textual narrative was about men exploiting women by forcing them to have sex. In this narrative, sex for money is linked to gang rape. This linkage devalues money as the defining condition of prostitution because rape is so powerful in its denotative and connotative value that it controls the meaning. Gang rape turns prostitution into a form of male domination through an exertion of power; by exploiting the prostitute's economic needs, males force her to have unwanted sex. Sallie Tisdale's textual narrative is about discrimination against women by making prostitution illegal. In this narrative, sex for money is linked to a chosen line of work (sex work) that is professionalized via unions (e.g. COYOTE). This linkage underscores money as the defining condition of prostitution. By "professionalizing" it, her narrative makes legal restrictions appear to be unjust treatment of women by limiting their right to earn a living as they choose. By thoughtful word choices, such as Dworkin's and Tisdale's, rhetors can influence greatly whether the audience actually receives the "correct" (intended) meaning.

Imagery. A third way in which the interinanimation within an utterance may be modified and meanings managed is through the use of **imagery**. Such usage is referred to as *figures of diction* or *speech*, sometimes called *tropes*. These figures alter a word or phrase from its proper meaning to another.

When we use language in unusual ways, we attract attention to our thoughts. For this reason, rhetoricians historically have stressed the importance of word choice to enliven ideas. When a politician refers to his opponent as a "pusillanimous pussyfooter" (**alliteration**: repetition of identical sounds in successive words) or a restaurant menu urges us to order "Jumbo Shrimp" (**oxymoron**: a seeming contradiction), they put ideas into unusual and even incongruous relationships. As these expressions "wheel across the landscape of our fancy" (**metaphor**: application of a term or phrase to something to which it is not literally applicable), they attract attention. In this way they may ornament ideas through conscious expression.

Of course, excessive use of imagery may leave your audience with the impression of *overdrawn* ornamentation substituted for *underdeveloped* ideas (**antithesis**: the balancing of two contrastive words, phrases, or clauses against each other). Rhetors who seem more intent on *sound* effects than *sound* reasoning (**epanaphora**: repeating the same word to begin successive phrases or clauses) may delight the ear but disappoint the *brain* (**synecdoche**: the use of a part to express the whole). We use imagery not only to beautify but also to create relationships that give new meaning.

Chaim Perelman and Lucie Olbrechts-Tyteca remind us that figures can argue. "Choice of terms to express the speaker's thought is rarely without significance in the argumentation."[13] This observation reinforces the thesis we developed in chapter 11: There is very little in language use that is neutral. Most contemporary rhetoricians agree that language in use *induces attitudes*; it is *sermonic* (**apposition**: restatement of a word or phrase next to another so that the second adds to or explains the first). In his work on the criticism of oral rhetoric, Carroll Arnold has shown that tropes may be grouped according to how they argue.[14] He reminds us that imagistic devices are practical means to *repeat, compare, enlarge, constrain,* and *contrast.* (**cumulation**: listing related items together).

The three preceding paragraphs identified devices of imagery that occurred in my attempt to communicate my understanding of imagery to you. These devices were noted after the fact of composition. They were the product of my worrying over word choices and sentence structures to explain the concept of tropes. The frequency of these parenthetical observations indicates that while tropes may have strange-sounding names, they are not esoteric considerations when communicating rhetorically. We cannot help but use them. The issue is never whether you will use imagery, but which tropes you will use and how well you will use them. As both makers and consumers of rhetoric, we must attend to how the interaction among symbols creates meaning. Figures of speech and of thought suggest an attitudinal disposition that invites and shapes perceptions in and through images used.

Extended Verbal Contexts

We experience meanings within larger frameworks of verbal context through the ways in which ideas interact. This may be the unit of a paragraph or an argument, or it may extend to the considerations of an entire work. Expressed ideas illuminate and modify one another, giving each argument a special sense for those who experience it as a whole. For example, former president Bill Clinton spoke at the annual White House prayer breakfast for clergy on September 11, 1998. The event followed his grand jury testimony and address to the nation on the Monica Lewinsky affair a few weeks earlier. That testimony (which was available on the Internet) and his nationally televised speech had raised questions about his contriteness for actions that citizens overwhelmingly found inappropriate and disappointing, if not illegal. Consequently, his audience heard his profession of repentance at the prayer breakfast in terms of the earlier events.

> I agree with those who have said that in my first statement after I tes-
> tified I was not contrite enough. I don't think there is a fancy way to
> say that I have sinned.

As a confessed sinner, his apology required a request for forgiveness.

> It is important to me that everybody who has been hurt know that the
> sorrow I feel is genuine: First and most important, my family; also my
> friends, my staff, my cabinet, Monica Lewinsky and her family, and the
> American people. I have asked all for their forgiveness.

For these comments to be heard as genuinely felt sorrow for the pain he
had caused others, he had to admit that his earlier remarks had not shown
him to be sufficiently contrite. But Clinton then sets forth additional criteria for forgiveness:

> First, genuine repentance—a determination to change and to repair
> breaches of my own making. I have repented. Second, what my Bible
> calls a "broken spirit"; an understanding that I must have God's help
> to be the person that I want to be; a willingness to give the very for-
> giveness I seek; a renunciation of the pride and the anger which
> cloud judgment, lead people to excuse and compare and to blame
> and complain.

He then linked his apology to a basic Judeo-Christian precept that true repentance must be accompanied by a commitment to change his ways, and
he listed the implications of this commitment for him.

> First, I will instruct my lawyers to mount a vigorous defense, using all
> available appropriate arguments. But legal language must not obscure
> the fact that I have done wrong. Second, I will continue on the path of
> repentance, seeking pastoral support and that of other caring people
> so that they can hold me accountable for my own commitment.
>
>   Third, I will intensify my efforts to lead our country and the world
> toward peace and freedom, prosperity and harmony, in the hope that
> with a broken spirit and a still strong heart I can be used for greater
> good, for we have many blessings and many challenges and so much
> work to do.[15]

The effectiveness of Clinton's apology rested in part on the coherence of
his expressions of remorse as it interacted with his acknowledgement that
his first apology was inadequate and how he proposed to satisfy the moral
framework he invoked: genuine repentance and acknowledgement of a
"broken spirit" that only God's help could mend.

External Contexts

As powerful as these internal sources of interaction are, they are not
without modification by the forces present in the external context. Meanings alter as we take into account how a particular rhetorical transaction is
situated in an action event. Concerns like the rhetorical situation, the per-

son of the rhetor, the perceived intentions of the rhetor, the functions the message is thought to serve, and the needs and potencies of the audience act as modifying factors on the meanings that emerge.

Kennedy's speech at the Berlin wall is a clear case. The meaning experienced by his audience was greatly influenced by significant external factors: The physical proximity of the wall (the distance of a football field from where JFK spoke) served as a grim reminder of the Berliners' desperate straits. The presence of American military leaders familiar to the audience was an external reminder of the American military safeguard against communist coercion. The speaker was the American president, singular in his power to make a pledge that would resolve the Berliners' fears. Finally, the audience of Berliners had a history of tense relations with the East German government. These immediate circumstances called forth the context of Berlin's post-World War II history as a source of experience from which Kennedy might draw and of which he had to remain cognizant in presenting his remarks. Everything he said predictably interacted with what his listeners had lived through. How Kennedy put those experiences into meaningful relationships influenced the measure of hope those Berliners had for their future.

In this section we have considered at some length the dynamic interaction that occurs in an experiential account of meaning. We have seen that our language use is tied in basic ways to our experience, that the context of our experiences shapes our perceptions, and that our language usage contains frameworks that conceptualize what we experience. Finally, we saw that meaning in rhetoric emerges from the interaction among symbols within the context of usage.

This last claim is most important. Through our management of language, we structure our perceptions of reality, preserving the past and creating new possibilities for the future. A rhetorical perspective toward language use considers our intellectual, moral, and emotional lives to be the product of meaning making and meaning sharing. Nowhere is this interactive function more apparent than in our use of metaphor. By examining how metaphors create meanings, we can gain greater insight into the practical dynamics of language in use.

᭰

Metaphor

The concept of metaphor has been a major concern of rhetoricians and other students of language since Aristotle wrote on the subject in his *Rhetoric* and his *Poetics*. Aristotle believed that skill at creating metaphors was the mark of genius because metaphor united ideas in ways that were extraordinary and indiscernible in any other fashion.[16] Unfortunately, Aristotle's views never caught on until the last century. In the 1920s and 1930s, I. A. Richards argued that metaphor was more than a stylistic device. It was the cornerstone of meaning and of thought. At first this seemed like a radical contention. How was metaphor "thought"? And why was metaphor the cornerstone of "meaning"? Richards's claim makes perfectly good sense within the framework we have been developing.

We have been examining how our language provides us with conceptual systems for understanding our experiences. These systems begin with the basic relationship between language and experience. We saw these to be orientational and ontological in their most basic form. The research of Lakoff and Johnson indicates that ontological and orientational systems can be combined to form structural systems.[17] Structural systems are ones in which we talk about one thing in terms of another. Take learning. We talk about learning as a journey ("You've come a long way in your understanding of rhetoric"), as a building ("He has a solid foundation in argumentation"), as an organism ("You've grown in your understanding of stylistics"). Each of these structures implies a set of relationships that constitute a conceptual scheme. Journeys are over surfaces ("Let's cover the ground"); there are detours ("Why didn't you go directly to the point?"); and we even get lost ("I don't know where Mike is going with his study"). Similarly, buildings have superstructures, floors, windows, and doors and are prized for interesting design and sturdiness of structure. Organisms, on the other hand, have divisions of plant and animal life, with roots, branches, fruits, and harvest, or with heart, limbs, the need for nourishment, and the capacity for motion.

These structures are metaphorical. They provide us with elaborate networks of relationships with which we think and communicate about our experience. It is so common for us to think in terms of structures like these that we do not notice how pervasive metaphoric systems are in our everyday lives. In fact, most of the metaphors we encounter are not used as imagery intended for stylistic embellishment. They are patterns of thought that we have adopted through their repeated use in our culture. They are so commonly used that we hardly notice that they are metaphors, let alone how they provide conceptual schemes for understanding and sharing experiences. Yet their operation as a mode of linguistic interinanimation is not substantially different from that found in metaphors that express novel ideas and relationships. Metaphors that catch our attention as interesting expressions of novelty we call **metaphoric statements**, and it is this aspect of metaphor we wish to examine more closely.

A metaphoric statement uses metaphoric expression as more than a literary device. A literary device may be discarded as a stylistic flourish. We cannot discard a metaphoric statement in this way because the statement relies on a metaphor in an essential way to constitute its very meaning. When a metaphor is essential to the meaning of a statement, it has several important characteristics. These characteristics were noted and organized in a most influential study by Max Black.[18] Because Black's terminology is so clear and fits so well with the rhetorical view of language use, we will adopt it here.

The first defining condition of a metaphoric statement is that another expression cannot substitute for its metaphoric component. Take as an example the statement "Our moments together are portraits hung in the gallery of my life." No literal equivalent can be used in its place without destroying the essential meaning of this statement; nor can it be paraphrased adequately. As a metaphoric statement, it relies exclusively on the conceptual scheme of art introduced by the metaphor. If we change the metaphor, we change the whole conceptual pattern.

Further, we cannot translate this metaphoric statement into a mere comparison where the metaphoric system is considered as an analogy. To illustrate, complete the following: "Shared moments are like portraits in that . . ." "Life is like a gallery in that . . ." If you can complete these statements without omitting a host of suggestions contained in the original metaphor, we can conclude that the metaphor was used for stylistic purposes. But comparisons of this sort are impossible with a metaphoric statement because it does not use metaphor for style. The metaphor *creates* the meaning. For ease of expression in this discussion, we will use metaphor as shorthand for "metaphoric statement." Our interest will be to discover how metaphors develop meaning interactively.

Every metaphor has the basic feature of one thing talked about in terms of another. The metaphoric expression is understood as a metaphor precisely because it does not fit literally in its context of use. We understand the sentence "Jeff argues with intelligence and zeal" to be a literal expression, whereas we understand "Jeff is a tiger in debate" to be a non-literal statement, since Jeff is not a tiger but a man. "Tiger" refers to some mode of behavior, namely, the savage and cunning character of his arguments.

In this metaphor, *tiger* is the salient term and is called the metaphor's **focus**, while the rest of the sentence is called the **frame**. The *frame thus consists of the literal portion of the utterance*. Frame and focus interplay to create their unique meaning. If the frame is changed, this will cause some alteration in the frame-focus interplay and may result in separate metaphors.

For example, compare the two statements in figure 12.1. By changing the frame, we emphasize different characteristics of the focus. In the first utterance, the way a snake moves is highlighted; in the second, our cultural aversion to snakes as sneaky creatures comes to the fore. In both cases, there is an interactive frame-focus relationship. Both serve as sources of thought, and both thoughts (Bob's behavior and a snake's behavior) are now supported by a single phrase whose meaning results from their interaction. "Bob is a snake" is a metaphoric statement, a metaphor that can only be accounted for in an **interactive view** of how metaphoric meaning emerges.

What are the elements of this interaction? As noted earlier, metaphor develops meaning by talking about one thing in terms of another. The thing talked about is called the **principal subject**, and what is applied to the principal subject is called the **subsidiary subject**. Thus in the sentence "Bob is a snake," Bob is the principal subject and snake the subsidiary subject.

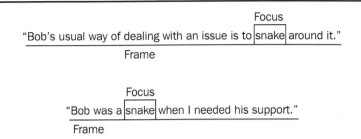

Figure 12.1

While the metaphor's meaning is a result of the interaction between these elements, readers and listeners who lack the meaning of snake and of Bob won't find the metaphor illuminating. More important than the dictionary meaning of snake or the indication of which Bob I mean by pointing him out is the **system of associated commonplaces** that attends each. *A system of associated commonplaces consists of the standard beliefs that are shared by members of the same speech community when they use a term literally.* These are the associations that grow from our cultural and historical experiences with these terms. They are the residues of the contexts in which these terms have been used. In metaphors that derive their meanings through interaction between frame and focus, these systems must be evoked freely. For metaphors of this type to work, we rely on the audience to supply relevant associations without special instruction.

These associated commonplaces affect our interpretation of the principal subject. These interpretations are not normally found in the associated commonplaces of the principal subject when used literally. Take the metaphor "Love is madness" (*Love* is the principal subject, *madness* the subsidiary subject). For our culture, *madness* and *love* have extensive systems of associated commonplaces. Here are some of the more obvious ones:

Love	Madness
affection	insanity
attachment	mental illness
fondness	psychopathology
worship	paranoia
respect	schizophrenia
generosity	catatonia
frustration	depression
commitment	anger
friendship	derangement
sentiment	caprice
tenderness	uncontrollability
protectiveness	irresponsibility

enchantment	dementia
captivation	foolishness
romance	feeblemindedness
amorousness	idiocy
passion	abnormality
ecstasy	hysteria

The two systems become interactive when supported in a single metaphoric expression. Their interaction highlights some elements of the system and hides others. Usually we don't think of lovers as idiots or feebleminded, although spurned lovers sometimes speak of themselves in precisely such terms; nor do we think of ourselves as literally suffering from a mental illness that requires institutional treatment. But we do find our moods to be unsettled and to experience abnormal states of mind. Lovers sometimes do appear to act compulsively or irresponsibly. Similarly, not all aspects of love pertain to madness. Normally we don't think of those who are mad as motivated to act out of respect, selflessness, or affection. We do see them occasionally as captivated or enchanted, as given to passion, and as suffering violent fluctuations of moods. Together these systems delimit each other to relevant associated commonplaces that are mutually illuminating and that create unique meanings.

From the expression "Love is madness" we form the general image of lovers as people not totally responsible for what they do. Contrast this with the images in "Love is a work of art" or "Falling in love is a free ride; staying in love carries a cost." These are entirely different ways of organizing our love experiences into a meaningful form. They bring different elements to the fore as most salient for understanding romantic love. They shape our perceptions in wholly different ways and encourage different anticipations of the future.

The different anticipations encouraged by each of these love metaphors illustrates once more how our language gives us conceptual frameworks for experience. In this case, our conceptual frameworks for love stem from the dynamic character of symbols interacting in a single expression. Metaphors project on the principal subject a set of associated commonplaces that have implications of attitude, value, and behavior.

Yet meaning is not in the utterance itself, as we saw earlier, but in the interaction that occurs between symbols and symbol users. Meaning is the creative response on the part of listeners who are able to comprehend what is being said and to project the significance of that utterance. In metaphor, listeners and readers play an especially active role because they must find a common understanding with the rhetor for the words used. This common understanding requires a shift from a normal or literal meaning to a nonliteral one. Thus rhetor and audience work together to create the meaning of a metaphor.

The elements of metaphoric interaction we have been considering apply to metaphors in general as they influence our perceptions and provide conceptual schemata. All effective metaphors develop meaning through dynamic interaction. This is true for trivial metaphors like "Richard is a lion" and novel metaphors like John Crowe Ransom's depiction of the human as an "oscillating mechanism."

Novel metaphors do have two features, however, that distinguish them from trivial ones: **emphasis** and **resonance**. These features contribute to the degree of interesting meaning evoked by a metaphor. *Emphasis refers to the degree to which the focus is essential for the meaning of the metaphor.* An emphatic metaphor will not permit substitution for its focus. By changing the word, we change the meaning. Emphatic metaphors require our thought. When metaphors create new meanings, we must reflect on their unstated implications. There is no novel meaning without audience cooperation in perceiving what lies behind the producer's words. *Resonance refers to the number of implications we can draw from the interplay between the principal subject and the subsidiary subject.* Metaphors that are rich in implications are resonant; those that are not are nonresonant.

When a metaphor creates meaning, it generates new information. This information is the body of implications—the **implicative complex**—that restructures reality for us. Metaphors that are highly emphatic and resonant have this trait. These are strong metaphors, ones with the power to generate novel thought through the implicative weight of their frame-focus interaction.

What is the interplay of such a metaphor? It is the interaction between sameness and difference. It is the tension that exists by violating the normal semantic sense of a term. It is a tension that forces us actively to consider a commonly held schemata or conceptual pattern with a new one apparently incongruous with the frame in which it is set.

Importantly, this power to present sameness in difference does not exist in the lexicon of a language. Metaphors are not found in dictionaries. They exist only in discourse. They exist only in the interaction experienced during language use. The meanings that emerge are not ones that can be produced in any other terms or in any other way. We began this chapter by indicating that rhetoric's concerns with meaning focused on how our use of language shaped our perception and understanding of our world. The power of metaphor to give birth to new meaning through utterance demonstrates how thoroughly the human world is the product of the interpretations we develop in and through discourse.

☙

Summary

The concept of metaphor brings the considerations of chapters 10, 11, and 12 full circle: the use of language to establish identification. We have explored how the resources of language create a world of meaning in which we find ourselves situated as participants in a narrative. Narratives both draw on our past experiences to constitute new understandings and, through their emplotted relationships, constitute a self-involving logic of action. We enlarged this action orientation to form a dramatistic perspective toward symbol use as the means by which humans induce attitudes. Our uses of symbols structure our realities because they structure our perceptions. Further, as symbols work in harmony with one another, they provide conceptual patterns that organize experience and how it is understood. When these patterns are shared, we identify with one another. The basic way in which these symbolic actions induce identification is through shared motives. In a sense, we speak the same language when we share the same vocabulary of motives.

The motivational dynamics of any message constitute the meaning of that message for listeners. If we know what a message is likely to mean to receivers, we can understand better why they respond as they do. A rhetorician's concern with how people use language requires a theory of meaning suited to rhetorical action. From a rhetorical perspective, meanings are not in the words themselves but evolve from the contexts in which symbols appear or are used. These contexts are historical, situational, linguistic, and sometimes personal.

The relationship between language or symbol usage and the shaping of perceptions is captured by Kenneth Burke's claim that rhetoric is "the use of language as a symbolic means of inducing cooperation in beings that by nature respond to symbols." His basic idea, and the idea generally adhered to in contemporary rhetorical theory, is that rhetoric persuades through establishing identification. Simply put, people identify in terms of shared motives, which are present in words, tones, gestures, actions, whatever has meaning for a rhetor and a listener or reader.

This set of relationships among identification, motives, and symbolic action raises a set of questions that guide our thinking about rhetorical actions:

1. What motives are present in a given symbolic exchange, a given instance of language usage?

2. What perceptions do these motives invite?

3. How do these motives work harmoniously to form an appeal to an audience?

4. What do our findings on the patterns of perceiving and thinking induced by motive appeals tell us about why listeners responded as they did, why they identified, misidentified, divided, and so forth?

One way to answer such questions is through inspection of how people actually use language. This requires hands-on conceptual tools we can use to dig into the dynamic interactions of language as it is used. Extensive development of such tools is beyond the scope of our present inquiry. We have set the stage for further exploration by discussing several basic ways in which meanings are created through the interaction of words in contexts. The concluding chapters will look at shared meanings in rhetorical strategies.

❧ 13 ❧

Rhetorical Form as Strategy

In January 1988, one month after the first Palestinian *intifada* broke out, a small group of Israeli women protested their government's occupation of Palestinian land on the West Bank and Gaza. The women gathered at a major intersection in Jerusalem to carry out their protest, dressed entirely in black and raising a black sign in the shape of a hand with white lettering that read "Stop the Occupation." They protested in silence, with only the sign to communicate the purpose of their vigil. Every week the women gathered at the same hour and in the same location. Word of their protest spread quickly and spontaneously, and within months vigils were occurring throughout the country. Women found the protest easy to enact; they could do it in their own locality, did not have to get a baby-sitter, and did not have to make signs, chant, or even march. This was the origin of the international movement called Women in Black.

Several months later solidarity vigils began to occur in other countries; sometimes the women were only Jewish but often Jews and Palestinians kept vigil together. Within two years Women in Black vigils took on a life of their own, as women in black garb gathered to protest a range of issues: war, foreign occupation of territory, Mafia crimes, neo-Nazism, attacks on foreigners and migrant workers, racism, nuclear arms, violence in neighborhoods, ill treatment of women by religious fundamentalists, interethnic conflict, political detention, and so forth. One of the most visible protests was the weekly interethnic gathering of women in Zagreb and Belgrade (beginning in 1991) to protest the war in Bosnia and the other former Yugoslavian states and the Serbian government's policies of nationalist aggression. In New York, Women in Black have gathered since 1993 on the last Wednesday of every month in front of the New York Public Library, where they have stood in solidarity with the Women in Black in Belgrade.[1]

The Women in Black Web site explains their silence:

> Our silence is visible. We invite women to stand with us, reflect about themselves and women who have been raped, tortured or killed in concentration camps, women who have disappeared, whose loved ones have disappeared or have been killed, whose homes have been demolished. We wear black as a symbol to mourn for all victims of war, to mourn the destruction of people, nature and the fabric of life.

The Web site continues to point out that Women in Black is not an organization but an international peace network, "a means for mobilization and a formula for action." An indication of its effectiveness as a movement of women of conscience is its international presence among women across nationalities and religions. While each group is autonomous and has its own cause, they are united in their commitment to justice and a world free of violence.

Without engaging in verbal discourse, the structure of Women in Black vigils has become an international call to conscience. Its attempt to disengage from the war of words that accompany repressive politics has been so moving that their efforts for peace and justice have received these distinguished recognitions: the Israeli Women in Black have received the Aachen Peace Prize (1991); the peace award of the city of San Giovanni d'Asso in Italy (1994); and the Jewish Peace Fellowship's "Peacemaker Award" (2001). In 2001, the international movement of Women in Black was honored with the Millennium Peace Prize for Women, awarded by the United Nations Development Fund for Women. Why have they achieved this level of affiliation and recognition? What is there about the visual appearance of women dressed in black that makes them so powerful? What does their silence communicate about their convictions of conscience? Does a visual display function rhetorically? These questions alert us to the power of rhetorical forms as strategies for coordinating social action.

As is apparent by now, the study of rhetoric is centrally concerned with the social uses of symbols to accomplish goals. Whether these goals are mundane or lofty, selfish or altruistic, base or noble makes little difference from the perspective of the capacity of symbols to induce cooperation. Goal-directed discourse is marked by its careful selection of symbols, construction of appeals, and engagement of listeners and readers as feeling and valuing as well as thinking beings. Unlike mathematical proofs, which are sound in and of themselves and are available for any and every competent mathematician to inspect, the appeals of rhetoric are *adapted* appeals. They are devised to suit an audience, an occasion, a presenting persona, a time, and a place. They are essentially *strategic* acts.

In the concluding chapters of this book we will consider rhetoric as a mode of **strategic action**. We will be concerned with how it "works" in the practices of any person who communicates with purposes to another. We will consider especially how the **form** of a rhetorical message always contains a strategic approach to the problem posed by a rhetorical situation. Moreover, we will see how rhetorical form is not limited to the selection of images. It extends beyond language to any structural feature that shapes a coherent inducement to perceive and respond in a particular way.

In this chapter we will consider the ways in which **structure in the large** functions as a source of identification. We will consider how rhetorical acts always involve form and how forms embody strategies. In well-formed rhetoric, these strategies are invariably geared to move the audience in some way that serves the rhetor's end—even if the goal is as direct as communicating information.

౨

Structure in the Large

We know from our studies of the sciences that nature percolates incessantly. Energy flows as atoms and molecules jounce and carom. Through a microscope we see organisms alive with eddies of cells that seem to jitterbug and bounce. Of course, to the naked eye none of this chaos is visible. We see only the outward forms of tables and cars, of people and trees. We see our world in the discernible patterns of visible structures. The claim that we perceive our world as structured patterns may seem like an obvious point. Still, it is an important point whose underlying reasons are relevant to understanding how rhetorical communication induces attitudes and actions.

At first glance it may seem that nature's chaos escapes detection because these motions are microscopic. Although it is true that atoms and molecules are not perceptible to the naked eye, this does not explain why our perceptions are always of structured wholes. Our perceptions tend to be holistic—more the result of cognitive processes than sensory experience. The topic of human cognitive processing is complex and beyond our concerns with the basic principles of rhetorical action. However, some of the findings on brain functioning are relevant to our undertaking, and we will briefly examine the important ideas.

Structures Are Basic to Perception

Neurological studies report that the brain does not take in sensory data as a mass of undifferentiated information. It engages in selective perception. This means that our brain separates certain elements from all the others, as the focus of its attention. This discriminative process is illustrated by our sense of sight. Researchers have found that light rays trigger responses in various parts of the brain. These responses tell us that our environment has regions of light and darkness. Moreover, our brain tells us about the qualities of light in these regions. For example, light regions may appear more intensely bright or more vibrantly colorful as the surrounding region is made darker or as its color changes. Studies of visual activity reveal a basic principle of perception: The human brain makes discriminations by **edging** and **bordering**.

In his study of the relationships among symbolic processes and mental processes, rhetorician Richard Gregg[2] indicates that without bordering, we could not stabilize the "ecological flux" that surrounds us. From the most rudimentary level of sensation to the most complex level of ideation, we require borders to perceive distinctions. In addition, Gregg notes that the bordering process is simultaneously a symbolic activity. In other words, our brains do not copy the external world but perceive the external environment in terms of forms that they are capable of perceiving. Gregg offers this summary observation:

> There is no experiencing but formed experiencing. To say that something is formless is usually only an acknowledgment that we have no handy label for what we are experiencing, but it cannot mean that we are experiencing something unformed, for this is a contradiction and a neurological impossibility.[3]

Of course, there are limits to what we can and cannot perceive. For example, humans are hardwired to interact with our environment in certain ways. We know that our sense of smell is inferior to a dog's, and our sight is less acute than a bird's. We do not detect some sights, sounds, and odors in our environment because our sense organs are insufficiently sensitive. Our "reality" is not the same as Rover's because our neurological capacities are different.

Gregg's investigation of neurological findings uncovered six basic patterns of human perception relevant to our immediate concerns with rhetorical inducements.[4]

1. *The principle of "edging" or formulating "boundaries."* The brain perceives data in terms of wholes. This principle is so important to perception that the brain will construct or fill in borders as necessary to render data meaningful.

2. *Rhythm.* The brain perceives data in terms of motion. Not only are the brain's activities rhythmic, but so too are human perceptions. Rhythm is fundamental to structuring "realities."

3. *Association.* The brain perceives identities. Likeness and difference are basic to discrimination. Comparison and contrast require detection of identical features.

4. *Classification.* The brain perceives groupings. The result of contrast and comparison is clustering of like with like. The brain "groups" likeness at all levels of activity.

5. *Abstraction.* The brain perceives by abstracting data from the ecological flux of its total environment. While abstraction is continuous and helps efficiency of perception, it also distorts because it is always partial.

6. *Hierarchy*. The brain seeks closure on structures of perception. These structures tend to be interrelated as superordinate and subordinate elements and systems. These hierarchical structures influence the meanings of perceptions.

Perception and Structure in the Large

These six basic principles of perception are rife with suggestions for how structures influence us. First, they suggest that all human perception is selective perception. We do not take in all of the sensory data "out there," only what we are equipped to detect. Our brains abstract, group, bound, and in other ways shape the data we do perceive. Other data are left behind. Although we form an intelligible perception of "reality," it is a partial perception and necessarily a distorted perception.

Second, our perception of reality requires structure. There can be no perception without structure of some sort. Consequently, the "realities" that we know and their meanings for us are welded to the structures we perceive.

Third, the structures we perceive have a variety of forms. Their defining traits have shape, movement, grouping, and likeness and difference, among other things. In other words, structures are not just material forms but any pattern that can be perceived by the brain.

Fourth, all of our experiences have structure or form. In every episode of motion and action, there are patterns of sense, feeling, and thought. Unless and until their patterns are grasped, these episodes remain unintelligible aspects of reality.

Fifth, because all experience is tied to structure, it is apparent that changes of structure lead to changes of experience. As changing the speed of an engine or rotating the eyepiece of a kaleidoscope alters what we hear or see, manipulating the structure of events changes the way they are perceived and experienced.

Significantly, these five points indicate the extent to which we play an active role in structuring our realities. From top to bottom, the only realities we have are the realities we perceive. The brain does not record exact images of the external world like a camera does. The camera frames entities; the brain creates events. The brain is selective in what it perceives and adroit in forming perceptions. Our experiences are not of what is "out there" but of the symbolic presentations of our mental structuring. Our experience grows from the variety of forms in which our senses, feelings, and thoughts are engaged. It grows from **structure in the large**.

৯৹

Structure and Strategy

The neurophysiological patterns of perception we have just described suggest that all structures are symbolic inducements to some extent. *All structures invite a particular expectation of patterned development and com-*

pletion. Why is this important to rhetoric? Because all our choices of argument, organization, language, action, occasion, setting, medium, and the like are actually choices of structures. In rhetoric, these structures are referred to as **forms**. The unique feature of *rhetorical forms* is that *they encourage an anticipation of an outcome*. If developed properly, they also *satisfy this anticipation*.[5]

In a sense we have been examining rhetorical forms throughout this book. Enthymemes, the passions, narratives, and resources of language are major forms we have considered. Each of these forms shares this quality of involving a listener or a reader in a participatory way: They are ways for getting our audience to anticipate where we're going. Because they arouse anticipations, forms also establish relationships between our audience and us. Consequently, our selection of forms bears directly on the type of relationship we want and the one we actually get. Considerations like these are **strategic**; they concern how best to achieve a goal.

Structure and Strategic Choice

We find an important clue for understanding the rhetorical character of structure in the earliest known Roman textbook on rhetoric, *Rhetorica ad Herennium* (*Rhetoric to Herennius*). After advising the reader on how to arrange arguments so that they will have a strong and lasting impression, the unknown author (pseudo Cicero) says, "This arrangement of topics in speaking, like the arraying of soldiers in battle, can readily bring victory."[6] The choice of a military metaphor is both dramatic and informative. Pseudo Cicero conceptualized the structure of a message—its introduction, body of proofs and refutations, and conclusion—as a design with strategic intent. Just as a military general arrays troops to exploit terrain, weaknesses of enemy position and numbers, and conditions of weather, so too the rhetor deploys the available means of persuasion with an eye toward gaining the advantage. What was true for ancient speeches remains true for contemporary rhetorical events. We still must structure our messages. We still select a specific structure (such as the visual structure of black apparel in the example that opened this chapter), because it arrays our points in the desired light (we should grieve for the victims of war and injustice) or marshalls the desired connection (our vigil requires witnesses).

The ancient suggestion that dispositional thinking is strategic thinking opens a broad range of possibilities for our consideration. Once we focus on the strategic value of structures, virtually any and every symbolic structure can have a rhetorical function. The world may bombard us with a montage of sensory data, but we perceive its sights and sounds in terms of structures, and we respond to holistic patterns that give coherent form to elements bebopping about chaotically in our environment.

Humans emit sounds strung together, but we hear a coherent utterance. Humans express utterances serially, but we recognize a reasoning pattern. Humans converse by communicative turn taking, but we grasp each turn as a move that opens some possibilities and closes others for coherent response. Humans inhabit physical spaces containing physical objects, but we respond to these as environments that encourage some modes of communication and discourage others. Humans are confronted at any given moment by the utter novelty of a world in flux, but our inherent disposition is to focus on the structural unities amid chaos. Amid novelty we find the familiar elements that permit anticipating the future of unfolding events. We perceive and conceptualize every aspect of physical and human environment as structured in some way. These structures, regardless of their character, function strategically to shape our attitudes, beliefs, and actions as responses to our world. For this reason, whenever a communicator provides verbal and nonverbal structures to an audience, these can be examined and understood for their strategic value.

Strategizing with Form

The strategic character of rhetorical thinking has been evident throughout our discussion. I want to underscore that our strategies are present in all the structural features of rhetoric, even those we don't tend to consciously. These structures profoundly influence audience perceptions and outcomes.

To illustrate the way in which structures are strategic, consider these examples of prose and how their form encourages different responses. Here's a passage from the beginning of a book:

> We usually use the term literature to refer either to (1) imaginative, enduring works or (2) bodies of writing that deal with particular topics of study (e.g., the "literature" on nuclear fission). The second is a fairly specialized usage; "literature" more often carries the first meaning. The phrase "literary criticism" refers almost invariably to the analysis and judgment of imaginative, linguistic works. But the question of where one applies or does not apply the principles of "literary criticism" has never had an obvious answer.[7]

Here's another, quite different beginning:

> Her body moved with the frankness that comes from solitary habits. But solitude is only a human presumption. Every quiet step is thunder to beetle life underfoot; every choice is a world made new for the chosen. All secrets are witnessed.[8]

And here's rhetoric of still another order:

> Tonight at 8:30 come to a "fraternity party" on the terrace of the Beta Theta Pi house, 220 N. Burrows Street (on campus). The food and drinks are on the house, the setting is perfect for fraternizing, and the location is convenient to the Arts Festival and downtown, in case you want to keep partying after the party.

As we read these passages, we form three different sets of expectations as to what we have in store. The first passage is written in the style of scholarly prose. Not only is the subject technical, but the writer expresses himself in a scholarly manner. We note the use of "either . . . or," "(1), (2)," and "e.g.," and the definition of a term and a transitional question. All of these are the trappings of conceptual treatment, and we, literate in the ways of scholarly prose, can project from these signs the type of treatment to follow. The passage also establishes a relationship between the voice speaking through the text and us. It is a didactic relationship, and the lessons to be taught will be the conceptual lessons relevant to mastering abstractions about criticism.

The second passage takes a different tone. More conversational, it deals with the subject of our place in a world of relationships that are not always evident. A woman whose stride suggests she is unaware of being observed offers an image that will have a concrete referent for most readers. We have seen such people, walking as if they were oblivious to the gaze of others. We catch the author's point that even if no other human is around, solitude is an invention of our own making with respect to, say, other creatures of nature. At the same time, we are led to wonder what, exactly, is the "frankness" of movement she is exhibiting, what "worlds" will be created anew, and what the author means by, "all secrets are witnessed." We delay our judgments because, as sensitive readers of fiction, we have an expectation that the author will soon clarify what she meant. Like the previous passage, this one also establishes a relationship between the voice speaking through the text and us. Not only is it the more familiar relationship of a friend, perhaps, sharing a story, but there is a teaching function here as well. Unlike the abstract, technical lessons to be taught by the author expounding on criticism, the lessons here will be about experiences. The next passage reads:

> If someone in this forest had been watching her—a man with a gun, for instance, hiding inside a copse of leafy birch trees—he would have noticed how quickly she moved up the path and how directly she scowled at the ground ahead of her feet. He would have judged her to be an angry woman on the trail of something hateful.
> He would have been wrong.[9]

We have the answer to our first question. Her gait and expression were not intended to perform a particular persona for a witnessing audience. Her frankness came from not having to worry about how her bodily movement would be interpreted; she presumed she was alone in the forest. But someone (we suspect) was watching her. Now we wonder who the observer is and why his interpretation is wrong—anticipating that the author soon will tell us. We will have to wait awhile for the meaning of choices and worlds created anew.

And what of our third example, the notice about the fraternity party? Clearly the invitation sets an expectation of a good time. The author whimsically weaves forms of the same word into the message: "fraternizing" at a fraternity house and "partying after the party." Again, because we are literate in the structure of invitations, we understand the jokes and blandishments to be a sign that our host sincerely desires our presence at this affair. Moreover, the informal structure of this invitation creates a relationship quite different than if its authorial voice had adopted the impersonal formality of something like "The Head and Faculty of the English Department request the honor of your presence for buffet and cocktails." There's no denying that the language of the first leads us to anticipate a casual affair—jeans, T-shirts, and deck shoes. Few of us would be caught dead attending the second in that attire. We would anticipate the polite and decorous behavior that accompanies a sedate reception and would dress accordingly.

Each of these examples presents us with remarkably different situations. They ask us to think of ourselves in distinctly different ways. They arouse unrelated expectations of the future. They establish relationships completely unlike one another and call on us to respond in dissimilar fashions to sustain these relationships. Finally, and importantly, we are able to decipher these forms and respond in an appropriate fashion. As Burke says, we (humans) are uniquely able to respond to symbols. Because we are hereditarily equipped to do so, the management of symbolic structures can induce attitudes, motives, and social cooperation.

ॐ
Structures Reveal Motives

In an important sense, all rhetorical situations may be thought of as posing a question. We are asked, "What shall we believe or feel or do about this problem or concern?" In the same vein, rhetoric is an answer to the question posed by the situation in which it arises. Rhetorical responses are not merely answers but *strategic* answers and *stylized* answers. Their differences in strategy and style can be as marked as those between advertisements featuring Jamie Lee Curtis hawking cell phones and the solemn tones in advertisements for investment houses or as subtle as those between saying the word "yes" in a tone that implies "Thank God!" or in one that pleads "Alas!"

When we say that rhetoric is an answer to the questions posed by the situation in which it arises, we imply that rhetorical acts adopt certain strategies for encompassing these situations. When we desire concerted action but are uncertain of how others will act we need to consider carefully the strategies necessary to achieve social cooperation. We make these determinations best when we can answer such questions as: What kind of problem is this? What do we want our audience or this public to do? How are we potentially united in a common bond of sentiment and action toward a common world? As Kenneth Burke says, "These strategies size up the situations, name their structure and outstanding ingredients, and name them in a way that contains an attitude towards them."[10]

In chapter 11 we discussed the concept of motives. We saw that motive terms are cultural shorthand for situations that recur regularly for our group. They provide a definition for our situation and point us toward appropriate action. There we were interested in how language encourages identification; here our concern is with how specific structures answer the demands of a situation. The structure we choose to join events and values when we communicate is synonymous with our motivation for communicating. Whether or not we are consciously aware of it, implicit in our structuring and patterning of symbols are strategies for dealing with the situations in which we find ourselves. These strategies, in turn, are the ongoing constructions of ourselves as symbol-using (or misusing) creatures with individual identities. They construct our world and our place in it and invite others to share it with us. When Women in Black congregate at a busy intersection, they interrupt the normal structure of street traffic with an unanticipated form. The appearance of women dressed in mourning garb with only a sign to indicate the cause of their sorrow is sufficient to restructure our perception of the street scene into a protest statement—one that is difficult to refute. How do you refute an expression of grief? How do you not empathize with it? Their display of sorrow is a call to sympathy; it's a strategy to induce identification by the way it structures our perceptions.

Looked at from the analyst's perspective, we can represent this strategic process as a circle (figure 13.1). This circle indicates the considerable information we divulge about ourselves through the structures present in our rhetorical acts. In every case of rhetorical action, we adopt strategies that can be observed and deciphered. As rhetors, we perceive selected elements of our environment. When these elements create tensions of unresolved conflict, communication is a likely response. We issue messages to rectify these tensions. Our messages are necessarily constructed with structures of some sort, such as language, arguments, and idea development. These message structures reflect our implicit definitions of our respective situations. Further, they function as our strategies for coping with these situations. Our strategies, in turn, contain our motives for action, and those motives are likewise a basis for identification with our audience. Insofar as we achieve identification, our audience shares in our perceptions of the environment and our ways of dealing with it.

Importantly, these structures are not hidden persuaders in any sinister sense. We can detect them in all sorts of messages if we look for them. Whether we are examining a transcript of a Jesse Jackson speech, a Neil Simon script, a Susan Karr rendition of growing up in East Texas, a set of Eminem rap lyrics, or some other symbolic form with persuasive potential, such as a film or photograph or interpersonal dialogue, we will notice that it has patterns uniquely its own. A message will have structure because, as we just saw, all data that are perceived are perceived as structured in some way. Moreover, perceived structures are coherent to us in terms of the relationships among their parts.

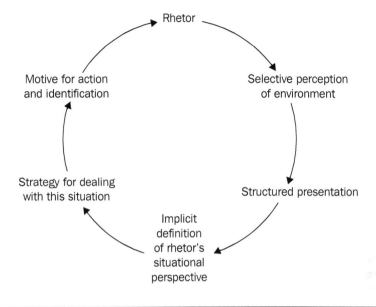

Figure 13.1

The same is true for language structures. Wherever there is purposeful, situated use of language relevant to the question posed by its situation we will find relationships among the rhetor's ideas. Among the most basic of these structures are **associational clusters**. Associational clusters are terms and ideas that congregate together. They modify one another, delimit the view of the world advanced by the speech or the text, articulate values, and establish intellectual, emotional, and value relationships as a basis for identification. For example, consider the way Maureen Dowd clusters images she observed in the presidential and vice presidential debates in the 2000 election.

> Let Al Gore sigh and roll his eyes and do his smarmy Eddie Haskell. (*"With all due respect, Mrs. Cleaver, for a mom you're quite a babe."*) Let W. snort and sniffle and get that look of thinly veiled terror when he hears a three-syllable name with too many consonants in it. Let Holy Joe gush about his personal odyssey of ethnic acceptance. Bring me the bald, pasty head of Big Time. . . . The other guys are always cuddling, kissing, misting, sharing family stories, and trying to Feel Deeply all the injustices of the world.
>
> Big Time is an unrepentant old-school guy, an insider's insider who blanches at glad-handing and gauzy handling. He does Feel Deeply, but he Feels Deeply that it was wrong for the press to hound him into giving up his stock options. He Feels Deeply, as he showed when he tried to restrict the press during Desert Storm, that he much prefers the Second Amendment to the First.
>
> He may be politically atavistic and autistic but at least he's authentic.[11]

Her portrayal contrasts the simulation of emotion and sentiment by three of the candidates with the authentic ones of Dick Cheney. Al Gore's eye-rolling, George W. Bush's halting delivery, and Joe Liebowitz's references to his family's emigration to the United States are associated with contrived ways of playing to the camera or to a lack of intelligence. By grouping these together Dowd encourages us to perceive them as signs that the debates are studied performances; the candidates are not offering candid insights into themselves or what they think. The suggestion is that the candidates are more committed to creating an image than to communicating with us about the issues and their position on them. The image projected by Cheney contrasts with this. He doesn't cuddle, kiss, or otherwise engage in public displays to show deep feeling. His deep feelings are not at the level of affect and emotion but policy. Her capitalization of "Feel Deeply" further groups and contrasts insincere and sincere feelings. Finally, her use of the terms "atavistic" and "autistic" to describe Cheney would be less than complimentary in most contexts, but contrasted with her representation of the other candidates they become political virtues because they are authentic.

Associational clusters like these are the typical ways in which rhetors enrich the texture of thoughts and feelings developed through their appeals. By examining messages for these clusters, we can disclose how they orchestrate various elements of thought and expression to shape responses. Associational clusters will tell us *what goes with what* in the speaker or writer's mind. The interrelationships among them will provide the rhetor's definition of the situation. In effect, these clusters are her situation, which as we just saw is another way of saying they are her motives: They are the capsule definitions of situations that imply the attitudes and actions she finds appropriate and with which she hopes her audience will identify.

To illustrate how the relationship between a message's structure and its strategy is concretely present in our speaking, let us examine a portion of Richard Nixon's speech delivered on April 30, 1970. Although this address was given more than 30 years ago, the effect on the American public was so dramatic that it bears continued scrutiny for the lessons we might learn. In this address he announced an American incursion into Cambodia for the purpose of finding and destroying North Vietnamese sanctuaries located there. These sanctuaries, close to the South Vietnamese border, enabled the North Vietnamese army to launch serious attacks that were slowing down the process of Vietnamizing the war—gradual withdrawal of American troops as South Vietnam assumed responsibility for waging the war. The speech triggered a violent domestic reaction. The antiwar movement, which had lost its steam in the months immediately preceding the address, had an upsurge of activity. Demonstrations swept across college campuses, and the conflict between the government and opponents to the war climaxed in the shooting of four students at Kent State University.[12]

When you examine statements by students, faculty, concerned citizens, national leaders, and politicians who opposed Nixon's action, you find they advanced a remarkably unified complaint. The president had cast the nation's worth in terms of its power. His critics thought this was a false issue; the world questioned our wisdom not our might. Nixon himself stated, "It is not our power but our will and character that [are] being tested tonight." In light of this disclaimer, why did so many Americans see the president as acting in an opposite way?

The answer can be found in several important structures of his speech. In a message of approximately 2,400 words, Nixon devoted about one-quarter of his remarks to reflections on the nation's character. Quite apart from announcing a military action and the rationale for it, he digressed into an area that went to the core of the nation's self-identity. These remarks were not called for by the situation itself and in fact transformed it from a military crisis into a crisis of integrity. Nixon invited the citizenry to reflect on how our willingness to use military force—or lack thereof—was a comment on our national values. This digression, a speech within the speech, highlighted his comments on character.

In addition to the structure of idea placement, the president's speech contained revealing clusters. After characterizing the Hanoi government as "intransigent," "belligerent," "aggressive attackers," and "killers," he decried their attitude as intolerable. The United States cannot be "plaintive" in response or its "credibility" will be destroyed "in every area of the world where only the power of the United States deters aggression." We try to be conciliatory; the enemy tries to "humiliate and defeat us." Thus we are a nation under attack and must defend ourselves. This was the prelude that trumpeted the centrality of power to our survival and the survival of the rest of the free world. In the next several paragraphs, notice how the clustering of ideas around power gave it a special role in defining Americans as a people:

Nixon's comments	What goes with what
1. "If, when the chips are down, the world's most powerful nation, the United States of America, acts like a pitiful, helpless giant, the forces of totalitarianism and anarchy will threaten the free institutions throughout the world."	1. Not using power now makes us helpless. Power must be used to be validated.
2. "It is not our power but our will and character that [are] being tested tonight."	2. Power, in turn, validates our national will and character.
3. "If we fail to meet this challenge, all other nations will be on notice that despite its overwhelming power, the United States, when a real crisis comes, will be found wanting."	3. Power's use is an index of our worth.

In a few brief moments, Nixon established a set of relationships that made power the central indicator of national character and that required power be used to validate character. The cluster of ideas about power reveals how Nixon defined this situation and simultaneously invited Americans to share in his definition. Those who decried the speech as misguided in its sense of America were not criticizing a mere digression in the address. The way the digression is set off and the structure of its appeal are strategies that call attention to this as a very crucial topic indeed. It informed the nation about some of its president's fundamental views about the United States, confronting them with the choice of identification or division.[13]

Shaping Audience Perceptions

So far we have considered that rhetorical form presents a structured message, that structures have identifiable features, that these features encourage relationships among rhetors and audiences, and that structural patterns such as placement and associational clusters provide an index to a rhetor's motives. Now we can extend these ideas to consider how various structural components function to shape an audience's perceptions.

When we recognize a pattern, we expect its completion. This expectation of the future allows us to listen with intelligence and to act with propriety. For example, sequences like "L, M, N, O, . . ." or "2, 4, 6, . . ." are easy to complete once we learn the pattern. In fact, we probably complete such patterns without consciously trying. Similarly, the patterns of common circumstances we experience repeatedly become ingrained in our thinking. Once initiated, we respond automatically. Patterns of weather lead farmers, sailors, and others whose livelihood depends on atmospheric conditions to set plans for the future. Patterns of the economy lead investors, bankers, and the business community to forecast the financial climate. Patterns of events allow us to predict what will follow and to foresee the likely consequences of our actions.

Rhetors can use our capacity to respond to patterns as a persuasive strategy. Uses of language, patterns of argument, and methods of appeal guide our reasoning and responses to arrive at and reinforce a selected conclusion. Recall the passages cited earlier concerning criticism, the frankness of solitary habits, and the party. Each of them selected and arranged ideas and expression with a goal in mind. Each sought to establish a thinking or feeling relationship with the reader. More than this, each channeled thoughts and feelings toward specific goals: It isn't clear where literary criticism does or does not apply; solitude is a human presumption, this character is not alone; we're going to have fun tonight. Once we know where a thought, argument, or theme is headed, we can anticipate what will come next, be alert for evidence and reasoning necessary to make a case, listen with increased critical sensitivity, and evaluate how the thought, argument, or theme fits with the overall pattern of the discourse.

For example, if a speaker tells us that the costs of college education are outstripping the ability of middle-class Americans to borrow money and to pay tuition, you anticipate that he will develop this observation as a problem and then propose a solution. A variety of themes are available for development, such as *magnitude* ("Fully one-third of those who now attend soon will no longer be able to afford college"), *expediency* ("It is contrary to the nation's economic well-being to reduce its numbers of technically trained and higher-educated citizens"), and *morale* ("Placing college beyond the hopes of these youths will deny them the American dream of opportunity for social and economic advancement"). Magnitude, expediency, and morale as distinct patterns of problem development encourage us to listen for different types of evidence, underlying assumptions, and even language. Because they are familiar patterns in American culture, each allows us to participate at some level in its development as we detect the overall pattern of the speech.

The rhetorical uses of form need not be artistically managed for them to influence us. Because all uses of language are necessarily structured, their strategies are implicitly present and waiting to be uncovered. Women in Black, for example, specifically refrain from verbal appeals. They wish to convey sorrow so deep that words cannot express it. Standing in public in a way that communicates grief and posting a sign that will communicate to everyone its source is sufficient to invite empathic responses. Would a single woman dressed in black be as effective? Would she even be noticed at a busy urban intersection? The gathering of a group is not incidental; its size conveys a sense of the depth of their feeling. Whenever we communicate seriously with another person, our use of symbols induces an attitude—even if it is the counterattitude of rejection.

Kenneth Burke suggests five major patterns by which audience expectations are aroused: syllogistic progression, qualitative progression, repetitive form, conventional form, and minor or incidental form.[14] Each of these patterns can guide reasoning and responses toward desired conclusions.

Syllogistic progression is the form of an argument that is perfectly conducted, with each premise leading to the next. We find this form in literary examples like mysteries, where each step leads to the next. It can take the form of historical progression in a lecturer's exposition of a topic. We would find it also in an attorney's tightly knit reasoning from facts to conclusions to prove a point in court. The important element to look for in this form is the logical progression from one element to the next. Given certain premises, others must follow. The audience participates in the framing of such an appeal. Their familiarity with the premises conditions them to know and feel the rightness of a conclusion. Thus when Richard Nixon presented his famous "Checkers" speech, he revealed his financial earnings and expenditures, what he owned and what he owed. Having done so, he prepared his audience for his later call that the other candidates for president and vice president make similar financial disclosures.

Qualitative progression is a form in which the presence of one quality prepares us for another. We do not have the pronounced anticipatory
response to qualitative progression that we do to syllogistic. Rather, we
recognize the rightness of the progression after the event. We do not demand that a premise follow so much as we are encouraged to adopt a
frame of mind that inclines us to accept a pattern of development. For instance, in the film *To Have and Have Not,* there is a memorable scene in
which the younger and well-heeled female character (Lauren Bacall) is
visiting the room of the older but financially strapped male character
(Humphrey Bogart). She flirts with him as she offers to help him out of his
financial troubles. Bogey declines, but Bacall is not about to let Bogey miss
the fact that she finds him attractive. As she moves to the door she turns
and says, "You don't have to say anything, and you don't have to do anything. Not a thing." As she is about to leave she says, "Oh, maybe just
whistle." Turning back to Bogart: "You know how to whistle don't you?
You just put your lips together . . . and blow." Mercy! The sequence of the
scene is organized so that each step leads to the next until the dramatic
leave-taking in which the whistle instruction, with lips puckered, imitates
a kiss. She had been talking about money, not kisses. But as soon as she ut-
ters her final line, the sexual undertones of the scene are brought together
in a way that make clear where the plot is headed.[15]

Repetitive form occurs when we consistently maintain a principle by
presenting it in different ways. It is restatement of the same idea in a new
guise. Lecturers do this when they state a principle and then provide an
example. The example repeats the principle, in the guise of a particular
case. A trial attorney uses this form when she parades a host of witnesses
to testify that her client is a person of sound character. An orator uses this
form by advising conduct that agrees with basic premises established
throughout the speech. By the consistency of repeating, the audience
comes to expect that the principle reasserted will be adhered to in other
aspects of the appeal. The Women in Black case offers a variant on this
principle in that they repeat the form of a silent vigil by women dressed as
in mourning. The specific event or circumstances over which they are
grieving will vary, however. The repeated form conveys a sense of protest,
while borrowing from the form of attire associated with grief to convey
their depth of emotion.

Conventional form relies on audience recognition of a familiar form.
"Once upon a time" and "They lived happily ever after" are conventional
forms in children's fairy tales. We expect them to be there. Unlike other
forms, in which anticipation is developed during the actual listening or
reading, anticipations of conventional forms exist prior to a performance.
For example, a homily is based on Scripture. We expect the preacher to
cite a biblical passage, explain it, and apply it to our lives. In an acceptance speech, we expect a presidential nominee to speak of the general
themes to be developed in the campaign. We do not expect a detailed ex-

position of specific proposals but broad and inclusive principles that will define the candidate's overall position. Women in Black could not gather as they do in celebration, since this would violate the conventions of mourning garb. In genres of formal and vernacular rhetoric, as in genres of literature, adhering to conventions provides a means for satisfying one set of audience demands, regardless of what we intend to say.

Minor forms are devices of expression, each of which can be regarded as a formal event in and of itself. Indirect question, metaphor, reduplication, antithesis, apostrophe, and other figures of speech and thought can be examined as though they were episodes within a discourse. Each form contains its own mode of appeal. All involve listeners in anticipation of how an expression will be completed or how one thought will lead to or amplify another. At the same time, taken together, they can enhance our anticipation of the whole. For example, John Kennedy's speeches were marked by the use of antithesis, a figure that sets one idea off against the other. ("We should never negotiate out of fear, but never fear to negotiate." "Ask not what your country can do for you, but what you can do for your country.") Each figure served as a vehicle for clarifying points JFK thought important. They also contributed to an overall perception of the United States as in transition from the postwar consolidation of the Eisenhower administration to the expansionist vision of Kennedy's New Frontier.

Burke's basic patterns of form can be extended to more complex systems of expression. Rhetorician Robert Hariman, working within the civic action tradition of rhetoric, has analyzed the way political cultures are influenced by their dominant rhetorical styles. Those who share political relations within that culture understand and use manners, taste, charm, charisma, as well as modes of reasoning and expression as public performances that communicate their relations to power. He finds these forms of expression constitute that culture's political style; its *"coherent repertoire of rhetorical conventions depending on aesthetic reactions for political effect."*[16] Hariman identifies four particular styles: **realist**, **courtly**, **republican**, and **bureaucratic**. Each represents a culture of power expressed in a distinctive form.

The **realist** style appears as a form of discourse that makes a radical separation between power and the artistry of public performance. It acts as if power were part of nature. Because it assumes power exists outside of rhetoric, politics becomes the use of force—as Machiavelli prescribed in *The Prince*—to achieve interests. We see this today in political rhetoric that emphasizes making a rational choice based on objective material circumstances. Verbal artistry is downplayed; the realist prefers the plain style because its lack of colorful expression helps to sustain the impression that decisions are being calculated in an objective fashion and arrived at on the basis of reason. Of course, this way of communicating is itself a form that encourages us to perceive and respond to its maker as if s/he were a reasonable person, informed, and acting in a way that depends on the power of the state rather than on her or his personal charisma. For example,

when Ali I. Al-Naimi, Saudi Arabia's minister of petroleum and mineral re-
serves, spoke in refutation of those who predicted a shortage of oil, he said
in part, "Let us look at the facts."

> The security-of-supply issue is global in nature. A price increase or
> decrease, a shortage or over-supply, will affect all countries in the free
> market system. . . . Today, the world political, economic and energy rela-
> tions are more favorable than ever. So are the conditions in the oil mar-
> ket. The expanded oil reserves, the excess production capacity, and the
> transparent market should all ease the concern over supply security.[17]

His argument relied on his audience's recognition of forces outside his
rhetoric were at work to insure supply would go unabated. It implied that
the rational choice was to heed the advice of the oil producing cartels and
not the "doomsayers" because objective circumstances would guarantee
supply and oil production was in everyone's best interests.

The **courtly** style develops from the relations of those at court with the
monarch. The monarch's body is at the center of court and the locus of
power. Those who are courtiers strive to be in proximity with the monarch
because that is a sign of status. It is a rhetoric that places heavy emphasis
on gesture. Although it is not particularly effective in coordinating the
pragmatic affairs of institutions, this style is highly visible in popular culture. Vamping by teens and young adults, entourages that surround popular entertainers, groupies following rock stars, and other gestures that
center on the individual as a person of power exemplify this style. By being
in the presence of these individuals, we exhibit our identification with
them and share in their aura of power. Of course, monarchs can be deposed or executed, and the power associated with this style lasts only as
long as the person at its center reigns and/or the subjects are permitted to
remain at court. This style of adulation supported by gestures of recognition, nonetheless, plays a significant role in the rhetorical displays addressed to a public constructed by mass media. It is a public that witnesses
and applauds; it does not discuss or otherwise actively participate in the
exercise of power.

The **republican** style is suited to the types of power we find in a parliamentary culture. It relies on the types of rhetorical skills emphasized in
classical rhetorical doctrine and discussed throughout this book. Hariman
says, "This model includes appreciation of verbal technique, a norm of
consensus, the embodiment of civic virtue, and a doctrine of civility that
exemplifies the difficulties facing contemporary liberalism."[18] This rhetoric finds power emerging from the agreements forged through deliberation
and persuasion. It assumes those in its political culture are committed to
the process of decision making and not to deciding matters in the streets.
This political style also assumes that a person's status in the parliamentary
arena is related to the community's vision of civic virtue. In earlier times,
this public reputation was the result of public deeds, such as might be en-

acted in the assemblies, courts, or military campaigns of the country. Today's mass society seems to have substituted accomplishments with the media craft of image building and image management. We have become leery of our politicians as individuals of inferior character who present us with an invented character rather than an authentic one. Be that as it may, while we may be leery of those who seek power through appearing to be virtuous, we still acknowledge the importance of the republican style to a democracy; most citizens still advocate deciding matters on the merits of the arguments. For that reason, those who master the republican style— people who are articulate spokespersons for their cause—often are regarded as having political power.

Finally, Hariman discusses **bureaucratic** style. This style organizes a great deal of institutional life, such as communication in offices, organizations, and agencies. The bureaucracy operates on a set of rational rules, which must be codified and, therefore, written. Rational *procedures* are set forth as *rules* drawn from the research and recommendations of *experts* and given objective status in the *documents* of the bureaucracy. Because documents must be written, the bureaucratic style emphasizes written over spoken communication. Memos, reports, and policy manuals abound. These messages are not addressed to swaying opinion but to codifying and clarifying procedures and policies, establishing jurisdiction, and formulating rules of equality. Its expression is impersonal and uses language that makes it difficult to identify the agent responsible for rulings that have been made. Hariman warns us not to underestimate the power of the bureaucratic style, because once it gains secure footing it can absorb the other styles and rewrite them as versions of itself.

Each of these styles is a source of identification and power; each establishes a particular form of culture of power. They extend the five forms identified by Burke as methods for managing symbols. Each, from the basic structural patterns of form to the complex style of a political culture, prepares an audience to receive ideas and participate in their development. By structuring our ideas, these styles also structure the orientation we bring to a rhetorical situation, the perceptions we frame of ourselves and our social realities, and our conceptions of power and our relation to it. In each case the rhetorical power of these forms relies on arousing our anticipations of feelings and actions that will be appropriate to our felt needs. Our ability to respond to form makes it possible for us to participate actively with the rhetor in the co-construction of our social worlds.

ॐ

Summary

Our discussion of strategy has focused on the fact that the human world is a perceived world of structures and patterns. These are prerequisites for human understanding and response, because of the way our brain and nervous system are "wired." Our mind finds shape, boundaries, and size in objects of its environment. It simplifies details by finding connections in them or imposing connections on them. These patterns eventually shape our cognitions of reality. Structures order the elements of our experience so that they have meaning and present motives for us to act.

As soon as we recognize that structures impose meaning and are necessary to frame appropriate action, we also recognize that structures argue for a particular vision of the world. Structures have a rhetorical quality to them; they make appeals. For this reason, they have psychological consequences. We find time a meaningful structure to organize events, for example, when we wish our account to proceéd in a chronological order. But perceiving the temporal quality of events also invites us to anticipate a future and events yet to transpire. In other words, time not only relates the elements of our current experience but it also induces us to frame an anticipation of what is to come. This relationship between structure and form can be found throughout human use of symbols, making all symbolic acts in some sense rhetorical.

The structural components of discourse—elements of language, argument, organization, setting, and the like that are available for all to notice—are resources for identification and persuasion. These structures reveal associational clusters among the rhetor's ideas that tell us *what goes with what* in the conceptual patterns that guide a message. They are the rhetor's strategic answer and stylized answer to the questions posed by the rhetorical situation. At the same time, structures function strategically with respect to establishing identification with audiences because they arouse audience anticipations. Specifically, there are five general patterns of arousal: syllogistic progression, qualitative progression, repetitive expression of the same essential idea in different ways, conventional expression, and minor or incidental forms as devices of expression.

Noting these aspects of structure, the questions we must address in any rhetorical transaction are whether and why a given use of symbols is geared to the audience's readiness to respond. Rhetorical concerns with humans as symbol-using animals focus on how our symbolic constructions arouse and satisfy an appetite and on how they enhance identification.

14

Strategic Forms of Argument Structures

In the fall of 1999, the Brooklyn Museum of Art had a major exhibit, "Sensation," that featured avant-garde works, some of which used dismembered animals or were constructed with organic matter, such as human blood. The exhibit included a work by Chris Offie, an African artist whose works often portrayed African themes. Offie's painting portrayed the Virgin Mary as a black woman. It swiftly became the center of public debate because it incorporated the use of elephant dung in its composition. The Catholic Church and other religious groups protested the exhibit and urged others to join them in a boycott. New York Mayor Rudy Giuliani threatened to withdraw the city's financial support from the museum. The museum, the mayor, the churches, the press, and interested citizens soon became embroiled in a massive controversy, which ended with two lawsuits filed: one by the museum to protect its right to display the painting without loss of public funds and one by the city to close the exhibit.

The Catholic Church objected that the use of elephant dung on a portrayal of the Virgin Mary was sacrilegious and offensive. The mayor maintained that public funds should not be used to support projects that were insensitive to the religious beliefs of others. The city's lawyers argued that the exhibit violated the museum's lease, which provided grounds to close it. The museum maintained that the painting was not intended to offend and that what one saw in a work of art was a matter of individual interpretation. The museum's lawyers argued that the First Amendment right to free speech protects artistic expression. Citizens writing to the New York newspapers were divided over the legal and cultural issues involved. Meanwhile, the artist expressed his surprise that anyone was offended. As a practicing Catholic his intention was not to offend, and he pointed out that in Africa elephant dung is often used in artwork to express veneration.

The "Sensation" controversy exemplifies some important rhetorical and civic precepts. Most obviously, it illustrates that all modes of human expression are open to interpretation; sometimes they evoke beliefs and sentiments other than their maker intended. It illustrates that although we commonly extol consensus as a civic goal, strong convictions can override that goal and lead to attempts to limit access to public spheres. It illustrates that supporting the First Amendment right to freedom of expression carries the risk that sometimes we will be offended by the rhetoric of others. It also illustrates the responsibility we have to pick our fights. Since the museum is a publicly funded institution, turning this into a *cause célèbre* struck many as a lose-lose battle. If the mayor won, the rights of free expression were endangered. If the museum won, it would imply authorization for using public money to underwrite exhibits that were offensive to many. For our purposes, the controversy illustrates that arguments rest on assumptions about what should count as an argument and what criteria should be applied to test them.[1]

In this chapter we will concern ourselves with arguments as strategic forms. We will consider arguments first in terms of several major perspectives on argument structures. Then we will consider how other dimensions of rhetorical form function as arguments. Throughout this chapter our primary interest will be to determine whether and why a given use of symbols functions as an argument structure and whether and why an argument structure is suited to the audience's readiness to respond.

☙
Aristotle's Syllogistic Structure

For centuries Western thinkers understood arguments in terms of Aristotle's syllogistic logic. Aristotle's syllogistic theory maintains that we can test the value of an argument by examining the relationships among its premises. Depending on the type of premises and how they are related, we either can or cannot deduce a conclusion. When we genuinely deduce a conclusion, the argument is called valid. For example, we know that summer winds are erratic and violent when a cold front passes through, and we know that sailboats handle best in a steady breeze. So when we hear that a cold front is predicted for later in the day, we may validly deduce that sailing will be treacherous. On the other hand, if we only pretend to deduce a conclusion, the argument is called invalid. For example, if we know that Joe is in the Coast Guard and that the Coast Guard patrols the navigable waters of the United States, it may appear to follow that Joe patrols the navigable waters of the United States. But this is not necessarily so. He may be a clerk or a mechanic who is always on shore. At best we only pretend to deduce a conclusion.

To test the validity of an argument, its premises are set forth in the form of a syllogism (an argument consisting of two premises and a conclusion), for example:

All members of the Cleveland Indians earn over $500,000 a year.

Fritz is a member of the Cleveland Indians.

Therefore, Fritz earns over $500,000 a year.

By examining the types of premises used and the relationships between their terms, Aristotle maintained that we could determine whether a valid conclusion follows.

Aristotle developed his theory of the syllogism in his *Prior Analytics*. There he discussed both valid and invalid syllogisms and the rules for testing each. For our purposes, the important point in Aristotle's theory is that he thought all reasoning could be expressed in syllogistic form. Consequently, he maintained that a single set of validity tests applied to all arguments, regardless of subject matter. This type of logic is called **field-invariant**. This means that all people and all arguments, regardless of whether they are in such disparate fields as history, biology, mathematics, politics, religion, or any other field, are subject to the same rules for valid inference.

Because Aristotle thought all arguments could be reduced to the same pattern of reasoning, he used this theory to describe rhetorical arguments. His rhetorical application of syllogism provides an intelligent form for speakers to use when they make arguments. As we saw in chapter 7, Aristotle thought the rhetorical use of this form, called the enthymeme, provided the reasoned basis for rhetorical appeals.

In addition to providing a reasoned basis for persuasion, enthymemes also serve strategic ends. As the basic unit of popular appeals, Aristotle discussed them as arguments geared to the psychology of the audience. Successful enthymemes use premises that connect with the audience's assumptions. They relate these assumptions to the speaker's desired conclusions. Because they draw on audience beliefs, the form of enthymematic arguments includes readers and listeners as active partners in the persuasive process.

૭

The Toulmin Model of Warranted Assent

Aristotle's views were not rigorously challenged until the twentieth century, when a number of thinkers took exception to the idea that reasoning in all fields was the same. Bosanquet's logic of linear inference and Fisher's narrative paradigm, discussed in chapter 10, are two examples of non-Aristotelian models. The most influential twentieth-century critique of the Aristotelian model on rhetorical conceptions of argument has been that of British philosopher and physicist Stephen Toulmin.[2]

Toulmin raised a twofold objection to Aristotle's syllogistic logic. First, it does not reflect the way people actually argue. In real life, people don't talk in syllogisms. Consequently, the analyst has to rearrange the parts of expression into the form of the syllogism to examine their logical relationships. Second, the syllogistic form is insensitive to different reasoning patterns as they develop in arguments. Syllogisms treat arguments as **closed systems**, like proofs in algebra or geometry. Relationships are evaluated by logical necessity. Toulmin believed arguments are actually **open systems** that develop more like legal reasoning. Their validity depends on the particular case, varying from field to field. Consequently, Toulmin held that arguments are **field-dependent**. What counts as a valid inference in theology, say, might be completely unacceptable in chemistry, and vice versa.

To clarify the open-ended character of the way people actually argue and the ways in which people argue in different contexts (or fields), Toulmin developed a new system for laying out an argument (figure 14.1).[3] The system consists of two triads of elements that show how evidence and assumptions combine to support conclusions. The first triad describes the main line of the argument and consists of **data**, **warrant**, and **claim**. *Data answers the question, "What have you got to go on?"* The arguer presents fact and opinion as data ("56 percent of entering freshmen at State University indicate a preference for a professional curriculum, compared to 40 percent five years ago"). *Claim is the inference drawn as a conclusion from the data.* It is where we are going with the argument ("State University must shift faculty lines from less popular curricula to professional programs"). *Warrant answers the question, "How did you get there?"* It provides the rationale for drawing an inference from the data to the claim ("Faculty distribution should reflect student demand"). Importantly, the warrant does not have to be explicitly stated.

Toulmin's second triad consists of elements that pertain to the force of the argument. Its elements are **backing**, **rebuttal**, and **qualifier**. *Backing contains evidence and argument to support a warrant.* It guarantees our

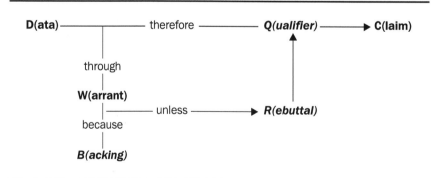

Figure 14.1 Toulmin's Layout of Arguments

confidence in the warrant as legitimate. ("Our land-grant charter estab-lishes the mission of State University as educating the sons and daughters of the working class.") *Rebuttal is the part of an argument that states excep-tions or reasons why the warrant shouldn't hold.* ("Student demand fluctu-ates too often to shift faculty; the general education requirements of State University cannot be met if faculty numbers are reduced in Arts or in Sci-ences; the costs outweigh the benefits.") Finally, *qualifier indicates the strength with which we hold the claim.* In other words, the force of the claim depends on the strength of the rebuttal. ("State University *must* shift lines" or "*probably* should shift lines" or "*perhaps* should shift lines" or "should *do nothing* at the present time—should send the matter to a com-mittee for further study.")

Toulmin's analysis of arguments was not intended to describe their rhetorical features. He was interested in the logical aspects of reasoning embedded in the ways people actually speak and write their arguments, but rhetoricians soon grasped the utility of his model for describing rhetor-ical structures as well. For example, soon after Toulmin's book appeared, Wayne Brockriede and Douglas Ehninger[4] noticed that the claims rhetors make correspond with the ends of arguments: establishing facts, defining problems, advancing values, establishing policies. These ends are tradi-tional ones not unlike the questions formalized in the ancient doctrine on stasis: conjectural, definitive, qualitative, and translative.

Brockriede and Ehninger also noticed that Toulmin's notion of warrant governed the mode of reasoning in an argument. Modes of reasoning have been traditional concerns of rhetoricians since Aristotle first classified ar-guments under logos, pathos, and ethos. Modernized, they suggested that warrants could be grouped as substantive (logos), motivational (pathos), and authoritative (ethos) rules that permitted the inference from data to claim. In this respect, warrants provide a line of reasoning much like topoi, as we saw in chapter 6. Thus, for example, review topics such as Wilson and Arnold described or material topics (*idia*) like those in Aristotle's *Rhet-oric* may provide bridges between events and how we respond to them. Whether stated explicitly or implied, like unstated premises in an en-thymeme, warrants provide authorization for judgments and actions.

Rhetorical arguments succeed only to the degree that they satisfy our requirements for acceptable evidence and relevant warrants. These vary with topic, audience, and rhetorical aim. The value of Toulmin's discussion to rhetoricians is that he provides a means to analyze how arguments are actually made. His model is sensitive to how the actual elements of the ar-gument interrelate to authorize an inference. In short, thinking of argu-ments in terms of data, warrant, and claim, backing, rebuttal, and qualifier improves our grasp of the structure of an argued appeal. It helps us form a clearer understanding of the rhetorical strategy for shaping perceptions.

Consider, for example, this argument advanced by Tamara Sobel. Ms. Sobel was addressing the gender differences in television coverage of the men's and women's NCAA national basketball championship tournament, aka "March Madness." Sobel writes:

[1]   Studies confirm that in general media coverage for women's and girls' sports lags far behind coverage for men's and boys' sports. A 1997 study of several newspapers found that female athletic events received only 11 percent of sports coverage while men's sports received 82 percent (6 percent covered sports where both genders compete). Although there are more male sports teams and events, it is still the case that female events and teams are often given less coverage and lower priority than comparable events for men and boys.

[2]   The CBS television network is a major offender this spring. While this week begins the play and viewing of most of the men's NCAA basketball tournaments on CBS, not one women's tournament will be shown on CBS or any other network station in most areas. . . .

[3]   What message do viewers receive when they turn on the TV? Even in the year 2000, when girls and women are participating and watching sports in record numbers, the networks and other news media still treat female athletes and their fans as second class. The airwaves may belong to the public, but so far there is no equity in the coverage of women's sports. It is up to viewers to show support for women's sports, and to voice our opinions about the unfair media coverage of women's sports events.[5]

Most of the materials in paragraphs 1 and 2 are presented as data, listing the respective amounts of coverage of men's and women's sports. Sobel begins paragraph 1 with the claim that studies "confirm" that girl's and women's coverage "lags far behind" that of boy's and men's sports. How does she get from these results to her conclusion? In paragraph 3 she makes her warrant explicit: These results indicate there is no equality in coverage; she calls on viewers to voice their "opinions about unfair media coverage of women's sports events." Notice also how earlier in paragraph 3 Sobel reinforces her point. By claiming that "the airwaves . . . belong to the public," she adds considerable force to her claim for equity. Without verbal fireworks or resorting to superlatives or exaggeration, her qualifying reference to "the airwaves . . . belong to the public" encourages the conclusion that the public interest is in equity of coverage and that this second-class treatment of women athletes is something citizens can correct.

As this illustration indicates, Toulmin's approach allows us to discover the structure of the argument as it is presented. By clarifying its form, we are better able to see how the structures of arguments are strategies for shaping audience perceptions of the rhetorical situation, the speaker, and themselves.

ಉം

Perelman and Olbrechts-Tyteca's
Associative and Dissociative Structures

Although students of rhetoric have adapted Toulmin's treatment of argument to meet their interests, the fact remains that his discussion focuses mostly on the logical requirements of validity in law, science, philosophy, and other fields of technical discourse. Accordingly, the bulk of his discussion explores whether and how inferences are authorized. It does not attempt to elucidate the argumentative function of rhetorical devices or the rhetorical potential of argument structures to induce attitudes. The scholars who have made the most impressive contribution in these areas are Chaim Perelman and Lucie Olbrechts-Tyteca. These Belgian scholars maintained that all argumentation is a rhetorical process and that rhetoric provides a logic for making rational appeals.

For Perelman and Olbrechts-Tyteca, the test of whether an argument is rational or irrational rests with the audience. They contend that audiences judge an argued case in terms of how they process and remake the appeals they hear. Argument structures are important to this remaking process because they supply patterns of theme and information that listeners regard as valid. Argument structures guide thought.[6]

This guiding function is important. Perelman and Olbrechts-Tyteca remind us that rhetorical arguments are different from proofs. Proofs lead to certainty. They are demonstrations that occur in isolated systems. For instance, geometry is such a system. Given its axioms and postulates, we learn to deduce correct conclusions about lines, planes, and angles. Arguments do not occur in isolated systems. They occur in contexts that are complex, dynamic, evolving, and open-ended. Consequently, the conclusions to arguments are not certainties in the absolute sense of geometric proofs. They are "characterized by a constant interaction among all [their] elements."[7]

Perelman and Olbrechts-Tyteca identify a number of these schemes as structures of **association** and **dissociation**. These are structures commonly used and accepted to show the presence or absence of relationships. As accepted common practices of reasoning, they lend authority to an argument, since "only agreement on their validity can justify their application to particular cases."[8] Perelman and Olbrechts-Tyteca show how these argument structures themselves function as topoi.

Processes of *association* are *"schemes which bring separate elements together and allow us to establish a unity among them, which aims at organizing them or at evaluating them, positively or negatively, by means of one another"*[9] (emphasis added). These processes are similar to the associative clusters discussed in chapter 13. They function, much along Burkean lines of determining what goes with what, to produce identification. The counterpart processes of *dissociation* are *"techniques of separation which have the purpose of dissociating, separating, disuniting elements which are regarded as forming a whole or at least a unified group within some system of thought: dissociation modifies such a system by modifying certain concepts which make up its essential parts"*[10] (emphasis added). Dissociations are schemes that highlight division; they are the opposing process to identification. Perelman and Olbrechts-Tyteca make this joining-dividing pattern concrete in terms of associative processes related to structures of logic and of reality and in terms of dissociative processes separating the apparent from the real. Considering these schemes more carefully will help us to see how argument structures can shape perceptions.

Quasi-logical Arguments

Sometimes we argue in ways that resemble formal reasoning. These patterns are called **quasi-logical** because they borrow the form of logic to present informal reasoning about everyday affairs. Speakers use quasi-logical arguments to imply that there are formal relationships among data that compel a conclusion (or the reverse: formal relationships have been violated and require rejection). Most commonly we employ this pattern whenever we criticize another person's arguments. Our criticism suggests that the reasoning process is faulty. Our objection is intended to straighten out an error of logic. For example, when we say, "You contradicted yourself" or "You made an ad hominem appeal," our suggestion is that this person needs to work on the logic of his argument.

Arguments from contradiction, identity, reciprocity, and transitivity (see table 14.1) get their persuasiveness from the appearance of being rigorous, formal reasoning. They borrow the prestige of logic through their form. These schemes encourage a perception of their maker as a clear thinker and of their contents as being thoroughly reasoned.

Let's consider the first example in the table. Contradiction attempts to indicate glaring inconsistencies in a person's position. These flaws undermine the rational basis for a person's claims. For example, about a month after the terrorist attack destroyed the twin towers of the World Trade Center, Saudi billionaire Prince Alwaleed bin Talal toured the WTC ruins. Afterward he handed Mayor Rudy Giuliani a check for $10 million for the disaster relief fund. He then proclaimed that it was time to get to the root of the problem of terrorism, which he defined as U.S. failure to pressure Israel to stop "slaughtering" Palestinians and to make a peace settlement with them. The mayor responded by returning the check. A few days later Thomas Friedman, in an editorial column in the *New York Times*, referred to the prince's statement as "the virgin birth problem."

> To listen to Saudi officials, or read the Arab press, you would never know that most of the hijackers were young Saudis, or that the main financing for Osama bin Laden—a Saudi—has been coming from other wealthy Saudis, or that Saudi Arabia's government was the main

funder of the Taliban. No, to listen to them you would think that all these young men had virgin births: they came from nowhere, no society is responsible for them, and no Arab state need reflect on how perpetrators of such a grotesque act could have come from its womb. [11]

Mr. Friedman argues that the prince's view of the cause of the terrorist act ignores the relationships present in the facts. He makes the relationship concrete by reciting the facts of Saudi connection to terrorists; because Saudi funds have supported terrorists, the Saudis bear responsibility for the destruction brought by terrorism. Note how Friedman characterizes the Saudi position as absurd by analogy to "virgin birth." This creates a dilemma for the Saudis: either you require us to believe something that is contrary to fact or you have to change your position. Either way, Prince Alwaleed bin Talal's opinion is not one we can take seriously. Perelman and Olbrechts-Tyteca think that the ridicule that results from exposing an inconsistency is the source of contradiction's persuasive force. [12]

Perelman and Olbrechts-Tyteca alert readers to the fact that quasi-logical schemes are sometimes based on mathematical relations, such as whole-part relationships, relative quantities of more and less, and the frequency of

---

Table 14.1   Quasi-logical Arguments[13]

1. *Contradiction*: attempts to indicate glaring inconsistencies in a person's position ("You claim to be for equal rights, yet you oppose an equal rights amendment.")

2. *Identity or difference*: reduction of elements to points they share in common or that divide them ("All men are created equal.")

3. *Reciprocity*: gives equal treatment to two elements that are counterparts of one another ("If it is no disgrace to allow the accused his day in court, it is no disgrace to provide for his defense.")

4. *Transitivity*: states that because one set of relationships holds (between A and B and between B and C), another relationship follows (between A and C) ("Any friend of Michael's is a friend of mine.")

5. *Inclusion of the part in the whole*: the whole includes the part and therefore is more important ("We are a government of justice for all, not privilege for a few.")

6. *Division of the whole into its parts*: the constituent parts of the whole are enumerable and can be recombined to give a different whole ("Dr. Kervorkian administered a lethal injection to put the woman out of her misery and because she asked him to do it, you should not consider acts of euthanasia as murder.")

7. *Comparison*: consideration of several objects in order to evaluate them through their relations to each other ("Jay is handsomer than Adonis.")

8. *Sacrifice*: consideration of what one is willing to surrender to achieve a certain result ("I'd rather lose the election than lose your friendship.")

9. *Probabilities*: calculation of likelihood based on the reduction of the real to a series or collection of beings or events, similar in some ways and different in others ("If Anne were not serious about her work, she would not spend so much time away from her family and in the library.")

occurrences (table 14.1). These argument structures have "the general effect of imparting an empirical character to [their] problems."[14] Such arguments give the impression that values and likelihoods attached to the data can share the logic of measurement, although this is seldom, if ever, the case.

For instance, in *The Book of Laughter and Forgetting* (1981), Milan Kundera provides a dramatic expression of the relevance a people's national consciousness bears to the political struggles that lie at the heart of defining society. Reflecting on the role of cultural memory in post-war Czechoslovakia, his narrator remarks, "People are always shouting they want to create a better future. It's not true. The future is an apathetic void of no interest to anyone. The past is full of life, eager to irritate us, provoke and insult us, tempt us to destroy or repaint it. The only reason people want to be masters of the future is to change the past."[15] Here Kundera comments about the values of people by making a comparison of the relative volume, so to speak, of the past and future. The future is a void of life (and therefore of no interest), the past is full of life (and therefore of great interest). Based on this relationship of relative volume, he is then able to reason to a conclusion that reverses the normal expectation: we want to control the future so we can change the past, i.e., control the narrative of our political and cultural identity.

Reality-Structure Arguments

Arguments that rest on various reality structures form a second major group of associative schemes. Arguments from sequential relations and relations of coexistence influence perceptions and judgments by arguing

---

Table 14.2   Reality-Structure Arguments[16]

Sequential Relations

1. *Causal link*: attributes a causal connection between events, objects, processes, etc. ("The past seven years of economic growth have caused American's to assume it would continue and acquire debt.")

2. *Pragmatic argument*: permits the evaluation of an act or event in terms of its favorable or unfavorable consequences ("Although allowing students on work-study programs more hours of employment relives their financial needs, it also reduces their time for course work and jeopardizes their grades.")

3. *Waste*: the loss of previous effort if an activity is stopped ("All our success in reducing pollution from industrial sites will be to no avail without strong auto emission regulations.)

4. *Direction*: criticizes acts or events on the basis of tendencies that fill us with alarm ("By continuing to limit growth in the University's budget to the rate of increase in the Consumer Price Index, we will not be able to retain our most accomplished faculty members, who can command higher salaries elsewhere.")

5. *Unlimited development*: the absence of foreseeable limits permits optimistic projections for continuing unimpeded on a course ("Their relationship is well on its way to recovery; each day they draw closer and closer.")

Relations of Coexistence

6. *Person and act*: evaluates an individual in terms of relationships that stress the essence of the individual and the character of that person's deeds ("It is one thing not to love and confess it; it is another not to love but pretend to. One party can earn our eventual respect, the other only our contempt.")

7. *Group and its members*: evaluates the relationships of an organization as they influence and are influenced by the characteristics of its membership ("I do not rest easy knowing that academic priorities are being set by accountants and politicians rather than scholars.")

8. *Act and essence*: evaluates relationships between deeds and their defining characteristics ("Patty's harsh comment was a sign of frustration, not meanness of spirit.")

9. *Symbolic relation*: the integration of symbol and referent into a common reality ("Uncle Sam is striking back at terrorists.")

10. *Double hierarchy*: correlates an accepted set of criteria with a second, sometimes contested set ("Extremism in the pursuit of freedom is no vice.")

11. *Degree and order*: assesses acts and events in terms of differences of quantity and quality ("Mother Theresa, frail of body, moved the earth with her compassion and love.")

Establishing Reality Structures

12. *Example*: the use of particular cases to make a generalization possible ("We lowered taxes in 1962 and the economy improved; we lowered them in 1968 and 1981 with similar results. Now is no time to raise taxes.")

13. *Illustration*: the use of a particular case to provide support for an already established regularity ("It isn't what happens to you but what you do with it that matters. So in times of difficulty, remember that your fate, like that of a person cast overboard, can be reversed only if you exert the effort.")

14. *Model*: the use of a particular case to encourage imitation ("Christian charity can best be practiced by following the pope's lead when he forgave his would-be assassin.")

15. *Analogy*: the use of relationships placed in juxtaposition to establish a new understanding ("The effects of these policies on the poor will be as deadly as a viper's bite.")

from reality structures we already accept. Other reality-structure arguments persuade by constructing new reality structures.

Arguments based on the structure of reality encourage associative patterns quite different from quasi-logical arguments. Quasi-logical arguments seek the appearance of validity through the form they build into the appeal. Arguments based on the structure of reality make use of what people accept as real to build a bridge to a new assertion that we wish to promote. Reality-structure arguments require that their basis in reality be sufficiently secure that it goes unchallenged. Once we accept that reality is actually as it has been presented, we are likely to accept further, previously unnoticed implications.

The following excerpt from *In Search of Excellence*, a study of successful corporations by Thomas J. Peters and Robert H. Waterman, illustrates the advantage of using what is known and accepted to move to a new reality. Here they are making a point about how actions and words get divorced:

> Probably few of us would disagree that actions speak louder than words, but we behave as if we don't believe it. We behave as if the proclamation of policy and its execution were synonymous. "But I made quality our number one goal years ago," goes the lament. Managers can't drive forklifts anymore. Yet they do still act. They do something. In short, they pay attention to some things and not to others. Their action expresses their priorities, and it speaks much louder than words. In the quality case alluded to above, a president's subordinate clarified the message. "Of course, he's for quality. That is, he's never said, 'I don't care about quality.' It's just that he's for everything. He says, 'I'm for quality,' twice a year and he acts, 'I'm for shipping products,' twice a day."[17]

Their discussion of the relationship between actions and words reminds us of the many times we have experienced inconsistencies between saying and doing. It encourages us to focus on these inconsistencies and to agree that actions speak louder than words, that reality frequently does reveal a split between words and deeds. Agreeing to this, we are less likely to resist their major claim several paragraphs later concerning employee motivation: "Only if you get people acting, even in small ways, the way you want them to, will they come to believe in what they're doing."[18]

Typical arguments based on the structure of reality include sequential relations, where emphasis is placed on the order of events leading to some significant conclusion. These schemes depend on the pattern of ordered series as an argument strategy. These reality structures are of coequal parts. However, not all reality structures are equal. This fact accounts for another pattern of schemes that depend on relations of coexistence in which items on different levels are united. The result of their union is a reconstruction of reality.

A third group of reality-structure arguments uses schemes of relationships especially suited to establishing the structure of reality. Typically, these arguments are invoked when we have an implied disagreement over the rules that describe our world. Arguments are essential in these cases. If people are willing to talk seriously and to work toward resolving their differences, they can create a new, more satisfying reality for all parties.

Perelman and Olbrechts-Tyteca outline two general patterns that reality-structure arguments follow. The first points to particular cases, much as paradigms discussed in chapter 7. A particular case may be used in a variety of roles: "As an example, it makes generalization possible; as an illustration, it provides support for an already established regularity; as a model, it encourages imitation."[19] The second pattern establishes reality structures through analogy. By careful choice of terms, ratios are set in proportion (A:B::C:D). As we saw in chapter 12, terms in proximity interact to create meaning by, in Perelman's words, "increasing or decreasing the value of the terms."[20]

Dissociation of Concepts

The patterns we just discussed establish connecting links. They are associative patterns. Dissociation does the opposite; it breaks links. Dissociative patterns call into question accepted, assumed, or hoped for associative links on the grounds that these connections do not exist. If the links don't exist, the arguments resting on them may be discounted as irrelevant. On the constructive side, dissociation encourages us to perceive divided elements as independent. In other words, it resolves problems of incompatibility by remodeling our conceptions of reality.

That probably sounds terribly abstract, but if you reflect for a moment, you will recognize that this *remodeling* function has been our major concern throughout our study of rhetoric. Every time we persuade or are persuaded, our outlook on reality is altered in some way.

Perelman and Olbrechts-Tyteca help us recognize the application of dissociation to concrete problems of speaking and writing by indicating that this argument structure frequently signals differences between appearance and reality. This is the difference between things as they seem and things as they actually are. We can imagine this type of argument presented by lawyers arguing over the letter and the spirit of the law, legislators deliberating the social and individual impacts of a bill, and nutritionists distinguishing between the natural and artificial properties of the foods we eat. The consequence of driving an appearance vs. reality wedge is that acts and ideas may be freed from old relationships and considered anew in fresh relationships, and our understanding of our world may be modified as a result.

Consider, for example, how Ali I. Al-Naimi, Saudi Arabia's minister of petroleum and mineral resources, uses the theme of "transformation" to dissociate the new realities of the economy of oil production from the past. Speaking at the Center for Strategic and International Studies, he said:

> The oil market underwent a process of transformation. Increasing competition and liberalization of oil production helped in making the market more transparent. The entry of financial houses and the use of futures, options and swaps have added to the factors influencing oil prices.
>
> Yet, there is a paradox in all of this. Remarkably, in most studies analyzing energy trends, little note is made of the oil decline, in terms of its share of international gross domestic product, global trade, and relative wealth of the industry.
>
> Over the last 20 years, we have seen startling changes in the relationship between energy and economic growth. The energy-to-GDP ratio—a traditional measure of the average amount of energy needed to produce a unit of output—has dropped dramatically. This is due both to greater efficiencies in energy usage and to a shift in the product mix—away from energy intensive sectors to services and information technology, particularly in the industrialized countries.[21]

Al-Naimi points out a paradox. While there is great concern that the oil producing nations raise prices to reap unfair profits, oil's actual share of the international gross domestic product has declined. In fact, he goes on to say, over the last 20 years the amount of energy needed to produce a unit of output has declined. The dissociation allows him to advance an argument that points to other conditions of the global economy that are influencing oil production and price levels.

In these illustrations we see how argument schemes can encourage a perception of reality. Perelman and Olbrechts-Tyteca's account reveals the persuasive dynamics of argument structures. Through the structures of their reasoning patterns, arguments build a sense of validity, of empirical foundation, or of remodeled understanding into the very way in which ideas are related. Argument forms not only control the types of inferences we are encouraged to draw, but they also anchor these inferences in patterns of thought and experience that we already accept as valid.

৯৫

Rhetorical Structures of Dramatic Enactment

The approaches of Aristotle, Toulmin, and Perelman and Olbrechts-Tyteca tell us a great deal about argument structures as forms that shape perceptions. Each provides major insights, especially into arguments as forms of reasoning—certifying the validity of claims. All four theorists emphasize the logical scaffolding from which rhetorical premises are hung. Apart from its "logic," what else may we say about how the structure of a message encourages us to agree with it? We can find a clue by stepping back for a moment to consider how *form in the large*, as represented by **genres** of discourse, argues.

When we consider a genre of symbolic acts, such as painting, dance, literature, or oratory from a rhetorical point of view, we invariably focus on how audiences respond to these performances. The most interesting responses are thoughts, emotions, and values that lead to the acceptance or rejection of an attitude, proposition, belief, or action. Consequently, genres become important when their typical structures become a source of influence urging audiences to think and respond in certain ways. Dramatic *form*, for example, urges us to look for revelation of motives, for a clash among competing motives, for resolution of the clash, for intimation of this resolution's implications in the lives of the characters.

Drama focuses our attention on motivations because it is a genre of action. It portrays the encounters of life and the motivations for resolving them. Moreover, dramatic portrayal is unique. In a film, we see the action through the eye of the camera. It necessarily focuses on one character at a time. We see that character's experience of the action. Film is selective in this respect. But in drama all the characters are before us, and we witness simultaneously their diverse experiences. In addition, in drama we typically know more than the characters portrayed. We know that A hates B for loving C and seeks revenge, while B trusts A but is insecure about C's love and could be moved to kill out of jealousy, and C thinks A and B are bosom buddies though she distrusts A and is totally devoted to B. While we know all of this, the characters know only a few of these things. Thus the form of a drama brings us into a relationship with the characters in which we see them before us as in life and weigh the consequences that will follow from what each character does, but we are helpless to intercede. That is why we are fascinated and moved by drama. We experience the heightened tension and emotion of knowing all this while the characters are sitting about the parlor engaged in conversation and not fully aware of what will result from their words and actions.

The very form of a drama thus influences what will count as "reality" and how we will respond to it. Considered rhetorically, drama establishes a relationship with its audience. It asks us to think, feel, and value in certain ways while we are in this relationship. In fact, we must do so to sustain the relationship between the dramatic performance and ourselves. In accepting the playwright's terms, we actually create a world with its own matrix of thoughts, emotions, and values as a proper motivational basis for action.

What counts as an argument for or against such action is conditioned by the terms of this symbolically constructed world. The form brings words and deeds before us. The form creates a need for A to respond to B. Something will happen. The form requires that the characters have a motivation for what they do. Their motivations will elicit our sympathies or evoke our resistances toward the characters. In all of this, we will not give primacy to the formal codes of legal rules or to the theoretical laws of nature. The form urges us to judge the rightness or wrongness of what transpires on the basis of how the characters acted. In sum, arguments in drama are products of dramatic form and the way symbols are used in it.

Having said that dramatic form shapes the way arguments develop, we still face the question of patterns that specific arguments take in dramatic development. Considering a play with a romantic theme, we might expect to find courtship. Courtship is itself a symbolic form with discernible elements and a pattern of development: Boy meets girl, boy courts girl, girl falls for boy, they marry and live happily ever after. Even in this oversimplified version, there is more to be said. All along the path from first encounter to the blessed nuptials, we witness partisan blandishments designed to secure the girl's affections: praising her virtues; bestowing gifts; showing himself as intelligent, sensitive, and humorous. Each enactment of the courtship is an argument for his sincerity and worth.

Now take the same pattern as it is developed in *Evita*. On balance, we are encouraged to reject Eva Peron; she is not a sympathetic character. There is pathos in her humble origins, but she is not unique in this respect. Men victimize her early on when she arrives in Buenos Aires, but she accepts this as necessary to achieving her ambitions. Soon she appears consumed with the lust for power. We reject her primarily because her life is a corruption of courtship. She is equally insincere whether teasing men or the people of Buenos Aires. We do not need the conscience of Che to tell us this; her own actions belie the sincerity of her words. How do we know this? Because the playwright develops his play through a montage of public and private scenes. The form of juxtaposing her public words with her private deeds has a doubling effect. We see her arguments as deceitful, and we see the play itself arguing against her vision of reality.

Drama reveals most clearly how a form of life unfolds in a way that argues. From a rhetorical perspective, this dramatic unfolding is not unique to the stage. On the stage we see in capsule form the highlights of events marked by tension and emotion marching toward their resolution. The same is true, though in tones more generally muted, of all discursive forms. As we noted earlier, all symbolic acts are dramatic in character; they unfold in a pattern of action. We have enactments whose impacts as symbolic forms are profoundly influenced by their patterns of development and of audience involvement. This occurs quite apart from their specific subjects and yet may reinforce or undermine their specific premises.

Abraham Lincoln's speech at Cooper Union[22] illustrates the way rhetoric argues through dramatic enactment. His speech addressed the question of slavery, but his address was also an enactment of leadership in which a local politician from Illinois thrust himself into a position to claim the Republican nomination for the presidency. Lincoln reasoned a case against the expansion of slavery based on the criteria of his opponents. He addressed Southerners to refute their objections against the Republicans and to confound them with the self-contradictions of their words and deeds. He spoke to his fellow Republicans, urging them to be true to their principles in the face of criticism. As the speech unfolded, its form reinforced his specific contentions. He said things that could only have infuriated the South. But to a northern audience looking for an articulate spokesman, he displayed himself as a qualified candidate. The structure of his arguments and their order in the speech themselves were a means of enticement. They encouraged identification with Lincoln as a leader capable of influencing the fate of his party and of his nation.

Some 120 years later, Edward Kennedy addressed the Democratic national convention with similar hopes. In a different era, with economic issues as the central focus, he attempted to wrest the leadership of his party from Jimmy Carter. Kennedy did not gain the nomination. The party rules made Carter's renomination a foregone conclusion, but Kennedy won sufficient support to force significant changes in the Democratic platform.

Kennedy's major contention held that his campaign was a "cause." Consider the implicative complex of his metaphor. If we have a cause, we have a goal. Such a goal is pursued over time. Achieving it requires sustained effort. Causes tend to have a moral impulse and justification. Therefore, they require fervent, even zealous commitment. Causes run into obstacles that must be overcome. Usually, the more formidable the obstacle, the more worthy the goal. By using "cause" to frame his campaign, Kennedy invoked a reservoir of implications that defined and gave value to his quest. In advancing his case, he meticulously provided appeals that played on this implicative complex. The very way in which he discussed the cause—the form of his address—encouraged the people in the convention hall and those viewing him on television to identify with him as a patrician warrior—the slayer of Ronald Reagan, the heir of Franklin D. Roosevelt, the champion of the common and the needy American. His manner of arguing was itself an enticement to share his vision of reality.

Every symbolic act considered as a whole has patterns that serve strategic ends. Each form in the large involves us in a creative relationship with the rhetor: we cocreate a world. This world unfolds through the patterns of evidence and reasoning presented much as a drama on stage. We are enticed to see our world as this symbolic form presents it because the very structure of rhetoric considered holistically enacts its realities, replete with the unifying links of associations and values. In addition to argument types, the ways in which rhetorical forms argue serve as powerful strategies suited to our readiness to respond and capable of remodeling the truths we live by.

৵
Scenic Structures as Arguments

We know from experience that a setting can have meaning or symbolic value. Further, we can respond to a **scene** in terms of its symbolic value. Take the middle of your hometown. If you come from a New England village, chances are that there is a village green with trees and benches; most likely it is surrounded by shops. It's a good place to gather and meet with your neighbors. The space is designed to encourage social congregation. If you come from a large city, the center of your town probably has a square that is purely monumental. It may have a circle designed to handle traffic flow; there may be offices and department stores around it, but it is not a place that encourages congregating. One scene invites meeting with neighbors and strangers; the other invites continued movement. One encourages conversation; the other discourages it.

The floor plan of an office has a similar effect. Office planners have found that if there are private places, such as individual offices or partitioned areas, workers will use them as places to congregate. Here they will interact with greater ease than if there were no partitions. In an open space, workers lose their sense of privacy. For self-protection, they retreat into themselves; socialization declines, and work output increases. By manipulating the space, managers can influence workers' behaviors.

Consider also the way your communication is influenced by your instructor's office arrangement. If your instructor's desk allows her to sit behind it, the desk acts as a barrier between you and lends her an air of authority. But if your instructor moved her desk so that she sat facing the wall, the barrier would be removed, and the openness of your body positions to each other would suggest greater equality.

Physical surroundings are significant in public address as well. Hitler, for example, was given to exploiting the suasive potential of scene by holding his mass meetings outdoors at twilight in monumental settings. The scene of a mass of enthusiasts lent the reinforcement of collective emotional energy to his exhortations. The scene of twilight had special significance for the Germans, since this was the bewitching hour when the mythical Nibelungs were alleged to be about. It was a magical time. Holding meetings outdoors opened the heavens to his oratory, suggesting that no barriers existed between his pleas and the throne of God. Finally, the backdrop of statues, pillars, arches, and massive buildings were symbols of solidity and visual grandeur. Here was scaffolding worthy of great causes! For Hitler, all these features conspired to form a whole that conferred righteousness on his pronouncements—and encouraged a perception of the man quite the opposite of his nature. In this setting, Hitler seemed larger than life.

Quite apart from their visual aspects, scenes encourage and thwart audience responses through the ways in which they induce rhetorical responses. One way in which scenic inducements are enacted is by structuring the elements in a setting in a way that suggests a possible course of future action. As we saw in chapter 3, when we succeed in imposing our definition on a scene, we set expectations of what should occur. A classic case of structuring scenarios occurred during the Nixon administration following student protests in the wake of the Kent State shootings. The president indicated that students would be invited to Washington to discuss matters of mutual concern regarding the war in Vietnam and student protests against it. By labeling the purpose of the meetings as discussion, Nixon set expectations of what should transpire. In our culture, discussion assumes open exchange, give-and-take, willingness to compromise, and seeking of common ground on which to build agreement. We also expect norms of civility and decorum to prevail. Chanting antiwar slogans, singing protest songs, shouting obscenities, delivering ad hominem invectives, and the like are inappropriate modes of communication while engaging in discussion. For many of the students, the rhetoric that they had perfected to radicalize their peers was ruled out of bounds. An expectation was set for communication of the type at which administrators were especially skilled.

The president invited the students to come to Washington. The nation's capital is our primary location for official meetings to decide weighty public questions. Accepting Nixon's invitation meant that the students would meet on the government's turf. The scenic constraints of meeting rooms that were paneled, carpeted, and had plush chairs invited the moderate tones of reasoned talk. The scene even denied the students their familiar garb, for these were places where business attire was in order.

When President Nixon invited the students, he also labeled the nature of the problem as a communication breakdown. This labeling imposed the assumption that the students' differences with the Nixon administration were more a matter of misunderstanding than substance. They were resolvable if the participants were reasonable. This assumption reinforced the rhetorical constraints imposed by the scenic frame of Washington. Moreover, the strategic advantage of structuring the communication event in scenic terms meant that the only information available to an observing public were summary reports of discussions that they never got to witness. If discussion stopped, the purpose went unfulfilled, and someone had to be at fault for that. We assume, after all, that a communication breakdown can be repaired if both parties try hard enough. The structure of the scene as a whole functioned as a rhetorical strategy. By orchestrating the setting (Washington), by defining the scenario of what was to transpire there (discussion), and by labeling the problem that motivated the participants' efforts (communication breakdown), the president exerted enormous control over public perceptions. These elements structured events in a manner that argued for a particular interpretation of reality. Together they set expectations for what would transpire. Consequently, when students finally broke off discussion in frustration, the administration could point its finger in dismay and bemoan the fact that the students obviously were not serious or they would have continued talking. By labeling the scenario as one for discussion and by reducing the differences to a communication breakdown, Nixon exploited the form of these meetings to shape public perceptions more favorably toward his administration.[23]

Another way in which we argue with scenic elements is through the location of the scene. Where we picture events occurring greatly influences what we perceive as the event and the nature of its concerns. For example, consider the way in which American television located the scene of the Iranian hostage event of 1979–81. Where was the story, in the embassy or in the streets? If we go by what appeared on American television each evening, we would have to say that it was in the streets. Viewers hardly saw the hostages during their 444 days of captivity, but they saw mobs of shouting Iranians burning effigies of the president and Uncle Sam, destroying the flag, and hurling invectives that vilified the United States. What was the story about? Was it about the plight of the hostages? They remained unseen; their story barely told. Was it about Iranian grievances? Those were not articulated. Street speakers shouted slogans, they did not offer rationales.

How were Americans to respond to such a sight? The serious and extreme nature of the hostage situation notwithstanding, the point remains that the setting in which this story was told worked as an argument structure; it argued for a response. The grievances of Iranian militants were not set in a deliberative assembly but in the streets. For Americans watching this event unfold on television, judgments were not invited through reasoned appeals but through actions. Televised behaviors were the focus of attention; they were also premises in the Iranian case. Because they so violated the Western cultural norms of the American viewing audience, is it any wonder that the argument of this scene solidified a nationalistic prejudice against Iran? Largely ignorant of Muslims, lacking in historical perspective on their country's 35-year involvement in Iranian affairs, Americans had only the vivid elements of scene to respond to. Off camera were Americans held hostage; on camera were mobs of aliens acting hatefully toward the United States. This crisis was presented as street theater; its scenic structure made a dramatic argument. The setting for these episodes controlled the story in a way guaranteed to arouse domestic anger and frustration at seemingly irrational behavior.

The important feature in each of these rhetorical scenes is summarized in the commonly used expression "Don't lose sight of the forest for the trees." This admonition warns against the danger of getting lost in details. The fact is that details, in and of themselves, are not terribly meaningful. As raw data, they are what they are, isolated and lacking connection to anything else. We need some way to relate individual bits and pieces of data to one another so that we can understand their meaning in terms of a unit or whole. We require patterns. Structural features such as those we have examined simplify details by finding among them or imposing on them patterns that relate ideas to audiences in meaningful ways, that provide arguments of some sort for an interpretation of reality, and that shape perceptions and encourage specific responses.

ॐ
Summary

We have considered how patterning a message plays an important role in inducing social cooperation. We have seen how structural patterns shape perceptions that in turn encourage audiences to see a subject in a similar light. This led us to inquire into why audiences respond as they do, and analysis of structures proved a useful explanation.

Rhetorical works composed with an eye toward the audience go beyond the informational level to consider how each element of the work establishes a relationship of thought and feeling that involves the audience in the composition. They argue, through their structures of thought and composition, for a view of reality. We recognize in a Shakespearean play, for example, how a protagonist's speech draws us into the play and shapes our desires for what is to follow. We don't just observe Othello's anguish, we share in the horror of his jealous rage. We don't just see the Roman mob turned against Brutus by Antony's speech, we are moved ourselves to desire revenge against his crime. In reading the Gettysburg Address, we don't just witness the dedication of the cemetery, we are pulled into a sympathetic relationship with basic American values. In each case, the composition affects us because its form is attuned to our capacities to feel and think and value—our capacities to respond. It is not the facts but the pattern of development or form that shapes our perceptions and gives us an active role as participants who identify with the rhetor.

Audience-involving rhetoric of this sort is artful. Its artfulness isn't in the truth of its facts but in the rightness of its structure to express something in a way that pulls us into sympathy with the rhetor's cause. We are in a sense stuck with the facts. Art consists in how the facts are presented, related, and juxtaposed to create arguments. In short, art resides in the form. This, after all, is the source of true eloquence: appeals attuned to our inherent appetites for meaning, life, community, and happiness.

Afterword
Inviting Rhetoric

Rhetoric has been essential to the development of civilization and remains essential to the well-being of our age—an age of diversity, of complexity, and of rapid change. We typically think that rhetorical communication requires common ground, and the factors just listed could work against consensus on values, principles, interests, or ends. However, we live in an age of increasing interdependence, and rhetoric involves us in relationships. Constructive possibilities reside in relationships.

Rhetorical communication is the form of human action so frequently forgotten in relationships that disintegrate, whether they are the interpersonal ties of romantic partners or the bonds of mutual dependency among global partners. Whenever two or more people communicate, each relies on the other to speak his or her mind and to support those expressions of opinion with reliable information. We count on each other to listen with an open mind, even when our views disagree, and to take one another's arguments seriously. Whenever two or more of us communicate in any serious sense, we must assume that each of us is competent to say what we mean and have reasons for the things we say. From the outset, genuine communication establishes a bond that enables us to exchange ideas and feelings and to achieve mutual understanding.

We need the cooperation of others for our physical survival. We need cooperation for our personal relationships to thrive, to accomplish group goals, to prosper as a community, to act in union as a nation, and to live in harmony as brothers and sisters in the family of humankind. From the couple trying to make their relationship work to world leaders seeking peace, the common thread that binds us to one another is our openness to communication and the possibilities it can create. So long as we are talking and listening, our communication relationship already has us cooperating in a way that can lead to a more cooperative world.

In simpler times, people shared unifying visions, a common set of values, to help them find meaning in their lives. Today it is harder to locate beliefs, values, or goals that everyone shares. Some people react to this by trying to force their views on others. Others go to the opposite extreme, talking and acting as if truth is whatever they believe it to be. But these views of privilege for one ism over another or of the relativity of everything are ill suited for our problems. Such approaches are more likely to intensify problems than resolve them. In these circumstances we need the mediating influence of rhetoric.

Rhetoric doesn't require that we share the same dogma. It does require that we use the same procedure: that of having open discussion with an audience we take seriously in order to advance our understanding of what is true and to act in ways that are just and right. Rightly practiced, rhetorical communication fosters cooperation. We become partners in the shared procedure of giving reasons and making appeals that take one another into account. A rhetoric of this sort gives us a procedure for working out agreements on our truths. It requires that we be tolerant of others, open to their criticisms, and willing to consider that change may be for the better.

We know that there have been, are, and will continue to be people who use rhetorical means to lie and to mislead. That is a fact of life. But their false and corrupt practices do not diminish this essential point: The human world is one we make through countless acts of social cooperation that are symbolically induced. It is a product of rhetoric. Every time we speak and write, we give voice to what we would like to transpire, to a world we would prefer. Amid our many differences, rhetoric provides the means to forge an expression of the future that all concerned can abide. Rhetoric is our last best alternative to a world run by power or privilege; it offers a world run by the people. In the final analysis, it may also be our last best hope for avoiding mutual obliteration and creating a world of amity and trust.

Notes

Chapter 1

1. Robert Craig, "Communication as a Field," *Communication Theory* 9, no. 2 (1999): 119–61.
2. For example, Carroll C. Arnold and John Waite Bowers, eds., *Handbook of Rhetorical and Communication Theory* (Boston: Allyn & Bacon, 1984) reviews research across the areas of specialization in communication. Noteworthy is the prominence of "process" as an anchoring concept.
3. See Henry W. Johnstone, "Rhetoric and Death," in *Rhetoric in Transition: Studies in the Nature and Uses of Rhetoric*, ed. E. E. White (University Park: Pennsylvania State University Press, 1980), pp. 61–70. My discussion borrows heavily from Johnstone's fine presentation.
4. Ibid., p. 62.
5. Michel Foucault, *The Archaeology of Knowledge*, trans. A. M. Sheridan (New York: Pantheon Books, 1972).
6. The concept of situated action is prominent in the rhetorical theory of Lloyd Bitzer, which is discussed in greater detail in chapter 3. See Bitzer, "The Rhetorical Situation," *Philosophy and Rhetoric* 1, no. 1 (1968): 1–12, and "Functional Communication: A Situational Perspective," in *Rhetoric in Transition*, pp. 21–38.
7. The concept of symbolic action is prominent in the rhetorical theory of Kenneth Burke, which is discussed in greater detail in chapter 12. See Burke, *A Rhetoric of Motives* (Berkeley: University of California Press, 1969 [1950]).
8. The concept of rhetoric as transactional is prominent across most of contemporary rhetorical theory. An exemplary discussion of the role of the audience as an active partner with the rhetor in rhetorical actions may be found in Ch. Perelman and L. Olbrechts-Tyteca, *The New Rhetoric*, trans. John Wilkinson and Purcell Weaver (Notre Dame, IN: University of Notre Dame Press, 1969 [1957]).
9. The concept of rhetoric as social action can be found in many sociological treatments of the subject. See, for example, Hugh Dalziel Duncan, *Communication and Social Order* (New York: Bedminster Press, 1962), and Joseph Gusfield, *The Culture of Public Problems: Drinking-Driving and the Symbolic Order* (Chicago: University of Chicago Press, 1981).
10. The concept of rhetoric as strategic action is most commonly found in theories that stress persuasion. Aristotle's *Rhetoric* is often interpreted to hold this view. We will consider Aristotle's views in greater depth in chapters 6–9.

11. The concept of rhetoric as constitutive action has become the dominant theoretical school among rhetoricians in the United States since the late 1980s. We will consider this view throughout our discussion of rhetorical theory. For an important statement of this theory, see Maurice Charland, "Constitutive Rhetoric: The Case of the *Peuple Québécois*," *Quarterly Journal of Speech* 73, no. 2 (1987): 133–50.

ఌ
Chapter 2

1. David Broder, "Ballot Initiatives Subvert Election Process," *The Denver Post*, May 14, 2000, p. 1K.
2. John Dewey, *The Public and its Problems* (Chicago: Swallow Press, 1954 [1927]).
3. Jeffrey Fleishman, "Italian Vendors Irked at Pilgrims," *Boulder Daily Camera*, May 30, 2000, p. 3A.
4. Dewey, p. 208.
5. Broder, p. 1K.
6. Thucydides, *The Peloponnesian War*, trans. John H. Finley, Jr. (New York: Random House, 1951).
7. William Grimaldi, *Aristotle, Rhetoric I: A Commentary* (New York: Fordham University Press 1980), pp. 349–56.
8. For a discussion of the ways in which women might occupy a pubic leadership role in the ancient Athenian polis, see Christine Sourvinou-Inwood, "Male and Female, Public and Private, Ancient and Modern," in *Pandora's Box: Women in Classical Greece*, ed. Ellen D. Reeder (Princeton: Princeton University, 1995), pp. 111–20.
9. For example, see Richard Weaver, *Visions of Order* (Baton Rouge: Louisiana State University Press, 1964), chs. 1–4; Jean-Francois Lyotard, *The Postmodern Condition: A Report on Knowledge*, trans. Geoff Bennington and Brian Massumi (Minneapolis: University of Minnesota Press, 1984).
10. Richard Weaver, *The Ethics of Rhetoric* (Chicago: Henry Regnery, 1953), p. 28.
11. "Soccer Balls From Space," *Discover* 21, no. 6 (June 2000): 20.
12. "A Slick Little Alien," *op. cit.*, p. 20.
13. W. Robert Connor, *The New Politicians of Fifth-Century Athens* (Princeton: Princeton University Press, 1971), chs. 3 and 4.
14. For extended discussion of Sophistic rhetoric, see Susan Jarratt, *Rereading the Sophists: Classical Rhetoric Refigured* (Carbondale: Southern Illinois University Press, 1991); John Poulakos, *Sophistical Rhetoric in Classical Greece* (Columbia: University of South Carolina Press, 1995); Takis Poulakos, *Speaking for the Polis: Isocrates' Rhetorical Education* (Columbia: University of South Carolina Press, 1997); and Edward Schiappa, *Protagoras and Logos: A Study in Greek Philosophy and Rhetoric* (Columbia: University of South Carolina Press, 1991).
15. For an excellent discussion of Protagoras' philosophy of socially established truths, see Eric Havelock, *The Liberal Temper of Greek Politics* (New Haven: Yale University Press, 1957), pp. 163–231.
16. Gorgias, "On the Nonexistent or on Nature," trans. George Kennedy, in *The Older Sophists*, ed. Rosamond Kent Sprague (Columbia: University of South Carolina Press, 1972), pp. 42–43.
17. Gorgias, "Encomium on Helen," trans. George Kennedy, in *The Older Sophists*, p. 72.

ఌ
Chapter 3

1. Lloyd Bitzer, "The Rhetorical Situation," *Philosophy and Rhetoric* 1, no. 1 (1968): 1–12; and "Functional Communication: A Situational Perspective," in *Rhetoric in Transition*, ed. E. E. White (University Park: Pennsylvania State University Press, 1981), pp. 21–38.

2. Peter McHugh, *Defining the Situation* (Indianapolis: Bobbs-Merrill, 1968), pp. 23–32.

3. Bitzer, "The Rhetorical Situation," 6.

4. "Aerial Mosquito Spraying Planned in Nassau," *New York Times*, October 1, 1999, p. A24.

5. Donald C. Bryant, "Rhetoric: Its Function and Scope," *Quarterly Journal of Speech* 39, no. 4 (1953): 413.

6. Bitzer, "Functional Communication," pp. 21–22.

7. Bitzer, "The Rhetorical Situation," 8.

8. Maurice Charland, "Constitutive Rhetoric: The Case of the *Peuple Québécois*," *Quarterly Journal of Speech* 73, no. 2 (1987): 133–50.

9. See Barbara A. Biesecker, "Rethinking the Rhetorical Situation from Within the Thematic of Différance," *Philosophy and Rhetoric* 22, no. 2 (1989): 110–30.

10. Biesecker, 126.

❧
Chapter 4

1. Henry W. Johnstone, Jr., "Some Reflections on Argumentation," in *Philosophy, Rhetoric, and Argumentation*, ed. Maurice Natanson and Henry W. Johnstone, Jr. (University Park: Pennsylvania State University Press, 1965), pp. 1–10.

2. Henry W. Johnstone, Jr., "Bilaterality in Argument and Communication," in *Advances in Argumentation Theory and Research*, ed. J. Robert Cox and Charles Arthur Willard (Carbondale: Southern Illinois University Press, 1982), pp. 95–102.

3. Ibid., p. 95.

4. Ibid., p. 99.

5. Ibid.

6. Thomas Farrell and G. Thomas Goodnight, "Accidental Rhetoric: The Root Metaphors of Three Mile Island," *Communication Monographs* 48, no. 4 (1981): 271–300.

7. Johnstone, "Bilaterality in Argument and Communication," p. 101.

8. Richard Weaver, *The Ethics of Rhetoric* (Chicago: Henry Regnery, 1953), pp. 55–114. Also see Edwin Black, "Second Persona," *Quarterly Journal of Speech* 56, no. 2 (1970): 109–19.

9. Maurice Charland, "Constitutive Rhetoric: The Case of the *Peuple Québécois*," *Quarterly Journal of Speech* 73, no. 2 (1987): 133–50. Also see Black, op cit.

10. Hank Johnston, "New Social Movements and Old Regional Nationalisms," in *New Social Movements: From Ideology to Identity*, ed. Enrique Laraña, Hank Johnston, and Joseph R. Gusfield (Philadelphia: Temple University Press, 1994), p. 278.

11. Richard B. Gregg, "The Ego Function of Protest Rhetoric," *Philosophy and Rhetoric* 4, no. 2 (Spring 1971): 71–91.

12. Doug McAdam, "Culture and Social Movement," in *New Social Movements*, p. 38.

13. Robert Bellah, et al., *Habits of the Heart: Individualism and Commitment in American Life*, (Berkeley: University of California Press, 1985) p. 249.

14. McAdam, p. 38.

15. Scott A. Hunt, Robert Benford, and David A. Snow, "Identity Fields: Framing Processes and the Social Construction of Movement Identities," in *New Social Movements*, p. 201.

16. Gregg, 87.

❧
Chapter 5

1. Clifford Geertz, *The Interpretation of Cultures* (New York: Basic Books, 1973).

2. Alain Touraine, *Return of the Actor: Social Theory in Postindustrial Society*, trans. Myrna Godzich (Minneapolis: University of Minnesota Press, 1988), ch. 1.

3. Samuel L. Popkin, *The Reasoning Voter: Communication and Persuasion in Presidential Campaigns* (Chicago: University of Chicago Press, 1991). For a good initial source for

learning about the role of media in making the link between the average person and public issues, see Shanto Iyengar and Donald Kinder, *News That Matters: Television and American Opinion* (Chicago: University of Chicago Press, 1987).

4. Joseph Gusfield, *The Culture of Public Problems: Drinking-Driving and the Symbolic Order* (Chicago: University of Chicago Press, 1981), p. 7.

5. Gusfield, p. 12.

6. John Dewey, *The Public and its Problems* (Chicago: Swallow Press, 1954 [1927]); and Walter Lippmann, *Public Opinion* (New York: Free Press, 1949 [1922]).

7. Dewey, p. 208.

8. Cited in Christopher Lasch, *The Culture of Narcissism* (New York: W. W. Norton, 1978), p. 77.

9. G. Thomas Goodnight, "The Personal, Technical, and Public Spheres of Argument: A Speculative Inquiry into the Art of Public Deliberation," *Journal of the American Forensic Association* 18, no. 2 (1982): 214–27.

10. Lloyd Bitzer, "Rhetoric and Public Knowledge," in *Rhetoric, Philosophy and Literature: An Exploration*, ed. Don M. Burks (West Lafayette, IN: Purdue University Press, 1978), pp. 67–95; Jürgen Habermas, *The Structural Transformation of the Public Sphere*, trans. Thomas Burger with the assistance of Frederick Lawrence (Cambridge: MIT Press, 1989).

11. Gerard A. Hauser, *Vernacular Voices: The Rhetoric of Publics and Public Spheres* (Columbia: University of South Carolina Press, 1999), p. 32.

12. James Fishkin, *The Voice of the People* (New Haven, Yale University Press, 1995).

13. Jürgen Habermas, "The Public Sphere: An Encyclopaedia Article," *New German Critique* 3 (1973): 49–55.

14. Hauser, p. 61.

15. Ibid., p. 98.

16. Ibid., pp. 73–76.

17. Elisabeth Noelle-Neumann, *The Spiral of Silence: Public Opinion—Our Social Skin*, 2nd ed. (Chicago: University of Chicago Press, 1993).

18. Hauser, *Vernacular Voices*, p. 78.

ॐ

Chapter 6

1. Matthew Miller, "The Poor Man's Capitalist," *New York Times Magazine*, July 1, 2001, pp. 44–47.

2. Quoted in Matt Bai, "Running from Office," *New York Times Magazine*, July 15, 2001, p. 28.

3. John Leonard, "Funny, Funky, and, ah, Flip," *Life*, January 11, 1971, p. 12.

4. Bruce Handy, "Comedian: Chris Rock," *Time*, July 29, 2001, p. 67.

5. Rodney Douglas and Carroll C. Arnold, "On Analysis of Logos: A Methodological Inquiry," *Quarterly Journal of Speech* 56, no. 1 (February 1970): 22–32.

6. Susan Jarratt and Rory Ong, "Aspasia: Rhetoric, Gender, and Colonial Ideology," in *Reclaiming Rhetorica: Women in the Rhetorical Tradition*, ed. Andrea A. Lunsford (Pittsburgh: University of Pittsburgh Press, 1995), p. 14.

7. C. Jan Swearingen, "A Lover's Discourse: Diotima, Logos, and Desire," in Lunsford, p. 33.

8. Christine Sourvinou-Inwood, "Male and Female, Public and Private, Ancient and Modern," in *Pandora's Box: Women in Classical Greece*, ed. Ellen D. Reeder (Princeton: Princeton University, 1995), pp. 111–20.

9. John F. Wilson and Carroll C. Arnold, *Public Speaking as a Liberal Art*, 5th ed. (Boston: Allyn & Bacon, 1983), pp. 83–88.

10. Ibid., p. 84.

෫

Chapter 7

1. Karl Wallace, "The Substance of Rhetoric; Good Reasons," *Quarterly Journal of Speech* 49, no. 2 (1963): 239–49.
2. William Grimaldi, *Aristotle, Rhetoric I: A Commentary* (New York: Fordham University Press, 1980), p. 8.
3. See Gerard A. Hauser, "The Example in Aristotle's Rhetoric. Bifurcation or Contradiction?" *Philosophy and Rhetoric* 1, no. 2 (1968): 78–90; Hauser, "Aristotle's Example Revisited," *P&R* 18, no. 3 (1985): 171–80; Scott Consigny, "The Rhetorical Example," *Southern Speech Communication Journal* 41, no. 2 (1976): 121–32; and William Lyon Benoit, "Aristotle's Example: The Rhetorical Induction," *Quarterly Journal of Speech* 66, no. 2 (1980): 182–92.
4. This feature was first noted in Lloyd Bitzer, "Aristotle's Enthymeme Revisited," *Quarterly Journal of Speech* 45, no. 4 (1959): 399–408.
5. Edward D. Steele and W. Charles Redding, "The American Value System: Premises for Persuasion," *Western Speech* 26, no. 1 (1962): 83–91.
6. Ibid.
7. Image restoration is a concept describing rhetoric intended to address a tarnished public image of an individual, group, organization, or institution. For example, the discourse of the Firestone Tire company following the rash of failures by their tires on Ford motor vehicles was intended to restore public confidence in the safety of its product. For a convenient and thorough discussion of image restoration see William L. Benoit, *Accounts, Excuses, and Apologies: A Theory of Image Restoration Strategies* (Albany: SUNY Press, 1995).
8. Gresham M. Sykes and David Matza, "Techniques of Neutralization: A Theory of Delinquency," *American Sociological Review* 22, no. 4 (1957): 664–70.
9. C. Wright Mills, "Situated Actions and Vocabularies of Motive," *American Sociological Review* 5, no. 4 (1940): 904–13.
10. Sykes and Matza, 667–69.
11. Marvin B. Scott and Stanford M. Lyman, "Accounts," *American Sociological Review* 33, no. 1 (1968): 46–62.
12. Ibid., 46.
13. Ibid., 47–52.
14. Jackson Toby, "Some Variables in Role Conflict Analysis," *Social Forces* 30 (March 1952): 323–27.
15. Ibid.

෫

Chapter 8

1. Richard Sennett, *Authority* (New York: Knopf, 1980), pp. 16–17. One imagines that Sennett, himself a cellist, had this experience face-to-face as an orchestra member, not as a sideline observer.
2. Ibid., pp. 20–27.
3. Ibid., p. 196.
4. See Gary Cronkhite and Jo Liska, "A Critique of Factor Analytic Approaches to the Study of Credibility," *Communication Monographs* 43, no. 2 (1976): 91–107.
5. Otis Walter, "Toward an Analysis of Ethos," *Pennsylvania Speech Annual* 21 (1964): 37–45.
6. Robert D. Brooks and Thomas M. Scheidel, "Speech as Process: A Case Study," *Speech Monographs* 35, no. 1 (1968): 1–7.
7. For example, in the 1960 presidential debates, a majority of viewers who saw the first debate on television thought John Kennedy won, while a majority of the radio audience

thought Richard Nixon won. The crucial variable was Nixon's nonverbal cues: He was poorly made up, and his heavy beard gave him a sinister appearance. History repeated itself in 1984. In the second Reagan-Mondale debate, Mondale appeared haggard, with dark bags under his eyes. Again, this was the result of makeup plus studio lighting. Viewers translated this as a sign that Mondale was nearly exhausted in a desperate effort to overcome his opponent's lead.

8. George Kennedy, trans., *Aristotle, On Rhetoric* (New York: Oxford University Press, 1991), p. 38.

9. Eric Havelock, *The Liberal Temper of Greek Politics* (New Haven, CT: Yale University Press, 1957), pp. 191–239.

10. John Herman Randall, Jr., *Aristotle* (New York: Columbia University Press, 1962), pp. 253–54.

11. Gerard Hauser, "Aristotle on Epideictic: The Formation of Public Morality," *Rhetoric Society Quarterly* 29, no. 1 (1999): 5–23.

12. Martha Nussbaum, *The Fragility of Goodness* (New York: Cambridge University Press, 1986), pp. 290–317.

13. Arthur B. Miller, "Aristotle on Habit (εθος) and Character (ηφος): Implications for the Rhetoric," *Speech Monographs* 41, no. 4 (1974): 309–16.

14. Jim Rutenberg, "Levy Case Brings Out Cable's Instinct for the Racy and Repetitive," *The New York Times on the Web*, July 30, 2001 (http://www.nytimes.com/).

15. Associated Press, "F.B.I. Investigates Internet Tip on Missing Intern," *The New York Times on the Web*, August 2, 2001 (http://www.nytimes.com/).

16. See, for example, Mike Litwin, "End May Be Getting Near for Condit," *Rocky Mountain News*, August 25, 2001, p. 2B; and the front page and opinion page of the on-line *Modesto Bee* for August 26, 2001 (http://modbee.com/).

17. "Deep Thoughts by Dan Quale" [sic] (http://www.duke.edu/~pms5/humor/quale.html/)

18. As students of Aristotle will recognize, these virtues are discussed in *Rhetoric* I.9. They remain a sound basic list for assessing ideal moral habits that should attract or repel audiences.

19. Kennedy delivered this speech on August 12, 1980.

20. For example, see William F. Fore, "There Is No Such Thing as a TV Pastor," *TV Guide*, July 19, 1980, pp. 15–18; Charles E. Swan, "The Electronic Church," *Presbyterian Survey*, May 1979, pp. 9–16; and Allan Dodds Frank, "Mr. Ed and the Gospel," *Forbes*, May 21, 1984, pp. 84–89.

21. Henry W. Johnstone, Jr., "Bilaterality in Argument and Communication," in *Advances in Argumentation Theory and Research*, ed. J. Robert Cox and Charles Arthur Willard (Carbondale: Southern Illinois University Press, 1982), p. 95.

22. The technical aspects of Aristotle's distinction between rhetoric as a power and as an art are elaborated in a variety of places. See especially Thomas Farrell, *Norms of Rhetorical Culture* (New Haven: Yale University Press, 1993), pp. 51–100; William Grimaldi, *Aristotle, Rhetoric I: A Commentary* (New York: Fordham University Press, 1980), pp. 349–56; George Kennedy, "Introduction," *Aristotle, On Rhetoric* (New York: Oxford University Press, 1991), pp. 12–13; Richard McKeon, "The Uses of Rhetoric in a Technological Age: Architectonic Productive Arts," in *The Prospect of Rhetoric*, ed. Lloyd F. Bitzer and Edwin Black (Englewood Cliffs, NJ: Prentice-Hall, 1971), pp. 44–63; McKeon, "General Introduction," *Introduction to Aristotle*, 2nd ed. (Chicago: University of Chicago Press, 1973), pp. xxvi–xli; and Elder Olson, "The Poetic Method of Aristotle: Its Powers and Limitations," in *On Value Judgments in the Arts, and Other Essays* (Chicago: University of Chicago Press, 1976), pp. 186–99.

23. George Yoos, "A Revision of the Concept of Ethical Appeal," *Philosophy and Rhetoric* 12, no. 1 (1979): 41–58.

24. Ibid., pp. 50–55.

25. George Yoos, "Rational Appeal and the Ethics of Advocacy," in *Essays on Classical Rhetoric and Modern Discourse*, ed. Robert J. Connors et al. (Carbondale: Southern Illinois University Press, 1984), pp. 82–97.

26. Tim Rice, "Don't Cry for Me, Argentina," copyright © 1976 by Evita Music, Ltd. Reprinted with Permission.

❧
Chapter 9

1. *The New York Times on the Web*, August 15, 2001 (http://www.nytimes.com/).
2. John Watson, *Behaviorism* (Chicago: University of Chicago Press, 1930), p. 268.
3. See G. E. M. Anscombe, *Intention* (London: Oxford University Press, 1957), and G. H. von Wright, "Practical Inference," *Philosophical Review* 72, no. 2 (1963): 159–79.
4. Robert C. Solomon, *The Passions* (Garden City, NY: Anchor Press, 1976), p. xvii.
5. Solomon develops this point in detail in chapter 9 of *The Passions*.
6. Andrea Dworkin, "Prostitution and Male Supremacy" University of Michigan Law School, October 31, 1992, *Gifts of Speech* (http://gos. sbc. edu/d.html#dworkin).
7. Sallie Tisdale, *Talk Dirty to Me: An Intimate Philosophy of Sex* (New York: Anchor Books, 1994), p. 197.
8. Solomon, pp. 282–368.

❧
Chapter 10

1. Osama bin Laden, "Text of bin Laden Video Statement," *The New York Times on the Web*, October 8, 2001 (http://www.nytimes.com/).
2. Donald P. Verene, "Philosophy, Argument, and Narration," *Philosophy and Rhetoric* 22, no. 2 (1989): 143.
3. Alisdair MacIntyre, *After Virtue* (Notre Dame, IN: University of Notre Dame Press, 1981), pp. 190–209.
4. Jerome Bruner, "Life as Narrative," *Social Research* 54, no. 1 (1987): 11.
5. Ibid., 13.
6. Hayden White, "The Value of Narrativity in the Representation of Reality," *Critical Inquiry* 7, no. 1 (1980): 13.
7. Paul Ricoeur, "The Narrative Function," in *Paul Ricoeur: Hermeneutics and the Human Sciences*, ed. and trans. John B. Thompson (Cambridge: Cambridge University Press, 1981), p. 278
8. Ibid., p. 294.
9. Robert N. Bellah, et al., *Habits of the Heart: Individualism and Commitment in American Life* (Berkeley: University of California Press, 1985).
10. Richard M. Weaver, *Visions of Order: The Cultural Analysis of Our Time* (Baton Rouge: LSU Press, 1964).
11. Bellah, et al., pp. 152–55.
12. Hans Georg Gadamer, *Truth and Method* (New York: Seabury Press, 1975), p. 15.
13. Ibid., p. 264.
14. MacIntyre, p. 201.
15. Bernard Bosanquet, *Implication and Linear Inference* (London: Macmillan and Co., 1920).
16. Walter Fisher, *Human Communication as Narration: Toward a Philosophy of Reason, Value, and Action* (Columbia: University of South Carolina Press, 1987).
17. Bruce Ballenger, "Methds of Memory: On Native American Storytelling," *College English* 59 (1997): 792.
18. Tamar Katriel, "Sites of Memory: Discourses of the Past in Israeli Pioneering Settlement Museums," *Quarterly Journal of Speech* 80, no. 1 (1994): 1–20.
19. John Bodner, *Remaking America: Public Memory, Commemoration, and Patriotism in the Twentieth Century* (Princeton, NJ: Princeton University Press, 1992), p. 15.
20. Stephen H. Browne, "Reading, Rhetoric, and the Texture of Public Memory," *Quarterly Journal of Speech* 81, no. 2 (1995): 244.
21. Gerard A. Hauser, *Vernacular Voices: The Rhetoric of Publics and Public Spheres* (Columbia: University of South Carolina Press, 1999), p. 115.

22. Fisher, p. 107.

23. Adam Michnik, "Why You Are Not Signing," *Letters From Prison*, trans. Maya Latynski (Berkeley: University of California Press, 1985), pp. 3–15.

24. Gerard A. Hauser, "Prisoners of Conscience and the Counterpublic Sphere of Prison Writing: The Stones That Start the Avalanche," in *Counterpublics and the State*, eds. Robert Asen and Daniel C. Brouwer (Albany: SUNY Press, 2001), pp. 35–58.

25. Gerard A. Hauser, "Demonstrative Qualities of Dissident Rhetoric: The Case of Prisoner 885/63," in *The Rhetoric of Display*, ed. Lawrence Prelli (Columbia: University of South Carolina Press, forthcoming).

26. Paul Ricoeur, *Time and Narrative* vol. 3, trans. Kathleen Blamey and David Pellauer (Chicago: University of Chicago Press, 1990 [1985]), p. 186.

ভ্ণ
Chapter 11

1. B. F. Skinner is a behavioral psychologist who maintains that all behavior is conditioned response. His contentions regarding operant conditioning rely heavily on studies of the effects of positive and negative reinforcement on the behavior of pigeons.

2. Kenneth Burke, "Dramatism," in *Communication: Concepts and Perspectives*, ed. Lee Thayer (Washington, DC: Spartan Books, 1967), p. 336.

3. Kenneth Burke, *Language as Symbolic Action* (Berkeley: University of California Press, 1970), p. 16. This section is based primarily on Burke's discussion in his essay "Definition of Man," contained in this book as chapter 1.

4. Kenneth Burke, "(Nonsymbolic) Motion/(Symbolic) Action," *Critical Inquiry* 4 (Summer 1978): 810.

5. C. Wright Mills, "Situated Actions and Vocabularies of Motives," *American Sociological Review* 5, no. 4 (December 1940): 906.

6. Burke provides a book-length development of the pentad in *A Grammar of Motives* (Englewood Cliffs, NJ: Prentice-Hall, 1945).

7. Burke, "Dramatism," p. 332.

8. Edward J. Keller, "Address to District Council 90 Leadership Conference," December 1, 1984 (unpublished typescript). AFSCME stands for American Federation of State, County, and Municipal Employees.

9. Kenneth Burke, *Permanence and Change*, 3rd rev. ed. (Berkeley: University of California Press, 1984), p. 30.

10. Ibid.

11. Kenneth Burke, *A Rhetoric of Motives* (Berkeley: University of California Press, 1969), p. 43.

12. Richard Weaver, "Language Is Sermonic," in *Dimensions of Rhetorical Scholarship*, ed. Roger E. Nebergall (Norman: University of Oklahoma Press, 1963), pp. 49–63.

ভ্ণ
Chapter 12

1. Bronislaw Malinowski, "The Problem of Meaning in Primitive Language," in *The Meaning of Meaning*, ed. C. K. Ogden and I. A. Richards (Orlando: Harcourt Brace Jovanovich, 1923), pp. 296–336.

2. Richard Weaver, *The Ethics of Rhetoric* (Chicago: Henry Rignery, 1953), pp. 164–85.

3. Dana Cloud, *Control and Consolation in American Culture and Politics* (Thousand Oaks, CA: Sage, 1994); Gerard A. Hauser and Susan A. Whalen, "New Rhetoric and New Social Movements," in *Emerging Theories of Human Communication*, eds. Donald Cushman and Branislav Kovacic (Albany: SUNY Press, 1997); and Enrique Laraña, Hank

Johnson, and Joseph R. Gusfield, eds., *New Social Movements* (Philadelphia: Temple University Press, 1994).

4. The most far-ranging yet accessible discussion of this point can be found in George Lakoff and Mark Johnson, *Metaphors We Live By* (Chicago: University of Chicago Press, 1980). I have relied on their treatment extensively in this section.

5. Lakoff and Johnson, pp. 3–22.

6. Ibid., p. 57.

7. Francis A. Beer, *Meanings of War and Peace* (College Station: Texas A & M University Press, 2001), pp. 8–14.

8. Ibid., pp. 8–9.

9. I. A. Richards, *The Philosophy of Rhetoric* (New York: Oxford University Press, 1936), pp. 47–66.

10. James Boyd White, *When Words Lose Their Meaning* (Chicago: University of Chicago Press, 1984), p. x.

11. Steven Mailloux, *Rhetorical Power* (Ithaca: Cornell University Press, 1989), p. 167.

12. Beer, p. 33.

13. Chaim Perelman and L. Olbrechts-Tyteca, *The New Rhetoric: A Treatise on Argumentation*, trans. John Wilkinson and Purcell Weaver (Notre Dame, IN: University of Notre Dame Press, 1969), pp. 149ff.

14. Carroll C. Arnold, *Criticism of Oral Rhetoric* (Columbus, OH: Charles E. Merrill, 1974), p. 199.

15. Bill Clinton, "President Bill Clinton speaks at the annual White House prayer breakfast for clergy following his testimony and address to the nation on the Monica Lewinsky affair, Washington, D.C. September 11, 1998," *PBS, Great American Speeches* (http://www.pbs.org/greatspeeches/timeline/clinton_prayer_s.html).

16. Aristotle takes this up in Book III of the *Rhetoric*, especially at 1404b–1405a.

17. Lakoff and Johnson, pp. 77–105.

18. Max Black, *Models and Metaphors* (Ithaca, NY: Cornell University Press, 1962), pp. 25–47. Black updated his views in "More About Metaphor," *Dialectica* 31 (1977): 431–57.

ॐ

Chapter 13

1. "Women in Black" (http://www.igc.org/balkans/wib); "Women in Black: An International Movement of Women for Peace" (http://adot.com/green/wib.html).

2. Richard B. Gregg, *Symbolic Inducement and Knowing: A Study in the Foundations of Rhetoric* (Columbia: University of South Carolina Press, 1984), pp. 49ff.

3. Ibid., p. 41.

4. Ibid., p. 50.

5. Kenneth Burke, *Counter-statement*, 2nd ed. (Los Altos, CA: Hermes, 1953), p. 31.

6. Harry Caplan, trans., *Ad Herennium* (Cambridge, MA: Harvard University Press, 1954), p. 189.

7. Carroll C. Arnold, *Criticism of Oral Rhetoric* (Columbus, OH: Charles E. Merrill, 1974), p. 4.

8. Barbara Kingslover, *Prodigal Summer* (New York: HarperCollins, 2000), p. 1.

9. Ibid.

10. Kenneth Burke, *The Philosophy of Literary Form*, 3rd ed., rev. (Berkeley: University of California Press, 1974), p. 1.

11. Maureen Dowd, "West Wing Chaperone," *New York Times*, October 8, 2000, p. WK15.

12. For an account of these events, see James Michener, *Kent State: What Happened and Why* (New York: Random House, 1971).

13. Richard Gregg and Gerard A. Hauser, "Richard Nixon's April 30, 1970 Address on Cambodia: The 'Ceremony' of Confrontation," *Speech Monographs* 40, no. 3 (1973): 167–81.

14. Burke, *Counter-statement*, pp. 124–28.

15. See Edwin Dobb, "A Kiss Is Still a Kiss," *Harper's* 292 (February 1996), p. 37 for a more complete discussion of this scene.

16. Robert Hariman, *Politcal Style: The Artistry of Power* (Chicago: University of Chicago Press, 1995), p. 4.

17. Ali I. Al-Naimi, "Geopolitics of Energy and Saudi Oil Policy," *Saudi Arabia* (http://www.saudiembassy.net/press_release/speech/energy-CSIS-12-99.html).

18. Hariman, p. 4.

ꕥ
Chapter 14

1. See David M. Herszenhorn, "Museum Accused of Conspiracy to Inflate Value of Art Show," *New York Times*, September 30, 1999, p. A1; William Glaberson, "Arguments Over Exhibition Intersect in Murky Legal Terrain," *New York Times*, September 30, 1999, p. A25; William Safire, "Manachean Madness," *New York Times*, September 30, 1999, p. A31 for a sampling of views on the "Sensations" exhibition.

2. Stephen Toulmin, *The Uses of Argument* (Cambridge: Cambridge University Press, 1958).

3. This diagram is based on Toulmin, pp. 94–146.

4. Wayne Brockriede and Douglas Ehninger, "Toulmin on Argument: An Interpretation and Application," *Quarterly Journal of Speech* 46, no. 1 (February 1960): 44–53.

5. Tamara Sobel, "March 'Madness' or March 'Unfairness'?" *National Organization for Women* (http://www.now.org/issues/media/watchout/report-3-13-00.html)

6. Chaim Perelman and L. Olbrechts-Tyteca, *The New Rhetoric: A Treatise on Argumentation*, trans. John Wilkenson and Purcell Weaver (Notre Dame, IN: University of Notre Dame Press, 1969), p. 189.

7. Ibid., p. 190.

8. Ibid.

9. Ibid.

10. Ibid.

11. Thomas Friedman, "Saudi Royals and Reality," *The New York Times on the Web*, October 16, 2001 (http://www.nytimes.com/).

12. Perelman and Olbrechts-Tyteca, p. 205.

13. Based on Chaim Perelman and L. Olbrechts-Tyteca, *The New Rhetoric: A Treatise on Argumentation*, trans. John Wilkenson and Purcell Weaver (Notre Dame, IN: University of Notre Dame Press, 1969), pp. 193–260.

14. Perelman and Olbrechts-Tyteca, p. 260.

15. Milan Kundera, *The Book of Laughter and Forgetting*, trans. M. H. Heim (Baltimore: Penguin Books, 1981), p. 22.

16. Based on Chaim Perelman and L. Olbrechts-Tyteca. *The New Rhetoric: A Treatise on Argumentation*, trans. John Wilkenson and Purcell Weaver (Notre Dame, IN: University of Notre Dame Press, 1969), pp. 261–292; 293–349; 350–410.

17. Thomas J. Peters and Robert H. Waterman, Jr., *In Search of Excellence* (New York: Warner Books, 1982), pp. 73–74.

18. Ibid.

19. Perelman and Olbrechts-Tyteca, p. 350.

20. Ibid., p. 378.

21. Ali I. Al-Naimi, "Geopolitics of Energy and Saudi Oil Policy," *Saudi Arabia* (http://www.saudiembassy.net/ press_release/speech/energy-CSIS-12-99.html).

22. Abraham Lincoln, "Cooper Union Address," February 27, 1860, *Abraham Lincoln Online* (http://showcase.netins.net/web/creative/lincoln/speeches/cooper.htm).

23. This discussion is drawn from Peter M. Hall and John P. Hewitt, "The Quasi-theory of Communication and the Management of Dissent," *Social Problems* (Summer 1970): 17–27.

Index